Pedro Calderón de la Barca, Denis Florence MacCarthy

Love, the Greatest Enchantment

Pedro Calderón de la Barca, Denis Florence MacCarthy

Love, the Greatest Enchantment

ISBN/EAN: 9783744695701

Printed in Europe, USA, Canada, Australia, Japan

Cover: Foto ©Thomas Meinert / pixelio.de

More available books at **www.hansebooks.com**

By the ſame Author.

I.

DRAMAS FROM THE SPANISH OF CALDERON.

2 VOLS. LONDON: C. DOLMAN.

*** Theſe Volumes contain unabridged Tranſlations of the following ſix celebrated Dramas:— *The Purgatory of St. Patrick*, *The Conſtant Prince*, *The Scarf and the Flower*, *The Phyſician of his own Honour*, *The Secret in Words*, and *To Love after Death*.

II.

BALLADS, POEMS, AND LYRICS, ORIGINAL AND TRANSLATED.

DUBLIN: M'GLASHAN.

*** A few Copies of this Edition may ſtill be had of Mr. Cornilh, Bookſeller and Publiſher, 18, Grafton Street, Dublin.

III.

THE BELL-FOUNDER, THE VOYAGE OF ST. BRENDAN, THE FORAY OF CON O'DONNELL, ALICE AND UNA, AND OTHER POEMS.

LONDON: KENT AND CO. (BOGUE). DUBLIN: M'GLASHAN AND GILL.

IV.

THE BRIDAL OF THE YEAR, THE YEAR KING, THE MEETING OF THE FLOWERS, THE PROGRESS OF THE ROSE, AND OTHER POEMS OF THE FANCY.

(UNDERGLIMPSES.)

LONDON: KENT AND CO. (BOGUE). DUBLIN: M'GLASHAN AND GILL.

LOVE THE GREATEST ENCHANTMENT, THE SORCERIES OF SIN, AND THE DEVOTION OF THE CROSS.

LOVE THE GREATEST ENCHANTMENT:

THE SORCERIES OF SIN:

THE DEVOTION OF THE CROSS.

FROM THE SPANISH OF CALDERON.

ATTEMPTED STRICTLY IN ENGLISH ASONANTE AND

OTHER IMITATIVE VERSE,

BY DENIS FLORENCE MAC-CARTHY, M.R.I.A.

WITH AN INTRODUCTION TO EACH DRAMA, AND NOTES BY THE TRANSLATOR, AND THE SPANISH TEXT FROM THE EDITIONS OF HARTZENBUSCH, KEIL, AND APONTES.

LONDON:

LONGMAN, GREEN, LONGMAN AND ROBERTS.

1861.

TO

GEORGE TICKNOR, ESQ.

THE HISTORIAN OF SPANISH LITERATURE,

This Volume

IS INSCRIBED IN GRATEFUL REMEMBRANCE OF INFORMATION

LIBERALLY COMMUNICATED,

AND PRAISE GENEROUSLY BESTOWED.

PREFACE.

IN 1853 I publiſhed two volumes of tranſlations from the Spaniſh of Calderon, which contained the firſt (as it ſtill continues to be the only) complete verſion of any of his plays that has ever been preſented to the Engliſh reader.* This attempt met with as much ſucceſs as I could have reaſonably anticipated for it, conſidering the circumſtances under which the work grew up, as detailed in the preface, and the timidity with which I ſhrunk from the whole metrical difficulties of my taſk—difficulties which then appeared to me to be ſo inſurmountable, that, had I the time, I ſcarcely would have had the courage to try and overcome. A forced leiſure, however, of many months, occurring at irregular intervals, but extending through the whole of the intervening period,

* The dramas contained in thoſe volumes are the following :—*The Purgatory of Saint Patrick*, *The Conſtant Prince*, *The Scarf and the Flower*, *The Phyſician of his own Honour*, *The Secret in Words*, and *Love after Death*. The remark in the text is by no means meant to diſparage Mr. Fitzgerald's *Six Plays of Calderon freely tranſlated*, London, 1853, the nervous blank verſe of which, though I think unſuited to Calderon, I greatly admire ; but ſurely a tranſlator who confeſſes that he has "ſunk, reduced, altered, and replaced" whatever did not ſeem to him particularly "fine" in his author, can ſcarcely be taken as a ſatisfactory interpreter of a poet whoſe very defects and extravagances are as characteriſtic of his genius as are his beauties.

having again induced me to resume my labours upon Calderon, I felt the very difficulties, which before I had left unattempted, an attraction and an incentive, as supplying a more laborious occupation, and a more engrossing distraction. I felt, too, a sincere artistic conviction that I was bound to do my best for a poet whom I had been, to some extent, instrumental in introducing to a foreign audience, and a determination that he should not suffer in their estimation by any wilful omission or neglect on the part of him at whose invitation he had appeared before them. Two things I set before me at the beginning of my renewed task, which, I trust, I have pretty faithfully observed to the end; namely, in the first place, to give the meaning of my author exactly, and in its integrity, neither departing from it through diffuseness, nor cramping it through condensation; and, secondly, to express it strictly in the form of the original, or not to express it at all.

It is by no means my intention to enter into the oft-debated question as to the principles which should guide or coerce the translator in his task. As far as the translator is concerned, it is a much easier thing to produce a popular and flowing version of any foreign poem or play, than a faithful and exact one; and the effect to be produced will so depend upon the capacity and culture of the reader,—whether, in a word, he will have his German or Spanish so thoroughly "done into English," as to have every particle of its original nature eliminated out of it, or will have it faithfully presented to him, with all its native peculiarities preserved,—is so much a matter of taste, that no definite rule can ever be arrived at in the matter. What Mr. Newman has said upon this subject so entirely agrees with my own impressions, that I print his observations here, the more readily, that I have been actuated independently by the same convictions long before I was aware that they were shared by him. Mr. Newman, alluding to some of his own critics, who had laid down, as axioms, certain principles which he considers to be utterly falſe and ruinous to tranſlation, thus proceeds:—"One of theſe is, that the reader ought, if poſſible, to forget that it is a tranſlation at all, and be lulled into the illuſion that he is reading an original work. Of courſe, a neceſſary inference from ſuch a dogma is, that whatever has a foreign colour is undeſirable, and is even a grave defect. The tranſlator, it ſeems, muſt carefully obliterate all that is characteriſtic of the original, unleſs it happens to be identical in ſpirit to ſomething already familiar in Engliſh. From ſuch a notion I cannot too ſtrongly expreſs my intenſe diſſent. I aim at preciſely the oppoſite;—to retain every peculiarity of the original, as far as I am able, *with the greater care, the more foreign it may happen to be*, whether it be matter of taſte, of intellect, or of morals."*

On this principle I have acted throughout the entire of this volume, with what ſucceſs, however, of courſe remains to be ſeen.

The peculiar feature, then, of this Tranſlation is its rigid adherence to the metres of the original, and particularly to that eſpecial Spaniſh one, the *aſonante* vowel rhyme, of which but a few ſcattered ſpecimens exiſt in Engliſh, and theſe rather as ſamples of what our language was incapable of producing to any conſiderable extent, than of what it could achieve. This metre is ſo very peculiar, and ſo oppoſed to anything that bears the ſemblance of rhyme in Engliſh, that I have known ſeveral perſons, who were able to read in the original a romance, or a ſcene from a Spaniſh play, and who, notwithſtanding, never perceived the delicate and moſt elaborate form of verſification they had been enjoying, until their attention was drawn to it; when once ſeen or heard, however, the diſcovery is hailed with delight, and we look or liſten for the ever-recurring ſimilarity of cadence or conſtruction, "the manifold wild chimes" of the Spaniſh aſonance, with pleaſure and ſurpriſe. The numerous examples of it throughout this volume will ſhow the reader

* *The Iliad of Homer, faithfully tranſlated into unrhymed Engliſh Metre*, by F. W. Newman. (London, 1856.) Preface, p. xv.

what it is more clearly, perhaps, than any explanation; and yet ſome definition of it may not be inappropriate in this place. "The Spaniſh *aſonante*,"* ſays the late Lord Holland, "is a word which reſembles another in the *vowel* on which the laſt accent falls, as well as the vowel, or vowels, that follow it; but every conſonant after the accented vowel muſt be different from that in the correſponding ſyllable. Thus: *tòs* and *amòr*, *orìlla* and *delìra*, *àlamo* and *pàxaro*, are all *aſonantes*." † This definition, though, perhaps, a little too limited for the boundleſs variety and freedom of the aſonance, may be conſidered tolerably ſatisfactory. The rhyme, ſuch as it is, is not confined, as in all other languages, to a few repetitions, of which thoſe in the octave ſtanza are, perhaps, the moſt frequent; but in Spaniſh, the *ſame* aſonance, that is, the ſame recurring ſimilarity of vowel, or vowels, in the laſt accented ſyllable, or ſyllables, of every ſecond line is kept up unchanged, however long may be the ballad or the ſcene in which it is commenced. In Spaniſh, from the open ſound of the vowels, and from the copiouſneſs of the language, this is eaſy. In fact, it is ſaid that the difficulty lies not in producing the *aſonante* where it is required, but in avoiding it in the intermediate lines, where it is ſuperfluous. But in Engliſh the caſe is very different; from the comparative weakneſs of the vowel ſounds,‡ from the rare poſſibility of combining them, and, what is ſtill more, from their per-

* This word is generally written *aſſonant* in Engliſh. For a thing ſo entirely Spaniſh, perhaps the Spaniſh form is the more appropriate one, and I have therefore followed Lord Holland and Mr. Ticknor in calling it by its original name.

† *Life of Lope de Vega*, vol. II. p. 215.

‡ Mr. Newman has a remark, in the Preface from which I have already quoted, which ſeems to be applicable here, eſpecially in reference to the general objection made againſt the introduction of the aſonance into northern languages, namely, its inſufficiency and incompleteneſs of *ſound*. "An accentual metre," he ſays, "in a language loaded with conſonants, cannot have the *ſame ſort* of ſounding beauty, as a quantitative metre in a highly vocalized language. It is not audible ſameneſs of metre, but a likeneſs of *moral genius* which is to be arrived at." P. xvii.

petual variation in quantity, anything like producing the ſame effect as in the Spaniſh is impoſſible. Yet this "ghoſt of a rhyme," as Dean Trench calls it,* is better than none at all; and I have found, from my own experience, that an inflexible determination to reproduce it, at whatever trouble, even though with imperfect ſucceſs, enables the tranſlator more cloſely to render the meaning of the original, and ſaves him from the danger of being tempted into diffuſeneſs by the facilities of expanſion which even the unrhymed trochaic, *without the aſonante*, too readily ſupplies. Tranſlators who have felt the weight of too much liberty might find within the reſtricted limits of the *aſonance* the ſame ſalutary reſtraints which Wordſworth diſcovered

"Within the ſonnet's ſcanty plot of ground"—

it is to be hoped with ſome ſlight portion of the ſame ſucceſs.

With regard to the dramas and *auto* ſelected for tranſlation in this

* In his charming little book on Calderon (*Life's a Dream, &c.* London, 1856), Dean Trench has the merit of being the firſt to attempt the tranſlation of any portion of Calderon into equivalent Engliſh *aſonantes*: his tranſlations having been made, as I infer from his preface, about eighteen years before they were publiſhed.

I may ſupply here an omiſſion in the Preface to my *Dramas from Calderon*, when noticing the contributions to a knowledge of the Spaniſh Drama which our early Engliſh literature ſupplies, an omiſſion alſo noticeable in that part of Dean Trench's Eſſay which goes over the ſame ground. I was not aware at the time that Preface was written that Sir Richard Fanſhaw, the tranſlator of Guarini and Camoens, had given, in 1649, a very pleaſing verſion in ſhort lyrical lines, almoſt Spaniſh in their felicity and grace, of Antonio de Mendoza's long and ſingular drama, *Querer por Solo Querer* ("To Love for Love's Sake"). This is the drama which took Charles Lamb three "well-waſted hours" to read, and, according to him, nine days to repreſent. (See the *Extracts from the Garrick Plays* in his *Specimens of Engliſh Dramatic Poets*, Bohn's Ed. 1854, p. 476.) "Five or ſix mortal hours," however, are the limits which Don Ramon de Meſoneros Romanos in the *Apuntes Biográficos* prefixed to his *Dramaticos Contemporaneos de Lope de Vega*, t. ii. p. 28, puts to the patience of the audience in liſtening to the ſix thouſand four hundred verſes of whch the original drama conſiſts.

volume, little requires to be ſaid in this place, as I have prefixed to each of them ſuch introductory remarks as ſeemed neceſſary for the proper underſtanding of the time and circumſtances of their production. They all may be conſidered repreſentative pieces—pieces that convey a fair idea of the claſs of drama, whether *Fieſta*, *Comedia*, or *Auto*, to which they belong. The firſt, *Love the Greateſt Enchantment*, which is the ſtory of Circe and Ulyſſes, is a favourable ſpecimen of the dramas which Calderon founded upon claſſical or mythological ſubjects. Of theſe he wrote altogether eighteen, and though they have been greatly admired, not alone in Germany, but in England, for the freedom with which the poet entered into poſſeſſion of theſe ancient fables, uſing them for his own purpoſes with a freſhneſs of invention ever new and ever delightful, but one only out of the eighteen has ever been even analyſed in Engliſh with anything like completeneſs or preciſion.*

The next piece, *The Sorceries of Sin*, is even ſtill more intereſting and more wonderful. It is an *auto*, and therefore, though dealing with the ſame ſtory as its foundation, is as different from the preceding play as ſpirit is to matter, or the ſoul to the body. In fact, the long dramatic ſpectacle in which the ancient Hellenic fable ſtarts into new life, in another climate, and at a different era, beneath the power of a new creator, ſeems to be worthleſs in the poet's eyes, unleſs he can deduce from it its *moral*, namely, the power of Man to reſiſt, or, at leaſt, to triumph over temptation, if he will only liſten to the voice of his own ſoul, and the ſilent whiſperings of repentance and of grace. This he has done in *The Sorceries of Sin*. In the introductory remarks which I have prefixed to it the reader will find ſome moſt intereſting and valuable bibliographical notes by Mr. Ticknor, relative to the firſt publication of the

* The drama alluded to is *Los Tres Mayores Prodigios*, on which there is a good paper in *Frazer's Magazine* for Auguſt 1849. *Eco y Narciſo* is referred to with great praiſe in the *Weſtminſter Review* for January 1851, pp. 295-307.

autos, taken from communications which he has had the kindneſs to addreſs to me upon the ſubject. Upon the general character of the *autos* I cannot do better than refer the reader to the third part of Dean Trench's eſſay, to which I have previouſly made alluſion.

The celebrity of the third piece which this volume contains, *The Devotion of the Croſs*, and the miſconceptions which exiſt as to its real character, will be, I truſt, ſufficient excuſe for my having tranſlated it. As in the other caſes, I refer the reader to the introductory remarks prefixed to this tragedy, which Dean Trench characterizes as, "deſpite of all its perverſity, a wonderful and terrible drama."*

The Spaniſh text, which I have printed for the convenience of the reader, is founded, as far as the *comedias* are concerned, partly on the edition of Keil, and partly on that of Hartzenbuſch. The *ſcenes* are altogether taken from the latter edition. Where any important difference exiſts between the text of the two editions, I have generally drawn attention to it in a foot-note. The *auto*, with the exception of a few ſlight corrections, is printed verbatim from the edition by Apontes (*Autos Sacramentales*, 6 vols. 4to. Madrid, 1759-60, vol. vi. p. 109).†

* For a ſupplementary note to *The Devotion of the Croſs* ſee next page.

† In addition to what has been ſaid in the note to p. xi. relative to Sir Richard Fanſhaw's tranſlation of *Querer por Solo Querer*, it may be mentioned that he alſo tranſlated another dramatic ſpectacle from the Spaniſh, called *Fieſtas de Aranjuez*. See *The Companion to the Play-houſe*, London, 1764, v. ii., under letter F, where it is erroneouſly attributed to Mendoza. This is doubtleſs the maſque written, by the unfortunate Count of Villa-Mediana, for the birth-day feſtivities of Philip IV. in 1622. See Ticknor, v. ii. p. 172, n.; ſee alſo Madame d'Aulnoy's *Relation du Voyage d'Eſpagne*, t. ii. pp. 20, 21. (La Haye, 1715,) for a very curious account of the exhibition of this ſpectacle, and for the author's premeditated act of daring gallantry towards the Queen, which, it is ſuppoſed, led to his immediate aſſaſſination.

Summerfield, Dalkey,
September, 1861.

SUPPLEMENTARY NOTE TO THE DEVOTION OF THE CROSS.

IN the Introduction to *The Devotion of the Croſs*, and at p. 284 of the Tranſlation, I have ſtated that *La Devocion de la Cruz* was firſt printed at Hueſca, in 1634, under the title of *La Cruz en la Sepultura*, and as the work of Lope de Vega. This miſtake, in a volume forming a portion of a collection containing the dramas of various authors, is perhaps not to be wondered at; but it ſeems ſtrange that the ſame error ſhould be repeated ſix years later, in a volume of the collection devoted excluſively to the dramas of Lope himſelf, in the twenty-fourth part or volume of which (Madrid, 1640) *La Cruz en la Sepultura* is again given as the work of Lope de Vega.* In a note to the exceedingly valuable catalogue of all the Comedias and Autos of Lope de Vega, compiled with ſuch care and labour by the diſtinguiſhed Spaniſh ſcholar Mr. J. R. Chorley, of London, and preſented by him with ſo much liberality to Señor Hartzenbuſch for his fourth volume of Lope's *Comedias Eſcogidas* (Madrid, 1853-60), it is ſtated that this twenty-fourth part is the only one out of the twenty-five to which the collection of Lope's comedias extended (1604-47), which is wanting to complete the copy in the Spaniſh Library of Lord Taunton, at Stoke Park, near London. It is preſerved, however, with the others in the National Library of Madrid. Mr. Chorley alſo mentions that according to Mr. Ticknor (under date October 1857), the edition of Hueſca, 1634, is to be found in the Library of the Arſenal at Paris, and in the Library of the Vatican at Rome. A volume of the collection of ſeparately-printed Spaniſh plays, brought from Spain by Lord Arlington in the reign of Charles the Second, and now preſerved in the Library of the Britiſh Muſeum, contains, according to Mr. Chorley, two of Calderon's dramas (one of them being *La Cruz en la Sepultura*), which are both attributed to Lope de Vega.†

---

* See Schack's *Geſchichte der Dramatiſchen Literatur und Kunſt in Spanien*, b. II. p. 696, Lord Holland's *Life of Lope de Vega*, vol. ii. p. 151, and Mr. Chorley's *Catalogo de Comedias y Autos de Frey Lope Felix de Vega Carpio*, referred to above.

† *Catalogo de Comedias, &c.* p. 542. I may add that the ſecond, *Amor, Honor, y Poder* is alſo given under another name in the twenty-fourth of Lope's Comedias above mentioned. The volume publiſhed at Hueſca in 1634 contains, in addition to theſe, a third of Calderon's dramas, erroneouſly attributed to Lope, namely *Un Caſtigo en Tres Venganzas*. See Hartzenbuſch's *Catalogo Cronologico, Comedias de Calderon*, t. iv. p. 669.

LOVE THE GREATEST ENCHANTMENT.

FROM THE SPANISH OF CALDERON.

INTRODUCTION.

THE Homeric Circe, previous to her becoming the heroine of this drama of Calderon, had figured under various names, and with various adventures, in the romances and romantic poetry of Europe, and we recognize her as the ſame perſon, whether called Morgana, as in Launcelot du Lac, and in Boiardo, Alcina, as in Arioſto, or Armida, as in Taſſo. To theſe may be added the Dueſſa of Spenſer, in 1590, and in 1634 (the year preceding the firſt performance of Calderon's drama) a male reproduction of the character in the "Comus" of Milton. Under her original name, Lope de Vega had devoted upwards of three thouſand lines to her adventures in his "Circe," a poem in octave ſtanzas, which he publiſhed in 1624. The ground-work of Calderon's Circe is to be found in Homer, *Odyſſey*, B. x. from line 135 to 574, and B. XII. from line 8 to 141. But he was under great obligations both to Arioſto and to Taſſo, the former of whom, in the Sixth Canto of the Orlando, and the latter, to a ſtill greater degree, in the Sixteenth Canto of the "Geruſalemme," ſupply him with many of his moſt intereſting incidents. Indeed the thirty-ſeventh ſtanza of the Sixteenth Canto of the latter poem may be taken as the key-note of his entire compoſition, and as ſuch I introduce it here in the quaint verſion of Fairfax, although the concluding couplet of the original—

Lascia gl' incanti, e vuol provar se vaga
E supplice beltà sia miglior maga—

more clearly expresses the meaning of Calderon :—

All what the witches of Thessalia land
  With lips unpure yet ever said or spake,
Words that could make heaven's rolling circles stand,
  And draw the damned ghosts from Limbo lake,
All well she knew, but yet no time she fand
  To use her knowledge or her charms to make,
But left her arts, and forth she ran to prove
If single beauty were best charm for love.

The experiment of recalling Ulysses to his martial tastes and duties, by placing before him the long-unused armour of Achilles, is probably suggested by the similar stratagem which gave Rinaldo courage to break from the enchantments of Armida; but both, no doubt, founded upon one of the later traditions of Achilles himself, who, when concealed in the court of Lycomedes of Scyros, under the disguise of a maiden, was discovered by Odysseus through a somewhat similar stratagem. The conduct of Armida herself upon her desertion also presents resemblances to the catastrophe in *El Mayor Encanto Amor*, detracting nothing, however, from the merits of Calderon's work, in which every incident of the ancient classical myth is recast, reborn, as it were, in the creative mind of the poet with a freshness (says Schack, from whom I have derived some of the foregoing references) which, while preserving all the charms of the old Hellenic Legend, impresses upon it the distinctive and not less delightful character of modern romance.*

The following curious paper I have translated from a document first published by Don Casiano Pellicer, in the second volume of his *Tratado Historico sobre el Origen y Progresos de la Comedia en España*, and introduced

* *Geschichte der dramatischen Literatur und Kunst in Spanien*, B. III. p. 190.

as a preface to this play by Hartzenbuſch in his edition of Calderon.* It is intereſting as well for ſhowing the labour which the great poet took in working upon the plan of the machiniſt, and in what reſpects he departed from it, as for the very remarkable proof which it gives of the mechanical reſources of the theatre in the reign of Philip the Fourth, and the unequalled magnificence with which this and ſimilar royal pageants were produced at the court of Madrid. The Maſques of Ben Jonſon,† which were about the ſame period the delight of "our James," are the only productions which can be compared with theſe dramatic ſpectacles of ſplendour and ingenuity; and while, in their united labours as dramatiſt and machiniſt, the palm for poetical excellence muſt be given to Calderon, it will be perceived that, in productions of this kind, the great Engliſh architect had no mean rival in the leſs widely known, but ſtill famous Italian artiſt, who had the honour of being Calderon's fellow-labourer in theſe magnificent ſhows.

"CIRCE,

"*A Dramatic Spectacle which was repreſented on the great pond of the Retiro,‡ the invention of Coſme Lotti, at the requeſt of her moſt excellent Ladyſhip, the Counteſs of Olivarez, Ducheſs of San Lucar la Mayor, on the night of St. John* [*June* 24, A.D. 1635].

"There will be formed in the middle of the pond a ſtationary iſland, raiſed ſeven feet above the ſurface of the water, with a winding aſcent, terminating at the entrance into the iſland, which will be ſurrounded by a parapet of looſe ſtones, adorned with corals and other curioſities of the

* *Biblioteca de Autores Eſpañoles*, T. VII. p. 385. Madrid, 1848. *Tratado Hiſtorico ſobre el Origen y Progreſos de la Comedia y del Hiſtrioniſmo en Eſpàña*, por D. Caſiano Pellicer. *Parte Segunda*, p. 146. Madrid, 1804.

† *Chloridia*, which he produced in conjunction with Inigo Jones in 1630, coſt 3000*l.* for decorations.

‡ The celebrated palace of the *Buen Retiro*.

ſea, ſuch as pearls and ſhells of different colours, with waterfalls and ſimilar decorations. In the midſt of this iſland will be ſituated a very lofty mountain of rugged aſcent, with precipices, and caverns, ſurrounded by a thick and darkſome wood of tall trees, ſome of which will be ſeen to exhibit the appearance of the human form covered with a rough bark, from the heads and arms of which will iſſue green boughs and branches, having ſuſpended from them various trophies of war and of the chaſe, the theatre during this opening ſcene being ſcantily lit with concealed lights: and, to make a beginning of the feſtival, a murmuring and a rippling noiſe of water having been heard, a great and magnificent car will be ſeen to advance along the pond, plated over with ſilver, and drawn by two monſtrous fiſhes, from whoſe mouths will continually iſſue great jets of water, the light of the theatre increaſing according as they advance; and on the ſummit of it will be ſeen ſeated in great pomp and majeſty the goddeſs Aqua, from whoſe head and curious veſture will iſſue an infinite abundance of little conduits of water; and at the ſame time will be ſeen another great ſupply flowing from an urn which the goddeſs will hold reverſed; and which, filled with a variety of fiſhes, that, leaping and playing in the torrent as it deſcends, and gliding over all the car, will fall at length into the pond. This admirable machine is to be accompanied by a choir of twenty nymphs of rivulets and fountains, who will advance, ſinging and playing, along the ſurface of the water: and, when this beautiful piece of mechaniſm ſtops in the preſence of His Majeſty, the goddeſs Aqua will commence the ſcene by repreſenting the Loa.* This being finiſhed, the ſound of various inſtruments will be heard, and the proceſſion will retire from the theatre in the ſame order, and with

* The *Loa* here mentioned is probably that which precedes the *Auto, Los Encantos de la Culpa* (*The Sorceries of Sin*), which is alſo founded on the ſtory of Ulyſſes and Circe, and a tranſlation of which forms the ſecond portion of this volume. This *Loa* has no connection with the incidents of either drama or auto, being merely a glorification of Madrid. In it, however, the goddeſs Aqua makes her appearance, which ſhe does not do in either *Love the Greateſt Enchantment*, or in *The Sorceries of Sin*, her

the ſame muſical accompaniment as it entered. Scarcely has it diſappeared, when a ſtirring ſound of clarions and trumpets will burſt forth, with diſcharges of muſketry and cannon, and the cry of *Land! Land!* will be heard from within: and a great and beauteous gilded bark will be diſcovered, adorned with ſtreamers, pendants, banneroles, and flags, which, with ſwelling ſails, will come to harbour, furling her ſails, and dropping her anchors and cables; and on her deck will be ſeen Ulyſſes and his companions, who, returning thanks to the gods for having reached land, will ſpeak of their paſt misfortunes and their preſent neceſſities, none of them having the daring to diſembark even to ſeek refreſhment, fearing the dangers that might enſue; on which account, lots being drawn, eighteen of them will be compelled to enter the long-boat, and to make the attempt: and they having tremblingly leaped on the iſland, a great number of various animals, ſuch as lions, tigers, dragons, bears, and others, will place themſelves before them, who, aſtoniſhed and full of terror, will form themſelves into a body for their defence; but the animals, with human intelligence, will approach them careſſingly, at which moment will be heard a ſad, but melodious ſtrain of muſic, proceeding from the trees and plants, which with human forms have been there metamorphoſed, at which muſical wail, the animals, in their various ways, will perform an extraordinary dance, and while this is kept up and continued, a terrible earthquake, with agitation of the air, will be felt, which, awakening flaſhes and peals of thunder, will dart forth a forked bolt, that, ſtriking the top and ſummit of the mountain, will ſo looſe and ſhatter it, that it will fall to pieces in various parts of the theatre, at which event the animals will diſappear, and the muſic will ceaſe, and the mariners will remain full of terror and amazement,

place in the car being filled, in the former, by the nymph Galatea, and in the latter by the perſonification of Penance. The car itſelf ſeems to have been uſed in other of theſe gorgeous ſpectacle-plays of Calderon. In his *Phaeton*, for inſtance, which was alſo acted on the pond of the Retiro a few years later, there are two references to its having been ſeen by the audience on ſeveral previous occaſions.—TRANSLATOR.

ſeeing, in the place where the mountain ſtood, a ſplendid palace appear, inlaid with precious ſtones of various colours, of a rich and well-deſigned architecture, with columns of agate and cryſtal, having baſes, capitals, and cornices of gold, and ſtatues of bronze and of marble, all arranged in their proper places. And the frightful and horrible wood will at the ſame time be transformed into a fair and delicious garden, encloſing a lofty edifice of ſpherical form, with corridors and porticos; and in the midſt of each delightful compartment will be ſeen fountains of running water, covered alleys, and numbers of domeſtic animals paſſing to and fro; and, at the appearance of this new wonder, the theatre will be illuminated by a brilliancy ſo great, that it will ſeem as if the ſun miniſtered its light, which will proceed from and be the reſult of the reflection which the jewels of this rich and ſumptuous palace will make, and from two ſplendid ſtars which, with ſingular and remarkable brilliancy, will iſſue from the waves and waters of the pond; and, in front of the porticos and corridors in the centre of the creſcent, Circe will be ſeen ſeated on a majeſtic throne, dreſſed magnificently in flower-embroidered robes of ſilk, attended by many ladies and damſels, ſome of whom will go about gathering herbs and flowers, which they will place in golden baſkets, and others will collect in cryſtal vaſes waters of various kinds, for the uſe and convenience of the ſorcereſs and her enchantments; and Circe, with a grave and compoſed countenance, holding a golden wand in one hand, and in the other a book, from which ſhe reads, (the timid companions of Ulyſſes being preſent, and beholding with wonder what has happened,) ſhe will direct one of her ladies to encourage and to lead them to her preſence, when, with an agreeable and deceitful countenance, ſhe will aſk them who they are, and for what object they have approached that iſland. To which they will give anſwer, referring to the events of the ſiege of Troy, and the ſubſequent misfortunes that had befallen them ſince its fall; and they will implore pity and ſuccour for themſelves and their diſmantled and ill-provided veſſel: and ſhe, feigning compaſſion for their miſery and misfortune, will promiſe them aſſiſtance, and, deſcending from her throne, on which, up to this time, ſhe has been ſeated, ſhe will ſtrike the earth with her golden wand, and at the inſtant a ſplendidly-furniſhed table will ariſe, at which banquet a potion in a golden cup will be adminiſtered to them which will transform them into ſwine, with the exception of one, who, flying a ſimilar metamorphoſis, and the treacherous hoſpitality of the ſorcereſs, will re-enter the boat, ſtill lying by the ſhore, and will relate this new adventure to Ulyſſes: and ſhe, enraged at the flight of their companion, will beat the ſeeming ſwine with her wand, ordering them away to the ſty, at which much amuſement will ariſe from their grunting; and ſhe will make one of them, who appears of a humorous turn, to ſtand upright, and ſpeak naturally as a man: and this one, ſerving as the *gracioſo*, will make entertaining jeſts and comic buffooneries with the ladies, endeavouring to ſit in their laps, and imitating the playfulneſs of a lap-dog: and, taking a fancy for one of them, he will fall in love with her, whom Circe will transform into a monkey, through anger and jealouſy that the appearance of any lady ſhould appear to the ſwine more beautiful and attractive than her own: from which will reſult a pleaſant and entertaining allegory, for the lady ſeeing herſelf transformed into a monkey, and great diſcord on this account enſuing between her and the ſwine, will under this metaphor point out the puniſhment which follows the vices and ſenſuality of men; and on the other hand a like allegory, under the metaphor and transformation of the lady into a monkey, the degradations which follow thoſe of women. In the meanwhile, the cavalier who fled the dangers and deceits of Circe, having come to the preſence of Ulyſſes, and having related the mournful fate of his companions, will move him to ſuch pity, that he will inſtantly go to their relief; and, making the land in his boat, he will hear a voice, without knowing from whom it proceedeth, and ſeeking the ſource of this voice, it will be found to proceed from one of thoſe cavaliers who, clothed in rugged bark, have been transformed into trees, who will exhort him not to proceed farther, nor expoſe himſelf to the certain danger that threatens him, but that he ſhould fly the enchantments of that iſland, originating in the deceptions of Circe, and in her magic and impure loves: at which Ulyſſes, wondering, will aſk him who he is, and what was the occaſion of ſo cruel an enchantment. To whom he with deep ſorrow will anſwer that he was one of the companions of King Picus, and will relate the tragic and mournful fate which had overtaken them and their king, all being, as their final miſfortune, either transformed into trees, or condemned to wander, in the ſhape of various animals, through the woods. At which Ulyſſes, compaſſionate and confuſed, will reſolve to undertake their reſtoration as a part of the conqueſt he was about undertaking; and ſcarcely will he have proceeded to put it into execution, when Mercury will be ſeen coming through the air, dazzling with various colours and reflections, who, as ambaſſador from Jupiter, will preſent him with a flower, by means of which he will be able to come triumphant out of the adventure which he had vowed, and from the ſnares and enchantments of Circe: to whom Ulyſſes will ſcarcely have given thanks, when from his preſence, cleaving the air, he will return to heaven: and Ulyſſes, recovering his breath, and thus ſecure of ſucceſs, will with freſh courage come in ſight of the beautiful palace, in which will be ſeen new wonders, ſince at the diſappearance of the throne on which Circe had been ſeated, under an arch in the middle of the porticos and corridors, will be diſcovered a moſt beautiful open portal, through which will be ſeen long and deep perſpectives, exciting great admiration; and while Ulyſſes ſtands in ſuſpenſe during the carrying out of this prodigy, that follower of his who, changed into a ſwine, acts the part of the *gracioſo*, will come before him, and recognizing him, will ſtrive to embrace him, and with his filthy ſnout attempt to kiſs him, calling to his companions, who, grunting in a comic way, will ſurround him, making altogether a groteſque tableau; and he, compaſſionating their miſery, will careſs them, aſking the talking ſwine to introduce him to the enchantreſs Circe; and they then, fearing greater evil, perceiving her preſence, will fly away, leaving Ulyſſes alone with her, whom, in an affable manner, the enchantreſs will receive, inviting him to drink, and offering him the ſame cup which had been preſented to his companions. Ulyſſes will excuſe himſelf, threatening her, in order that ſhe ſhould give them their liberty; and ſhe, refuſing, will ſo provoke the anger and fury of Ulyſſes, that he will put his hand to his ſword; but, ſeeing that his threats are of no avail, and his ſword equally ineffectual, he will change his anger and fury into flatteries and careſſes; and, pretending to be enamoured, will offer to dwell with her, and to comply with all her wiſhes and deſires, provided that ſhe will reſtore his companions to their original ſhape, which Circe offers to do, and, enamoured of him, embraces him; and, conducting him to his companions, ſhe will make them waſh in a beautiful fountain, the waters of which will reſtore them to their original ſhape of men, all except the *gracioſo*, who, for their greater pleaſure and entertainment, will remain transformed, gaining nothing from his ablutions but a ſtill longer ſnout, and the ſudden acquiſition of a pair of aſs's ears; at which, haraſſed and enraged, he will indulge in various comic and amuſing expreſſions, and will implore Circe to reſtore him, and of Ulyſſes he will aſk it, and of his companions in like manner: which ſhe will promiſe to do when he has done penance in that ſhape for having been attracted more by the beauty of the lady transformed into a monkey, than by hers. And, matters being thus arranged, there will appear in the pond ſix barks or ſloops, commanded and ſteered by ſix cupids, in which Circe will cauſe the companions of Ulyſſes to enter, aſſigning to each one the lady to whom he is to pay court, and to the gracioſo-ſwine the lady that was transformed into a monkey: and ſhe herſelf will enter with Ulyſſes into hers; and, ſinging to the ſound of various inſtruments, they will go through the pond, fiſhing with rods for freſh fiſh, which, wherever the tackle is thrown into the water, will nibble at the fly, and, being caught by the hook, will be raiſed up, plunging and bounding; but the ſwine-transformed gracioſo, in place of catching freſh fiſh, will only draw up thoſe that are ſalted and dried, ſuch as dog-fiſh and hake; and after this comic diverſion the little fleet will form a creſcent, the bark of Circe and Ulyſſes being in the centre, ſhe will command the ſea, in order to give pleaſure to her new lover, to bring forth and exhibit on its waves the diverſity of fiſhes and marine monſters which it contains in its womb: at which precept and command the pond will be ſeen filled with a variety of fiſhes, great and ſmall, which, playing with each other, will force up through their mouths and noſtrils frequent jets of odoriferous water, which, ſcattered in fragrant ſhowers upon the ſpectators, will diffuſe a ſweet and agreeable odour around. And at this time will come and appear ſuddenly upon the pond VIRTUE, diſguiſed under the form and figure of a female magician, ſeated upon a great ſea-tortoiſe, and ſeeming to Circe (in conſequence of her aſſumed diſguiſe of a magician) a great friend of hers, ſhe will be rejoiced to ſee her, and will compliment her on her arrival, at which they will all diſembark upon a flowery lawn in front of the palace, where they will ſit down; and then, converſing on various matters, and being much pleaſed at the viſit of her friend, Circe, to entertain her, will introduce a groteſque aſſemblage of ſirens and tritons, who, on the water of the pond, will perform a wonderful ſort of dance, the like of which has never been ſeen or heard of: at the end of which, they having diſappeared, and Circe, Virtue, and Ulyſſes having reſumed their converſation and diſcourſe, Circe will aſk Virtue the reaſon that has moved her to leave her ſtudies and magical purſuits to come and viſit her: and ſhe will anſwer, that the object of her coming is her love for Ulyſſes, whom, from the moment of his birth, ſhe had deſtined for herſelf, having experienced from him ſuch tender reſpect and attention, which have obliged her to ſeek him, and to come for him, in order to withdraw him from her hands, becauſe her great love allowed her no reſt, nor confidence in her ancient friendſhip with Circe. And the companions of Ulyſſes, hearing this explanation, wondering and confuſed at what had happened, will be aſtoniſhed, and not knowing Virtue under the diſguiſe of a magician, will believe her to be mad; but Circe, laughing, and treating what her friend had ſaid to her as a jeſt, will treat her with raillery, notwithſtanding which ſhe, through jealouſy, and to reaſſure herſelf, will make Ulyſſes and his companions perform a mimic tournament on foot, the tilting encloſure ſuddenly appearing for the occaſion: ſcarcely has this begun, when Virtue, praiſing the ſhape, the graceful deportment, the activity and courage of Ulyſſes, will cauſe great jealouſy to Circe, who will ſuſpend the tournament, cauſing the liſts to diſappear, and commanding Virtue on the inſtant to depart the iſland; but ſhe will not do ſo, unleſs ſhe can take Ulyſſes with her; at which Circe, angry and enraged, will make great incantations, ſhapes, ſpectres, and enchantments to overcome her and to drive her thence, which will produce in the air and on the iſland great prodigies and wonderful appearances, which will do no injury to Virtue, who will conquer them all; and Circe, finding that ſhe is powerleſs to ſubdue her, will go away in wrath, leaving Virtue alone with Ulyſſes, who will reveal herſelf to him, rebuking him for his way of life, and cenſuring him for his effeminacy, aſking him if it was he that ſhe had conducted out of Greece, and had made victorious over the Trojans, and recalling the other glorious achievements of Ulyſſes. He, grateful, and with his memory reſtored, will repent, and will promiſe to follow her, abandoning his vices, which, till then, had held him in forgetfulneſs, at which ſhe will lead him to the fountain, where, beholding himſelf as in a mirror, he will ſee himſelf ſo different from what he was in the days of his valour, that, with a fixed determination, he will reſolve to leave Circe. At which there will appear in the theatre a very old and deformed giant, wearing a venerable beard, dreſſed in the habit of a hermit, and with a ſtaff in his hand, whoſe preſence will compel Ulyſſes to inquire of Virtue who he is, and what was his buſineſs with him; to whom ſhe will give anſwer: "This is he whom thou art to follow, and whom thou oughteſt to congratulate in order to riſe from the abyſs of vices into which thou haſt fallen." With that Ulyſſes will turn to the giant, and aſk him to give him his protection, and to tell him who he is: and the other will aſſure him of it, ſaying that he is called the Buen Retiro, (the Happy Retreat,*) and telling Ulyſſes that what is neceſſary to obtain for him a place in the temple of eternity, and to make his name famous, illuſtrating it with glorious actions, is to follow him, the Happy Retreat, becauſe unleſs he followed that, he would not be able to renounce vice and love virtue, which could only be done by retiring from all that could divert him from her. With that Ulyſſes, determining to follow the Happy Retreat, will embrace Virtue, and being embraced by her, Circe will return in deſpair, and, ſeeing Ulyſſes embraced by Virtue, will aſk him if theſe were the attentions, the fond vows, the promiſes and flatteries, on account of which ſhe relied upon his ſteadfaſtneſs and fidelity: and ſhe will aſk him not to leave her, availing herſelf for that purpoſe of great threats, mingled with careſſes, at which, mocking her, Virtue will ſay, that not only is ſhe powerleſs to ſubjugate Ulyſſes, but that, for his greater triumph, he will take with him all whom that enchanted iſle contains, and, for the carrying out of this, it will be ſo arranged, that the trees will then burſt aſunder, and from their trunks and cavities all will iſſue forth who have been there confined."

Love the Greateſt Enchantment was firſt printed, in the year 1641, in the ſecond volume of the poet's dramas, publiſhed by his brother. It is thus deſcribed:—

"*El Mayor Encanto Amor*, a *fieſta* which was repreſented before his Majeſty on the night of St. John, in the year 1635, on the pond of the royal palace of the Buen Retiro." (*Segunda parte de Comedias de Calderon*. Collected by Don Joſé Calderon, his brother. Madrid, 1641.)

Previous to its repreſentation, however, in 1635, a ſtill earlier play on the ſame ſubject had been produced, to which the date of 1634 has been aſſigned, from an alluſion to it in the firſt act of *Love the Greateſt Enchantment*, to which I have more particularly referred where the paſſage

* "*El Buen Retiro*," a pun, doubtleſs, on the name of the palace in the gardens of which this ſpectacle was to be exhibited. In the phraſeology of the "Pilgrim's Progreſs," perhaps it might be tranſlated "Giant Good-path."—TRANSLATOR.

occurs. This drama was called *Polyphemus and Circe*, and was the united work of Mira de Mefcua, Perez de Montalvan, and Calderon. It is fuppofed to have been printed at Madrid in 1652, in the *fecond part* of the collection of *Comedias de varios Autores*,* as would appear from the MS. index, by Don Juan Ifidro Fajardo, of all the plays printed in Spain to the year 1716, which is preferved in the National Library of Madrid. Of this *fecond part*, however, there feems to have been two diftinct impreffions, the one above mentioned, in 1652, and another in 1653. Of thefe impreffions, no copy of the edition of 1652 is known to exift, and that of 1653 does not contain the drama of *Polyphemus and Circe*. A copy, however, has been made up by Señor Hartzenbufch from two manufcripts kindly placed at his difpofal by Señor Duran, (the editor of the moft complete *Romancero* that has yet been given to the world,) and publifhed by him in the fourth volume of his edition of Calderon.† In addition to the curious paper juft given, it may be interefting to give an analyfis of this hitherto unknown drama, as a further evidence of the care and deliberation with which Calderon

* It is fingular, as Mr. Ticknor remarks, that of this collection of the old dramas of Spain, which at leaft extended to forty-three volumes, (from the lift of Fajardo, above mentioned, it would appear there were forty-feven,) fo little fhould now be known. Of thefe volumes, at the date of the publication of his "Hiftory of Spanifh Literature" (1849), Mr. Ticknor himfelf poffeffed three, namely, the twenty-fifth (Saragoffa, 1633), the thirty-firft (Barcelona, 1638), and the forty-third (Saragoffa, 1650). He mentions two others, which he had not feen, namely, the twenty-ninth (Valencia, 1636), and the thirty-fecond (Saragoffa, 1640). In addition to the twenty-fifth (a copy of which, as has been already mentioned, is in the poffeffion of Mr. Ticknor), Señor Hartzenbufch mentions four others, the twenty-eighth (Huefca, 1634), the thirtieth (Saragoffa, 1636), the thirty-third (Valencia, 1642), and the part above defcribed as wanting the *Polifemo y Circe*. It is from the thirtieth volume of this collection he has taken the firft fketch of Calderon's *Armas de la Hermofura*, namely, *El Privilegio de las Mujeres*, which he wrote in conjunction with Montalvan and Antonio Coello. It is given in vol. iv. p. 397, of his edition. Madrid, 1848-50. Tr.

† *Comedias de Calderon.* Por Don Juan Eugenio Hartzenbufch, vol. iv. p. 413.

elaborated thofe dramas, the fubjects of which feem to have been favourites with himfelf.

POLYPHEMUS AND CIRCE.

Written by Doctor Mira de Mefcua, Doctor Juan Perez de Montalvan, and Don Pedro Calderon de la Barca.

The firft act is by Mira de Mefcua. The opening fcene, in the pofition of the fhip, &c. refembles the correfponding one in *Love the Greateft Enchantment*. It is a faint outline of the complete picture painted by Calderon.

In the tenth fcene Polyphemus quotes Gongora, and feems well read in Spanifh poetry.*

> " Un poeta me dijo que en la luna,
> Defde la cumbre defte monte, puedo
> Efcribir mis defdichas con el dedo."—Pp. 416-17.

The lines of Gongora referred to are—

> " Y en los cielos defde efta roca puedo
> Efcribir mis defdichas con el dedo?"
>
> *Fabula de Polifemo y Galatea*, Stanza 49.†

The firft act ends with a ftruggle between *Love* and *War* for the poffeffion of Ulyffes, as in Calderon's play. The fong in favour of the former is fung by the firens, the call to the latter is given by one of the Greeks called Turfelino. The refrain is the fame in both plays: Ulyffes yields to Love, and is overcome with fleep, as in *Love the Greateft Enchantment*. The experiment which Circe makes ufe of as a teft of his

* In Montalvan's fpecial Auto on the fame fubject, Polyphemus plays on a guitar. This Auto of *Polifemo*, which Montalvan fubfequently publifhed in his *Para Todos*, is fuppofed to have been written as early as 1619.

† *Poetas Liricas de Siglos* 16 *y* 17, in Biblioteca de Autores Efpañoles, vol. xxxii. p. 462.

affection, is to assume the appearance of a statue while he sleeps. Ulysses awakes, and, seeing his mistress turned to marble, bewails his loss, and declares that there is nothing now in the palace of Circe that can detain him. He rushes towards the sea, determined to embark; Circe follows, declaring she is still alive, and rejoiced in her heart at the success of her experiment.

The second act is by Montalvan.

In this act Montalvan introduces some harmonious verses, in octave stanzas, taken from his earlier *Auto* of *Polifemo*, which, as I have said, was probably written before 1619, but not published till 1632; or, as Señor Hartzenbusch says, 1633, in the edition of his *Para Todos*, which appeared at Huesca in that year. These verses are followed by a very spirited scene between Polyphemus and Galatea. The dialogue is kept up with great liveliness, each party scarcely using more than one line—a rhetorical forbearance very unusual in Spanish plays.

The third act is by Calderon. Ulysses relates that in consequence of his having preferred Irene, one of Circe's ladies, to the enchantress herself, for no other reason, he would have us believe, but her resemblance to the absent Penelope, the jealous and indignant Circe had taken a very summary way to put an end to that flirtation, by causing palace, ladies and all, to disappear. Indeed, at the end of the second act, the grated window at which Ulysses and Irene had been conversing at the moment of this catastrophe, and of which the thoughtful lady advised her lover to lay hold, is represented as flying away, with the hero himself hanging on. The story of Polyphemus then proceeds in the usual way. In this play, the disenthralment of Ulysses is effected by an appeal from Acis (the catastrophe connected with whom and Galatea takes place in the second act), who comes forth bleeding from the rock which Polyphemus had flung upon him, and at whose fountain Ulysses was about to drink. At the departure of the hero from the island, Circe makes the same appeal that is given in *Love the Greatest Enchantment*, occasionally in the same words. At the end the indulgence of the audience is aſked for the three poets who had joined in its compoſition.

It only remains to add that the reſemblance, which every one will perceive exiſts between the opening ſcene of *Love the Greateſt Enchantment* and *The Tempeſt*, in the poſition of the ſhip, the nautical phraſeology uſed by the ſeamen, and the jokes of the *gracioſos* and clowns, ſeems to be purely accidental. If Calderon were acquainted with the works of his great Engliſh predeceſſor, and he might eaſily have been ſo, as he was but twenty-three years of age when the firſt folio was publiſhed; and from the intercourſe then exiſting between Spain and England, it would not be at all ſurpriſing that the volume had found its way to the Peninſula; he would ſcarcely have confined his imitations to this one paſſage, and perhaps another in his *Saber del mal y del bien* (To know good and evil), where the idea conveyed in Shakeſpeare's famous lines—

> " All the world's a ſtage,
> And all the men and women merely players,"

is expreſſed by Calderon with almoſt equal power in the well-known reflection commencing,—

> " *En el teatro del mundo*
> *Todos ſon repreſentantes.*"

PERSONS REPRESENTED.

Ulíses.
Antístes.
Arquelao.
Polidoro.
Timántes.
Floro.
Lebrel.
Clarin.
Lísidas.
Arsidas.
Brutamonte, *gigante.*
Aquíles.
Circe.
Casandra.
Clori.
Tisbe.
Sirene.
Flérida.
Astrea.
Libia.
La Ninfa Iris.
Galatea.
Griegos, Soldados de Arſidas, Tritones, Sirenas.

Ulysses.
Antistes.
Archelaus.
Polydorus.
Timantes.
Florus.
Lebrel.
Clarin. } *Companions of Ulyſſes.*
Lysidas, *Prince of Tuſcany.*
Arsidas, *Prince of Sicily.*
Brutamonte, *a giant.*
Shade of Achilles.
Circe.
Cassandra.
Chloris.
Thisbe.
Sirene.
Flerida. } *Her ladies.*
Astrea.
Libia. } *Her attendants.*
Iris.
Galatea. } *Nymphs.*
Greek and Sicilian Soldiers, Tritons, Sirens.

Scene, *Sicily.*

LOVE THE GREATEST ENCHANTMENT.

JORNADA I.

MAR Y COSTA DE TRINACRIA.

Suena un clarin, y deſcúbreſe un navío, y en él ULÍSES, ANTÍSTES, ARQUELAO, LEBREL, POLIDORO, TIMÁNTES, FLORO, CLARIN *y otros Griegos.*

Antíſtes.

N vano forcejamos,
Cuando rendidos á la ſuerte
eſtamos,
Contra los elementos.

Arquelao.

Homicidas los mares y los vientos,
Hoy ſerán nueſtra ruina.

Timántes.

Iza el trinquete.

Polidoro.

Larga la bolina.

Floro.

Grande tormenta el huracan promete.

Antíſtes.

¡ Hola, iza !

ACT THE FIRST.

THE SEA AND COAST OF SICILY.

A ſhip is diſcovered ſtruggling with the waves: in it are ULYSSES, ANTISTES, ARCHELAUS, POLYDORUS, TIMANTES, FLORUS, LEBREL, CLARIN, *and others.*

Antiſtes.

E ſtrive in vain,
Fate frowns averſe, and drives
us o'er the main
Before the elements : —

Archelaus.

Death wings the wind, and the wild
waves immenſe
Will be our graves to day.

Timantes.

Brace up the foreſail.

Polydorus.

Give the bow-line way.

Florus.

The riſing wind a hurricane doth blow.

Antiſtes.

Hoiſt!

Lebrel.
A la eſcota!
Clarin.
Al chafaldete!
Ulíſes.
Júpiter ſoberano,
Que eſte golfo en eſpumas dejas cano,
Yo voto á tu deidad aras y altares,
Si la cólera templas deſtos mares.

Antíſtes.
¿ Sagrado Dios Neptuno,
Griegos ofendes á peſar de Juno?

Arquelao.
Cauſando eſtá deſmayos
El cielo con relámpagos y rayos.

Clarin.
¡ Piedad, Baco divino!
No muera en agua el que ha vivido en vino.
Lebrel.
¡ Piedad, Momo ſagrado!
No el que carne vivió, muera peſcado.

Timántes.
Monumentos de hielos
Hoy ſerán eſtas ondas.

Todos.
Piedad, cielos!
Polidoro.
Parece que han oido
Nueſtro lamento y míſero gemido,

Lebrel.
To the mainſheet!—
Clarin.
Let the clew-lines go!—
Ulyſſes.
O Sovereign Jove!
Thou who this gulf in mountainous foam doſt move,
Altars and ſacrifice to thee I vow,
If thou wilt tame theſe angry waters now.
Antiſtes.
God of the Sea, great Neptune! in deſpite
Of Juno's care, why thus the Greeks affright?
Archelaus.
And ſee, the kindling Heavens are all ablaze,
With angry bolts and lightning-wingèd rays.
Clarin.
Son of Silenus, truly called *divine!*
Save from a watery death theſe lips that lived on wine!
Lebrel.
Let not, O Momus! 'tis his lateſt wiſh,
A man who lived as fleſh now die as fiſh!—
Timantes.
This day, theſe waves that round about us riſe
Will be our icy tombs:—
All.
Have pity, O ye ſkies!—
Polydorus.
It ſeems that they have liſten'd to our prayer—
Our wild lament that pierced the darkſome air—

Pues calmaron los vientos.

Arquelao.

Paces publican ya los elementos.

Antíſtes.

Y para mas fortuna,
(Que la buena y la mala nunca es una)
Ya en aqueſte horizonte
Tierra enſeña la cima de aquel monte
Corona de eſa ſierra.

Timántes.

Celages ſe deſcubren.

Todos.

Tierra, tierra!

Ulíſes.

Pon en aquella punta,
Que el mar y el cielo, hecho biſagra, junta,
La proa.

Polidoro.

Ya toca el eſpolon la playa.

Antíſtes.

Vaya toda la gente á tierra.

Todos.

Vaya;

Antíſtes.

Del mar ceſó la guerra.

Ulíſes.

Vencimos el naufragio.

Todos.

A tierra, á tierra!

[*Llega el bajel y deſembarcan todos.*

Ulíſes.

Saluda el peregrino,
Que en ſalado criſtal abrió camino,

Since ſuddenly the winds begin to ceaſe.

Archelaus.

Yes, all the elements proclaim a peace:—

Antiſtes.

And for our greater happineſs,
(Since good and evil on each other preſs)
See, on the far horizon's verge
The golden ſummits of the hills emerge
From out the miſt that ſhrouds the lowlier ſtrand.

Timantes.

The clouds are ſcatter'd now;

All.

The land! the land!

Ulyſſes.

Beneath this promontory, which doth lie
A link of ſtone betwixt the ſea and ſky,
Turn the tired prow:

Polydorus.

The rock bends beetling o'er:—

Antiſtes.

All hands deſcend on ſhore:—

All.

All hands on ſhore!

Antiſtes.

After the war of waves the air grows bland:—

Ulyſſes.

Shipwreck we have ſubdued.

All.

To land! to land!

[*The veſſel anchors and all the crew diſembark.*

Ulyſſes.

Salute this hoſpitable land,
Whoſe curving ſhores like ſheltering arms expand

La tierra donde llega,
Cuando inconſtante y náufrago ſe niega
Del mar á la inconſtancia proceloſa.

Antiſtes.

¡Salve, y ſalve otra vez, madre piadoſa!

Arquelao.

Con rendidos deſpojos
Los labios te apellidan, y los ojos.

Clarin.

Del mar vengo enfadado;
Que no es gracioſo el mar, aunque es ſalado.

Lebrel.

No es aqueſo forzoſo
Que yo no ſoy ſalado, y ſoy gracioſo.

Ulíſes.

¿Qué tierra ſerá eſta?

Timántes.

¿Quién quieres que á tu duda dé reſpueſta,
Si, ſiempre derrotados,
Mares remotos, climas apartados
Habemos tantos años diſcurrido,
El rumbo, el norte y el iman perdido?

Polidoro.

Pues no nueſtras deſdichas han ceſado;
Que el monte, donde ahora has arribado,
No parece habitable

To claſp us to its breaſt:—
Storm-toſs'd and ſhip-wreck'd we awhile may reſt
Nor dread the ſea's wild rage, the ſtorm-wind's wilder mirth!

Antiſtes.

Hail! and thrice hail, O holy mother Earth!—

Archelaus.

To thee O land! our grateful tears and ſighs
Breathe from our lips, and tremble from our eyes:—

Clarin.

Loathing the tireſome ſea, I turn from it,—
So much of ſalt and yet ſo little wit!—

Lebrel.

That does not follow, ſince the ſalt ſea can
Make a good merman of a merry-man!—

Ulyſſes.

What land is this, what ſhore, what ſheltering creek?

Timantes.

Which of us all can anſwer what you ſeek?
Since ever driven along the watery waſte
Through diſtant ſeas and climes aſunder placed,
We for ſo many years have now been toſt—
Our route, our polar ſtar, our compaſs loſt?

Polydorus.

I fear new trials threaten us again;
Since from this hill where we have ſhelter ta'en,
The place looks all deſerted—hillocks piled

En lo inculto, intrincado y formidable.

Antistes.

En él las mas pequeñas
Ruinas, de gente humana no dan señas.

Arquelao.

Solo se vé de arroyos mil surcado,
Cuyo turbio cristal desentonado
Parece, á lo que creo,
Desperdiciado aborto del Leteo.

Lebrel.

Que habemos dado, temo,
En otro mayor mal, que el Polifemo.

Floro.

Quejas son lastimosas y severas,
Cuantas se escuchan, de robustas fieras,

Timántes.

Y si las copas rústicas miramos
Destos funestos ramos,
No pájaros suaves
Vemos, nocturnas sí, agoreras aves.

Arquelao.

Y entre sus ramos rotos y quebrados
Trofeos de guerra y caza están colgados.

Polidoro.

Todo el sitio es rigor.

Floro.

Todos es espanto.

Antistes.

Todo horror.

On woody plains, and heaths untrodden rude and wild.

Antistes.

From this I cannot see the slightest trace
Of human dwellings in this lonesome place.

Archelaus.

'Tis furrow'd by a thousand tiny streams
Whose troubled tide so hoarse and slimy seems,
That one could almost think
It burst and stray'd away from Lethe's leaden brink.

Lebrel.

Worse than the cave of Polyphemus, here
A greater evil threatens us I fear :—

Florus.

And hark! that distant sound appears the howl
Of famish'd beasts that through the forests prowl;

Timantes.

And if we turn our eyes
Unto the darksome boughs that hide us from the skies,
No gentle songsters warble from the trees,
But hoarse nocturnal birds of fatal auguries.

Archelaus.

Suspended from the boughs, methinks I trace
Some broken trophies of the war and chase.

Polydorus.

All here is gloomy.

Florus.

All is full of fear.

Antistes.

Horror!

Arquelao.
Todo aſombro.
Timántes.
Todo encanto.
Lebrel.
Abſorto de mirar ſus ſeñas quedo.
¿Creeráſmé una verdad, que tengo miedo?
Clarin.
Sí creeré, ſi es que arguyo,
Que por mi corazon ſe juzga el tuyo.
[*Vanſe todos, y quedan Ulíſes y Clarin.*

Ulíſes.
Pues los dos nos quedamos,
Por eſta parte penetrando vamos.
¡Qué boſque es de confuſion tan rara
Aqueſte que piſamos!
Clarin.
Y aun no para
En eſo, pues del triſte obſcuro centro
Suyo, miro ſalirnos al encuentro
Un eſcuadron de fieras,
Bárbara inculta hueſte, que en hileras
Mal formadas embiſte
A los dos.

Ulíſes.
Defendámonos (ay triſte!)
El uno al otro.—Pero cómo es eſto?
No ſolo á nueſtra oſenſa ſe han diſpueſto,
Pero humildes, poſtrados y vencidos,
Los pechos por la tierra eſtan rendidos.
[*Salen animales, y hacen lo que ſe va diciendo.*
Y el Rey de todos ellos,

Archelaus.
And terror!
Timantes.
And enchantments drear!
Lebrel.
At all theſe ſigns I ſtand and gape diſmay'd—
Can you believe it true that I'm afraid?—
Clarin.
Eaſily, truly, and for this alone,
I judge your heart and courage by my own.
[*Exeunt all but Ulyſſes and Clarin.*

Ulyſſes.
Since we alone of all our comrades ſtay,
Let us attempt to penetrate this way:
What tangled wood with thorny thickets blind,
Is this we tread?
Clarin.
And worſe remains behind,
For from its central ſad obſcurity,
My frighten'd eyes a fearful ſquadron ſee
Of banded wild-beaſts iſſuing through the gloom;
Hither the ſavage hoſt appears to come,
In broken ranks the dreadful foe flocks nigh
To attack us two!—
Ulyſſes.
O woe! then let us die
Defending one another!—Stranger ſtill,
They do not ſeem diſpoſed to do us ill:
But humbled, vanquiſh'd, crowd around,
And with their proſtrate breaſts ſalute the ground.
[*The Animals enter and act as they are deſcribed.*
And ſee the King of all the train—

El leon, coronado de cabellos,
En pie pueſto, una vez hácia las peñas,
Y otra hácia el mar, cortes nos hace
ſeñas.
O generoſo bruto,
Rey de tanta república abſoluto,
¿Qué me quieres decir, cuando á la
playa
Senalas? ¿que me vaya,
Y que no tale mas el boſque, donde
Tienes tu imperio? A todo me re-
ſponde,
Inclinada la teſta,
Con halagos firmando la reſpueſta.
Creamos pues al hado;
Que un bruto no mintiera coronado.—
Convoca á gritos fieros
A nueſtros compañeros,
Para que al mar volvamos,
Y agradecidos el peligro huyamos.

Clarin.

Compañeros de Uliſes,
Que diſcurris los bárbaros paiſes
Deſte encantado monte,
Deſamparad ſu bárbaro horizonte.

Uliſes.

Al mar volved, al mar, que triſtemente
Con halago las fieras obediente,
Cuando ſus voces nueſtras gentes llaman,
Quieren quejarſe, y por quejarſe, braman.

Clarin.

Todas con manſo eſtruendo,

The lordly Lion crown'd with his own
mane—
Standing erect, doth beckon courteouſly,
Now to the rocks, and now unto the
O generous and noble brute, [ſea.
Of thine own realm ſole monarch abſo-
lute! [to ſhow
What wouldſt thou ſay by ſeeming thus
My way to the ſtrand? Is it that I
ſhould go,
Nor ſeek to penetrate this myſtic wood,
Where thou doſt hold thy court? Oh!
I am underſtood! [imperial eye,
He bends his ſovereign head, his proud
And with careſſes ſtrengthens his
reply:—
On fate and on his word let us rely,
A King—even though of beaſts—can
never lie!
With hurried cries of hope and fear
Convoke our ſcatter'd comrades here,
That to the ſea we may return once
more, [ſhore.
And grateful fly the dangers of this

Clarin (calling).

Companions of Ulyſſes, who
Roam this ſavage region through,
Come, leave this land by fiends poſſeſt,
Come, fly this mountain's magic breaſt!

Ulyſſes.

To ſea! to ſea! with what a ſad aſſent
The wild beaſts' voices with our cries
are blent!
With us they call our people o'er and
o'er, [ing roar!
They wiſh to warn them, and in warn-

Clarin.

With gentle clamour through the woods
they flee,

Repitiendo las ſeñas, van huyendo.
Ulíſes.
Mucho es mi aſombro.
Clarin.
Y mi triſteza es mucha.
Ulíſes.
Dioſes, ¿ qué tierra es eſta ?
Sale huyendo Antistes.
Antíſtes.
Atiende, eſcucha :
Entramos en eſe monte,
Ulíſes, tus compañeros,
A examinar ſus entrañas.
A ſolicitar ſu centro,
Cuando á las varias fortunas
Del mar penſamos que el cielo
Nos habia dado amparo,
Nos habia dado puerto.
Mas ay triſte ! que el peligro
Es de mar y tierra dueño ;
Porque en la tierra y el mar
Tiene el peligro ſu imperio.
Digalo alli, coronado
De tantos naufragios ciertos,
Y aqui lo diga, ceñido
De tantos preciſos rieſgos :
Aunque ni el mar, ni la tierra
No tienen la culpa dellos,
Pues el hombre en tierra y mar
Lleva el peligro en sí meſmo.
Por diverſos laberintos,
Que labró, artífice dieſtro
Sin eſtudio y ſin cuidado,
El deſaliño del tiempo,
Diſcurrimos eſe monte,
Haſta que hallándonos dentro,
Vimos un rico palacio.
Tan vanamente ſoberbio,
Que embarazando los aires,

Still making ſigns and pointing to the ſea.
Ulyſſes.
Great is my wonder.
Clarin.
Great my mournful fear.
Ulyſſes.
What is this land, ye Gods ?—
[Antistes *ruſhes in.*
Antiſtes.
Oh ! liſten, thou ſhalt hear :—
We, Ulyſſes, thy companions,
Dared this mountain wild to enter,
Its interior to examine,
To explore its inmoſt centre,
For we thought the fickle fortune
Of the ſea at length had ended,
And that heaven had given us favour,
And the earth a welcome ſhelter ;
But, alas ! doth Danger lord it
Over land and ſea for ever,
Sea and land th' eternal kingdom
Ruled by Danger's deathleſs ſceptre ;
There his gloomy throne is builded
Of unnumber'd ſhipwreck'd veſſels,
Here his widening realm is bounded
By a ring of riſks unended,
Though nor land nor ſea ſhould juſtly
Bear the blame of theſe exceſſes,
Since on both, the ſeeds of danger
Man within his own breaſt beareth ;
Through the labyrinthine paſſes,
Which with careleſs hand Time cleaveth—
Time the cunning craftſman making
Moſt of that which he neglecteth,
Without ſeeming toil or effort,—
In through theſe the mount we enter'd,
And advanced, until with wonder
A rich palace we beheld there,

Y los montes afligiendo,
Era para aquellos nube,
Y peñaſco para eſtos,
Porque ſe daba la mano
Con uno y con otro extremo:
Pero aunque vicioſos eran,
La virtud no eſtaba en medio.
Saludamos ſus umbrales
Corteſanamente atentos,
Y apenas de nueſtras voces
La mitad nos hurtó el eco,
Cuando de Ninfas hermoſas
Un tejido coro bello
Las puertas abrió, moſtrando
Apacible y liſonjero,
Que habia de ſer ſu agaſajo
De nueſtros males conſuelo,
De nueſtras penas alivio,
De nueſtras tormentas puerto.
Mintió el deſeo; ¿ mas cuándo
Dijo verdad el deſeo?
Detras de todas venia,
Bien como el dorado Febo,
Acompañado de eſtrellas,
Y cercado de luceros,
Una muger tan hermoſa,
Que nos perſuadimos ciegos,
Que era, a envidia de Diana,
La dioſa deſtos deſiertos.
Eſta pues nos preguntó,
Quiénes eramos; y habiendo
Informádoſe de paſo
De los infortunios nueſtros,
Cauteloſamente humana,
Mandó ſervir al momento
A ſus Damas las bebidas
Mas generoſas, haciendo
Con urbanas ceremonias
Político el cumplimiento.

So ſuperbly proud and haughty,
That embarraſſing the zephyrs
And the mountains' ſides oppreſſing,
It to thoſe a vaſt cloud ſeemeth,
And to theſe a rock as mighty:—
Since at once to earth and heaven
Each of its extreme ends reaches;
But unlike the extremes of vices,
In its midſt no virtue dwelleth.
We, its threſholds fair ſaluted,
Courteouſly approaching nearer,
And the ſwift thief Echo ſcarce
Half our ſtolen words repeated,
When a linkèd choir of nymphs
Wide its ample doors extended,
Showing in their ſmiling looks
Such a ſweet and gracious preſence,
That we thought at length had come,
After all our toils, refreſhment,
After all our evils, good,
And a haven after tempeſts:—
Falſely ſpoke our wiſhes thus;
But, ah! when have wiſhes ever
Spoke the truth? Behind them all,
Like the golden ſun attended
By the morning ſtars, and girt
Round with roſy eaſtern ether,
Came a woman, ah! ſo fair,
That our dazzled eyes believed her
(To Diana's envy ſure)
The ſole goddeſs of thoſe deſerts:—
She inquired of us, at length,
Who we were: and when was ended
The brief outline of our woes,
She, with purpoſe well diſſembled,
Order'd her attendant dames
To ſupply us with whatever
Generous and refreſhing drinks
We in our condition needed,

Apenas de ſus licores
El veneno admitió el pecho,
Cuando corrió al corazon,
Y en un inſtante, un momento,
A delirar empezaron,
De todos los que bebieron,
Los ſentidos, tan mudados
De lo que fueron primero,
Que no ſolo la embriaguez
Entorpeció el ſentimiento
Del juicio, porcion del alma,
Sino tambien la del cuerpo;
Pues poco á poco extinguidos
Los proporcionados miembros,
Fueron mudando las formas.
¿Quién vió tan raro portento?
¿Quién vió tan extraño hechizo?
¿Quién vió prodigio tan nuevo?
¿Y quién vió, que, ſiendo hermoſa
Una muger con extremo,
Para hacer los hombres brutos,
Uſaſe de otros remedios,
Pues deſtas transformaciones
Es la hermoſura el veneno?
Cual era ya racional
Bruto, de pieles cubierto;
Cual, de manchas ſalpicado
Fiera con entendimiento;
Cual ſierpe armada de conchas,
Cual de agudas puntas lleno,
Cual animal mas immundo:
Y todos al fin á un tiempo
Articulaban gemidos,
Penſando que éran acentos.
La mágica entonces dijo:
"Hoy vereis, cobardes Griegos,
De la manera que Circe
Trata cuantos paſageros
Aqueſtos umbrales tocan."—

Greeting us the while with all
Courteous geſtures and addreſſes.
Scarcely of theſe poiſon'd drinks
Had the mouth received the eſſence,
When it reach'd the very heart;
So that quickly, in my preſence,
Strange delirium ſeized on all
Who had drunk what they preſented,
So that the ſwift drunkenneſs
Not alone benumb'd the ſenſes,
Or obſcured the reaſon, part
Of the immortal ſoul, but even
Reach'd the very frame itſelf;
So that the well-moulded members
Gradually began to loſe
Their fix'd outline and preſentment.
Who e'er ſaw ſo ſtrange a portent?
Who bewitchment ſo demented?
Who a prodigy ſo new?—
And who ſaw too this extremer
Wonder, that a woman deck'd
With ſuch charms as ſhe poſſeſſes,
If ſhe wiſh'd to make men brutes,
Should have other means invented,
When ſo well for ſuch transformings
Beauty's poiſonous power ſucceedeth?
One, though keeping reaſon ſtill,
Seem'd a rough-ſkinn'd beaſt untether'd;
One, with ſtain'd and ſpotted hide,
Seem'd a brute with human ſenſes;
This a ſerpent arm'd with ſcales,
That by prickly ſtings protected;
This became an animal
Moſt unclean, and all together
Utter'd howls and cries, believing
They were words that they accented.
Then the fair magician ſaid,
"Coward Greeks, this day's experience
Teacheth you how Circe treats

Yo, que por ſer el que haciendo
Eſtaba la relacion
De nueſtros varios ſuceſos,
Aun no habia al labio dado
El vaſo, el peligro viendo,
Sin que reparara en mí
Circe, corrí; que en efecto,
El que ſe ſabe librar
De los venenos mas fieros
De una hermoſura, es quien ſolo
Niega los labios á ellos.
Eſto en fin me ha ſucedido,
Y vengo à aviſarte dello,
Porque deſta Esfinge huyamos.
¿Pero dónde podrá el cielo
Librarnos de una muger
Con belleza y con ingenio?

Ulíſes.

¿Cuándo vengada eſtarás,
O injuſta deidad de Vénus!
De Grecia? ¿cuándo tendrán
Divinas cóleras medio?

Antíſtes.

No en laſtimoſos gemidos
La ocaſion embaracemos,
Que tenemos de librarnos:
Al mar volvamos huyendo.

Ulíſes.

¿Cómo, habemos de dejar
Aſi á nueſtros compañeros?

Clarin.

Perdernos, ſeñor, noſotros,
No es alivio para ellos.

Ulíſes.

Juno, ſi en deſprecio tuyo
Vénus ofende á los Griegos,
¿Cómo tú no los defiendes,

Every traveller who ſteppeth
From his ſhip upon theſe ſhores."
I, that I might be the bearer
Of this newer, ſtranger phaſe
Of the fate that dogs us ever,
Though the cup was at my lips,
Seeing what a danger threaten'd,
Fled ere Circe was aware.
For in truth the only ſecret
Antidote by which to eſcape
Beauty's poiſon'd influences,
Is to never truſt the lips
Even to touch what ſhe preſenteth.
This is my unhappy tale,
And of this I come to tell thee,
That we may this fair Sphinx fly.
But fly whither? ſince the heavens
Scarce can ſave us from a woman,
Ah! ſo lovely and ſo clever!

Ulyſſes.

Venus, cruel goddeſs fair,
When wilt thou enough avenge thee
Upon Greece? Ah! when will be
Thy divine diſpleaſure leſſen'd?

Antiſtes.

Let us not in mournful ſighs
Loſe the occaſion chance preſenteth
Of effecting our eſcape:—
Better ſeek the ſea's rude ſhelter.

Ulyſſes.

How! and can we leave them here,
Our companions thus deſerted?

Clarin.

But to loſe ourſelves, my lord,
Will, methinks, but little ſerve them.

Ulyſſes.

Juno, if through ſcorn of thee
Venus thus the Greeks oppreſſes;
Why, reſenting this her ſcorn,

Quejoſa de tu deſprecio?
Acuérdate, que, ofendida
De Páris, á nueſtro acero
Le fiaſte tu venganza:
Acuêrdate, que ſangrientos
Por tí abraſamos á Troya,
Cuyo no apagado incendio
Hoy en padrones de humo
Eſtá en cenizas ardiendo.
Si, por haberte vengado,
Tantos males padecemos,
Remédianos, Juno bella,
Contra la deidad de Vénus.

[*Tocan chirimías, y ſale en un arco la Ninfa* IRIS, *y canta la Múſica dentro.*

Múſica.

Iris, Ninfa de los aires,
El arco deſpliega bello,
Y menſagera de Juno,
Raſga los azules velos.

Iris (*canta*).

Ya la obedezco,
Y batiendo las alas,
Rompo los vientos.

Ulíſes.

Línea de púrpura y nieve,
Nube de roſa y de fuego,
Verde, roja y amarilla,
Nos deſlumbran a ſus reflejos.

Antíſtes.

¿Qué hermoſo raſgo corrido
En el papel de los cielos,
Bandera es de paz?

Ulíſes.

Y en él
Eſtá la Ninfa pendiendo,
Embajatriz de las dioſas,
Reina de dos elementos.—

Doſt thou not in turn defend them?
Oh! remember when thou wert
Wroth with Paris, to avenge thee,
Thou didſt truſt thee to our ſwords:—
And that bloody deed remember,
How it was for thee we burn'd
Ilium down, whoſe living embers
Raiſe red monuments of ſmoke
O'er its aſhes ſtill unquenchèd;
If for wreaking thy revenge,
Such unnumber'd ills have centred
All in us, O Juno fair,
Againſt Venus be our helper!

[*A ſound of clarions is heard, and the nymph* IRIS *appears in a rainbow, voices are heard ſinging within.*

Song within.

Iris, lovely nymph of air,
Now her beauteous bow extendeth,
And, ſwift meſſenger of Juno,
Rends the azure veil of heaven.

Iris (*ſings*).

I, the glad-obeying bearer
Of good tidings, float along,
Parting with my wings the ether.

Ulyſſes.

Curved lines of purpled ſnow,
Clouds of fire and roſe-hues blended,
Green and red, and golden yellow,
Dazzle us with their reflexes.

Antiſtes.

What fair ſtreak of light is this,
That, from heaven's blue walls projected,
Seems the flag of peace?

Ulyſſes.

And, lo!
In it is the nymph ſuſpended,
She who is embaſſadreſs
From the Goddeſſes, and regent

Iris, bellísima Ninfa,
Si tu respuesta merezco,
¿ Qué, dichosa, vas buscando ?
¿ Qué, infelice, vas huyendo ?

Iris (*canta*).

A tus fortunas atenta,
O nunca vencido Griego,
Juno tu amparo dispone,
Y yo de su parte vengo.
Este ramo, que te traigo,
De varias flores cubierto,
Hoy contra Circe será
Triaca de sus venenos.

[*Deja caer un ramillete.*

Toca con él sus hechizos,
Desvaneceránse luego,
Como al amor no te rindas :
Que con avisarte desto,
Ya la obedezco,
Y batiendo las alas,
Rompo los vientos.

Toda la Música.

Y batiendo las alas,
Rompo los vientos.

[*Tocan chirimías, y desaparece el arco y la Ninfa.*

Ulises.

Hermoso aliento de Juno,
No desvanezcas tan presto
Tanto aparato de estrellas,
Tanta pompa de luceros.
Espera, detente, aguarda,
Que te sacrifique el pecho
Estas lágrimas, que lleves
En señal de rendimiento.

Clarin.

Ya las esparcidas luces

Of two separate elements : —
Iris, lovely nymph, if ever
I thy answer have deserved,
Say, O happy, whom thou seekest ?
Say, unhappy, whom thou fleest ?

Iris (*sings*).

O thou never conquer'd Greek !
Thou whose fate is ever present
To great Juno's thoughtful care,
Unto thee she now has sent me.
See this floral branch I bear
Gemm'd with buds that Flora tended,
It will be the antidote
Against Circe's poison'd secrets,—

[*She lets fall a bunch of flowers.*

Touch with it her magic spells,
They will vanish, if thou yieldest
Not to love's more potent charm :—
With this parting hint I leave thee,
I, the glad-obeying bearer
Of good tidings, float along,
Parting with my wings the ether.

Chorus of voices within.

See ! the glad-obeying bearer
Of good tidings floats along,
Parting with her wings the ether,

[*The clarions sound, and the rainbow and Nymph disappear.*

Ulysses.

Sweet-sent breath from Juno's lips,
Ah ! do not so soon dismember
Such a glorious gleam of stars,
Such a crimson cloud of cressets,
Oh ! detain thee, listen, stay,
Till at least my breast present thee
With these sacrificial tears,
Of my feelings the mute emblems.

Clarin.

See, the scatter'd lights retire,

Va doblando y recogiendo,
Haſtaperderſe de viſta,
Por las campañas del viento.

Ulíſes.

Ya no hay que temer de Circe
Los encantos, pues ya veo
Tan de mi parte los hados,
Tan en mi favor los cielos.
A ſus palacias me guia,
Veráſme vencer en ellos
Sus hechizos, y librar
A todos mis compañeros.

Antiſtes.

No es meneſter que te guie
A ſus ojos; que ella, haciendo
Salva á tus peligros, ſale
Al ſon de mil inſtrumentos.

Aparece el Palacio de Circe.

Salen los Múſicos cantando, y deſpues CIRCE, CASANDRA, TISBE, CLORI *y* ASTREA, *que trae un vaſo en una ſalvilla, y* LIBIA *una toalla.*

Múſica.

En hora dichoſa venga
A los palacios de Circe
El ſiempre invencible Griego,
El nunca vencido Ulíſes.

Circe.

En hora dichoſa venga
Hoy á eſta palacio hermoſo
El Griego mas generoſo,
Que vió el ſol, donde prevenga
Blando albergue, y donde tenga
Dulce hoſpedage, y atento
A ſus fortunas, contento
Pueda en la tierra triunfar
De la cólera del mar,
Y de la ſaña del viento.

Now outgleaming, now condensèd
Till they wholly fade away
On the far-off plains of heaven!

Ulyſſes.

Now I have no cauſe to fear
Circe's magic rites, defended
As I am by friendly fates,
And by favouring ſkies protected.
To her palace lead the way,
Thou wilt ſee me there defend me
'Gainſt her ſorceries, and ſet free
My companions from their fetters.

Antiſtes.

Need there's none that I ſhould lead thee
To her preſence, ſince ſhe entereth
Here herſelf, with thouſand cymbals
Greeting thee and thy diſtreſſes.

The Palace of Circe appears.

Muſicians enter ſinging and playing, followed by CIRCE, CASSANDRA, THISBE, CHLORIS, ASTREA, *who carries a goblet on a ſalver, and* LIBIA, *bearing a napkin.*

Song.

Be the hour propitious when
To the palace-halls of Circe
Comes the ever-victor Greek,
The invincible Ulyſſes.

Circe.

Be the hour propitious when
To this beauteous palace here
Comes the nobleſt Greek that e'er
Has the ſun ſeen amongſt men;
Here ſhall he enjoy again
Sweet repoſe, and rapture find,
And attention the moſt kind,
Since in triumph cometh he
From the anger of the ſea,
And the raging of the wind.

Felice pues fueſe el dia,
Que eſtos piélagos ſulcó,
Felice fueſe el que halló
Abrigo en la patria mia,
Y felice la oſadía,
Con que ya vencer preſuma
En tranquila paz, en ſuma
Felicidad inmortal,
Eſe monſtruo de criſtal,
Sierpe eſcamada de eſpuma.
Que yo al cielo agradecida,
Pues ya mis venturas ſé,
De tanto huéſped daré
Parabienes á mi vida;
Y aſi, á tus plantas rendida,
Con aplauſos diferentes,
Vengo á recibir tus gentes,
Hurtando en ecos ſuaves
Las claúſulas á las aves,
Los compaſes á las fuentes.
Y porque al que en mar vivió,
Lo que mas en él le obliga
A ſentir, es la fatiga
De la ſed, que padeció,
(¿Quién ſed en tanta agua vió?)
A traerte aqui ſe atreven
Los aplauſos, que me mueven,
(En ſeñal de cuan piadoſo
Es mi afecto) el generoſo
Néctar, que los dioſes beben.
Bebe, y ſin pavor alguno
Brinda á la gran mageſtad
De Júpiter, la beldad
De Vénus, ciencias de Juno,
De Marte armas, de Neptuno
Ondas, de Diana honor,
Flores de Flora, eſplendor
De Apolo; y por varios modos,
Porque en uno aſiſten todos,

May the day thrice happy ſhine
When he plough'd theſe waves around,
Be it happy when he found
Shelter in this realm of mine:
Be that courage call'd divine,
With which he in peace doth come
Now to taſte the joys of home,
He who lately hath ſubdued
This cruel cryſtal monſter rude,
This azure ſerpent ſcaled with foam.
Gratefully, with glowing breaſt,
Do I thank the Gods for this,
That they crown my life with bliſs,
Giving me ſo great a gueſt:—
Therefore have I hither preſt
Thus to throw me at thy feet,
Thus melodiouſly to greet
Thy approach with ſongs, whoſe words
Seem the notes of warbling birds,
Or the fountains' murmurings ſweet.
And ſince dwellers on the ſea
'Mid each moment's miſery,
Feel of all their ills the worſt
Is the oppreſſive pang of thirſt—
(Can thirſt 'mid ſo much water be?)
Hither to the ocean's brink—
(By this zeal, O wanderer, think
How I value thy ſurviving!)
Have I brought thee the reviving
Nectar that the great Gods drink.
Drink, and without any fear
Pledge the ſovereign ſacredneſs
Of high Jove, the lovelineſs
Of fair Venus, Neptune's ſphere,
Juno's knowledge, the ſevere
Huntreſs Nymph who rules the grove,
Flora's flowers, the beams that move
Round Apollo's golden throne,
Or, to blend all praiſe in one,

Bebe y brinda al dios de Amor.
Ulíſes.
Bellíſima cazadora,
Que en eſte opaco horizonte,
Siendo noche todo el monte,
Todo el monte haces aurora,
Pues no amaneció, haſta ahora
Que te ví, la luz en él,
Admite rendido y fiel
Un peregrino del mar,
Que halló piadoſo al peſar,
Que halló á la dicha cruel.
Eſa nave derrotada,
Que con tanta ſed anhela,
Pez, que por las ondas vuela,
Ave, que en los aires nada,
A tu deidad conſagrada,
Víctima ya ſin ejemplo,
De tus aras la contemplo,
Pues aqui ſe ha de quedar
Por trofeo de tu altar,
Por deſpojo de tu templo.
[*Llegan* LIBIA *y* ASTREA.
El néctar, con que has brindado
Mi feliz venida, aceto,
Aunque temor y reſpeto
Me han ſuſpendido y turbado
Tanto, que de recatado,
No me atrevo á tus favores,
Sin que otros labios mejores
Liſonjeen tus agravios:
Y aſi, antes que con los labios,
Haré la ſalva con flores.
[*Mete el ramillete en el vaſo, y ſale fuego.*
Aſtrea.
En fuego el agua encendió.
Libia.
¿ Qué es lo que mis ojos ven ?

Drink and pledge the God of Love.
Ulyſſes.
Beauteous huntreſs, thou that makeſt
All this black horizon bright,
Flooding all the darkſome night
Of this mountain's vault opaqueſt
With the dawn that thou awakeſt,
Since thy face its orient is,—
Oh ! receive ſubdued, ſubmiſs,
A poor pilgrim of the ſea
Who in grief finds ſympathy,
Cruelty in ſeeming bliſs.
Our diſrupted bark that there
Gapes with thirſt, and ſtranded lies,
Fiſh that through the water flies,
Bird that ſwimmeth through the air,
Conſecrated, as it were,
Unto thee, fair nymph divine,
We to-day to thee reſign ;
Victim-like it muſt remain
As a trophy in thy fane,
As a relic at thy ſhrine.
[LIBIA *and* ASTREA *advance.*
And this nectar which you drink
To my happy coming here,
I accept, but with a fear
Mingled ſo with awe, I ſhrink
But to touch the goblet's brink ;
Terror even my thirſt o'erpowers,
Worthier lips than thoſe of ours
Should the draught a goddeſs ſips
Taſte, and thus before the lips
I ſalute it with theſe flowers.
[*He applies the flowers to the goblet, from which fire iſſues.*
Aſtrea.
Fire from water flaming high !
Libia.
Can my eyes believe this true ?

Circe.
¿Quién, cielos airados, quién
Mas ha ſabido que yo?

Ulíses.
Quien tus encantos venció
Deidad ſuperior ha ſido;
Y pues á tiempo he venido,
Que á tantos vengar eſpero,
Verás, mágica, eſte acero
En tu púrpura teñido.
[*Saca la eſpada.*

Circe.
Aunque llego à merecer
La muerte, es bien que te aſombre,
Que no es victoria de un hombre
El matar á una muger.
Valor, tan hecho á vencer,
No ha de ſer, no, mi homicida.
Rendida tienes mi vida:
Luego de tu acero hoy
Dos veces ſegura eſtoy,
Por muger, y por rendida.

Ulíses.
Por rendida, y por muger
Darte la muerte no quiero;
Vida tienes; mas primero
Que la vaina vuelva á ver
La cuchilla, has de traer
Mis compañeros aqui.

Circe.
Eſo y mas haré por tí.—
Oid, racionales fieras,
En vueſtras formas primeras
Trocad las formas que os dí.
[*Sale cada uno de por sí.*

Timántes.
¿Qué es lo que me ha ſucedido
Eſte rato que he ſoñado?

Circe.
Who, O angry heavens! who
Deeper lore has learn'd than I?

Ulyſſes.
One, a mightier deity,
Who thy charms hath all ſubdued;—
By my vengeful arm purſued
Thou the atoning ſtroke ſhalt feel,
Sorcereſs, thou ſhalt ſee this ſteel
With thy crimſon blood imbued.
[*Draws his ſword.*

Circe.
Though by me it is confeſt
That I merit death from thee,
Still to a man, no victory
Is it to pierce a woman's breaſt!
Valour hath a nobler teſt
Than the murderous ſtroke inhuman—
'Tis to ſpare a proſtrate foeman;—
To ſubdue is not to ſlay,
Doubly ſafe am I to-day
In being conquer'd and a woman.

Ulyſſes.
Then for being thus o'erpower'd,
Likewiſe for the form you wear,
I conſent your life to ſpare,
But before I ſheathe my ſword,
On the ſpot muſt be reſtored
My companions ſafe and free.

Circe.
That and more I'll do for thee:—
Reaſon-bearing wild beaſts, hear!
In your proper ſhapes appear,
Changing thoſe were given by me!
[*All the followers of* ULYSSES *enter one after the other.*

Timantes.
What a ſtrange deluſive dream
Slumbering fancy round me wrought!—

Polidoro.
En un leon transformado
Mi letargo me ha tenido.
Floro.
¡ Qué ageno de mi ſentido
Me ha uſurpado un freneſi !
Arquelao.
¡ Gracias á Dios, que te vi,
O campo azul criſtalino !

Lebrel.
Vive Dios ! que fui cochino,
Y aun me ſoy lo que me fui.
Circe.
Ya libres tus gentes ves.
Ulíſes.
Y ya aqui no hay que eſperar.—
¡ Alto, amigos, á embarcar !
Timántes.
A todos nos da tus pies
Por eſta ventura.
Circe.
Pues
Tan ſeguro eſtás de mí,
No te auſentes, no, de aqui,
Sin que llegue á ſaber yo
Mas deſpacio, quién venció
Mis encantos.
Ulíſes.
Oye.
Circe.
Di.
Ulíſes.
Si caben tantos ſuceſos
En el coto de unas voces :
La fértil Grecia es mi patria,
Y Ulíſes mi propio nombre ;
Aunque inclinado á las letras,
Militares eſcuadrones

Polydorus.
In my lethargy methought
That a lion I had been !
Florus.
What a frenzy came to ſcreen
Reaſon's light and nature's laws !
Archelaus.
Thanks to Heaven ! the cloud withdraws,
And I ſee the azure ſky !
Lebrel.
Bleſt be Jove ! a hog was I,
And I *am* juſt what I was !
Circe.
All thy people now are free.
Ulyſſes.
Let us hence, my friends, away !
Quick ! embark ; make no delay !
Timantes.
At thy feet permit that we
Kneel to thank thee.
Circe.
Since of me
Now all fear were worſe than weak,
Let me aſk you not to ſeek
Yonder wave, until I know
More of him who has laid low
My enchantments.
Ulyſſes.
Liſten !
Circe.
Speak !
Ulyſſes.
If ſuch ſtrange adventure can
By a ſingle voice be ſpoken :—
Fertile Greece my country is,
As Ulyſſes there they know me ;
Though inclined to letters firſt,
Martial camps and crowds I follow'd,

Seguí; que en mí ſe admiraron
Eſpada y pluma conformes.
Cerqué á Troya, y rendí á Troya:
No me permitas que torne
A la memoria ſus ruinas,
Baſta que Vénus las llore.
Heredero de las armas
De Aquíles fui; porque logren,
Si dueño no tan valiente,
Dueño á lo menos tan noble.
Al mar me entregué, penſando
Volver á mi patria, donde
Trocara el bélico eſtruendo
A regalados favores.
Engañóme mi eſperanza,
Mintióme mi amor, burlóme
Mi deſeo. ¡O cuanto fácil
Su dicha imagina el hombre!
Vénus, del Griego ofendida,
Mis venturas deſcompone;
Que es, aunque dioſa, muger,
En quien duran los rencores.
La cárcel abrió á los vientos,
Para mi agravio veloces;
Que para mis eſperanzas
Aun fueran los vientos torpes.
Ellos, que airados embiſten,
La fragil armada rompen,
Y yo turbado perdí
Con la confuſion el norte.
Huéſped viví de Neptuno
Seis años, y por ſalobres
Campañas de agua, ſoſpecho,
Que he dado una vuelta al orbe.
Entre Caríbdis y Scila
Me ví, y á las dulces voces
Del golfo de las Sirenas
Baſiliſco fui de bronce.
Llegué al pie del Lilibeo,

Since in me the ſword and pen
Woke in turn the ſame reſponſes,—
I laid ſeige to Troy, by me
Was the Trojan city conquer'd;
Little need of memory now
To go o'er that famous ſtory;
'Tis enough its proud walls fell
And that Venus weepeth o'er them.
I became, by public voice,
Of Achilles' arms the owner,
Since they needed a new lord
If not braver, ſtill as noble;—
Truſting to the ſea, I thought
Soon my country to recover,
Where I hoped, inſtead of ſteel,
Arms of fondneſs would enfold me.
Hope deceived me, love ſpoke falſely,
Fond deſire deluſive mock'd me.
Oh! how eaſily doth man
Dream of joy from doubtfuleſt omens!
Venus, wrathful with the Greeks,
All my plans, my ſchemes diſorder'd—
Since a goddeſs though ſhe be,
Woman-like her rage ſhe fondles—
She the priſon of the winds
For my quick deſtruction open'd;
Swift were they to do me wrong,
For my hopes ſo dead and torpid,
On my frail armada ſoon
Burſt they forth with rage ungovern'd,
So that I, confuſed, overwhelm'd
With amazement, loſt the pole-ſtar;
Six years lived I Neptune's gueſt,
And his ſalt ſeas ſailing over,
Muſt in that time I ſuſpect
Have encompaſsèd the whole earth.
Between Scylla and Charybdis
I beheld me, and a bronzèd
Baſiliſk grew to the ſyren's ſong,

Eſe gigante, que opone
Al cielo ſus puntas, ſiendo
Excelſa pira de flores,
Donde fui de Polifemo
Míſero cautivo, y donde
Con ſu muerte reſcaté
Mi vida de ſus priſiones,
El trágico fin vengando
De Acis, generoſo jóven,
Y la hermoſa Galatea,
Hija de Nereo y Dóris,
Que, lágrimas de un peñaſco,
Al mar en dos fuentes corren,
Cuando . . . . Mas deber no quiero
Tan poco á hazaña tan noble,
Que la deſluzca en contarla,
Preſumiendo que la ignores.
Baſta decir, que ſeguro
De ſus caſtigos atroces,
Tuvimos por agradables
De los vientos los rigores,
Porque tan airados fueron,
Que nos trajeron adonde
El rigor de una muger
Venciеſe al rigor de un hombre;
Pues venimos donde tú
Mágicas transformaciones
Uſas; llorando lo digan
Eſas fieras y eſos robles.
Y aſi, pues tan generoſas
Deidades mas ſuperiores
Me aſeguran, volveré,
Huyendo de tus rigores,

Though they ſang their ſweeteſt, ſofteſt;
Then I came unto the foot
Of Lilybœum, which oppoſes
Its gigantic mountain-peaks
To the heavens, and crown'd with roſes
Seems a pyramid of flowers,
Where I was awhile the hopeleſs
Captive thrall of Polyphemus,
Till my priſon-doors I open'd
By his death; and ſo preſerving
Life and limb, the ſelf-ſame moment
By the ſelf-ſame ſtroke avenging
Acis' tragic end, young lover,
And the beauteous Galatea,
Child of Nereus and of Doris,
Who, the ſwift tears of a rock,
Roll twin fountains to the ocean;—
There . . . . but I would wiſh to ſhow
More reſpect to a deed ſo noble
Than to ſpoil it by relating,
Thinking that it was forgotten.*
'Tis enough to ſay that ſafe
From his dread atrocious torments
We were wafted by the winds,
Pleaſant now, but with their former
Anger wing'd, ſince us they bore
Where the rigour of a woman
All man's rigour triumphs o'er,
Since we came where thou performeſt
Magic metamorphoſes:—
Weeping let theſe beaſt-ſhapes own them,
And the trees of this ſtrange foreſt.
Now ſince more indulgent powers

* Alluding to the drama of *Poliſemo y Circe*, which Calderon wrote in conjunction with Mira de Meſcua and Perez da Montalvan. It is the original draft of *El Mayor Encanto Amor*, and having been acted the year preceding that in which the latter drama was brought out (1635), was ſtill in the memory of the audience. See Hartzenbuſch's "Calderon," vol. iv. pp. 413 and 669, and, for an analyſis of it, the introduction to this tranſlation of *El Mayor Encanto Amor*, p. 16.

A quebrantar los criſtales
De eſe piélago, que ſobre
Sus eſpaldas tantos años
Huéſped me admitió. Deſcoge
O ſurto delfin, que vuelas,
Varado neblí, que corres,
Las alas, porque otra vez
La plata del agua cortes,
O con la quilla la rices,
O con el buque la entorches.
Torne pues al albedrío
De aire y mar la nave, y torne
A llevarme donde fuere
La voluntad de los dioſes.

Circe.

Retórico Griego, á quien
Eſe eſcollo criſtalino,
Eſe peñaſco de nieve,
Eſa campaña de vidrio
Náufrago huéſped te tuvo
Tantos años, pues, vencidos
Los hados, llegas, trayendo
Aqueſas flores contigo,
Que ſon antidoto hermoſo,
Que ſon conjuro divino
Contra mortales venenos,
Contra mágicos hechizos:
No tan preſto á peinar vuelvas
Al mar los cabellos rizos,
Que canos y ajados ſon
Hermoſos con deſaliño;
Deja deſcanſar las ondas,
Y eſe bajel, que al abrigo
De dos montes ſurto yace,
Permite, que agradecido

And divinities more potent
Reaſſure me, once again,
Flying from thy deeds of wonder,
I ſhall break the cryſtal glaſs
Of this ſea, upon whoſe ſhoulders
I, an outcaſt, have been carried
Many a year. Be then unfolded,
Flying dolphin anchor'd there—
Stranded-falcon ſo ſwift-footed,
Thy white wings, for thou once more
Muſt cut through the ſilver-molten
Surface of the ſea, thy prow
Daſhing up the curling foam-wreaths,
And thy keel wave-woven braid.
Give then, give the ſhip the open
Choice of ſea and air, that I
Borne on it may thus diſcover
Where the Gods deſire I go.

Circe.

Eloquent-tongued Greek King whom
Yonder rippling realm of cryſtal,
Yonder liquid hills of ſnow,
Yonder plains of glaſſy glitter,
Have a ſhipwreck'd gueſt detain'd
Such a length of years: ſince hither,
Conquering adverſe fate, thou haſt come,
Bearing theſe divine flowers with thee,
Which are beauteous antidotes,
Which are god-ſent exorciſms,
Againſt deadly poiſon'd draughts,
Againſt magical bewitchments,
Do not fly ſo quickly back
To outcomb the foam-white frizzled
Locks of ocean, which, though toſs'd
To and fro in wild-treſs'd whiteneſs,
Wear a beauteous negligence:—
Let the waves repoſe a little,
And that bark which in the ſhade
Of two hills at anchor lieth,—

A la piedad de los cielos,
De los hados al arbitrio,
Blanda, y no penoſamente
Bata las alas de lino,
En tanto que te reparas
De aquel paſado peligro,
Que derrotado te trajo
A aqueſtos montes altivos.
Y para que ſepas cuanto
Aſombro es el que has vencido,
Darte relacion de mí
Eſte inſtante ſolicito.
Eſa luminar antorcha,
Que deſde ſu plauſtro rico
El cielo ilumina á rayos,
El mundo deſcribe á giros,
Eſe planeta, que corre
Siempre hermoſo, ſiempre vivo,
Llevándoſe tras sí el dia,
Fue el luciente padre mio.
Prima nací de Medea
En Teſalia, donde fuimos
Aſombro de ſus eſtudios,
Y de ſus ciencias prodigio;
Porque enſeñadas las dos
De un gran mágico, nos hizo
Docto eſcándalo del mundo,
Sabio portento del ſiglo:
Que en fin las mugeres, cuando
Tal vez aplicar ſe han viſto
A las letras, ó á las armas,
Los hombres han excedido.
Y aſi, ellos envidioſos,
Viendo nueſtro ánimo invicto,
Viendo sútil* nueſtro ingenio,
Porque no fuera el dominio
Todo nueſtro, nos vedaron

* Hartzenbuſch reads *agudo*, ſee his edition, t. i. p. 304.—Tr.

Grant that, ſhowing thus thy thanks
To the heavens for their late pity,
For their mercy, to the fates,
It may beat its wings of linen
Tranquilly, without fatigue,
Whilſt thou doſt repair a little
The effects of that late danger
Which had flung thee almoſt ſhipwreck'd
At the foot of thoſe tall cliffs.
And, that thou mayſt know the mighty
Terror whom thou haſt ſubdued,
I will give to thee this inſtant
An account of who I am.
Yonder torch of dazzling brightneſs
Which, from out its car of gold,
Heaven with glorious beams enlightens,
Earth encircles as it rolls;
That great ſtar whoſe undiminiſh'd
Power and beauty lead along
Captive day untired, delighted,
Was my ſplendour-crownèd ſire:
Being of Medea's kindred,
I with her, a child, was rear'd
In Theſſalia as a ſiſter,
Where we were its ſchool's amazement,
And the wonder of its ſcience;
For being there well taught, we two,
By a greatly-ſkill'd magician,
We became the learnèd marvel
Of the world, a lore-enlighten'd
Lamp portentous to the age,
For 'tis aſcertain'd that women,
When to letters or to arms
They with reſolute will apply them,
Oftentimes ſurpaſs the men.
Thus it is, by envy blinded,
Fearing our unvanquiſh'd ſpirit,
Dreading the reſult to witneſs
Of our quick intelligence,

Las eſpadas y los libros.
No te digo, que eſtudié
Con generoſo motivo
Matemáticas, de quien
La filoſofía principio
Fue; no te digo, que al cielo
Los dos movimientos mido,
Natural y rapto, ſiendo
Ambos á un tiempo continuos;
No te digo, que del ſol
Los veloces curſos ſigo,
Siendo cambiante cuaderno
De tornaſoles y viſos;
No, que de la luna obſervo
Los reſplandores mendigos;
Pues una dádiva ſuya
Los hace pobres ó ricos;
No te digo, que los aſtros,
Bien errantes, ó bien fijos,
En eſe papel azul
Son mis letras: ſolo digo,
Que eſto, aunque es eſtudio noble,
Fue para mi ingenio indigno;
Pues paſando á mas empeños
La ambicion de mi albedrío,
El canto entiendo á las aves,
Y á las fieras los bramidos,
Siendo para mí patentes
Agüeros ó vaticinios.
Cuantos pájaros al aire
Vuelan, ramilletes vivos,
Dando á entender, que ſe llevan
La primavera conſigo,
Renglones ſon para mí,
Ni ſeñalados, ni eſcritos.
La harmonia de las flores,
Que en hermoſos laberintos
Parece que es natural,
Sé yo bien que es artificio;

Leſt all empire ſhould be given
Unto us, to us have they
Swords and books alike forbidden.
I ſay nothing of the zeal,
Truth inſpired, with which I ſtudied
Mathematics, on whoſe baſe
All philoſophy is builded,
Or with what ſucceſs I meaſured,
With a ſcientific niceneſs,
The two movements of the ſky,
Each by days and years divided,
Both continuous at one time.
I ſay nought of my untirèd
Watching of the ſun's ſwift courſe,
As it oped its ever-ſhifted
Gold-emblazon'd book of light,
Or the moon's poor pauper brightneſs,
Begg'd for from the ſun, like alms,
Since its poverty and riches
Are his beams, refuſed or given.
I ſay nothing of the fixèd
Or ſlow-moving orbs on high
Being to me but letters written
On the heaven's cerulean page.
This alone I ſay, this ſingly,
That the ſtudy of this ſcience,
Noble though it be, ſeem'd worthleſs
To my mind that ſought the higheſt,
Since its free flight, ſoaring ever
In purſuit of new achievements,
Learn'd what meant the birds' ſweet ditties,
And the howlings of the wild-beaſts,
They to me becoming patent
Auguries or propheſyings.
When the rich-plumed birds ſweep by me
Like to living noſegays lifted
High in air, the tidings telling
Of the ſweet ſpring they bear with them,

Pues ſon imprenta,* en que el cielo
Eſtampa raros aviſos.
Por las rayas de la mano
La quiromancía examino,
Cuando en ajadas arrugas
De la piel el fin admiro
Del hombre ; la geomancía
En la tierra, cuando eſcribo
Mis caractéres en ella ;
Y en ella tambien conſigo
La piromancía, cuando
De ſu centro, de ſu abiſmo,
Hago abrirſe las entrañas,
Y abortar á mis gemidos
Los difuntos, que reſponden,
De mi conjuro oprimidos.
¿ Mas qué mucho, ſi al infierno
Tal vez obediente he viſto
Temblar de mí ? ¿ ſi tal vez
Sus eſpíritus aflijo ?
¿ Pero para qué te canſo ?
¿ Pero para qué repito
Grandezas mias, ſi todas
En eſta ſola las cifro ?
Para que mejor pudieſe
Entregarme á mis deſignios,
A Trinacria vine, donde
En eſte apartado ſitio
Del Etna y del Lilibeo,
Eſtos palacios fabrico,
Deleitoſas ſelvas fundo,
Y montes incultos finjo.
Aqui pues, ſiendo bandida
Emperatriz de ſus riſcos,
La vida cobro en tributo
De todos los peregrinos,
Que náufragos en el mar,
A la ley de ſu deſtino,

* Hartzenbuſch reads *planas.*—Tr.

They to me are ſecret ciphers,
Legible although unwritten.
Then the harmony of flowers,
In wild beauteous mazes mingled,
Though ſo natural it ſeemeth,
Well I know is artificial ;
Since upon their lovely leaves
Rare advices heaven imprinteth.
By the lines upon the hand
Palmiſtry's ſtrange lore delights me,
When the deſtiny of man
In the ſkin's poor wither'd wrinkles
I can ſee. And geomancy
On the earth, when I inſcribe there
My myſterious characters ;
And with it I alſo mingle
Pyromancy, when from out
Earth's far centre, its abyſſes,
I command its womb to ope
And with groans bring forth the buried
Dead, who anſwer all I aſk,
To my magic ſpells ſubmitted.
And what wonder, when full oft
Hell itſelf is ſeen to ſhiver
With ſubmiſſive fear before me,
When I queſtion its loſt ſpirits ?
But for what ſhould I fatigue thee ?
But for what ſhould I thus fritter
Time away, my greatneſs telling,
When this ſingle proof ſuffices ?
That I might the better work
Out my plans uncheck'd, unwitneſs'd,
I Trinacria ſought, where here,
In this lonely ſpot, which circle
Ætna and wild Lilybœum,
I theſe palaces have builded,
Theſe delicious woods have planted
And with harveſts clothed theſe hills here.
Being thus the brigand queen

Cerrado puerto de nieve,
Oſaron abrir caminos.
Y porque fueſe mi imperio
Mas raro y mas exquiſito,
Eſas fieras y eſos troncos
Todos ſon vaſallos mios;
Que los troncos y las fieras
Viven aqui con inſtinto;
Pues árboles racionales
Son hombres vegetativos.
Eſta ſoy, y con mirar
El ſol á mi voz rendido,
La luna á mi accion atenta,
Obediente á mi ſuſpiro
Toda la caterva hermoſa
De los aſtros y los ſignos;
Con ſaber, que, cuando quiero,
El cielo empaño, que vibro
Los rayos, que de las nubes
Aborto piedra y granizo,
Que hago eſtremecer los montes,
Caducar los edificios,
Titubear todo eſe mar
Y penetrar los abiſmos;
Y finalmente trocarſe
Los hombres ſin albedrío
En varias formas, teniendo
Ya en las peñas obeliſcos,
Ya en las cortezas ſepulcro,
Y ya en las grutas aſilo:
Hoy á tus plantas me poſtro,
Hoy á tu valor me rindo,
Y como muger te ruego,
Como ſeñora té pido,
Como Emperatriz te mando,
Como ſabia te ſuplico,
No te auſentes, haſta tanto
Que hayas del hado vencido
El rigor, con que te trajo

Of this realm by rocks engirdled,
I as tribute claim the lives
Of all ſtrangers who are ſhipwreck'd;
Daring through this lonely ſea,
Yielding to a fate forewritten,
A preſumptuous path to cleave
Through this gulf by ſnow-foam ſilver'd.
And, in order that my realm
Should be rareſt and uniqueſt,
I have made as vaſſals mine
All theſe tree-trunks, all theſe wild beaſts;
For the wild beaſts and the trees
Here poſſeſs peculiar inſtincts,—
Vegetative men are they,
Trees with human reaſon gifted.
This I am. The ſun ſubmiſſive
At my potent voice inclineth,
At my beck the moon doth liſten,
At my breath, in prompt obedience,
All the beauteous troop of ſtars,
And the zodiac ſigns and circles.
With the knowledge then that I
Can, whene'er I chooſe, in miſt-wreaths
Hide the heavens, can launch the lightnings,
Can from out the clouds parturient
Bring forth frozen ſleet and ſtones;
That theſe mountains I can ſhiver,
Shake to duſt theſe edifices,
Cleave aſunder the abyſſes
Of the ſea, and look within them;
That, in fine, againſt their will
I can change men to the likeneſs
Of what form I pleaſe, ſome having
Obeliſks of rocks to gird them,
Some their tombs in rough bark finding,
Some in grottoes their aſylum;
Still I throw me at thy feet,
To thy might to-day I yield me,

Derrotado y perſeguipo
A inculcar* aqueſtos mares.
Quédate unos dias conmigo;
Verás trocado mi extremo
De riguroſo en benigno,
Con el guſto que te hoſpedo,
Con la atencion que te ſirvo;
Siendo el Flegra deſde hoy,
No ya fiero, no ya eſquivo
Hoſpedage de Saturno,
Siempre en roja ſangre tinto;
Selva sí de Amor y Vénus,
Deleitoſo Paraiſo,
Donde ſea todo guſto,
Todo aplauſo, todo alivio,
Todo paz, todo deſcanſo.
Y no quieras mas indicio
De mi piedad, que ſer hoy
El primero que ha venido
A aqueſtos montes, á quien
Con algun afecto miro,
Con algun agrado eſcucho,
Con algun cuidado aſiſto,
Con algun guſto deſeo,
Y con toda el alma eſtimo.

Ulíſes (aparte).

No fuera Ulíſes, ſi ya
Que á eſtos montes he venido,
La libertad no trajera
A cuantos aqui cautivos

* Probably a miſprint for *ſulcar*, which Hartzenbuſch adopts.—Tr.

And as ſimple woman aſk thee,
As a lady I deſire thee,
As a ſovereign I command thee,
As a ſage with tears invite thee,
Not to go from this, until
Thou haſt well ſubdued the rigour
Of the fate that hither drove thee,
Toſt, abandon'd, anger-ſmitten,
Through theſe dangerous ſeas to ſteer thee.
Here remain ſome few days with me,
And thou'lt ſee my rude behaviour
Change to more exceſſive mildneſs,
In thy joyful entertainment,
In the attention I will give thee.
Phlegra from this day ſhall be
Not that dreadful, not that fiery,
Dwelling-houſe of Saturn which
Ever is with red blood tinted;
But a grove of Love and Venus,
An elyſium where unmixèd
Joy ſhall reign, a bower of pleaſure,
Full of rapture, full of bliſſes,
Calm repoſe and ſweet refreſhment.
And thou needeſt have no higher
Proof of my good will than this,
That of all who have come hither
To theſe mountains, thou'rt the firſt
Whom I ſee with aught of kindneſs,
Whom I hear with any pleaſure,
Whom I have in aught aſſiſted,
Whom with any joy I wiſh for,
And whom all my ſoul deſireth.

Ulyſſes (aſide).

I were not Ulyſſes if,
Now that 'mid theſe hills I find me,
I did not reſtore to freedom
All thoſe captives whom bewitchment
Holds impriſon'd here. To-day

Tiene el encanto. Hoy ſeré
De aqueſta Esfinge el Edipo.

Antiſtes (aparte á el).

Señor, no de ſus liſonjas
Te creas, porque es fingido
Su halago.

Lebrel.

Huyamos de aqui.

Circe.

Qué dices, Ulíſes?

Ulíſes.

Digo,
Que no pudiera ſer noble
Quien no fueſe agradecido,
Y que conmigo he de ſer
Cruel, por ſer cortes contigo.

Caſandra (aparte).

Ay de tí! porque no ſabes
A lo que te has atrevido.

Circe.

Pídeme pues en albricias
Una merced.

Ulíſes.

Solo pido,
Que eſtos dos árboles, que hoy
A láſtima me han movido,
Porque fue mi acero cauſa
De aumentarles ſu martirio,
En pago de aqueſto, ſean
A la luz reſtituidos.

Circe.

Eſte árbol Flérida, una

I will prove myſelf this ſphinx's
Œdipus through all her lures.

Antiſtes (aſide to him).

Ah! my lord, do not confide thee
To her flatteries: her endearments
All are feign'd.

Lebrel.

Ah! let us fly hence.

Circe.

What, Ulyſſes, ſay'ſt thou?

Ulyſſes.

This,
That *his* nature were unknightly
Who could thankleſs be for kindneſs,
And that *I* muſt be ſelf-cruel,
Thee to treat with due politeneſs.

Caſſandra (aſide).

Woe to thee! thou little knoweſt
What thy boldneſs enterpriſeth.

Circe.

Aſk me then by way of earneſt
For ſome favour.

Ulyſſes.

I aſk ſimply
That theſe two trees which to-day
Moved ſo much my grief and pity,
Since my ſword unwittingly
Upon *them* new pain inflicted,*
Shall, in recompenſe of this,
Back to living light be given.

Circe.

This tree here was Flerida,

---

* This is not explained. Nothing is ſaid throughout the entire play from which it can be inferred how the ſword of Ulyſſes augmented the ſuffering which Flerida and Lyſidas endured under their transformation into trees. Perhaps in ſome paſſage which is ſuppreſſed there may have been a theatrical trick or artifice introduced to which this is an alluſion; for inſtance, Ulyſſes might have ſtruck with his ſword theſe trees, from which blood might have iſſued—HARTZENBUSCH.

Divina hermoſura, ha ſido,
Dama mia, y mi privanza.
Rindió al amor ſu albedrío,
Enamorada de un jóven,
Líſidas en ſu apellido,
Heredero de Toſcana,
Que de eſe mar peregrino
Salió á tierra; y porque oſados
Profanaron el retiro
De mi palacio, aſi yacen
En árboles convertidos;
Porque, aunque yo fiera y monſtruo,
Tan dada ſoy á los vicios,
Solos delitos de amor
Fueron para mí delitos;
Tanto, que Arſidas, valiente
Jóven y Príncipe invicto
De Trinacria, á cuyo imperio
Eſtos montes tiranizo,
Con ſaber que enamorado
De mi hermoſura ha venido,
No ha merecido tener
Mas favor, que volver vivo.
Pero ya que es la primera
Coſa, que tú me has pedido,
Flérida y Líſidas rompan
Las priſiones que han tenido.

[*Abrenſe dos árboles, y ſalen* Flérida *y* Lísidas.

Líſidas.

Torpe el diſcurſo, atado el penſamiento,
La razon ciega, el ánimo oprimido,
Sin uſo el alma, el corazon rendido,
Muda la voz, y tímido el aliento;
Sin voluntad, memoria, entendimiento,
Vivo cadáver de eſte tronco he ſido.
Ya pues, que me quitabas el ſentido,
Quitáraſme tambien el ſentimiento.

Who, with rareſt beauty gifted,
Was my confidential lady.
She to love her free heart yielded,
Being enamour'd of a youth,
Lyſidas by name, entitled
To the fair Etruſcan kingdom,
Who upon this ſea a pilgrim
Landed here: and for their daring
To profane the calm retirement
Of my palace, thus they lie,
Into two fair trees transfigured;
Since, though monſtrous I may ſeem,
Subject to ſo many vices,
Love's offences are by me
But the ſole ones unforgiven;
So much ſo, that Arſidas,
A brave youth, Trinacria's prince here,
From whoſe ſceptre theſe proud hills
I have ſever'd and divided,
Knowing that inflamed with love
Of my beauty he came hither,
Merited no greater boon
Than to get back with his life hence.
But as this is the firſt thing
Thou haſt aſk'd that I ſhould give thee,
Flerida and Lyſidas,
Burſt the priſon bonds that bind ye.

[*The trees open and* Flerida *and* Lysidas *come forth.*

Lyſidas.

Dull was my mind, embarraſs'd was my thought,
Blind was my reaſon, and my mind oppreſt,
Uſeleſs my ſoul, my heart by fear oppreſt,
Mute was my voice, and all my brain diſtraught;

Si de amar (ay de mí) á Flérida bella,
Caſtigo fue eſta forma, en vano quieres,
Que yo me olvide, porque vivo en ella.
Los troncos aman : luego mal infieres,
Que, por ſer tronco, venceré mi eſtrella,
Pues no la vences tú, y mas ſabia eres.

Without the power to will or think of aught,
A breathing corſe I lived this ſtrange tree's gueſt :
Ah ! ſince thou took'ſt the feeling from my breaſt,
Why not the pain that all this ſuffering wrought ?
If 'twas for loving Flerida the fair
I thus was puniſh'd, then how vainly tries
Thy wrath to kill the love that lives in her ;—
Trees even love ;—the ſtar that rules my ſkies
If thou doſt ſeek to darken, thou doſt err,
Since thou art foil'd although thou art more wiſe.

Flérida.

Racional, vegetable y ſenſitiva
Alma el cielo le dió al ſugeto humano ;
Vegetable y ſenſible al bruto ufano ;
Al tronco y á la flor vegetativa.
Tres almas ſon ; ſi de las dos me priva
Tu voz, porque amo á Líſidas, en vano
Solicitas mi olvido, pues es llano
Que, aun tronco, alma me dejas con que viva.
No de todo mi amor tendrá la palma
La parte, en que has querido conſervarme ;
De aquella sí, que permitió eſta calma :
Luego mudarme en tronco, no es mudarme ;
Porque ſi no me quitas toda el alma,
Todo el amor no has de poder quitarme

Flerida.

Life, reaſon, feeling, Heaven's all-wiſe decree
Unites commingled in man's heart and brain,
Feeling and life in beaſts that ſcour the plain,
And life alone in budding flower and tree.
Theſe are three ſouls : if two out of the three
I loſe for loving Lyſidas, in vain
Thou ſeek'ſt that I forget him, ſince 'tis plain
That, though a tree, a ſoul ſtill dwells in me.
Thoſe I have loſt do not contain the whole
Of that fond love that thy dread wrath could wake,

The one I keep is free from thy control;
To change me thus doth ſeem a ſtrange miſtake,
Becauſe if thou doſt take not all my ſoul,
All of my love thou haſt not power to take.

Circe.
Agradeced vueſtras vidas
Al huéſped, que me ha venido,
Y vivid los dos ſeguros
Por él ya de mis caſtigos,
Como de vueſtros amores
No deis el mas leve indicio.

Circe.
For your new-recover'd lives
Thank the gueſt who ſtands beſide me,
And be ſure henceforth that I
Shall not with new pains chaſtiſe ye,
If you give not of your loves
Any new hint to remind me.

Líſidas.
Siempre, Ulíſes, me tendrás
A tus pies agradecido.

Lyſidas.
Ever ſhalt thou ſee me lie
Grateful at thy feet, Ulyſſes.

Flérida.
Y ſiempre confeſaré,
Que por cuenta tuya vivo.

Flerida.
And for ever ſhall I own
Thine the life this day thou giv'ſt me.

Circe.
Pues porque empiecen á ſer
Deſde hoy aplauſos feſtivos
Todo el monte, todo el valle,
Todo el mar y todo el ſitio,
Volved á cantar, y todos
Con él volved, y conmigo.

Circe.
Then in order that from this
Our glad feſtive notes ſhould circle
Round the mountain, round the valley,
Round the ſea and all it girdles,
Raiſe the ſtrain once more, and lead
Him and me back thus united.

Múſica.
En hora dichoſa venga
A los palacios de Circe
El rayo de los Troyanos,
El diſcreto y fuerte Ulíſes:
En hora diſchoſa venga . . . .

Song.
Be the hour propitious when
To the palace-halls of Circe
Comes the terror-bolt of Troy
The diſcreet and bold Ulyſſes,—
Bright, propitious be the hour . . . .

Sale Arsidas.

Enter Arsidas.

Arſidas.
No venga en hora dichoſa,
Felice en deſprecio mio,

Arſidas.
Be it not propitious when
He comes here in my deſpiſal,

Ni el que fue ſepulcro á tantos,
Hoy á uno ſolo ſea alivio.
Peligre en la tierra quien
Por aqueſos mares vino,
En ſu ſombra tropezando,
De un peligro á otro peligro.
Eſe acento harmonioſo,
Que le ſaluda benigno,
Airado trueque en endechas
Triſtes, fúnebres caiſtros
Las cláuſulas, porque ſean
De ſus tragedias aviſo ;
Que no es juſto, no, que un Griego
Extrangero, advenedizo,
De tanto uſado rigor
Venga á mudar el eſtilo.
¿ Deſde cuándo, Circe bella,
Con tanto aplauſo feſtivo,
Con tan alegre aparato,
Tanto noble regocijo
Al foraſtero ſaludas,
Recibes al peregrino,
Sin que eſte mar, ó eſtas peñas
Le ſirvan de precipicio,
O ya convertido en fiera,
O ya en árbol convertido,
Tenga en las peñas ſu eſtancia,
Tenga en las grutas ſu aſilo ?
Príncipe ſoy de Trinacria :
No derrotado y perdido
Llegué á eſte puerto, pues vine
De mis afectos traido,
Porque aun aqueſto tambien
Debieſes á mi albedrío ;
Que no quiſo, no, el que ſolo
Porque le fue fuerza quiſo,
Ni es ſacrificio, no ſiendo
Voluntario el ſacrificio.
Y en cuanto tiempo eſtos montes,

Nor the grave-yard of ſo many
Prove a ſolace to him ſingly ;
Let him who theſe wild ſeas dared
On the land endure new riſks here,
From one danger to another
Ever treading as he flieth.
Let this ſoftly-cadenced ſtrain,
Which ſaluteth him benignly,
Change to mournful wails of woe,
Hoarſely change to funeral dirges,
Propheſying thus to him
What the tragic future bringeth.
For it is not fit that he,
A Greek ſtranger, a benighted
Alien, ſhould come here to change
Thine accuſtom'd form of rigour,
Since what time, O Circe fair !
With ſuch feſtal ſongs and timbrels,
With ſuch joyful preparation,
With a proud diſplay ſo princely,
Doſt thou thus ſalute the ſtranger,
Thus receive the wretch here driven,
Without making theſe ſteep rocks,
Sea-waſh'd, be his precipices,
Or transform'd into a tree,
Or tranſmuted to a wild-beaſt,
Make him hold 'mid cliffs his dwelling,
Amid grottoes his aſylum ?
Of Trinacria Prince am I :—
Not as one nigh loſt and ſhip-wreck'd
Came I to this port, but drawn
By my true love came I hither,
That my heart's free-will ſhould be
Thus a new claim to thy pity :—
Since he loves not, he who only
Loves becauſe ſome force inciteth,
And if not ſpontaneous, all
Sacrifice is worſe than idle.
And ſince ſight of thee has been

Por ſolo mirarte, vivo,
No he debido á tu rigor,
Ni á tu crueldad he debido
Una accion, á quien me mueſtre
Guſtoſo, ni agradecido;
Tanto, que aun de tus encantos
Libre, eſtos campos aſiſto,
Porque en tantos ſentimientos
No me faltaſen ſentidos.
Pues dos hombres ſolamente
Los que nos libramos fuimos,
Ulíſes y yo, porque
Todo hoy en deſprecio mio
Reſulte; pues ſi los dos
Nos reſervamos, ha ſido
Ulíſes para gozarlo,
Y Arſidas para ſentirlo.

'Mid theſe hills my ſole exiſtence,
I owe little to thy rigour,
To thy cruelty as little,
Nought for which to thee ſhould I
Joy or gratitude exhibit,
Only that exempt from all
Thy enchantments, I can viſit
Theſe dread fields, in order that
For the ſorrows that afflict me
Human ſenſes ſhould not fail.
Since then but two men are ſingled
Out of all the world, to whom
Freedom from thy ſpell is given,
This Ulyſſes and myſelf,—
Ah! the exemption but inflicteth
A new pang, a freſh deſpiſal,
Since if we are both preſerved,
'Tis with more malign refinement
To give pain to Arſidas,
To give rapture to Ulyſſes.

Ulíſes.

Si de mi dicha envidioſo,
Si de mi ſuerte ofendido . . . .

Ulyſſes.

If thou envieſt my good fortune,
If my happier fate afflicts thee . . . .

Circe.

Calla, Arſidas, ſi conoces,
Que la vida te permito,
Porque es la mayor venganza
Que tomo, como tú has dicho,
Dejarte vivir, teniendo
Sentimientos y ſentidos.
Quejarte de mí, es decirme,
Que lo que buſco conſigo;
Y aſí, porque tú te quejes,
Yo la cauſa no te quito.—
Cantad, cantad, y tú ven,
Ulíſes, al lado mio.

Circe.

Ceaſe, O Arſidas! if thou
Knoweſt that I have permitted
Thee to live, ſince greater vengeance
I could take not, as admitted
By thyſelf, than with thy life
Feelings and their food to give thee.
To complain is but to tell me
That I have obtain'd my wiſhes,
And that thou mayſt ſtill complain,
I the cauſe ſhall ſtill leave with thee.
Sing, ſing, and at my ſide
Come unto my court, Ulyſſes.

Lebrel (á Clarin).

No ſon muy malas las dos
Circecillas de poquito.

Lebrel (aſide to Clarin).

Not ſo very bad theſe two,
Circe's little ſervant Circelets.

Clarin (á Lebrel).
No hay que volver á dar cartas;
Que yo las tomo, y no miro.

Aſtrea (aparte).
Habíanme dicho, que eran
Los Griegos feos y eſquivos,
Y ni eſquivos ſon, ni feos,
Tanto como me habian dicho.

Líſidas.
¡Gracias á Amor, que otra vez,
Flérida hermoſa, te miro!

Flérida.
¡Gracias, Líſidas, á Amor
Que otra vez á amarte vivo!

Circe (aparte).
Venceràle mi hermoſura,
Pues mi ciencia no ha podido.

Ulíſes (aparte).
Libraré de aquelta fiera
A Trinacria, ſi amor finjo.

Arſidas (aparte).
Solo zelos me faltaban,
Ya eſtá todo el mal cumplido.

Muſica.
En hora dichoſa venga, &c.

Clarin (to Lebrel).
Don't mind ſhuffling; I will take
My chance of trumps and win though blinded.

Aſtrea (aſide).
They have told me that the Greeks
All were ſcornful and unſightly;
But nor ugly nor ſo coy
Are they as they have been libell'd.

Lyſidas.
Thanks to Love, fair Flerida,
That once more thy face I witneſs!

Flerida.
Thanks to Love, I live once more,
Lyſidas, my heart to give thee!

Circe (aſide).
Let my beauty him ſubdue,
Since ſo powerleſs was my ſcience!

Ulyſſes (aſide).
I, by feigning love, may free
Fair Trinacria from this wild-beaſt.

Arſidas (aſide).
I but needed jealouſy
My full cup of woe to embitter.

Song.
Be the hour propitious when
To the palace-halls of Circe
Comes the never-vanquiſh'd Greek,
The invincible Ulyſſes!

[*Exeunt, all ſinging.*

JORNADA II.

Palacio de Circe.

Salen Circe, *llorando*, Flerida, Tisbe, Casandra, Astrea, Libia, *y* Clori.

Libia.

EÑORA, qué llanto es eſte ?

Aſtrea.

¿ Qué pena, ſeñora, es eſta ?

Clori.

¿ Tú lágrimas en los ojos ?

Flérida.

¿ Tú ſuſpiros, y tú quejas ?

Tiſbe.

¿ Qué ocaſion pudo moverte
A que ſentimientos tengas ?

Caſandra.

Los males comunicados,
Si no ſe vencen, ſe templan.

Circe.

¡ Quien tiene de que quejarſe,
O cuanto en quejarſe yerra !
Que la juſticia del llanto
Hace apacibles las penas.
Yo aſi mi triſteza quiero,
Que tan poco no me deba,

ACT THE SECOND.

Circe's Palace.

Enter Circe *in tears, attended by* Flerida, Thisbe, Cassandra, Astrea, Libia *and* Chloris.

Libia.

LADY, what lament is this ?

Aſtrea.

Ah, my lady, whence this
ſadneſs ?

Chloris.

Canſt thou fill thine eyes with tears ?

Flerida.

Sob and ſigh like one diſtracted ?

Thiſbe.

Say what ſudden cauſe of grief
Can thy ſenſes thus have maſter'd ?

Caſſandra.

The confiding of our ills
If it cures not, mitigates them.

Circe.

He who for complaint hath cauſe,
Oh ! how errs he who complaineth !
Since the juſtice of his plaining
Turns his very grief to gladneſs.
I ſo love my ſource of ſorrow,
Feel ſo much its ſweet advantage,

Que en repetirla procure
Hacer menor mi triſteza.
Dejadme ſola.

Aſtrea (*aparte las dos*).

Oyes, Libia?

Libia.

Razonablemente, Aſtrea.

Aſtrea.

¡ Plegue á Amor, que eſtos extremos
Lo que yo pienſo no ſean!

Libia.

¡ Plegue al Amor, que ſi haga!
Que es lo que plegamos pienſa:
Pues ſi es amor la ocaſion
Dellos, y ella á verſe llega
Enamorada, dará . . . .

Aſtrea.

Qué?

Libia.

Libertad de conciencia.

Aſtrea.

Holgaréme de ſalir
De religion tan eſtrecha,
Como es el honor. Veſtales
Vírgenes Diana celebra
Entre gentes, mas noſotras
Entre animales y fieras
Somos vírgenes beſtíales.

Libia.

Calla, porque no lo entienda.

[*Vanſe todas las Damas, menos* FLERIDA.

Circe.

Flérida, tú no te auſentes:
Sola conmigo te queda,
Que tengo que hablarte ſola.

That I would not by repeating
Take one ſting from out my ſadneſs.
Leave me here alone.

Aſtrea (*to Libia*).

Canſt hearken,
Libia?

Libia.

Pretty well, Aſtrea.

Aſtrea.

Love but grant that theſe exceſſes
Are not what my fear doth fancy!

Libia.

Love but grant they are, if it
Fancieth what we both ſigh after!
Since if their true ſource be love,
If ſhe has her own heart granted
To love's ſway, ſhe'll give us . . . .

Aſtrea.

What?

Libia.

Liberty of conſcience, may be.

Aſtrea.

I indeed were glad to free me
From a worſhip ſo contracted,
And ſo ſtrict as honour is.
Great Diana celebrateth
Among men her feſtal choirs
Of veſtal virgins, but, unhappy!
We poor beſtial virgins ſeem
Among beaſts who growl and chatter.

Libia.

Silence, leſt ſhe overhear us!

[*Exeunt all the ladies and attendants but* FLERIDA.

Circe.

Flerida, in the others' abſence
I would ſpeak with thee alone
Of a certain private matter:
Stay thou here with me.

Flérida (aparte).
Sin duda, cielos, que intenta
Darme caſtigo mayor,
Que el que en la dura corteza
Tuve, porque hablé eſta tarde
A Líſidas.

Circe.
Oye atenta:
Eſte Ulíſes, eſte Griego,
Que eſa marítima beſtia
Sorbió ſin duda en el mar,
Para eſcupirle en la tierra;
Eſte, que á la diſcrecion
De los vientos, con deſhecha
Fortuna, tan derrotado
Llegó á tocar eſtas ſelvas;
Eſte, que trajo deidad
Superior en ſu defenſa,
Pues, burlando mis encantos,
Les tiraniza la fuerza;
Eſte pues, que mi hoſpedage
Corteſanamente acepta,
Adonde hoy tan divertido
Vive, olvidado de Grecia:
Como ſi fuera mi vida
Troya, ha introducido en ella
Tanto fuego, que en cenizas
No dudo que ſe reſuelva;
Y con razon; porque ya
En callado fuego envuelta,
Cada aliento es un Volcan,
Cada ſuſpiro es un Etna.
Quiſiera . . . . quiſiera dije?
Mal empecé; pues ſi es fuerza
Querer, Flérida, y ya quiero,
Erré en decir, que quiſiera.
Quiero, digo; pero quiero
Tanto á mi ambicion atenta,
Que quiero á Ulíſes, y no

Flerida (aſide).
O heavens!
Doubtleſs now her anger planneth
Some new puniſhment, ſeverer
Than the hard bark that enwrapp'd me,
Since this evening I have ſpoken
Unto Lyſidas.

Circe.
Now, mark me;
This Ulyſſes, this Greek king,
Whom the ſea—that mighty kraken—
Doubtleſs ſwallow'd on the ocean
To outſpew him on the land here;
He who at the wild wind's liſting,
So forſaken, ſo ſtorm-ſhaken,
Came to anchor by theſe groves;
He who calleth in his danger
On ſome mightier god to aid him,
Since deſpiſing my enchantments
O'er their power he tyranniſeth:
He who courteouſly hath granted
All my hoſpitable wiſhes,
And a glad gueſt at my table,
Lives forgetful now of Greece.
He it is who in my heart here
(Ah! as if 'twere Troy) hath kindled
Such a fire, that ſoon in aſhes
Doubtleſs it muſt be diſſolved;
And with reaſon, ſince already
Wrapp'd in hidden flames it burns,
Every breath it breathes volcanic,
Every ſigh an Ætna ſeems.
I would love him . . . . *would* love!—badly
I begin in ſaying "would;"
Since, if doom'd to love, I madly
Yield to Fate, I err in ſaying
I *would* love when love hath happen'd.
Him I ſay I love, but love

Quiero, que Ulíſes lo entienda.
Ahora te admirarás
De que yo, que tan ſoberbia
Tu amor reñí, te fie el mio ;
Pero admiraráſte necia ;
Porque la cauſa mayor,
Porque la ocaſion mas cierta
De incurrir en una culpa,
Es haber dicho mal della.
Y porque el contar delitos,
A quien es cómplice, cueſta
Menos vergüenza, yo quiſe
Recatear eſta vergüenza,
Y porque me cueſte menos,
Decirlos á quien los ſepa.
Yo amo en fin, Flérida mia ;
Vengada eſtás de mi ofenſa.
¡ Pluguiera á Júpiter ſanto,
Tú trasformarme pudieras
A mí en inſenſible planta,
Que yo te lo agradeciera !
Porque ſi ſupiera entonces
Lo que es amor, mas quiſiera
Verte enamorada y viva,
Que no enamorada y muerta.
Enamorada en efecto
Llego, y pues tú á ſaber llegas.
Qué es amor, de tí pretendo
Ayudar una cautela ;
Y es, que para poder yo
Hablar con él, ſin que él ſepa
Que ſoy yo la que le habla,
Tú con ruegos y finezas
Le has de enamorar de dia,
Y diciéndole que venga
De noche á hablarte, eſtaré
Yo con tu nombre encubierta,
Donde mi altivez, mi honor,
Mi vanidad, mi ſoberbia,

With an eye of ſuch exactneſs
To decorum, that I wiſh
He ſhould know not my attachment.
Wonder now that I who late
Chid thy love with ſo much anger,
Should confide to thee my own ;
But thy wonder is the vaineſt,
Since the greateſt cauſe of all,
The ſure ſource that never faileth,
Of committing any fault,
Is ſometimes to reprimand it.
And becauſe confeſſing crimes
To an accomplice doth o'ermantle
The fluſh'd face with bluſhes leſs,
I deſire to drive this hardeſt
Bargain with my bluſhes thus,
And to make my heart's crimes ſtand me
A leſs price, to tell them thee,
Who ſo well can underſtand them.
Ah ! my Flerida, I love !—
Now thou art avenged with ample
Juſtice for my bygone wrong.
Would that ſacred Jove might grant thee
Power, through magic transformation,
To a ſenſeleſs plant to change me !
Oh ! how thankful would I be !
Since, if at that time, exactly
I knew what was love, enamour'd
I would ſee thee living, rather
Than enamour'd not and dead.
Since then love is ſuperadded
To my paſt experience, and
Thou too knoweſt love's enthralments,
In a little ſtratagem
I expect that thou wilt aid me ;
And it is,—that I may ſpeak
With him, without any danger
Of his knowing that 'tis I [thee
Who ſpeak *with* him ; thou muſt maſk

Mi reſpeto, mi decoro
No ſe rindan, y . . . .

Flérida.

Oye, eſpera,
Que quieres hacer en mí
Dos coſtoſas experiencias.
Yo amo á Líſidas, y tú
Cruel, ſeñora, me ordenas,
Que diſimule el amarle;
Yo no amo á Ulíſes, é intentas,
Que finja amarle. ¿Pues cómo,
A dos afectos atenta,
Quieres, que olvide á quien quiero,
Y que á quien olvido quiera?
Damas tienes con quien hoy
Partir los afectos puedas;
A una alma baſta un cuidado.

Circe.

Y aun la miſma cauſa es eſa;
Yo ſé, que quien llega á eſtar
Enamorada, no deja
Lugar para otro cuidado
En el alma: luego acierta
Quien á ella el ſuyo le fia,
Porque no peligra en ella
El rieſgo de enamorarſe,
Pues ya lo eſtá; de manera,
Que tú no me darás zelos,
Y otra sí, cuando te vea
Con Ulíſes; pues tu amor
Sanea la contingencia.

So in ſoft requeſts and ſmiles,
So by day his heart entangle,
That when thou requir'ſt that he
Meet thee nightly in the garden,
I may take thy place, conceal'd
'Neath thy name as 'neath a mantle,
Where my haughtineſs, my honour,
Where the pride on which I trample,
My decorum, ſelf-reſpect
May be ſafe from . . . .

Flerida.

Hear, oh! hearken:
For thou wouldſt attempt on me
Two experiments the hardeſt.
I love Lyſidas, and thou,
Lady, ſternly wouldſt command me
To diſſemble that I love him;
I Ulyſſes love not, nathleſs
Thou deſireſt I ſhould feign ſo;
How, by two deſires diſtracted,
Can I think of the ne'er thought of,
And forget the never abſent?—
Ladies haſt thou here with whom
Thou thy feelings thus may parcel;
To one heart one care's enough.

Circe.

It is therefore that I aſk thee,
Since I know that whoſoever
Is in love, can keep vacated
Heart-ſpace for no alien care:
Safe then is he who imparteth
His heart's love to ſuch an one,
Since in love itſelf, the latter
Runs no danger of becoming
His friend's rival; in this manner
Thou no jealouſy wilt give me,
Even when I ſee thou ſtandeſt
By Ulyſſes ſide,—thy love
Bailing the contingent danger.

Eſto ha de ſer en efecto.—
¿Mas qué ruido es eſe?

Flérida.

Llegan
Dos criados aqui, y traen
Sin duda alguna pendencia.

Circe.

Retírate; que no quiero,
Que á todas horas me vean,
Y eſcuchemos deſde aqui
Lo que tratan en mi auſencia.
[*Retíranſe.*

Sale Lebrel *y* Clarin.

Lebrel.

Digo, que es la mejor vida,
Que tuve en mi vida, aqueſta.

Clarin.

Eſo dices?

Lebrel.

Eſto digo;
Y que en el mundo no hay tierra
Como Trinacria, y que Circe
Es un ángel en belleza
Y condicion.

Clarin.

Eſtás loco?

Lebrel.

Dime, ¿ella no nos hoſpeda
Como á unos reyes?

Clarin.

Es cierto;
Mas mucho mejor nos fuera,
Que en ſus palacios, eſtar
En un bodegon de Grecia.

Lebrel.

¿No comemos lindamente?

Clarin.

No; que no hay comida buena

This thou muſt in fine contrive.—
But what noiſe is this?

Flerida.

Two valets
Hither come, engaged no doubt
In ſome ſcolding match or quarrel.

Circe.

Step a little back, I would not
Have them every moment paſs me,
And we'll hear from this, how they
Treat me when they think me abſent.
[*They retire.*

Enter Lebrel *and* Clarin.

Lebrel.

I ſtill ſay, no ſweeter life
Have I in my whole life taſted.

Clarin.

Can you ſay ſo?

Lebrel.

This I ſay,—
That Trinacria is the marvel
Of the whole world, and that Circe
Is in form and face an angel
Of perfection.

Clarin.

Art thou mad?

Lebrel.

Tell me, are we not here treated
As if we were kings?

Clarin.

'Tis true,
But a better place, I fancy,
For us were a Grecian cook-ſhop,
Than theſe palaces of marble.

Lebrel.

Don't we eat though ſumptuouſly?

Clarin.

No, 'tis not a pleaſant banquet

Adonde no doy bocado,
Que no pienſe, que me deja
Hecho un cochino.

Lebrel.

No es eſo
Tan malo como tú pienſas;
Que yo lo fui, y no me hallaba
Mal con ſerlo; de manera,
Que á cuantos cochinos hay
Sin aliño y ſin limpieza,
Diſculpo, porque ſe ahorran
De muchas impertinencias.
Y al caſo, ¿dónde hallarás
Una cama tan compueſta?

Clarin.

No eſtá el deſcanſo en la cama;
Ni hay pícaro, que no duerma
Sin penas en un pajar
Mejor, que un ſeñor con ellas
En una cama dorada.

Lebrel.

¿Dónde eſtos jardines vieras?

Clarin.

¿Para qué quiero jardines?

Lebrel.

Cogíte: ¿dónde tuvieras
Dos mozas de tan buen aire,
Como ſon Libia y Aſtrea?

Clarin.

Daréme por concluido
En tocándome eſa tecla;
Pero no confeſaré,
Que Circe no es una fiera,
Nigromante, encantadora,
Energúmena, hechicera,
Súcuba, íncuba; y en fin
Es, por acabar el tema,
Con los demonios demonia,

Where I ſcarce can take a mouthful,
But I think I'm tranſmigrated
To a hog.

Lebrel.

That's not ſo bad
By one half as you imagine;
I was one ſome time, and found me
Nought the worſe for what had happen'd;
So that now when I behold
Happy pigs, unkempt, untrammell'd,
Wallowing in the mire, I give them
My forgiveneſs, ſince their manners
Save them from much uſeleſs trouble.
To the point though; where, my maſter,
Have you ſuch a ſoft bed found?

Clarin.

Reſt comes not from bed or blanket;
Not a beggar but ſleeps better
On his ſcanty ſtraw-ſtrewn pallet,
Free of care, than doth a lord
Rack'd with *his*, upon his grand bed.

Lebrel.

Where ſuch gardens have you ſeen?

Clarin.

Gardens? what care I for gardens?

Lebrel.

Now I have you, tell me where
Have you ſeen two girls, the matches
Of fair Lybia and Aſtrea?

Clarin.

Well to that there's but one anſwer;
You have touch'd the chord at laſt;
But I won't confeſs ſo gladly,
Circe is not a wild-beaſt,
A demoniac, a witch-charmer,
An hobgoblin, a wild vampire;
And in fine to end our quarrel,
A ſhe-devil among demons,
A duenda among fairies.

Como, con los duendes duenda.
Circe (aparte á Flérida).
No puedo ſufrir ya mas
El eſcuchar mis ofenſas.
Flérida.
No te des por entendida.
Clarin.
Y es Circe . . . .

Salen CIRCE *y* FLERIDA.

Circe.
Qué es?
Clarin.
Una Reina,
Y á quien dijere otra coſa,
Le daré, porque no mienta,
Dos mil palos, como uno.—
[*á Lebrel.*
Y á tí, porque no te atrevas
A hablar mal de las ſeñoras
Doñas Circes en ſu auſencia,
Yo te haré . . . .
Lebrel.
¿Pues quién hablaba
Mal, ſino tú?
Clarin.
Buena es eſa;
¿A mí por los filos?
Circe.
Baſta.
Lebrel.
Yo . . . .
Circe.
Bien eſtá.
Clarin (aparte).
El cielo quiera,
Que no oyeſe lo demas.
Lebrel.
¡Que tan gran mentira creas!

Circe (aſide to Flerida).
Oh! I can't endure to let
This inſulting ſcene go farther.
Flerida.
Do not ſeem as if you heard them.
Clarin.
Circe is . . . .

CIRCE *and* FLERIDA *advance.*

Circe.
Pray what?
Clarin.
A lady,
And a queen, and who denies it
I will teach him better manners,
By two thouſand blows at leaſt.
[*to Lebrel.*
As for you becauſe you gabbled
Something naughty of the noble
Lady Circes in their abſence,
I will make . . . .
Lebrel.
Why, who ſpoke badly
But yourſelf?
Clarin.
Well, that is cool!
Would you turn the tables?
Circe.
Mark me.
Lebrel.
I . . . .
Circe.
'Tis well.
Clarin (aſide).
Heaven grant that ſhe
Did not hear our tittle-tattle!
Lebrel.
Who'd believe ſo great a liar?

Circe.
Yo ſé bien lo que es verdad.
Vos os ſalid allá fuera ;
Que yo haré, que mi caſtigo
Hoy eſcarmiente la lengua,
Que habló mal de mí.

Clarin.
Y ſerá
Muy juſto.

Lebrel.
Que eſto ſuceda ! [*Vaſe.*

Circe.
A tí, en pago de que aſi
Hoy mis acciones defiendas,
Te quiero dar un teſoro,
Con que á Grecia rico vuelvas.
De eſe monte en lo intrincado
Llamarás con voces fieras
Tres veces á Brutamonte ;
Que él te dará la reſpueſta.

Clarin.
Mil veces tus plantas beſo ;
Que bien tu gran valor mueſtras.
A toda ley, hablar bien.
¡ Qué haya hombres de mala lengua !
[*Vaſe.*

Flérida.
¿Cómo caſtigas, ſeñora,
Al que te defiende, y premias
Al que te ofende ?

Circe.
A ſu tiempo
Verás el premio que lleva.

Sale Astrea.

Aſtrea.
Ulíſes deſde ſu cuarto

Circe.
I know well the truth of the matter.
Go, and wait without : to-day
I ſhall make a dread example
Of the ſaucy tongue that dared
To inſult me.

Clarin.
And 't will be
Only juſt.

Lebrel.
That this ſhould happen !
[*Exit.*

Circe.
As for thee, to pay thy zeal
In defence of the way I act here,
I intend a gift to give thee,
With which rich to Greece thou'lt travel :—
Deep within this mountain's thickets,
Thou ſhalt call out loud and ſharply
Three times upon Brutamonte,
Who will give to thee thy anſwer.

Clarin.
At thy feet a thouſand kiſſes,
Thou, who knoweſt to act ſo grandly :
Civil ſpeaking is my motto,
Oh ! that men ſhould uſe bad language !
[*Exit.*

Flerida.
How is it thou doſt puniſh, lady,
Thy defender, and rewardeſt
Him who wronged thee ?

Circe.
In due time,
Thou'lt perceive why thus I've acted.

Enter Astrea.

Aſtrea.
From his quarter comes Ulyſſes

Al tuyo paſa.

Circe.

Aqui empieza
Del amor y la altivez
La mas cauteloſa guerra,
Pues no he de dar por vencida
La que quiero que ſe venza.

[*Vanſe.*

JARDIN.

Salen ULÍSES, CIRCE, FLÉRIDA, LÍSIDAS, ANTÍSTES, ARQUELAO, LEBREL, CLARIN, CASANDRA, *Damas*, *Griegos*, *Muſicos*.

Ulíſes (*aparte*).

Temeroſo vengo, ay triſte!
A ver á Circe, ſi es fuerza
Que como ſabia la admire,
Y la admire como bella.
¡Quién no ſe hubiera fiado
Tanto de sí! ¡quién no hubiera
Hecho cautela el quedarſe!
Pues ya contra ſu cautela
Es impoſible olvidarla,
Y es impoſible quererla.

Circe.

En eſte hermoſo jardin,
Adonde la primavera
Llamó las flores á cortes,
Para jurar por ſu reina
A la roſa, que teñida
En ſangre de Vénus bella
Púrpura viſte real,
Generoſo honor de Grecia,
En tanto que de una caza
Boreal el término llega,
Que ſerá luego que el ſol
Vaya perdiendo la fuerza,

To wait on thee.

Circe.

Here at laſt then
'Twixt my love and pride commences
The moſt ſingular of battles;
Since I'd wiſh that one were victor,
Yet the other not be maſter'd.

[*Exeunt.*

THE GARDEN.

Enter ULYSSES, CIRCE, FLERIDA, LYSIDAS, ANTISTES, ARCHELAUS, LEBREL, CLARIN, CASSANDRA, *Ladies*, *Greeks*, *Muſicians*.

Ulyſſes (*aſide*).

Tremblingly I come, O ſorrow!
To ſee Circe, ſince I'm fated
For her wiſdom to admire her,
To adore her for her graces.
Who would not have ſo far truſted
In himſelf? oh! who that waits here
Would not need a ſage's caution?
Since, deſpite of all his calmneſs,
It is hopeleſs to forget her,
And to love her is but madneſs.

Circe.

Here—where Spring has call'd together
In this bright and beauteous garden
Her ſweet parliament of flowers
To ſwear fealty to the faireſt,
To their queen, the roſe, who wears
Her imperial purple mantle,
Dyed in the blood of Venus fair,—
I await thee, pride and marvel
Of all Greece, until the chaſe
Circles o'er our northern lands here,
Which will be when ſinks the ſun
With his burning beams abated.

Con múſicas y feſtines
Te eſpero, porque la auſencia,
Y memorias de tu patria
Entretenido diviertas.

Ulíſes.

Bellíſima Circe, en quien
Por lo hermoſa y lo diſcreta,
O eſtá de mas el ingenio,
O eſtá de mas la belleza,
No es meneſter, que mi vida
Tantas liſonjas te deba,
Para que rendido ſiempre
A tus plantas la agradezca;
Que el merecer adorar
Tu hermoſura . . . .

Circe.

Aguarda, eſpera;
Que eſte cortes cumplimiento
No quiero, Ulíſes, que ſea
Carta de favor, con que
A mi reſpeto te atrevas;
Que una coſa es hoſpedarte,
Agradecida á tus prendas,
Y otra es eſcucharte amores.

Ulíſes.

Ni yo, Circe, me atreviera
A decirlos; que una coſa
Es corteſana fineza,
Y otra fineza amoroſa.

Circe (aparte).

¡Pluguiera á Dios que lo fuera!—
En eſta tejida alfombra,
Que de colores diverſas
Labró el Abril, á quien ſirve
De doſel la copa amena
De un laurel, al ſol hagamos
Apacible reſiſtencia.
Vayan tomando lugares
Todos, y tú aqui te ſienta.

Here with ſongs and feſtive muſic
I await thee, that the abſence
And the memory of thy country,
Thus amuſed, may not unman thee.

Ulyſſes.

Lovelieſt Circe, thou in whom
Beauty ſo to ſenſe is added,
That ſuperfluous ſeems the ſenſe,
Or the beauty ſeems not wanted.
Needleſs is it that my life
Owe thee for ſuch liberal largeſs
Of all kindneſs, though thus kneeling
Ever at thy feet 'twould thank thee;
Since to merit leave to worſhip
Thy fair beauty . . . .

Circe.

Stay, detain thee;
Since this courteous compliment,
I, Ulyſſes, would not have thee
Uſe againſt me as a licenſe
To o'erſtep reſpect's exactneſs.
One thing is a gueſt's warm welcome,
Such as worth like thine demandeth,
And another, love to liſt to.

Ulyſſes.

Nor would I, fair Circe, aſk thee
So to liſten; it is one thing
With a courtier's tongue to flatter,
With a lover's is another.

Circe (aſide)

Would to God, he uſed the latter!—
On this flower-inwoven floor,
Spread as with a coloured carpet
By rich April's hand, beneath
Theſe o'erhanging laurel branches,
Which—a green-leaf'd canopy,
Tremble o'er it—to the ardent
Sun a ſoft ſhade let us make.
All take ſeats, thine here, I aſk thee.

Ulíses.
Temo enojarte otra vez.
Circe (aparte á Flérida).
Flérida, á entabler empieza
Lo que has de fingir.
[*Van tomando lugares las damas y los galanes, y* ULÍSES *se asienta en medio de* CIRCE *y* FLERIDA.

Flérida (aparte á Ulíses).
Aqui
Me siento, porque quisiera
Daros á entender, Ulíses,
Lo que me debeis.
Lísidas (aparte).
¿ Qué llegan
¿ A ver mis ojos ? ay cielos !
¿ Flérida al lado se sienta
De Ulíses, y con él habla ?
¡ Denme los cielos paciencia !
Antístes (aparte).
¡ Infelices de nosotros,
Si á estas lisonjas se entrega
Ulíses ! pues tarde, ó nunca
Daremos la vuelta á Grecia. [*Vase.*

Música.
Solo el silencio testigo
Ha de ser de mi tormento,
Y aun no cabe lo que siento
En todo lo que no digo.

Sale ARSIDAS.

Arsidas (á Circe).
Si para ver sus desdichas
Siempre ha tenido licencia
Un triste, porque el pesar
A nadie cerró las puertas,
No te admires que la tome

Ulysses.
Once again I fear to offend thee.
Circe (aside to Flerida.)
Flerida, be now enacted
The feign'd part I gave thee.
[*The ladies and gentlemen take their places, so that* ULYSSES *has* CIRCE *at one side of him, and* FLERIDA *at the other.*
Flerida.
Here
I my place select, to make thee
Feel, Ulysses, what thou owest
To my favour.
Lysidas (aside).
O unhappy
Eyes of mine, what sight to see!
Can my mistress by this stranger
Sit and whisper in his ear?—
O ye heavens, full patience grant me!
Antistes (aside).
Ah! unhappy we, if now,
By these false fair flatteries dazzled,
Yields Ulysses, late or never
Shall we back to Greece be wafted.
[*Exit.*

Song with Music.
Silence only, ah! I feel
Must be witness of my woe;
Though my suffering doth outgrow
Even the all that I conceal.

Enter ARSIDAS.

Arsidas (to Circe).
If to see his own misfortunes
Ever hath a wretch free access,
Since the gloomy gates of grief
Shut not out the humblest sadness,
Wonder not that I avail me

Yo, y que á tus jardines venga,
Pues he de mirar mis zelos,
A mirarlos de mas cerca.

Circe.

Yo no doy ſatisfacciones;
Pero huélgome que ſeas
Teſtigo de eſto, porque,
Sin que yo las dé, las tengas.

Arſidas.

Pues ſiendo aſi, y que ya Ulíſes
Eſtá á la mano derecha,
Como eſcogido, yo tomo,
Como dejado, la izquierda.

Circe.

Pues habemos de paſar
Aqui el ardor de la ſieſta,
Porque una aguda cueſtion
Mas á todos entretenga,
Haz, Flérida, una pregunta,
Y cada uno la defienda.

Flérida (aparte).

Diré lo que á mí me paſa,
Porque Líſidas lo entienda.—
Danteo ama á Liſis bella,
Y Liſis manda á Danteo
Diſimular ſu deſeo;
Silvio olvida á Clori, y ella
Manda, que finja querella;
Danteo, amando, ha de callar;
Silvio, no amando, moſtrar
Que ama: ſiendo eſto forzoſo,
¿Cuál es mas dificultoſo,
Fingir, ó diſimular?

Ulíſes.

Diſimular el que amó,
Lo mas difícil ha ſido.

Arſidas.

Fingir el que no ha querido,
Mas difícil juzgo yo.

Of the boon, and ſeek thy gardens;
Since if I muſt jealouſy ſee,
Beſt to ſee it near and naked.

Circe.

Satisfaction for ſuſpicions
I ne'er give, although it glads me
That you witneſs this, ſince I
Give them not, and yet you have them.

Arſidas.

This then being ſo, and ſince
On thy right hand ſits the favour'd
Gueſt, Ulyſſes, on thy left
Will I ſeat me, the forſaken.

Circe.

Since we here intend to paſs
The ſieſta's burning ardour,
That ſome ſubtle play of wit
May amuſe us while it laſteth,—
Flerida, a queſtion ſtart
Which we all in turn muſt anſwer.

Flerida (aſide).

What has paſs'd I'll tell, and truſt
Lyſidas may underſtand me.—
Laon loveth Lyſis fair,
Yet ſhe doth of him require
To diſſemble his deſire;
Silvio is free as air,
Yet is forced to affect deſpair;
Laon loves, yet hides his pain;
Silvio's free, yet wears the chain.
Thus coerced the two, I aſk,
Which is the ſeverer taſk,—
To diſſemble or to feign?

Ulyſſes.

The moſt difficult muſt be
To diſſemble where one loves.

Arſidas.

Feigning when no paſſion moves
Seems more difficult to me.

Caſandra.
Eſta opinion me agradó.
Arquelao.
Yo eſtotra pienſo ſeguir.
Clori.
¿ Quién diſimula el ſentir ?
Liſidas.
¿ Y quién fingirá el amar ?
Thiſbe.
Lo mas es diſimular.
Timántes.
Lo menos es el fingir.
Ulíſes.
El hombre, que enamorado
Eſtá, (quien lo eſtá no ignora,
Que eſto es aſi) á cualquier hora
Trae conſigo ſu cuidado;
El que finge no; olvidado
Puede eſtar, haſta llegar
De fingir tiempo y lugar:
Luego, ſi ſu afecto es juez,
Uno ſiempre, otro tal vez,
Mas cueſta el diſimular.
Arſidas.
La miſma razon ha ſido
La que me da la victoria.
Conſigo trae ſu memoria
Quien ama; quien finge, olvido:
Luego el que ama no ha podido
Olvidarſe de ſentir;
Quien finge sí, pues ha de ir
Tras la ocaſion que ſe pierde,
Sin que nadie ſe lo acuerde:
Luego mas cueſta el fingir.
Ulíſes.
El fingir ſe trae conſigo
Un cuidado tambien, pues
Batalla es fingir; mas es
Batalla ſin enemigo;

Caſſandra.
That I hold inſtinctively.
Archelaus.
I the other view maintain.
Chloris.
Who can hide the heart's fond pain?
Lyſidas.
Love can have no imitator.
Thiſbe.
To diſſemble is the greater.
Timantes.
'Tis the leſſer taſk to feign.
Ulyſſes.
He who loves (it is confeſs'd
By all hearts that own Love's power),
Carries with him every hour
Care and trouble in his breaſt;
He who feigneth love's unreſt
Feeleth nought that theſe reſemble
Till the time and place to tremble
At and in come round; deciding
'Twixt the fleeting and abiding;
Then 'tis greater to diſſemble.
Arſidas.
For the reaſon you expreſs
I may claim the victory:
He who loves brings memory,
He who feigns, forgetfulneſs;
One is powerleſs to repreſs
The remembrance of his pain;
That the other can is plain,
Since 'tis uſed but as a cover,
And forgotten when 'tis over;
Therefore greater 'tis to feign.
Ulyſſes.
He who feigns muſt alſo know
Conſtant care, for feigning is
A warfare; but this war of his
Is a fight without a foe;

La del que ama no ; teſtigo
Es uno, y otro peſar :
Eſte tiene que triunfar
De muchos afectos ciego ;
Aquel de uno ſolo : luego
Mas es el diſimular.

Arſidas.

Mayores afectos miente,
Que el que ſiente un mal cruel,
Y le diſimula, aquel
Que le dice, y no le ſiente.
Pruébaſe eſto claramente,
Si un repreſentante á oir
Vamos, porque perſuadir
Nos hace entonces que amó,
Y un enamorado no :
Luego mas es el fingir.

Ulíſes.

Yo ſiento eſto.

Arſidas.

Eſtotro yo.

[*Meten mano á la eſpada.*

Circe.

¿ Qué es eſto ? ¿ pues como aſi
Hablais delante de mí ?
Duelos del ingenio no
El acero los lidió :
Y aſi, para que ſalgamos
De la cueſtion en que eſtamos,
Deſde el empuñado acero
Hoy á la experiencia, quiero,
Que la duda remitamos.
Ulíſes no ama, y defiende
Que es mas zelar un ardor ;
Arſidas ama en rigor,
Y que es mas fingirle entiende ;
Y aſi mi ingenio pretende
La cueſtion averiguar :
Los dos la habeis de moſtrar

That the lover's is not ſo,
Witneſs ſorrows that aſſemble,
Witneſs fears that make him tremble
For his leaguer'd hope nigh loſt :
This fights one, but that a hoſt ;
Then 'tis greater to diſſemble.

Arſidas.

Hard albeit to conceal,
Yet 'tis falſe to ſay one feeleth
Equal heart-pangs who concealeth,
And who feigns but does not feel ;
This I prove by an appeal
To the actor's mimic pain ;
When we liſten to his ſtrain,
We believe his paſſion real,
Though we know 'tis all ideal ;—
Therefore greater 'tis to feign.

Ulyſſes.

This I feel.

Arſidas.

The other I.

[*They put their hands to their ſwords.*

Circe.

What is this ? and can it be
That you ſpeak thus before *me ?*
With the ſword we ne'er ſhould try
Wit-jouſts to conclude thereby.
Thus that we may pretermit
The diſpute that here is knit,
Without clenching ſwords to aid it,
By a trial I'll evade it,
And refer the doubt to it.
Free of love, Ulyſſes holdeth
Harder 'tis to hide love's fire ;
Arſidas, who's all deſire,
Thinks to feign, more pain enfoldeth.
Of the truth that each upholdeth
Thus I mean to manifeſt :—
Let the two be put to teſt

Hoy conmigo; y ſin reñir,
Tú, Ulíſes, has de fingir,
Tú, Arſidas, diſimular.
Y el que en la experiencia hiciere
Primera demoſtracion,
Por premio de la cueſtion
Una rica joya eſpere.

Arſidas.

Mi amor aceptar no quiere
El partido, pues la llama
Ha de ocultar que le inflama;
Y Ulíſes no ha de fingir,
Pues nada finge en decir
Que te ama, ſi te ama.

Circe.

Soſpechas ſon de tus zelos,
Y eſto ha de ſer.

Ulíſes.

Deſde aqui
Finjo ſer tu amante.

Circe (aparte).

Aſi
Abran camino los cielos,
Para explicar mis deſvelos.

Arſidas.

Yo diſimulo, que no
Te quiero, pues me obligó
Tu precepto.

Circe (aparte).

Deſta ſuerte
Al uno y al otro advierte
Mi amor lo que deſeó.

Flérida (aparte á Circe).

Si le das á cada uno
Un cuidado, ¿cómo, ay Dios!
Quieres, que yo tenga dos?
Pues en mal tan importuno
Son muchos cuidados uno.

In my perſon; uncomplaining
Thou, Ulyſſes, play love's feigning;
Arſidas, conceal thy beſt.
And who better doth affect
His aſſignèd part to-day,
Guerdon of this mimic fray,
A rich jewel may expect.

Arſidas.

My true love cannot accept
A partition which concealeth
What my burning heart revealeth.
Light the part Ulyſſes playeth,
Since he feigns not if he ſayeth
That he loves, when love he feeleth.

Circe.

This thy jealous thoughts betray;
Be it ſo, howe'er it move thee.

Ulyſſes.

I henceforth pretend to love thee.

Circe (aſide).

Heaven but point me out a way
That to ſhow I dare not ſay.

Arſidas.

I henceforth pretend that I
Love thee not, and thus comply
With thy precept.

Circe (aſide).

In this faſhion,
I my heart's new waken'd paſſion
Indicate to both thereby.

Flerida (aſide to Circe).

If from thee in ſeparate ſhares
Each a ſingle care muſt rue,
Canſt thou wiſh that I have two?
Since in hapleſs love affairs
One care holds a thouſand cares.

Circe.	*Circe.*
¿Si ambos los has de tener,	If thou'rt forced the two to hold,
Quien te metió, di, en saber	Thou thereby art less controll'd;
Cual de los dos en rigor	What availeth thee to know
Era cuidado mayor,	Which care works the weightier woe,
Pues no habias de escoger?	Since to choose thou art not told.
[*Quiere irse.*	[*She is about retiring.*
Arsidas.	*Arsidas.*
Circe se va, ingrata y bella,	Circe goes, and though my trembling
Y aunque su ausencia sentí,	Heart may for her absence ache,
No la seguiré; que así	I the cruel fair forsake,
Disimularé el querella.	Thus my love of her dissembling.
Ulises.	*Ulysses.*
Circe se ausenta; tras ella	Circe goes, and I resembling
Iré, aunque mi mal infiero,	One who 'neath some charm doth move,
Por mostrarla que la quiero.	Follow her to show my love.
Circe.	*Circe.*
¿Dónde, Ulíses, vas?	Whither goest thou?
Ulises.	*Ulysses.*
Tras tí,	After thee,
Que eres el sol, de quien fui	Sun, whose sun-flower I must be;—
Girasol; vida no espero,	Till thy sweet light from above
Ausente tu rosicler;	Dawns on me no life I know;
Y así tus reflejos sigo.	Therefore where thou shin'st, I go.
Circe.	*Circe.*
Arsidas, ven tú conmigo.	Arsidas, come thou with me.
Arsidas.	*Arsidas.*
Tengo otra cosa que hacer;	Pardon me, it cannot be,
Perdona, no puede ser. [*Vase.*	I a different duty owe. [*Exit.*
Circe (aparte).	*Circe (aside).*
Bien á los dos considero	In this primal test the two
En el combate primero.	Have the fight gone bravely through.
¡O si este amor, si este olvido,	Thus adored, and thus disdain'd,
Uno no fuera fingido,	Would the real love were feign'd!
Y otro fuera verdadero!	And the feign'd love were but true!
[*Vanse todos, y* FLERIDA *detiene á* ULÍSES.	[*Exeunt all but* FLERIDA, *who detains* ULYSSES.
Flérida.	*Flerida.*
¡Oye, Ulíses!	Lift, Ulysses!

Ulíses.

¿Qué me quieres?

Flérida.

Estoy tan agradecida
A la deuda de mi vida,
Que hasta decirte, que eres
Quien hoy en ella prefieres
Sus sentidos, no tendré
Sosiego en ellos; porque
Es el agradecimiento
El mas preciso argumento
Para probar una fe.

Ulíses.

De tus penas obligado,
Decir puedo, y afligido,
Que antes de haberlas sabido,
Ya me habian lastimado.
No debes á mi cuidado
Lo que por tí no hice alli,
Cuando á la luz te volví;
Porque tú no tienes, no,
Que agradecer lo que yo
No supe que hacia por tí.
Ahora sí que debieras
Mi deseo agradecer,
Pues almas quisiera ser,
Para que tú las tuvieras.

Flérida.

Aunque acciones lisonjeras,
Agradezca su trofeo
Con mis brazos mi deseo :—
[*Abrázale.*
¡Yo misma de mí me admiro!
[*aparte.*
[*Al ir á darse los brazos salen por dos puertas* CIRCE *y* LÍSIDAS.

Lísidas (*Cada uno aparte*).

¿Qué es esto, cielos, que miro?

Ulysses.

Call'st thou me?

Flerida.

Ah! the gratitude I'd show thee
For the debt of life I owe thee
Is so great, that, till to thee
I declare it openly,
I can find nor peace nor rest
In the senses thou hast blest;
Since a warm acknowledgment
Is the strongest argument
Of a true and faithful breast.

Ulysses.

Though thy pain's unnatural laws
Must have moved the flintiest heart,
I can say their bitter smart
Pain'd me ere I knew their cause.
Then before you thank me, pause;
Thanks to me you do not owe,
Thanks you do not owe me, no,
For restoring you to light.
Service can at best be slight
Given to one we do not know.
Wouldst thou now my wishes meet,
Trust me, if that debt survives,
If I had a thousand lives,
I would lay them at thy feet.

Flerida.

Let this flattering act complete
What my words have fail'd to prove,
All my gratitude and love :—
[*Embraces him.*
Self-surprise amazeth me!
[*At the moment of their embracing,* CIRCE *and* LYSIDAS *appear at different doors.*

Lysidas (*aside.*)

What is this, O heavens! I see?

Circe.
¿ Qué es esto, dioses, que veo ?
Lísidas.
El Griego Ulíses es quien
Darme vida y muerte espera.
Circe.
Bien que fingiese quisiera,
No que fingiese tan bien.
Lísidas.
Muerte mis zelos me den.
Circe.
¿ Mas de qué debo quejarme ?
Lisidas.
¡ La vida intenta quitarme,
Que me ha dado Ulíses, cielos !
Porque darme vida y zelos,
No deja de ser matarme.
Flérida (á Ulíses).
Estaré, como te digo,
De noche en ese jardin,
Que cae sobre el mar, á fin
De que él solo sea testigo
Del afecto á que me obligo.
Ulíses.
Flérida, no es grosería
Que responda la voz mia
Que no te ha de obedecer ;
Pues es mas desaire ser
Amada por cortesía.
Yo he de fingir ser amante
De Circe, y no lo fingiera,
Si otro favor admitiera
Tan poco firme y constante.
No el desengaño te espante ;
Que aunque de mi pensamiento
Otro haya sido el intento,
Cesó ; que en el mal que sigo,
Solo el silencio testigo
Ha de ser de mi tormento. [*Vase.*

Circe (aside).
What a sight ! ye powers above !
Lysidas (aside).
By the Greek Ulysses' spell
Must I death as life attain ?
Circe (aside).
Though I wish'd that you should feign,
Ah ! you should not feign so well.
Lysidas (aside).
Jealousy doth ring my knell !—
Circe (aside).
Wherefore though should I complain ?
Lysidas.
Heavens ! Ulysses would again
Of that life he gave deprive me !
Since 'tis worse than death to give me
Life so link'd with jealous pain.
Flerida to Ulysses.
I to-night will wait for thee
In the garden o'er the sea,
Since my grateful heart would only,
Of its utterance, have that lonely
Silent scene its witness be.
Ulysses.
Lady, if my voice replieth
With refusal, it denieth
Not through want of courtesy,
Since affected love to thee
Far less courtesy implieth.
I, thou know'st, must feign to be
Circe's lover : 'twere not feigning,
If my suit to her disdaining,
I elsewhere should bend the knee ;
Let my candour pain not thee :—
Other homage do I owe,
Other love I fain would show,
But unspoken must conceal.
Silence only, ah ! I feel,
Must be witness of my woe ! [*Exit.*

Flérida.
No pudiera reſponder
Mas á mi contento nada ;
Pues de verme deſpreciada,
Soy la primera muger,
Que guſto llegó á tener.
Líſidas (*aparte*).
Qué eſpero ? Mas ay de mí !
Que eſtá Circe ingrata alli.
Ocaſion eſperaré
De quejarme, ſi podré.
Flérida.
¿ Aqui eſtás, ſeñora ?
Circe.
Sí.
Flérida.
¿ Luego ya bien entablado
Lo que me has mandado habrás
Viſto ?
Circe.
Sí, Flérida, y mas
De lo que te habia mandado.
Flérida.
Encarecí mi cuidado
Con afecto, ay de mí ! cuanto
Supe.
Circe.
Deja afecto tanto,
Flérida, que amando muero ;
Y bien que lo finjas quiero,
Mas no que lo finjas tanto.
Demas, que ſi en los primeros
Lances pierdo los ſentidos,
No quiero zelos fingidos,
Que ſepan á verdaderos.
Tus afectos liſonjeros
Ceſen, pues que ſu caſtigo
Fingido fue tal conmigo,
Que no digo ſu tormento ;

Flerida.
A more fortunate reply
Fate could never have deviſed !
Since to ſee myſelf deſpiſed
Firſt of womankind am I
Who a pleaſure feel thereby.
Lyſidas (*aſide*).
Why delay ? But, dire diſtreſs !
Circe's there, the mercileſs.
I a better time muſt plan
To expoſtulate, if I can.
Flerida.
Wert thou here, Señora ?
Circe.
Yes.
Flerida.
Saw you then how I expended
All my art in the part I play'd
By your orders ?
Circe.
You obey'd
Even more than I intended.
Flerida.
Woe is me ! I thus offended,
Fancying that you wiſh'd for ſuch
Feint of fondneſs.
Circe.
Ceaſe ! Thy touch
Ice-like chill'd my heart and brain ;
Ah ! I die of love !—to feign ?
Yes, but not to feign ſo much.
Nay, if thus I ſadly rue
This firſt feint ſo unpropitious,
I deſire not by fictitious
Jealouſies to learn the true.
Ceaſe then with fond wiles to woo,
Since I pay for thy appeal
With ſuch feign'd pain, that I feel
Words are weak to ſpeak my woe,

Y aun no cabe lo que ſiento
En todo lo que no digo. [*Vaſe.*

Flérida.

¿ Quién mas necio extremo vió ?
¿ Hay mas penas, que por mí
Paſen eſte inſtante ?

Líſidas.

Sí ;
Que aun ahora falto yo.
No, Flérida hermoſa, no
Porque á quejarme me obligo,
Porque para mi caſtigo,
Que eſto hable, que eſto vea,
No quiero mas de que ſea
Solo el ſilencio teſtigo.

Flérida.

Líſidas, ſi has eſcuchado
Lo que á Ulíſes dije aqui,
Tambien lo que Circe á mí
Es fuerza que hayas notado.
No lince para el cuidado,
Y ciego para el contento
Eſtés ; que eſte fingimiento,
Si fue cauſa de mi engaño,
Tambien, tambien deſengaño
Ha de ſer de mi tormento.

Líſidas.

De un triſte el rigor es tal,
Que, aunque mal y bien eſtên
Iguales, duda del bien
El crédito que da al mal.
Uno y otro en mí es mortal ;
Y aſi, al bien y al mal atento,
Flérida, auſentarme intento
De aqueſte monte cruel,
Que con ſer tan grande, en él
Aun no cabe lo que ſiento. [*Vaſe.*

Flérida.

Oye, eſcucha !—Mas ¡ ay cielos !

Though my ſuffering doth outgrow
Even the all that I conceal. [*Exit.*

Flerida.

Who has ſeen more wild conceit ?
Can this moment bring exceſs
Of the pain I ſuffer ?

Lyſidas (*advancing*).

Yes ;
Without me 'twere incomplete :
But I come not to repeat
Vain complaints, alas ! not ſo,
Since, fair Flerida, I know
From the things I hear and ſee,
Silence only, woe is me !
Muſt be witneſs of my woe.

Flerida.

Lyſidas, if audibly
What I told Ulyſſes floated
To thine ear, thou muſt have noted
Alſo Circe's words to me,
Be not then to miſery
Lynx-eyed, and to joy but blind :—
If the part to me aſſign'd
Cauſes grief by its deceiving
Likewiſe too in undeceiving
Muſt I ſtill my torment find.

Lyſidas.

'Tis the torment of the ſad,
That though good and evil ſhould
Seem alike, they doubt the good,
And give credence to the bad.
Both a mortal anguiſh add
To my ſuffering, I would fain
Flerida forget the twain,
And this cruel mountain flee,
Which however vaſt it be
Cannot compaſs all my pain. [*Exit.*

Flerida.

Liſten ! hear me !—But, ah me !

¿Con qué podrán mis enojos
Detenerle, si los ojos
No pueden, que en sus desvelos
Rémoras son de los zelos?
En vano, ay de mí! le sigo;
No á explicar mi mal me obligo,
Pues que no cabe, no ignoro,
Aun nada de lo que lloro,
En todo lo que no digo. [*Vase.*

How can all my tears and sighs
Hold him here, when even the eyes
Cannot do so, though we see
Oft their light scares jealousy.
It is vain, oh! woe the day!
To pursue him, vain to stay
Doubts that o'er his heart are creeping,
Let me then in silent weeping
Wail the grief I must not say. [*Exit.*

MONTE.

Sale CLARIN.

Clarin.

Engañada Circe bella
(Que en efecto las mugeres,
Que saben mas en el mundo,
Se engañan mas fácilmente),
Agradecida me dijo
Que á este monte me viniese,
Y que en hallándome solo,
A Brutamonte le diese
Voces, que al instante el tal
Brutamonte, sea quien fuere,
Me traeria un gran tesoro.
Solo estoy, ya no hay que espere.
Brutamonte!—No responde;
Brutamonte!—No me entiende;
A tres irá la vencida:
Brutamonte!

Sale BRUTAMONTE *gigante.*

Brutamonte.

Qué me quieres?

Clarin.

Nada, si fuere posible,
Es cuanto puedo quererte.

Brutamonte.

Ya me has llamado, y ya sé

A MOUNTAIN.

Enter CLARIN.

Clarin.

Circe fair, by me deceived
(Since 'tis easiest of all women
To impose on those who are
Wisest in all kinds of knowledge),
Circe fair, as I have said,
In a grateful moment told me
To this mountain to repair,
And to shout out Brutamonte
When I found myself alone,
And that he upon the moment
Would, whoe'er he be, confer
Some most precious gift upon me.
I am now alone, why wait?
Brutamonte!—No responses;
Brutamonte!—No one hears me;
Third and last time,—Brutamonte!

Enter BRUTAMONTE, *a giant.*

Brutamonte.

At your service, what's your business?

Clarin.

Nothing, faith, an it were only
Possible to get away.

Brutamonte.

You have call'd me, and the object

A lo que vengo; que es eſte
Recado que traigo.

Clarin.

¿Y no
La ſeñora Circe tiene
Otros pagecicos mas
Mañeros, que le trajeſen?
Porque para mí baſtara
Menor ſeis varas, ó ſiete.

Brutamonte.

De mí ſe ſirve, que ſoy
De Cíclopes deſcendiente,
Por mas mageſtad, y eſpero,
Antes que de aqui ſe auſenten
Los Griegos, vengar en todos
De Polifemo la muerte.

[*Sacan una arca dos animales.*

Clarin.

Poco hay que vengar en mí;
Que yo no le toqué, y ſiempre
Le tuve, viven los cielos!
Tanto miedo como eſte;
Que otro hipérbole no sé,
Con que mas encarecerle.

Brutamonte.

Toma eſta caja, que traigo
Para tí.

Clarin.

Bien.

Brutamonte.

Y agradece
A Circe, que ſu obediencia
Atadas mis manos tiene,
Para que no te arrebate
De un brazo, y contigo dieſe
De eſotra parte del mar.

Clarin.

Lindo ſaque fuera eſe;

Of your coming I diſcover
By the diſpatch I carry.

Clarin.

Can
Lady Circe have no other
Little page but you to run
On her errands through the foreſt?
Quite enough for me were one
Who was ſix or ſeven yards ſhorter.

Brutamonte.

She makes uſe of me, who am
From the Cyclops ſprung, to ſhow her
Greater grandeur, and I hope,
Ere the Greeks depart theſe coaſts here,
For the death of Polyphemus
To take vengeance on the whole herd.

[*Two animals draw in a cheſt.*

Clarin.

Little need you take on *me*:—
Since I never touch'd him, no then,
But the ſame fear felt, by Heaven!
Towards him then, that now comes o'er
me;
I know no hyperbole
Better can my terror ſhow thee.

Brutamonte.

See this cheſt I here have brought thee,
Take it.

Clarin.

Good.

Brutamonte.

And thank the goddeſs
Circe, that obedient duty
Unto her my ſtrong hand holds here,
So that I do not uplift thee
With one arm, and hurl thee yonder
Far amid the whelming ſea-waves.

Clarin.

What a game of ball, to hop there

Pero, aunque hiciera buen bote,
¿Quién de allá habia de volverme?

Brutamonte.

Y ſi eſto no hiciera, hiciera
Otra coſa.

Clarin.

Cuál?

Brutamonte.

Comerte
De un bocado.

Clarin.

Y aun no hubiera
Harto para untar un diente.

Brutamonte.

¡O llegue el dia en que tenga
Eſta licencia!

Clarin.

¡O no llegue
Nunca, ſino deſpeado
En el camino ſe quede!

Brutamonte.

Toma la caja, y en ella
Hallarás mas que quiſieres.

Clarin.

Un modo de deſpedirte
Quiſiera hallar ſolamente.

Brutamonte.

Pues yo me voy.

Clarin.

Haces bien.—
¡Qué gigantes tan corteſes [*aparte.*
En eſta tierra ſe uſan,
Que poquito ſe detienen
En converſaciones donde
Eſtorban!

Brutamonte.

Y cuantas veces
Me nombrares . . . .

Out ſo far! But, when I bounded
On the ſea, who'd hit me home here?

Brutamonte.

If I didn't do that, I'd do
Something better.

Clarin.

What?

Brutamonte.

Juſt gobble
You up in a bit.

Clarin.

'Twould ſcarcely whet
One of your teeth, ſo ſmall a morſel.

Brutamonte.

May the day come ſoon when I
Have that licence!

Clarin.

May it not then
Ever come, but rather ſounder
On the road before it comes here.

Brutamonte.

Take the cheſt, and you will find
In it more than you could covet.

Clarin.

How to get you to take leave
Is juſt now my only problem.

Brutamonte.

Then I go.

Clarin.

You do quite right;—
How obliging and how courteous
[*aſide.*
Are the giants of this country,
Who their viſitations ſhorten,
When they find their converſation
Grows a bore!

Brutamonte.

And I, as often
As you call me . . . .

Clarin.

Qué?

Brutamonte.

Vendré
A eſtos paiſes á verte. [*Vaſe.*

Clarin.

Yo le ahorraré eſe trabajo
Cuantas veces yo pudiere.—
Fueſe? Parece que sí,
Aunque aqui no lo parece.
¿Pero de qué tengo miedo,
Si es humilde y obediente,
Un novicio de gigantes?
Y pues el teſoro viene,
¿Quién me mete en diſcurrir?
Tráigale quien le trajere.
¡Alto pues, abro la caja!
Que la llave en ella tiene.
¿Quién duda, que habrá diamantes
Como el puño, como nueces
Perlas, y como las bolas
De los bolos los claveques?

[*Abre la caja, y ſale una Dueña.*

Mas, cielos! qué miro?

Dueña.

Miras
A una míſera ſirviente,
Que para ſervir de eſcucha,
Y parlar cuanto dijeres
De Circe, me manda que ande
Contigo acechando ſiempre.
Por eſo en trage de dueña
Me envia, para que aceche.

Clarin.

¡Lindo teſoro de chiſmes
En la tal arca me viene!
¿Yo dueña, tras un gigante?
Aqui falta ſolamente,

Clarin.

Well?

Brutamonte.

Will come
Here to ſee you on the moment. [*Exit.*

Clarin.

Well, that trouble I will ſpare you
Every time I can, good monſter.—
Has he gone? It ſeems he has,
Though perhaps it ſeems ſo only.
But what need I fear? He is
Mild and meek in his deportment,
Quite a novice among giants.
Since a treaſure I have gotten,
'Bout the bearer, or the bringer
Why ſhould I diſturb my noddle?
Courage then! the cheſt I'll open.
With the key that's in the lock here,
Who can doubt that here are diamonds
Bigger than my fiſt, and whole heaps
Of large pearls like nuts, and gems
That like bowls roll o'er each other?

[*He opens the box, from which a Duenna ariſes.*

Heavens! what's this I ſee?

Duenna.

You ſee
A poor wretched ſervant body,
Who to play the part of ſpy,
And to tell what may be ſpoken
Againſt Circe, is commanded
Ever-liſtening to eſcort thee.
Since I'm ſent to liſten, I
Thus duenna-like am clothèd.

Clarin.

What a treaſure-trove of rags
Have I in this cheſt diſcover'd!
Firſt comes giant, then duenna:—
Now the thing that's only wanted

Para que el triunfigurato
De caballeros noveles
Eſté cabal, un enano.

Dueña.

Pues no faltará, ſi es eſe
El defecto.—Brunelillo!
Sal al punto.

Sale un Enano.

Enano.

¿Qué me quieres,
Doña Brianda?

Clarin.

¿De dónde
Sales, átomo viviente?

Enano.

De mi caſa, que lo es
Eſta caja, donde ſiempre
Acueſtas me has de traer.

Clarin.

¿Pues cómo aqui caber pueden
Un enano y una dueña,
Si cualquiera de ellos ſuele
No caber en todo el mundo?

Dueña.

Brunelillo, gente viene,
Y no es juſto que nos vean.—
Oye, dóblenos, y cierre
La caja.

Enano.

Circe lo manda,
Que ſiempre al hombro nos lleve,
Y lo que dijere oigamos.

Dueña.

Y aun mas de lo que dijere.

[*Métenſe en la caja y cierran.*

Clarin.

¿Señores, qué es lo que paſa
Por mí? qué teſoro es eſte?

To make all this transformation
(Like to a knight-errant novel)
Finiſh finely, is a dwarf.

Duenna.

Then if that be ſo, no longer
Need you wait.—Here! Brunelillo,
On the inſtant.

A Dwarf comes out.

Dwarf.

For what object,
Dame Brianda?

Clarin.

Where did you come from,
Living atom, pigmy wonder?

Dwarf.

From my manſion, which you ſee
Is this box, where on your ſhoulder
You muſt carry me henceforth.

Clarin.

How I marvel, can this box here
Hold a dwarf and a duenna,
When there's ſcarce for either of them
Room enough in all the whole earth?

Duenna.

Brunelillo, men come yonder,
And 'twere wrong that they ſhould ſee us.
Hark you! fold us ſmooth, and cover
Up the cheſt.

Dwarf.

Remember, Circe
Bids you bear us on your ſhoulder,
And that what you ſpeak we'll hear.

Duenna.

Ay, and more than will be ſpoken.

[*They enter the box, which cloſes.*

Clarin.

What on earth am I to do
With my treaſure, good Señores?

Vive Júpiter! que juntos
A ſu caſcara ſe vuelven.
Aqui hay trampa, vive Dios!
Mas no, en la caja no tienen
Por donde haberſe ſalido.
¿Qué haré en confuſion tan fuerte?
Si de Circe no obedezco
El caſtigo que me ofrece,
Otro mayor me dará,
Si es que otro ſer mayor puede
Que levar la caja. Pues
Ahora veo claramente,
Por qué el gigante la trajo,
Y los animales fuertes;
Porque coſa tan peſada,
Como una dueña, no puede
Sufrirla, ſino un gigante
Y dos beſtias ſolamente.—
¿Quién compra dueñas y enanos,
Como peines y alfileres?

Sale LEBREL.

Lebrel (*Para ſi*).
¡Que tal penſaſe de mí
Circe, y que á Clarin creyeſe!
Huyendo vengo á eſte monte,
Donde á los dioſes pluguieſe,
Que al caſtigo, que me eſpera,
Hallaſe donde eſconderme.
Pondré, que aqueſta es la hora,
Que eſtá trazando de hacerme
Sabandija deſtos montes,
Guſarapo deſtas fuentes.
Eſte es Clarin, y aqui dél
Será razon que me vengue.—
Huélgome de haberte hallado,
Clarin.

Clarin.
Por mas que te huelgues,

Jupiter! my precious gems
In their caſket now are cover'd:
Oh! there muſt be trap-doors here!
Yet the box contains no open,
Out through which they could have gone.
In ſuch ſtrong fix, how comport me?
If the puniſhment rejecting
Which to me hath Circe offer'd,
She a greater one may give me,
If a greater is concocted
Than to bear this box. I now
Clearly can explain the problem
Why a giant had to draw it,
And two beaſts as big as oxen;
Since ſuch heavy baggage is
A duenna, that the ſtrongeſt
Giant and two beaſts to match him
Muſt unite them to uphold her.—
Dwarfs! Duennas! come, who'll buy?
Like the man who pins and combs ſells.

Enter LEBREL.

Lebrel (*ſoliloquiſing*).
Oh! that thus could think of me
Circe, and truſt Clarin's nonſenſe!
Flying do I ſeek this mountain,
And its guardian gods invoke here,
That I may perchance find ſhelter,
From the wrath impending o'er me.
Now I'll bet ſhe's thinking how
In the beſt way to transform me
To a beetle of theſe mountains,
To a wet worm of theſe ponds here.
Here is Clarin, and here I
Will revenge the wrong he has done me.
Clarin, I'm o'erwhelm'd with joy
To have met thee.

Clarin.
If thy load, then,

No tanto como me pefa.

Lebrel.

Que vengo á darte la muerte.

Clarin.

Yo vengo á darte la vida.

Lebrel.

De qué fuerte?

Clarin.

Defta fuerte:
Circe, obligada de mí,
En efta caja me ofrece
Un teforo, y yo con él
Pretendo fatisfacerte;
Porque fi del bien hablar
El premio, Lebrel, es efte,
Con dártele á tí, tendrás
El premio, que tú mereces.
¿Puedes obligarme á mas
De que todo te lo entregue?
Toma la caja.

Lebrel.

No quiero,
Que todo á dármelo llegues,
Sino, pues me defenojas,
Que partamos igualmente.

Clarin.

Pues llevarâfte la dueña,
Y yo el enano.

Lebrel.

¿Qué quieres
Decir en efo?

Clarin.

No fé,
Tú lo verás, fi la abrieres.

[*Pone la caja en otra parte, y ábrela* Lebrel.

Lebrel.

Ponla aqui. Ya abierta eftá.

Is fo great, mine's not lefs weighty.

Lebrel.

Since to kill thee I'm devoted.

Clarin.

And to give thee life am I.

Lebrel.

In what way?

Clarin.

In *this* way, know then.
Circe being obliged to me,
In this cheft to me has offer'd
A great treafure, which as thine
I'm determined to reftore thee;
Since, if it is the reward,
Friend Lebrel, of the civil-fpoken,
By my giving it thee, thou'lt have
The reward thou'ft won fo nobly.
Can you then oblige me more
Than I do in giving the whole heap?
Take the cheft.

Lebrel.

I do not wifh you
To beftow the whole upon me;
But fince you've appeafed my wrath,
Be one half to each allotted.

Clarin.

Then do *you* take the duenna,
And I'll take the dwarf.

Lebrel.

You mock me;
What do you mean?

Clarin.

I do not know;
But you'll fee all when you open.

[*He places the cheft in another place, and* Lebrel *opens it.*

Lebrel.

Place it here, 'tis open now.

[*Saca* Lebrel *todo lo que dice.*

¡ Qué joyas tan excelentes !

Clarin.

Son muy excelentes joyas . . . .
(Para el diablo, que las lleve.) [*aparte.*

Lebrel.

Aquefta cadena efcojo,
Y efta para tí fe quede.

Clarin.

Ca . . . . qué ?

Lebrel.

Cadena ; y ahora
Dé diamantes efte Fénix
Para mí, y efta Sirena,
Toda de efmeraldas verdes,
Te dejo.

Clarin (*aparte*).

¡ Viven los cielos,
Que es impofible, que hubiefe
Diamantes donde hubo dueñas !

Lebrel.

Yo no quiero parecerte
Codiciofo ; efto me bafta,
Lo demas es bien te deje.—
¿ Quién no fe defenojara [*aparte.*
Con teforo como efte ?
A bufcar á Libia voy,
Y á darla cuanto quifiere. [*Vafe.*

Clarin.

O yo eftoy borracho, ó yo
Sueño cofas diferentes,
O he perdido mi juicio,
O tengo un grande accidente,
O de Circe he hablado mal.
¡ Que joyas hallar pudiefe

[*He takes out each article as he defcribes it.*

Oh ! what rich gems I behold here !

Clarin.

Very precious gems they are . . . .
(For the devil himfelf who bore them.) [*afide.*

Lebrel.

I felect this pretty chain,
And for you remains this other.

Clarin.

Pretty what ?

Lebrel.

This pretty chain ;
Now in turn to me belongeth
This refplendent diamond Phœnix,
And this Siren emerald brooch here,
I leave *thee.*

Clarin (*afide*).

Good gracious heavens !
Can it be that he difcovers
Diamonds now where I found dwarfs ?

Lebrel.

I don't wifh that you fuppofe me
Greedy ; fo I've had enough :
Of the reft I make thee owner.—
Who would not forego his anger [*afide.*
For a prize like this I hold here ?
Libia now I go to feek,
And I'll give her what fhe choofes. [*Exit.*

Clarin.

Either I am drunk, or I
Dream now this, and now the other ;
Or I have my fenfes loft,
Or have got fome grief in ftore yet,
Or 'gainft Circe wagg'd my tongue.—
Jewels how could *he* behold here,

Donde yo dueñas y enanos !
Mas yo las ví claramente,
Y ſupueſto que las hay,
Tomaré las que pudiere.
[*Sale la Dueña no mas del medio cuerpo.*

Dueña.
Señor, diga á Brunelillo
Vueſa merced, que me deje
Hacer mi labor.
[*Sale el Enano.*

Enano.
Señor,
Dígala uſted, que no llegue
A lamerme la merienda.

Dueña.
Tú mientes.

Enano.
Tú eres quien miente.
[*Aporréanſe y búndenſe.*

Clarin.
¿ Qué es lo que paſa por mí ?
¡ Valedme, dioſes, valedme !
¿ Eſta trajo Brutamonte ?

Sale BRUTAMONTE.

Brutamonte.
Qué me mandas ?

Clarin.
¡ Qué obediente
Es toda aqueſta familia !
¡ Con la preſteza que vienen
En llamándolos !—Señor
Brutamonte, á quien proſpere
Júpiter con la ſalud,
Que ſu gigantez merece,
Yo he viſto la caja, y yo
Le ruego, que ſe la lleve.

Where I ſaw but dwarfs and damſels ?
But I ſaw the gems with open
Eyes, and now with open hands too
Shall I make a haul and bolt hence.
[*The Duenna ariſes half her height in the box.*

Duenna.
Speak to Brunelillo, Sir,
Bid him leave me at my work here
Quietly, your worſhip.
[*The Dwarf riſes up.*

Dwarf.
Sir,
Tell her not to ſpoil my poſſet,
Pleaſe your worſhip, with her licking.

Duenna.
Oh ! a lie.

Dwarf.
On thy ſide only.
[*They beat each other, and ſink down.*

Clarin.
What, oh ! what fate will befall me ?
Help me ! help me ! all ye Gods here.
Was it this brought Brutamonte ?

Enter BRUTAMONTE.

Brutamonte.
What are your commands ?

Clarin.
The promptneſs
Of the family's ſurpriſing !
With what quickneſs they all hop here
When you call them !—Brutamonte,
Noble Sir, whom Jove may proſper
With ſufficiency of health
For your giantſhip's big body,
I have ſeen the cheſt, and I
Aſk thee now to take it home hence ;

Quédese para señores
Esto de trastos vivientes;
Que no he menester alhajas,
Que coman, y no aprovechen.

Brutamonte.

¿Para eso se llama á un hombre
Como yo? Estoy por hacerle . . . .

Clarin.

Por deshacerme dirá.

Brutamonte.

Piezas; y si le sucede
Llamarme otra vez . . . .

Clarin.

No hará.

Brutamonte.

Por Júpiter! que le eche
Tan alto de un puntapie,
Que cuando á los cielos llegue,
Ya llegue muerto de hambre;
Y vuelva, si acaso vuelve,
De los pájaros comido.

[*Vase.*

Clarin.

¡Puntapie bien excelente!
¿Dónde le hacen puntapies?
No sé, vive Dios! que hacerme
Entre los tres enemigos
Del cuerpo.

Salen Astrea, Libia *y* Lebrel.

Lebrel.

Un instante breve
Habrá, que le dejé aqui
Con las joyas.

Astrea.

Tiempo es este
De buscarle, que está rico.
Ven, Libia, conmigo á verle.

Living lumber like to this
May be fit for grand señores,
But fine furniture that eats,
And is useless, I don't covet.

Brutamonte.

Is't for this, a man like me
Thou dar'st call on? I am prompted . . .

Clarin.

To do something pleasant, doubtless.

Brutamonte.

To make bits of thee; another
Time if thou dost call . . . .

Clarin.

I won't then.

Brutamonte.

By great Jove! so high I'll toss thee
With a kick, that when thou reachest
The remote celestial bodies,
Thou'lt have long since died of hunger;
And thou'lt drop, if e'er thou droppest,
On the earth, by birds half eaten.

[*Exit.*

Clarin.

Kick supreme! of kicks the model!
Where are such kicks to be purchased?
I know not, as God's above me,
What to do against these three foes
Of my body.

Enter Astrea, Libia, *and* Lebrel.

Lebrel.

Scarce a moment
Is it since I left him here
With the jewels.

Astrea.

Then 'tis proper
That we seek him, since he is rich.
Libia, come, let's seek our old friend.

Libia.
Aqui eſtá.—Clarin, qué hay?
Lebrel.
De qué ſuſpiras?
Aſtrea.
Qué tienes?
Clarin.
Tengo dueña, tengo enano,
Y tengo gigante.
Aſtrea.
Vuelve,
Y dinos, qué es eſo?
Clarin.
Es
La dueña, que me atormente,
El enano, que me valga,
Y el gigante, que me lleve.

Aſtrea.
Eſtás loco?
Clarin.
A Dios pluguiera!
Aſtrea.
¿Qué modo de hablarme es eſe?
De otra manera Lebrel
A Libia habla, adora y quiere;
Pues una joya la ha dado,
Y tu ninguna me ofreces
De tantas.
Clarin.
Déjame, Aſtrea,
Y no de joyas me tientes,
Que me harás deſeſperar,
Si á hablar mas en eſo vuelves.
Voces (dentro).
Por acá, por acá!
Circe (dentro).
Sube,
Remontada garza, á hacerte

Libia.
Here he is.—How goes it, Clarin?
Lebrel.
Why thus ſigh?
Aſtrea.
What haſt thou got there?
Clarin.
I've a dwarf here, a duenna,
And a giant alſo.
Aſtrea.
Nonſenſe,
Tell us what it is.
Clarin.
It is
The duenna who's my torment,
'Tis the dwarf with whom I'm bleſs'd ſo,
'Tis the giant ſworn to flog me.
Aſtrea.
Are you mad?
Clarin.
I would I were ſo!
Aſtrea.
What a way is this to have ſpoken!
In another ſtyle Lebrel
Speaks to Libia, worſhips, loves her,
Since a jewel he has given her;
And to me not one thou'ſt offer'd
Of ſo many.
Clarin.
Ceaſe, Aſtrea!
And on jewels touch no longer,
Since you'll drive me to deſpair,
If again you harp upon them.
Voices (within).
Hither! hither!—
Circe (within).
Upward ſtill,
Soaring heron, and transform thee

Eſtrella viva de pluma.

Aſtrea.

Circe es eſta, que aqui viene ;
Yo no quiero que me vea.

Lebrel.

¡ A Júpiter para ſiempre !

[*Vanſe* Libia, Astrea *y* Lebrel.

Sale Circe.

Circe.

Por ver ſi Ulíſes me ſigue,
Me he perdido de mi gente,
Y dejando á un tronco atado
Eſe zéfiro obediente,
Que fatigué, he de eſperar
Entre eſtos álamos verdes.—
Quién eſtá aqui ?

Clarin.

Un mentecato,
Un ſucio, un impertinente,
Un necio, un loco, un menguado,
Y un cuanto vuſted quiſiere.
Sáqueme, por Dios ! de dueñas,
De hombres largos, y hombres breves,
Aunque me convierta en mona.

Circe.

Yo lo haré, ſi eſo pretendes.

Clarin.

No me tome la palabra
Tan preſto, ſi le parece.

Circe.

Y porque me debas mas
Que otros, que mi voz convierte,
Haré, que tengas tu voz
Y tu entendimiento. Vete
De aqui.

To a living ſtar of plumes !

Aſtrea.

Circe's voice ! this way ſhe cometh :
Here I would not have her ſee me.

Lebrel.

Jove ! nor I upon the whole earth !

[*Exeunt* Libia, Astrea, *and* Lebrel.

Enter Circe.

Circe.

To diſcover if Ulyſſes
Follows, from my train I've loſt me,
And unto a tree-trunk tying
My obedient zephyr courſer,
Wearied with the chaſe, I'll wait here
Underneath theſe dark green poplars.—
Who is there ?

Clarin.

A ſimple ninny,
A poor moon-calf, a big blockhead,
A born fool, an aſs, a madman,
And what elſe your worſhip chooſes.
Free me, God's life ! from duennas,
From theſe tall men, from theſe ſhort men,
Though you make of me a monkey.

Circe.

So I'll do, ſince you have told me.

Clarin.

Do not take me at my word
Quite ſo quickly, I implore thee.

Circe.

And that you may owe me more
Than the others I transform here,
I will leave to you your ſenſes
And your voice. And now begone hence,
Quick !

Clarin.
No lo dije yo
Por tanto.
Circe.
Un punto no eſperes.—
Haſta mirarſe á un eſpejo, [*aparte.*
Ya en ſu forma no ha de verſe.
Clarin.
Si es que mona me has de hacer,
Solo quiero merecerte,
Que ſea mona de lo caro,
Mas que dormilona, alegre.—
Hombres monas, preſto habrá
Otro mas de vueſtra eſpecie. [*Vaſe.*

Sale Ulíses.

Ulíſes.
Por mas que te he ſeguido,
Corto el aliento de eſe bruto ha ſido,
Si bien con harto raſtro te ſeguia,
Pues llevabas por ſeñas todo el dia.

Circe.
De la caza canſada,
A eſte apacible ſitio retirada
Me vine. Qué has volado?
Ulíſes.
Un deſeo, ay de mí! tan remontado,
Que oſó con alto vuelo
Calarſe entre las nubes de algun cielo,
Donde al fuego vecino,
Con ligereza ſuma,
Abraſada la pluma,
Subió deſeo, y maripoſo vino.

Clarin.
In faith, I didn't mean it
Seriouſly.
Circe.
Don't wait a moment.—
Till he looks into a mirror, [*aſide.*
He his own ſhape won't recover.
Clarin.
If a monkey you will make me,
Let me for this favour hope then,
That you make a nice ape of me,
Briſk and lively, and no ſnorer.—
Monkey-men there, ſoon you'll have
One more member of your order.
[*Exit.*

Enter Ulysses.

Ulyſſes.
The quicker was my ſpeed,
The quicker fail'd the hot breath of my ſteed,
Following thy track along the devious way,
Since in thy flight thou haſt outſtripp'd the day.
Circe.
Aweary with the chaſe,
To this retired and ſylvan-ſhaded place
I came. Say, what has riſen?
Ulyſſes.
A fond deſire, ah me! from out its priſon,
Which dared in lofty flight
To pierce the clouds of one ſweet heaven ſo bright,
That from the glowing ſky
Through which it ſoar'd a paſſion-wing'd deſire,
With plumage all afire,

Circe.
¿ De la caza, pregunto, qué has volado ?

Ulises.
En ella te respondo, que un cuidado.

Circe.
¿ Pues cómo á mí en sentido
Equívoco respondes atrevido ?

Ulises.
Como pienso que sabes, que esta culpa
Anticipada tiene la disculpa.

Circe.
Ah sí, no me acordaba . . . .

Ulises (aparte).
Yo estoy loco.

Circe.
De la porfía de hoy.

Ulises (aparte).
Ni yo tampoco.

Circe.
Qué dices ?

Ulises.
Que por ella me atrevia.

Circe.
Por ella ?

Ulises.
Sí.

Circe (aparte).
¡ O mal haya la porfía !—
Mas pues fingidos son esos extremos,
Hablemos en la caza sola.

Ulises.
Hablemos.
Luego que tú te retiraste de una

Fell back to earth, a flame-singed butterfly.

Circe.
I spoke of hawking, when I ask'd, What rose ?

Ulysses.
And I replied, a woe of tenderest woes.

Circe.
Why thus forgetful of my dignity,
Dost thou still make equivocal reply ?

Ulysses.
Because I thought the task thyself had given,
Might have supposed such fault would be forgiven.

Circe.
Ah ! yes, I had forgotten . . . .

Ulysses (aside).
I am mad.

Circe.
To-day's dispute.

Ulysses (aside).
'Twere better that I had.

Circe.
What do you say ?

Ulysses.
'Twas that impell'd my suit.

Circe.
That only ?

Ulysses.
Yes.

Circe (aside).
Accursed be the dispute !—
Well, since these feignings but false flatteries seek,
Let us speak of the chase alone.

Ulysses.
So let us speak :—
You scarce had gone, when near

Guarnecida laguna,
Efpejo de la hermofa primavera,
Se remontó una garza, que altanera
Tanto á los cielos fube,
Que fue á un tiempo aqui pájaro, alli
mube;
Y entre el fuego y el viento,
Arbitro igual, (o válgome fu aliento!)
De fuerte fe interpufo, que las alas
En la diáfana esfera, en la fuprema,
O las hiela, ó las quema,
Cuando las enarbola, ó las abate,
Tan á compas entre las dos las bate,
Que aqui elevadas é inclinadas luego,
Aqui dan en el aire, alli en el fuego.
Geroglífico era
La garza entre la una y otra esfera
De alguno, que aqui ofado, alli cobarde,
Se hiela á un tiempo, y arde,
Y entre el aire y el fuego fe embaraza.

Circe.
Efo no es de la caza.

Ulifes.
Es de la pena mia,
Que es en parte tambien volatería.

Circe.
Hubiérame ofendido,
Si no fupiera, Ulífes, que es fingido.

Ulifes (aparte).
¡A Júpiter pluguiera!

The margin of a lake, that cryftal-clear
Seem'd a fmooth mirror for the beauteous
Spring,
A heron rofe, fo fudden its quick wing
Bore it amid the fky elate and proud,
That at one moment it was bird and
cloud,
And 'twixt the wind and fire,
(Would that fuch courage had my heart's
defire!)
So interpofed itfelf, that its bold wings
Wheeling alternate near,
Now the diaphanous, now the higher
fphere,
Were burnt or froze,
As down they fank or upward foaring
rofe,
In all the ficklenefs of fond defire,
Now in the air and now amid the fire.
An emblem as it were,
This heron was, betwixt each oppofite
fphere,
Of one who is both cowardly and bold,
Can burn with paffion, and yet freeze
with cold,
And 'twixt the air and fire ftill doubts
his place.

Circe.
You fpeak not of the chafe.

Ulyffes.
I fpeak of my heart's care,
Which feems a quarry for each fond
defpair.

Circe.
This would have offended me again,
Did I not know, Ulyffes, that you
feign.

Ulyffes (afide).
Ah! would to Jupiter, 'twere fo.

Circe (aparte).
¡ Pluguiera al cielo, ay Dios ! que no lo fuera !
Y pues que ſolo eſtás aqui conmigo,
No finjas, y proſigue.

Ulíſes.
Ya proſigo.
Atomo ya la garza apenas era,
Cuando, deſenhetrada la cimera
Que el capirote enlaza,
Mi mano un gerifalte deſembraza,
A quien, porque en priſion no ſe preſuma,
La pluma le halagaba con la pluma,
Y él, como hambriento eſtaba,
Duro el laton del caſcabel picaba.
Apenas á la luz reſtituidos
Se vieron otro y él, cuando atrevidos,
Cuanta eſtacion vacía
Paleſtra es de los átomos del dia,
Corren los dos por páramos del viento,
Y en una y otra punta,
Eſte ſe aleja, cuando aquel ſe junta ;
Y el bajel ceniciento
(Que bajel ceniciento entonces era
La garza, que velera
Los piélagos ſulcó de otro elemento)
Librarſe determina diligente,
Aunque navega ſola,
Hechos remos los pies, proa la frente,
La vela el ala, y el timon la cola.
¡ Míſera garza, dije, combatida
De dos contrarios ! bien, bien de mi vida
Imágen eres, pues ſitiar la veo
De uno y otro deſeo.

Circe (aſide).
Ah ! would to Heaven, 'twere otherwiſe I know !—
And ſince you're here alone with me, you need
Not further feign ; proceed.

Ulyſſes.
I thus proceed :—
Scarce had the heron dwindled to a ſpeck
On the far ſky, when from about the neck
Of a gerfalcon I unlooſed the band
Which held his hood ; a moment on my hand
I ſoothed the impatient captive, his dark brown
Proud feathers ſmoothing with careſſings down ;
While he, as if his hunger did ſurpaſs
All bounds, pick'd ſharply on his bells of braſs.
Scarce were they back reſtored to light,
He and another, when in daring flight
They ſcaled heaven's vault, the vaſt void ſpace where play
In whirling dance the mote-beams of the day,
Then down the deſerts of the wind they float,
And up and down the ſky
One flies away as the other ſwoopeth nigh ;
And then the aſhen-colour'd boat
(An aſhen-colour'd boat it ſurely were,
That heron, that through ſhining waves of air
Furrow'd its way to fields remote)
Reſolving to be free and not to fail,
Although alone it ſaileth now,
Of feet made oars, of curved beak a prow,

Sails of its wings, and rudder of its tail;—
Poor wretched heron, ſaid I then, thy ſtrife
'Gainſt two oppoſing ills, are of my life
Too true an image; ſince it is to-day
Of two diſtinct deſires the hapleſs prey.

Circe.

Ahora diſculparte no has podido,
Pues yerras, ſi es fingido, ó no es fingido.

Circe.

Now thou canſt not excuſe thee, ſince 'tis plain
Thou offendeſt, whether thou feigneſt, or don't feign.

Ulíſes.

Sí puedo; ſer tu amante no fingiera,
Si á la primera vez te obedeciera.—
A uno pues, y otro embate,
Coge las alas, ó las velas bate,
Y poniendo debajo de la una
La cabeza, ſe deja á ſu fortuna
Venir á pique, cuando
Nos pareció caer revoloteando
Una encarnada eſtrella,
Y los dos gerifaltes ſiempre en ella.
Si ejemplo eres, o tú, á mi penſamiento,
Sé tambien eſcarmiento,
Y no me ofrezcas eſperanza alguna,
Si ha de deſengañarme tu fortuna.

Ulyſſes.

I can; thy lover's part I would badly play,
If at thy firſt command I could obey.—
'Gainſt this, 'gainſt that, as either doth aſſail,
It furl'd its wing, and droop'd its languid ſail,
And placing its dazed head beneath the one,
Truſting to fortune, like a plummet-ſtone
Straight down it fell, we looking, from afar
Saw it deſcending, an incarnate ſtar
Through the dark ſky,
With the purſuing falcons ever nigh.
O thou! if thou'rt the image of my thought,
Be thou a warning too, with wiſdom fraught,
Let no deluſive hope by thee be ſhown,
If in thy fate I muſt foreſee my own.

Circe.

Aunque ſea fingido, todavía
Es ya en ofenſa mia,
Pues ſi te habia mandado
Fingir antes de ahora tu cuidado,
Tambien te mandé ahora
A ſolas no fingirle.

Circe.

Though this be feigning, it offends no leſs,
Than if the feigning were all truthfulneſs;
Since if I bade thee feign,
At another time, the lover's anxious pain,
I alſo bade thee now not feign again,

Ulíses.
Pues, feñora,
Si tu caftigo efpero,
Siendo fingido, y fiendo verdadero,
De verdadero ya el caftigo pido,
Pues folo efto es fingido en fer fingido.

Circe.
¿ Cómo, di, tan ofado
Refpondes ?

Ulíses.
Como eftoy defefperado.

Circe.
¿ Cómo tan atrevido
Te defvaneces . . . .

Ulíses.
Como eftoy perdido.

Circe.
A hablarme defta fuerte ?

Ulíses.
Como finjo quererte.

Circe.
¿ Luego aquefto es fingido todavía ?

Ulíses.
No, feñora.

Circe (*aparte*).
¡ O bien haya la porfía !—
Ulífes, aunque fuera
Jufto, que de efcarmiento te firviera
Tu ofadís, conviene
Difimular, porque la gente viene,
Que hafta aqui me hà feguido ;
En fu fuerza fe quede lo fingido.

Since we are here alone.

Ulyffes.
O Lady ! then
If I alike thy chaftifement muft rue,
Whether my paffionate fpeech be feign'd or true ;
Then let the true be punifh'd or difdain'd,
Since it is only feign'd in being feign'd.

Circe.
How haft thou, fay, fuch courage as to dare
So bold a reply ?

Ulyffes.
Becaufe I muft defpair.

Circe.
Why thus prefuming to the uttermoft,
Ventureft thou now again . . . .

Ulyffes.
Becaufe I am loft.

Circe.
To fpeak though I reprove thee ?

Ulyffes.
Becaufe I feign I love thee.

Circe.
Is this then alfo feign'd as was thy fuit ?

Ulyffes.
Señora, no.

Circe (*afide*).
Oh ! bleft be the difpute !—
Ulyffes, though it were
But juft, that thou fhouldft pay by thy defpair
For thy prefumption ; ftill it needs that we
Diffemble, fince my people feeking me
Have hither come ; thus there is no refource,
And the command to feign muft ftill remain in force.

Salen todos, excepto CLARIN.

Arſidas (*aparte*).

Aunque en tantos deſvelos
Mis agravios ſe valgan de mis zelos,
No darme intentaré por intendido.
¿ Mas cómo diſimula un ofendido ?
Volverme es ya moſtrar mi ſentimiento ;
Deſpejo quiero hacer de mi tormento.—
Siguiéndote, ſeñora, con tu gente
Por la florida márgen deſta fuente
Vine, que ella pautada de colores,
Las ſeñas de tu pie daba con flores.

Circe.

Hácia eſta parte vine,
Porque es donde la cena ahora previne.

Lebrel.

¡ Qué bien, qué bien me ſuena
Eſta palabra, cena!
Mas no veo entre ramas, ni entre flores
Meſas, ni aparadores,
Ni ocupada en doméſtico trabajo
A la familia de eſcalera abajo
Cruzar muy diligente.

Circe.

Todos os id ſentando brevemente,
Porque en el campo todos
Cenemos juntos, y de varios modos
Se ſirvan las viandas.—
¡ Hola, la meſa !

Lebrel.

Dime, á quién lo mandas ?

Enter all, except CLARIN.

Arſidas (*aſide*).

Although theſe watchings bring no eaſe
Unto my wrongful pangs but jealouſies,
Still I would feel as if I did not feel them ;
But how can *he* who knows his wrongs conceal them ?
Now to turn back would all my wounds lay bare,
And ſo I'll maſk them with this lightſome air.
Lady, I've follow'd with thy people here
Unto this flower-encinctured fountain clear,
Whoſe margin, colour'd by its cryſtal ſhowers,
Gave us the impreſs of thy feet with flowers.

Circe.

I led unto this ſhade,
As here I order'd ſupper to be laid.

Lebrel.

Supper ! delicious word !
Oh ! how my heart by the ſweet ſound is ſtirr'd !
But beneath the boughs, nor on the lea,
Tables nor ſideboards can I ſee,
Nor on needful houſe affairs
The family down-ſtairs
Buſtling about all buſy and all heated.

Circe.

Here I deſire that you would all be ſeated,
Since in the open field ſhall we
Together ſup, and with variety
Of meats be ſerved ; and ſo as time is preſſing,
The table there !—

Lebrel.

Now who are you addreſſing ?

Circe.
A quien ya me ha entendido.
[*Por debajo del tablado ſale una meſa muy compueſta y con luces, y ſiéntanſe* ULÍSES, CIRCE, *y* ARSIDAS, *y los demas en el ſuelo.*

Lebrel.
Linda meſa, pardiez! nos ha venido.
¿ No me dirás, ſi deſto no te peſa,
Cuanto habrá que ſembraron eſto meſa?

Circe.
¡ Hola, cantad! cantad, y divertido
Uno y otro ſentido
Eſté con las viandas y las voces,
Que ſuenen en los zéfiros veloces.
[*Canta la Múſica.*

Múſica.
Olvidado de ſu patria,
En los palacios de Circe
Vive el mas valiente Griego,
Si, quien vive amando, vive.

Tocan dentro cojas y ſale LIBIA.

Circe.
¿ Pero qué es eſto que eſcucho?

Ulíſes.
¿ Pero qué es eſto que oigo?

Flérida.
¿ Qué es eſto, cielos, que veo?

Arſidas.
¿ Qué es eſto, cielos, que noto?

Circe.
¿ Qué bélico eſtruendo, qué
Marcial ruido, qué alboroto
Deja la luz del ſol ciega,

Circe.
One who can underſtand me, do not fear.
[*A table riſes from the ground, well furniſhed, and with lights.* CIRCE, ULYSSES, *and* ARSIDAS *ſeat themſelves at it, the others on the graſs.*

Lebrel.
Jove! what a crop of table ſpringeth here!
Will you not tell me though, if you are able,
How long it took the ſowing of this table?

Circe.
Sing, ſing! and with the influence
Of muſic pleaſe a double ſenſe,
Let voice to voice replying
Blend with the zephyrs o'er our banquet flying. [*Muſic within.*

Song.
Native land and home forgetting,
In the palace-halls of Circe
Lives the braveſt Grecian hero;
If *he* lives, who loving, liveth.

A ſound of drums is heard from within, and LIBIA *enters.*

Circe.
But what noiſe is this I hear?

Ulyſſes.
But what ſound is this that ſtirs me?

Flerida.
What, O heavens! muſt I behold?

Arſidas.
Heavens! to what ſtrain muſt I liſten?

Circe.
Say, what warlike clangour, what
Martial noiſe is this that filleth
Heaven with darkneſs, blinds the ſun,

Y el eco del aire ſordo?

Libia.

Eſe fiero Brutamonte,
Eſe gigante furioſo,
Que preſo, ſeñora, tienes,
Por guarda de tus hermoſos
Jardines, porque no robe
Nadie ſus manzanas de oro,
Ofendido que á los Griegos
Blanda paz y ſuave ocio
En tus palacios divierta,
Olvidados de sí propios,
Habiendo ſido homicidas
De Polifemo, que aſombro
Era monſtruo de los hombres,
Y era hombre de los monſtruos:
Comunero de tu imperio,
Para vengarſe de todos,
Convocó del Lilibeo
Cuantos Cíclopes famoſos,
Eſpurios hijos del ſol,
Hoy viven de darle enojos;
Y dándoles paſo al Flegra
Brutamonte cauteloſo,
Vienen contra tí en eſcuadras
Mal ordenadas, de modo,
Que viendo vagar los riſcos,
Diſcurrir los promontorios,
Parece que aqueſtos montes
Deſcienden unos de otros,
A cuyo eſtrépito, á cuyas
Voces y ſuſpiros roncos,
El ſol ſe turba, y del cielo
Caducan los ejes rotos.

Circe.

¡Ay de mí, en qué gran peligro
Eſtoy! en qué grande ahogo!

And the deaſen'd echo dinneth?

Libia.

That ferocious Brutamonte,
That gigantic form of grimneſs,
Whom, a captive, lady, thou
Makeſt guardian of the richneſs
Of thy gardens fair, that none
May their golden apples pilfer,
Being offended that the Greeks,
Gentle peace, and reſt, and mirth, here
In thy palaces enjoy,
Home-forgetting, and when drifted
Here erewhile, that they had ſlain
Polyphemus, who was mingled
Man and monſter—man 'mongſt monſters,
And a monſter 'mong man's kindred,
Now a rebel of thy realm,
In revenge his foes to kill here,
Hath convoked from Lilybœum
All the famous ſpurious children
Of the ſun, the giant Cyclops,
Who in ſpite of thee ſtill live here.
By the cunning Brutamonte
They through Phlegra's paſs admitted,
Come againſt thee in diſorder'd
Squadrons, ſo that up the cliffs here
Climbing, o'er the promontories
Striding, each huge bulk uplifted
'Gainſt the ſky, they look like mountains
O'er each other roll'd and rifted,
At whoſe clamour, at whoſe tumult,
Hoarſe halloos, and hollow whiſpers,
The ſun groweth dark, and downward
Fall heaven's axes crack'd and ſhiver'd.

Circe.

Woe is me! in what great danger
Am I! oh! how I'm afflicted!

Ulíſes.
Dadme mis armas, que yo
Saldré á reciberlos ſolo ; . . . .
Arſidas.
No temas, que yo á tu lado
Te defenderé de todo ; . . . .
Ulíſes.
Porque para mi valor
Son tantos Cíclopes pocos.
[ULÍSES *va hácia afuera, y* ARSIDAS *acude á* CIRCE.
Arſidas.
Porque no quiero mas vida,
No, que morir á tus ojos.
Lebrel.
Como y cordelejo, dicen,
Que es en el mundo uno propio ;
Mas la cena que eſperaba
Es cordelejo, y no como.
Circe.
¡ Deteneos, deteneos !
Que eſte aparato ruidoſo
Solo ha ſido ma experiencia,
Exámen ha ſido ſolo,
Para ver, cual de los dos
En un peligro notorio
Acudia á ſus afectos
Mas noble y mas generoſo ;
Y aſi en campañas del aire
Fantáſticas hueſtes formo.
Arſidas.
Pues ſi ha ſido eſto experiencia,
Yo ſoy el que me corono
Vencedor, y el que merezco,
Circe, tu favor hermoſo,
Ya pue Ulíſes, acudiendo
A ſus armas tan heróico,
Dejó de moſtrarſe amante,
Pues en rieſgo tan forzoſo,

Ulyſſes.
Bring me here my arms, for I
Shall go forth and meet them ſingly ; . . . .
Arſidas.
Do not fear, for at thy ſide
I ſhall guard thee from all ills here . . . .
Ulyſſes.
Since for valour ſuch as mine
All the Cyclops' ſtrength ſeems little.
[ULYSSES *goes to the ſide, and* ARSIDAS *approaches* CIRCE.
Arſidas.
Since I only wiſh for life,
That thou may'ſt my death here witneſs.
Lebrel.
Mirth is juſt as good as meat,
So they ſay, but all within me
Yearneth for the miſſing ſupper
As the fitter thing to fill me.
Circe.
Stay ! oh, ſtay here ! ſtay ! oh, ſtay here !
For this ſeeming ſound that ſtirs thee,
Is but an experiment,
Is but only a ſlight trial,
To diſcover, of the two,
Which of you in dangerous riſks here,
Would more generouſly, more nobly
Show the love that in him liveth ;
Therefore on the fields of air
Have I phantom hoſts depicted.
Arſidas.
Then if this has been a trial,
I am he, who, as the victor,
Crown me, as the one who merits
Thy divineſt favour, Circe,
Since Ulyſſes when he hurried
Hero-like to his arms ſo ſwiftly,
Ceaſed to ſhow himſelf thy lover,
Since in ſuch a needful riſk, he

No acudió luego á ſu dama,
Que en un amante es impropio.
Ulíſes.
Que acudí á las armas mias,
No niego; pero tampoco
Niego, que de amante ha ſido
El afecto mas forzoſo;
Porque ſi tomo mis armas,
Para defenſa las tomo
Suya.
Arſidas.
Nunca en un acaſo
Eſtá el diſcurſo tan pronto,
Que eſpere á cauſa ſegunda;
Lo primero es lo mas propio:
A las armas fuiſte, luego
Ya perdiſte.
Ulíſes.
De eſe modo
Tú tambien; pues ſi me acuſas
De poco amante, de poco
Fino, porque no acudí
A Circe, con eſo propio
Te convenzo, pues que tú
Acudiſte á ſus enojos,
Y ya te moſtraſte amante.
Arſidas.
Si las nobles leyes noto
De caballería, acudir
A las damas es forzoſo;
Y aſi, como caballero,
No como amante, ſocorro
A Circe.
Ulíſes.
En las de milicia
Es ley, ſiempre que armas oigo,
Acudir á tomar armas;
Y aſi, con valor heróico,
Yo, ſoldado, caballero

Did not haſten to his lady,
As a lover would from inſtinct!
Ulyſſes.
That I hurried to my armour
I admit, but unadmitted
Is it, that in this, my action
From a lover's impulſe differ'd,
Since if I took arms, it was
But in her defence I girt me
With them.
Arſidas.
Ne'er in ſudden need
Can the reaſon have ſuch quickneſs
As to think of ſecond cauſes;
The firſt impulſe is the fitteſt.
To your arms you went, and therefore
You've already loſt.
Ulyſſes.
In *this* way,
Have you alſo; ſince if *me*
Thou doſt charge with ſhowing little
Love-zeal, for my not approaching
Circe, I can now convict thee
On thine own ground, ſince thou haſt
Sought her, though it was forbidden
To avow thyſelf her lover.
Arſidas.
If I underſtand the firmeſt
Law of knighthood, 'tis to ſuccour
Ladies when ſome wrong afflicts them,
Therefore it was not as lover,
But as cavalier, that Circe
I thus guarded.
Ulyſſes.
In war's code too,
'Tis the law, that when the firſt peal
Calls to arms, we then ſhould arm us;
And thus, valorous, as befits me,
I, as ſoldier, knight, and lover,

Y amante, he acudido á todo.
Arſidas.
Ya ſé, que por la elocuencia
Has de quedar ſiempre airoſo ;
Que no heredaras de Aquíles
El grabado arnes de oro,
Si por el valor humbiera
De dárſele á Telamonio.
Ulíſes.
El valor le mereció ;
Y ahora verás ſi es forzoſo,
[*Saca la eſpada.*
Pues de eſa voz en ofenſa,
El Flegra volará en polvo.

Arſidas.
Primero arderá en cenizas
Con el fuego de mis ojos,
Porque á los dos de Trinacria
Volcanes ſe añadan otros.
[*Saca la eſpada.*
Circe.
Pues qué es eſto ? ¿ en mi preſencia
Sacais el acero ? cómo ?
Arſidas.
Tu reſpeto me perdone.
Ulíſes.
Perdóneme tu decoro.
Arſidas.
Que no hay reſpeto con zelos.
Ulíſes.
Ni decoro con oprobios.
Lebrel.
En mi vida me hallé en cena,
Que no paraſe en lo propio.
Ulíſes.
Aqui de Grecia !
Arſidas.
¡ Y aqui

Wholly have myſelf acquitted.
Arſidas.
Yes I know, thy eloquence
Ever proveth thee keen-witted,
Elſe thou hadſt not won the golden
Graven armour of Achilles,
Which had been the Telamonian's,
If to valour it were given.
Ulyſſes.
'Twas by valour it was won,
This thou'lt own when thou doſt witneſs
Phlegra into duſt down ſhaken
By my voice in anger lifted.
[*Draws his ſword.*
Arſidas.
By the fire-flames from mine eyes,
It will firſt be burnt to cinders,
As if two volcanoes more,
With Trinacrias two, were lit here.
[*Draws his ſword.*
Circe.
How is this ? and in my preſence
Dar'ſt thou draw thy ſword ? can this be ?
Arſidas.
May the reſpect that's due thee, pardon.
Ulyſſes.
May thy due deſerts forgive me.
Arſidas.
Since reſpect no jealous heart knows.
Ulyſſes.
No deſert makes inſult ſtingleſs.
Lebrel.
Never in my life, a ſupper
Have I waited for, like this here.
Ulyſſes.
Here for Greece !
Arſidas.
And here, on my ſide

De Trinacria! Que aunque ſolo
Me ves, mis vaſallos ſon
Eſos brutos y eſos troncos.—
¡ Fieras de Trinacria humanas,
Dad á vueſtro Rey ſocorro!

Salen todas las fieras, y pónenſe al lado de Arsidas, *y los Griegos al lado de* Ulíses.

Ulíſes.

Aunque á tus voces ſe muevan
Mejor, que al eco ſonoro
De Orfeo, troncos y fieras,
Haciendo en ellas deſtrozo,
Apuraré eſtas montañas
Bruto á bruto, y tronco á tronco
[*Riñen.*

Sale Clarin *de mona.*

Clarin.

Entre Griegos y animales
Mal trabadas lides noto.
No ſé á cual debo acudir;
Porque obligado de todos,
Soy por una parte Griego,
Y por otra parte mono.

Circe.

Pues no puedo reportaros
Con mis voces, con mi aſombro
Podré. Los aires cubiertos
De vapor caliginoſo,
Segunda noche parezca,
Y á tanto fracaſo abſortos,
Del embrion de las nubes
Sean los rayos abortos,
Y el ſol y la luna hoy,
Viéndoſe vivir tan poco,
Pienſen, que el camino erraron

For Trinacria! For though ſingle
Here you ſee me, I as vaſſals
Have theſe wild-beaſts and theſe fir-trees.
Human wild-herds of Trinacria,
Succour! ſuccour! to your king here!

Enter all the animals and place themſelves beſide Arsidas, *and the Greeks beſide* Ulysses.

Ulyſſes.

Though unto thy accents move,
Better than when Orpheus' fingers
Touch'd the lyre, the woods and wild-beaſts,
Swift deſtruction dealing 'midſt them,
Brute by brute, and tree by tree now
Shall I purify theſe hills here.
[*They fight.*

Enter Clarin, *as a monkey.*

Clarin.

'Twixt the Greeks and animals,
I the conflict watch bewilder'd:
Which of them to join I know not.
Since they're both of them my kinſmen,
Being half monkey, and half Greek,
On my outer ſide and inner.

Circe.

Since I cannot hold you back
By my words, my dread bewitchments
May be ſtronger. Let the air
Cover'd with a miſt's black thickneſs
Seem to ſpread a ſecond night,
And the clouds, by terror ſtricken,
From their wombs in ſudden travail
Give the abortive bolts exiſtence;
And the ſun and moon to-day
Seeing how their brief life flitted,
Let them think they've loſt their way

De ſus celeſtiales tornos,
O que yo deſde la tierra
Apagué ſu luz de un ſoplo.

[*Truenos y relámpagos, obſcurécese el teatro, y riñen á obſcuras.*

Arſidas.

¿ Adónde, Ulíses, eſtás ?

Ulíſes.

Con mi acero te reſpondo.

[*Pelean todos.*

Floro.

Qué pena !

Caſandra.

Qué ciego abiſmo !

Arquelao.

Qué llanto !

Chloris.

Qué triſte enojo !

Antíſtes.

Qué obſcura noche !

Clarin.

Ha ſeñores !
¿ Somos Griegos, ó qué ſomos ?

Lebrel.

En tanto que todos andan
Tropezando unos con otros . . . .

Clarin.

En tanto que cada uno
Buſca de eſcaparſe modo . . . .

Lebrel.

Yo á la meſa me remito.

Clarin.

Y yo á la cena me acojo.

[*Suben ſobre la meſa, y abrázanſe uno con otro.*

Lebrel.

Pero qué es eſto ? un leon
Dió conmigo.

'Mid the fix'd celeſtial circles,
Or that I from off the earth
With a breath their light eclipsèd.

[*Thunder and lightning ; the theatre becomes darkened, and in the obſcurity the fighting is ſtill continued.*

Arſidas.

Say, Ulyſſes, ſay, where art thou ?

Ulyſſes.

Let my ſword an anſwer give thee.

[*All fight.*

Florus.

Oh ! what pain !

Caſſandra.

What blind abyſm !

Archelaus.

Oh ! what yells !

Chloris.

What mournful ſhrill ſcreams !

Antiſtes.

What a night !

Clarin.

Oh ! are we Greeks,
Or what are we elſe, good miſters ?

Lebrel.

While they all o'er one another
Tread and trample, hither, thither . . . .

Clarin.

While each one of them is thinking
Of the ſafeſt way to flit hence . . . .

Lebrel.

I'll unbend me at the table.

Clarin.

I'll take refuge 'mong the diſhes.

[*They leap on the table, and fall into each other's arms.*

Lebrel.

But what's this ? a mighty lion
Seizes me !

Clarin.
Mas qué toco?
Conmigo ha dado un gigante.

Circe.
Húndase este suelo todo,
Y ponga paz la distancia.

Clarin.
Todo se hunde con nosotros.
[*Húndese la mesa, y los dos graciosos sobre ella, y con la batalla y la tempestad se van todos.*

Clarin.
What's this that grips me?
I am seized here by a giant!

Circe.
Let the whole ground sink down with them,
And let peace spring from their severance.

Clarin.
All things sink, as down we sink here.
[*The table sinks into the earth, with the graciosos upon it, and with the cessation of the battle and the tempest, the scene closes.*

JORNADA III.

MARINA, E IMMEDIATOS A ELLA LAS JARDINES DE CIRCE.

Salen ANTÍSTES, ARQUELAO, POLIDORO, FLORO, TIMANTES *y* LEBREL.

Antíſtes.

UNQUE ya todos ſepais
Lo que repetiros trata
Mi voz, oidme ; que tal vez
En pena, en deſdicha tanta,
Aun mas que noticias propias,
Mueven agenas palabras ;
Porque en efecto ninguno
Es juez en ſu miſma cauſa.
Siempre á la cólera expueſtos,
Siempre expueſtos á la ſaña
De los hados riguroſos,
Deſpues de fortunas varias,
Arraſtrados del deſtino,
Dimos en aqueſta playa
Del Flegra, exentos vaſallos
Del imperio de Trinacria.
Aqui, contra los venenos
De eſa fiera, eſa tirana,
Antídoto nos dió Juno
En las flores de oro y nácar,
Que Iris trajo, deſplegando

ACT THE THIRD.

THE SEA-COAST, AND NEAR IT CIRCE'S GARDENS.

Enter ANTISTES, ARCHELAUS, POLYDORUS, FLORUS, TIMANTES *and* LEBREL.

Antiſtes.

HOUGH ye all perchance
may know
What my voice would fain
impart ye,
Hear me ſtill: for many a time,
In ſuch pain, in ſuch-like ſadneſs
More than to one's own thoughts even,
To a ſtranger's words we hearken ;
Since no judge in his own cauſe
Can in truth be thought impartial.
Still unto the wrath expoſed,
Still exposèd to the anger
Of the ever-rigorous fates,
After fortune's various chances,
Dragg'd along by deſtiny,
Came we to this Phlegra's ſtrand here,
Free-born and unfetter'd vaſſals
Of the kingdom of Trinacria.
Here againſt the venom'd draughts
Of this tyrant-queen, this adder,
Juno gave us antidotes

Arcos de carmin y gualda.
Libres pues de ſus priſiones
Nos vimos, y cuando trata
Ulíſes volver al mar,
Que ya tuvimos por patria,
El blando halago de Circe,
Que cuando vé que no baſtan
Mortales venenos, uſa
De mas venenoſas trazas,
Perſuadió á Ulíſes, que aqui
Unos dias ſe quedara
A reparar de los vientos
La repetida inconſtancia.
El, fiado en ſus cautelas,
Perſuadido á que quedaba
A dar libertad á cuantos
En eſtas rudas montañas
Bárbara priſion padecen,
Se quedó, donde á la rara
Beldad de Circe rendido
Vive, ſin mas eſperanzas.
¿ Quién creerá, que, no baſtando
Tantos encantos, ni tantas
Ciencias, á vencer ſus hados,
Una hermoſura baſtara ?
Mas todos lo creerán, todos,
Pues todos á ver alcanzan,
Que un amor y una hermoſura
Son el veneno del alma.
Rendidos pues al amor,
Tanto los dos ſe declaran,
Deſde la noche que fueron
Argumento las eſpadas,
Y puſieron paz las nubes
Denſas, obſcuras y pardas,
Que Arſidas, zeloſo y triſté,
Lleno de zeloſa rabia,
Se fue á ſu corte, quizá
A diſponer ſu venganza.

In the flowers of gold and nacre,
Which fair Iris brought amid
Arcs of crocus and of carmine.
Free then from her threaten'd chains
We beheld us, and thereafter,
When Ulyſſes would to ſea—
Which our country we regarded—
Circe with her flatteries ſoft,
Seeing that her mortal draughts were
Inſufficient, had recourſe to
Means whoſe venom nought could
maſter;
Him perſuading, that ſome days
Here he would remain at anchor,
To repair the oft-repeated
Fickleneſs of the winds' diſaſters;
He, confiding in his caution,
Thinking that he could enfranchiſe
All who in the barbarous priſons
Of theſe rude hills are held captive,
Here remain'd, where he, o'ercome
By the charms, the unexampled
Loveline ſs of Circe, lives
Without hope or aim or plan here.
Who'll believe, that when had fail'd
Every ſcience, all enchantments
To ſubdue his fate, the beauty
Of one face was more than ample ?
But all *will* believe it, all,
Since all hearts this truth have maſter'd
That wild love and woman's beauty
Are to the ſoul as poiſonous aſps are.
Thus ſurrender'd up to love,
Have the two their wild attachment
So avow'd, ſince that night when
Swords cut through the word-entangled
Argument, and black clouds brought
Peace 'amid their miſts of darkneſs,
That Prince Arſidas, ſad, jealous,

Ulíses pues, ſin rezelo,
Solo de ſus guſtos trata,
Siempre en los brazos de Circe,
Y aſiſtido de ſus damas,
En academias de amores,
Saraos, feſtines y danzas.
Yo pues, viéndonos perdidos,
Hoy he penſado una traza,
Con que á ſu olvido le acuerde
De ſu honor, y de ſu fama:
Y es, que pues el otro dia,
Cuando oyó tocar al arma,
Se olvidó de amor, y fue
Tras la trompeta y la caja,
A todas horas eſtemos
Deſde el bajel, que en el agua
Surto eſtá, tocando á guerra,
Como que á Circe hacen ſalva;
Cuya voz noble recuerdo
Será de ſu olvido, clara
Sirena, que tras ſu acento
Los ſentidos arrebata.

Polidoro.

Dices bien, y yo el primero
Seré, que eſta tarde haga
La experiencia.

Timántes.

Pues ahora
Es tiempo; que Ulíſes anda
Eſtos jardines, que hermoſos
Narciſos ſon de eſmeralda,
Y enamorados de sí,
Se eſtan mirando en las aguas.

Arquelao.

Yo ſeré el que deſde el mar

Driven by jealous rage to madneſs,
To his Court retired, where he
Doubtleſs ſome dread vengeance
planneth;
Whilſt Ulyſſes, uncontroll'd,
All his time in pleaſure paſſes,
Ever in the arms of Circe,
And aſſiſted by her damſels,
In academies of love
Studieth balls and feaſts and dances;
I then, ſeeing we are loſt,
Have to-day deviſed a plan here,
By whoſe means to fame and honour
We may wake him from his trances.
This 'tis, ſince, the other day,
When he heard arms clang and jangle,
He forgot his love, and went
After the drum's and trumpet's rattle,
We at every hour, from out
Yonder bark, that lieth anchor'd
On the ſhore, will ſound a war-charge,
As if to Circe 'twere a ſalvo;
Whoſe voice will a noble memory
Of the forgotten glorious paſt be,
A clear Syren, at whoſe ſtrain
All his ſenſes will be raviſh'd.

Polydorus.

You ſpeak well, and I'll be firſt
To attempt the experiment after
Evening cloſes.

Timantes.

Then the preſent
Is the time; for through the gardens
Walks Ulyſſes, through the emerald-
Hued Narciſſi ſelf-enamour'd,
Gazing on their own ſoft green
In the water's clear expanſes.

Archelaus.

I will be the one to ſound

Haré que toquen al arma ;
Antíſtes aqui ſe quede,
Para prevenir, que es ſalva,
Que á Circe hace nueſtra gente.

Lebrel.

Si entre tantos votos halla
Lugar un juro, yo juro
A la deidad ſoberana
De Júpiter, que haceis mal
En prevenir eſta traza.

Floro.

Por qué?

Lebrel.

Porque Circe ſabe
Mejor lo que aqui ſe habla,
Que noſotros, y podrá
Tomar de todos venganza.
Eſcarmentad en Clarin,
Que habló mal della, y airada
Se vengó, pues no ſabemos
Qué hay dél, ni por donde anda.

Floro.

Todo eſo es temor.

Lebrel.

Es cierto.

Arquelao.

Dejadle, no le creais nada,
Y vamos á nueſtro intento.

Todos.

Vamos.

[*Vanſe todos, y quédaſe* LEBREL.

Lebrel.

Vueſarcedes vayan,
Que yo me quedo á tratar
Coſas de mas importancia.
De todos los animales,
Que por eſtos campos andan,
Quiſiera coger alguno,
Que á Grecia deſpues llevara,

From the ſea the martial clang then ;
Thou, Antiſtes, here remain,
To explain, it is a ſalvo
Given to Circe by our people.

Lebrel.

If there's room, amid ſo many
Vows, for a good oath, I ſwear
By great Jove, the ſovereign father
Of the Gods, that you do wrong
In attempting what you plan here.

Florus.

Why?

Lebrel.

Becauſe of Circe knowing
Better about what we chat here
Than we do ourſelves ; and ſhe
Will take vengeance for it, mark me !
On us all. Be warn'd by Clarin
Who ſpoke ill of her ; in anger
She revenged herſelf, and no one
Knows his fate or what has happen'd.

Florus.

All this is but fear.

Lebrel.

That's certain.

Archelaus.

Leave him there, don't mind his tattle,
And let's go and try our project.

All.

Let us go. [*Exeunt all but* LEBREL.

Lebrel.

My worſhipful maſters,
You may go, but I'll remain
For a more important matter.
Of the many animals
That acroſs theſe wild plains wander,
I am anxious to catch one,
Which I may to Greece hereafter

Cuando quiſieren los dioſes
Eſcaparnos de Trinacria;
Porque fuera para allá
Importantíſima alhaja
Uno dellos, pues á verle
Solamente ſe juntara
Toda Grecia, y yo tuviera
Con él ſegura ganancia.
Cierta mona aqueſtos dias
Siempre cocándome anda
Con geſtos y con viaſages,
Y á eſta quiſiera peſcarla,
Para cuyo efecto traigo
Eſte cordel con que atarla
Luego que la vea, porque
Es juguetona, y es manſa.

Sale Clarin *de mona.*

Clarin.

Hácia aqui, ſi no me engaño,
Mis compañeros eſtaban,
Aunque, deſpues que ſoy mona,
Por donde quiera que vaya,
Hallaré mis compañeros.
Por ſeñas les diré, que hagan,
Que me dé libertad Circe,
Pues ya lo enmonado baſta.

Lebrel.

Vela aqui; yo quiero echarle
Eſte lazo á la garganta.
Ahora es tiempo. ¿Qué me eſtorba,
Qué me turba, ó qué me eſpanta,
Si una mona diz que es fácil
De coger?* Díganlo tantas
Como cogidas me eſcuchan.

* *Coger una mona*, literally, to catch a monkey, means to be intoxicated. I have paraphraſed it by a ſomewhat ſimilar expreſſion in the tranſlation.

Bring back with me, when the Fates
Let us fly free from Trinacria.
One of them would be at home
Quite a treaſure, a full harveſt
Of fine profit, for all Greece
Would flock round to ſee his gambols,
And I'll make of him clear gain
By exhibiting his antics;
For ſome days a certain monkey
Have I ſeen that grins and chatters
With odd geſtures and grimaces;
'Tis for him I wiſh to angle;
For which purpoſe I have brought
This good cord wherewith to catch him
When again I ſee him, ſince
He's ſo playful and ſo active.

Enter Clarin *as a monkey.*

Clarin.

'Twas but now, unleſs I err,
My companions here were gather'd—
Though ſince I a monkey grew,
Whereſoe'er I roam or ramble
I can't meet with my companions.
By theſe geſtures I would aſk them
Circe to implore to free me,
Since with monkeyhood I'm ſated.

Lebrel.

There he is! around his throat
I this nooſe would like to faſten.
Now's the time. But whence this fear?
What diſturbs me? What unmans me?
Since ſo eaſy, as 'tis ſaid,
Is it to ſuck a monkey?* Maſters,
Ye who hear me, own how eaſy:—

* "*To ſuck the monkey*, to drink at an alehouſe at the expenſe of another."—Halliwell's *Dictionary*.

No eſcapareis de mis garras.
[*Echale un cordel al cuello.*
Clarin.
¡ Ay, que me ahogas, Lebrel !
No en el peſcuezo me hagas
La preſa.
Lebrel.
Por mas que coques,
No te irás.
Clarin.
¿ No es coſa extraña,
Que hable para mi, y diſcurra
Con ſentidos, vida y alma,
Y con los otros no pueda
Articular las palabras ?
Lebrel, mira que ſoy yo.
Lebrel.
¡ Como brinca, y como ſalta !
No puedo llevar á Grecia
Coſa de mas importancia.
Señora mona, deſde hoy
Hemos de ſer camaradas,
No hay ſino tener paciencia,
Y venir conmigo.
Clarin.
Baſta,
Que no me entiende.
Lebrel.
¡ Qué geſtos
Hace, y con qué linda gracia !

Salen Astrea *y* Libia.

Libia.
En todo el dia no hay verte,
Lebrel ; dime, dónde andas ?
Lebrel.
He andado á caza de monas,
Y á fe que no es mala caza,
Y eſta he cogido.

But you won't eſcape my hands here.
[*Flings the cord round* Clarin's *neck.*
Clarin.
Ah ! you're choking me, Lebrel !
I'm your priſoner, but don't catch me
By the throat thus.
Lebrel.
Mouth away,
Come you will though.
Clarin.
What a marvel !
That I ſpeak to myſelf, make uſe of
All my ſenſes, ſoul and heart have,
Yet I can't articulate words,
To make others underſtand me.
Ah ! Lebrel, think who I am.
Lebrel.
How he bounces ! how he dances !
Nothing could I bring to Greece
More important or attractive.
From this day, Sir Monkey, we
Will be comrades in my travels.
Nothing for't but patience, ſo
Come along.
Clarin.
'Tis plain and patent
He don't underſtand me.
Lebrel.
How
Gracefully he grins and chatters !

Enter Astrea *and* Libia.

Libia.
Why, Lebrel, I haven't ſeen you
All the day : what were you after ?
Lebrel.
I've been after apes and monkeys,
And with good ſucceſs : this charmer
I have captured.

Libia.	*Libia.*
¡Ay, qué linda	What a pretty
Monica!	Little monkey!
Lebrel.	*Lebrel.*
Cocala, Marta.	Jock, grin at her.
Libia.	*Libia.*
¿Qué pienſas hacer con ella?	What, though, do you purpoſe with him?
Lebrel.	*Lebrel.*
Pienſo, Libia mia, llevarla	Him, my Libia, I ſhall carry
A Grecia, enſeñarla allá	Back to Greece, and have him taught
A tocar una guitarra,	To touch lightly the guitar there,
A andar por una maroma,	On the tight-rope there to tumble,
Y hacer vueltas en las tablas.	And to dance in booths and taverns.
Clarin.	*Clarin.*
Yo por maroma? yo vueltas?	I a dancer! I a tumbler!
Eſto ſolo me faltaba.	Only this alone was wanted.
Aſtrea.	*Aſtrea.*
Dime, Lebrel, ¿y Clarin	Tell me, though, Lebrel, of Clarin,
Dónde eſtá?	Where's he gone?
Clarin.	*Clarin.*
Aqui.	He's here.
Aſtrea.	*Aſtrea.*
Allá te aparta!	Keep back there!
Lebrel.	*Lebrel.*
Deſde el dia que quedó	Since the day I left him laden
Cargado de joyas tantas	With his jewels, gems, and jaſpers ...
Clarin.	*Clarin.*
¡Tal tengas tú la ſalud!	May you have the like good fortune!
Lebrel.	*Lebrel.*
No le ví, ni ſé que ſe haya	I haven't ſeen him, nor his abſence
Hecho.	Can I account for.
Clarin.	*Clarin.*
Yo sí.	*I* can.
Aſtrea.	*Aſtrea.*
Su codicia	Doubtleſs
Le ha eſcondido.	Avarice hides him.
Clarin.	*Clarin.*
Hay mayor rabia!	Oh! 'tis madneſs!

Libia.
Circe hácia eſta parte viene.
Lebrel.
Pues por ſi acaſo ſe enfada
De que cogieſe eſta mona,
Me voy. Ven conmigo, Marta.
Clarin.
Si me ahoga, qué he de hacer?

Lebrel.
¡O cómo he de regalarla! [*Vanſe.*

Salen ULÍSES, CIRCE *y todas las Damas.*

Circe.
En eſta florida márgen,
Deſde cuya verde eſtancia
Se juzgan de tierra y mar
Las dos viſtoſas campañas,
Tan contrariamente hermoſas,
Y hermoſamente contrarias,
Que neutral la viſta duda,
Cual es la yerba, ó el agua,
Porque aqui en golfos de flores,
Y allí en ſelvas de eſmeraldas,
Unas miſmas ondas hacen
Las eſpumas y las matas,
A los ſuſpiros del noto,
Y á los alientos del aura,
Puedes deſcanſar, Ulíſes,
Las fatigas de la caza
En mis brazos.

Ulíſes.
Dices bien;
Pues ſolo en ellos deſcanſa
El alma, porque ellos ſolos
El centro han ſido del alma.

Libia.
Circe comes in this direction.
Lebrel.
Leſt perchance ſhe ſhould be angry
With me for my monkey prize here,
Off I go. Come with me, Maſſa.
Clarin.
What's to be done though, if he choke
me?
Lebrel.
Faith, to hold him I'll be hard ſet.
[*Exeunt all.*

Enter ULYSSES, CIRCE *and her Ladies.*

Circe.
On this flowery margin here,
From whoſe green ſlopes ſoftly ſlanted,
The two lovely level plains
Of the land and ſea expand them,
So contraſted in their beauty,
In their beauty ſo contraſted,
That the neutral viſion doubts
Which is graſs and which is water,
Since in bright bays here of flowers,
In green groves of emerald glaſs there,
The ſame waves together make
Now the foam-wreaths, now the
branches,
When the ſunny ſouth wind ſigheth,
When the ſofter zephyr panteth,
From the labours of the chaſe
Thou, Ulyſſes, in mine arms here
Canſt refreſh thee.
Ulyſſes.
Thou ſpeak'ſt well;
Since in them alone comes any
Reſt unto my ſoul, for they
Are its centre, its ſole magnet.

Circe.
Con todas eſtas finezas,
Temo, Ulíſes, que me engañas.
Ulíſes.
Por qué?
Circe.
Por penſar, que dura
Aquella ficcion paſada.
Ulíſes.
Nunca lo fue para mí.
Circe.
Quién lo aſegura?
Ulíſes.
Mis anſias.
Circe.
Quién lo dice?
Ulíſes.
Mis deſeos.
Circe.
Es engaño.
Ulíſes.
Es verdad clara.
Circe.
¡Quién, Ulíſes, la ſupiera!
Ulíſes.
Eſcucha, Circe, y ſabráſla:
Vengativa deidad, deidad ingrata,
Que á la de Juno y Júpiter ſe atreve,
Huéſped de eſa república de nieve,
Vecino de eſe piélago de plata,
Tantos años la patria me dilata,
Y tantos contra mí peligros mueve,
Que, porque fueſe mi vivir mas breve,
A tus umbrales derrotarme trata.
A ellos llegué, ſeguro y defendido
De eſcándalo, de horror, de aſombro tanto,
Como has en tierra y mar introducido.
Tus encantos vencí, mas no tu llanto;

Circe.
Ah! I fear thou ſtill deceiv'ſt me,
Howſoe'er thy tongue doth flatter.
Ulyſſes.
Why?
Circe.
Becauſe I think that ſtill
That falſe feint of loving laſteth.
Ulyſſes.
Falſe it never was with me.
Circe.
Who doth make that ſure?
Ulyſſes.
My anguiſh.
Circe.
Who doth ſay it?
Ulyſſes.
My heart's hope.
Circe.
'Tis deceit.
Ulyſſes.
'Tis truth's own language.
Circe.
Who, Ulyſſes, that can know?
Ulyſſes.
Hear me, Circe, and I'll anſwer:—
A vengeful goddeſs, a dread deity,
One who with Jove and Juno dares compete,—
An ill-fared gueſt where ſnow-white breakers meet,
A lonely loiterer on the ſilver ſea,—
Long from my country had belated me,
And with new tempeſts every day would beat
My ſtruggling ſhip, to make my fate complete
Led me at length unto thy ſhores and thee.

Pudo el amor lo que ellos no han podido:
Luego el amor es el mayor encanto.

Circe.

Con toda aquesa fineza,
La que me debes no pagas,
Porque fue mayor la mia.

Ulises.

De qué suerte?

Circe.

Oye, y sabrásla:
Vengativa y cruel, porque te asombres,
A pesar de deidades lisonjeras,
Reina desta república de fieras,
Señora deste piélago de hombres,
Viví; y porque mas bárbara me nombres,
Ninguno abortó el mar á estas riberas,
Que á mi sangrienta mágica no vieras
Trocar las formas, y mudar los nombres.
Llegaste tú, y queriendo tu homicida
Ser, burlaste mis ciencias, con espanto,
Queriéndote vencer, quedé vencida.
Si mi encanto, al mirar asombro tanto,
Al encanto de amor rindió mi vida,
Luego el amor es el mayor encanto.
[*Duérmese* Ulises.

Hither I came, my fearless path pursuing,
All fears of thee, all horrors raised above,
Thy vain enchantments in a trice subduing,
But not thy tears, which still could victor prove,
Since love could do what they had fail'd in doing
Then is the greatest of enchantments, love.

Circe.

Even with all thy flatteries
Thou thy debt to me canst cancel,
Since still greater far were mine.

Ulysses.

In what way?

Circe.

Attend, I'll answer:—
Vengeful and cruel (fear-inspiring then)
Spite of all goddesses of gentler mien,
Of this wild kingdom of wild beasts the queen,
The mistress of this wilderness of men,
Long lived I here in my enchanted den,
No one approach'd these shores of smiling green
But by my bloody magic soon was seen
Transform'd and prison'd in a bestial pen:
At length you came, by power still mightier shielded,
You laugh'd my spells to scorn, and when I strove
To conquer you, the subtler power you wielded
Enmesh'd me in the net-work that I wove,

Since then my life to love's enchantments
yielded,
Then is the greateſt of enchantments,
love. [ULYSSES *ſleeps.*

Sale LIBIA.

Libia.

La múſica, que has mandado
Prevenir, eſtá, ſeñora,
Eſperando.

Circe.

Por ahora
No canteis; que deſvelado
Se da Ulíſes por vencido
A la deidad de Morfeo,
A cuyo letal trofeo
Las potencias ha rendido,
Haciendo de todas dueño
Eſta macilenta ſombra,
Que á un tiempo halaga y aſombra,
Pues es deſcanſo, y es ſueño.
Infundid, aves y flores,
Para aliviar ſus congojas,
Silencio en templadas hojas,
Suſpended vueſtros amores.
No hagan ruido los criſtales
De los arroyos, callando
Corran las fuentes, moſtrando
Obedientes y leales
El amor, que en mí ſe encierra;
Y en retórico ſilencio
Digan, cuanto reverencio
Su deſcanſo.

Voces (dentro).

Guerra, guerra!
[*Tocan dentro cajas hácia un lado.*

Enter LIBIA.

Libia.

Lady, as you have deſired,
The muſicians now are ſtaying
In the ante-room.

Circe.

Their playing
Muſt be now poſtponed, ſince tired,
Hath Ulyſſes yielded up
All his ſenſes to the keeping
Of the god of ſleep, and ſleeping
Taſtes the god's lethean cup—
That pale power, death's ſhadowy
brother,
Who a curſe or bleſſing ſeems,
As he gives ſweet reſt or dreams
Which the conſcience fain would
ſmother;—
Give, ye birds and flowers and groves,
Give, for that light breath he heaves,
Silence 'mid your trembling leaves,
Brief ſuſpenſion to your loves;
Streamlets, down in ſoft attrition
Let your cryſtals glide, ye flowing
Fountains, now be ſilent, ſhowing
Your obedience and ſubmiſſion
To the love my breaſt that charms,
And in ſilent rhetoric ſay
How you reverence to-day
His repoſe.

Voices within.

To arms! to arms!—
[*Drums and trumpets are heard
from the ſame ſide.*

Circe.
Qué es esto? ¿cuándo pretendo
Silencio, hay quien le interrompa?
[*Despierta* ULÍSES.
Ulíses.
Guerra publica esta trompa,
Guerra publica este estruendo.
¿Pues cómo, ay dioses! así
Es hoy perezoso el sueño,
De nobles sentidos dueño?
No soy, sin duda, el que fui,
Pues á delicias suaves
Entregado, ay de mí? estoy,
Y tras los ecos no voy
Mas belicosos y graves.—
Perdona, Circe, que así,
Habiendo guerra y furor,
No me ha de tener tu amor.
Circe.
Detente, escucha! ay de mí!
¿Quién ese clarin tocó?

Sale ANTÍSTES.

Antístes.
Quien, pensando que seria
Lisonja, la salva hacia,
Cuando desde el mar te vió.
Ulíses.
Aqui no hay ya que esperar;
La guerra me ha despertado,
Porque en el alma ha tocado
La sirena militar.
Circe.
Para templar el furor,
Cantad de amor, cantad pues.
[*La Música al otro lado.*
Música.
¿Dónde vas, Ulíses, si es
El mayor encanto amor?

Circe.
What is this, that thus destroys
Silence, that so late I claim'd?
[ULYSSES *awakes.*
Ulysses.
War, that trumpet hath proclaim'd,
War, that clang of martial noise.
But, ye Gods! from what base cause
Is, to-day, dull sleep abhorr'd,
Of my nobler senses lord?
Ah! I am not what I was;
Since by its soft sway subdued,
Woe is me! when bugles vie,
Ah! my heart doth not reply,
Bold, responsive, as it should.
Pardon me, O Circe, see!
War and woe are in my ear,
And love must not keep me here.
Circe.
Listen, stay! ah! woe is me,
Who produced this wild uproar?

Enter ANTISTES.

Antistes.
We with trumpets long so mute,
From our ship did thee salute,
When we saw thee on the shore.
Ulysses.
Here delay disgraceful seems,
Battle leads my steps afar;
Since the siren song of war
Wakes my soul from all its dreams.
Circe.
Sing of love, sing rapturously,
Sing, and thus his rage remove.
[*Music and song from the other side.*
Song.
Stay, Ulysses, stay, if love
Greatest of enchantments be.

Ulíses.
¿ Qué blandas voces ſuaves,
Repetidas en los vientos,
Son con ſonoros acentos
Dulce envidia de las aves ?
¡ Qué bien el amor me ſuena !
¿ Cómo tu amor me ha podido,
Circe hermoſa, haber vencido
Aquella paſada pena ?
Ya me vuelvo á tu favor.

Griegos (*dentro*).
Guerra, guerra !

Ulíses.
Mas ¿ qué eſpero ?
Las armas me llaman, quiero
Seguirlas.

Múſica (*dentro*).
Amor, amor !

Ulíses.
¡ Qué blanda, qué dulcemente
Suena eſta voz repetida !

Antíſtes (*aparte*).
Aunque me cueſte la vida,
Tengo de hablar claramente.—
Ulíſes, invicto Griego,
¿ Cómo, cuando aſi te llama
La trompeta de la fama,
En delicioſo ſoſiego
Sordo yaces ? ¿ Cuánto yerra,
No ſabes, el que rendido
A ſu amor, labra ſu olvido ?
Oye eſta voz !

Griegos (*dentro*).
Guerra, guerra !

Ulíses.
Tienes, Antíſtes, razon ;
Torpes mis ſentidos tuve,
Ciego eſtuve, ſordo eſtuve ;
Mas ya que eſtas voces ſon

Ulyſſes.
Ah ! what ſweet ſeductive words !
Ah ! what ſounds are thoſe I hear ?
Sounds whoſe ſoften'd echoes clear
Wake the envy of the birds.
Ah ! how ſweet to me love's ſtrain,
Sweet and with a ſtrange power too,
Lovely Circe, to ſubdue
All that paſt perturbèd pain :—
'Neath thy ſway once more I move.

The Greeks (*within*).
To arms ! to arms !

Ulyſſes.
But why delay ?
Battle calls, I muſt away
To the combat.

Song (*within*).
Love, ſweet love !

Ulyſſes.
Ah ! how ſweetly on the wind
Sounds again that warbled ſigh !

Antiſtes (*aſide*).
Though I loſe my life thereby
Plainly I muſt ſpeak my mind :—
O Ulyſſes, victor Greek !
When the trumpet of thy fame
Calls thee to a loftier aim,
Canſt thou, lull'd in luxury, ſeek
Not to hear it ? Of love's charms
Know'ſt thou not the dire effect ?
How they work ſad ſelf-neglect ?
Lift *this* voice.

The Greeks (*within*).
To arms ! to arms !

Ulyſſes.
Yes, Antiſtes, thou art right,
Torpor held my ſpell-bound mind.
I was deaf, and I was blind,
But my ſenſes and my ſight

Recuerdos de mi ofadía,
Las prifiones rompere.

Circe.

¿Tan ingrata prifion fue,
Ulífes, la prifion mia?
¿Cómo, cuando entre mis brazos
Envidia á las flores das,
Tras otro afecto te vas?
¿Tan fáciles fon mis lazos
De romper? ¿Tanto rigor
Premio es de tantos favores?
Efcucha en hojas y en flores
Efta voz.

Múfica (dentro).

Amor, amor!

Antíftes.

No calle el marcial furor.

Circe.

Amor digan mar y tierra.

Múfica (dentro).

Amor, amor!

Griegos (dentro).

Guerra, guerra!
Guerra, guerra!

Múfica (dentro).

Amor, amor!

Ulífes.

Aqui guerra, amor aqui
Oigo, y cuando afi me veo,
Conmigo mifmo peleo;
Defiéndame yo de mí.

Antiftes.

Efto es honor.

Ulífes.

Dices bien,
Todo el honor lo atropella.

Circe.

Efto es gloria.

By thefe voices are reftored;
I fhall break my chains and flee.

Circe.

To be captive unto me,
Was it thraldom fo abhorr'd?
How, when in my arms thou'ft given
Envy to the lovelieft flowers,
Canft thou figh for ftormier hours?
Can my fweet bonds then be riven
Thus fo lightly? Doft thou prove
Grateful thus for bygone bliffes?
Hear this voice, that as it kiffes
Flowers and leaves, fings—

Song (within).

Love, fweet love!

Antiftes.

Ceafe not, founds that warriors move!

Circe.

Land and fea fing love's foft charms.

Song (within).

Love, fweet love!

The Greeks (within).

To arms! to arms!
To arms! to arms!

Song (within).

Love, fweet love!

Ulyffes.

Love and war falute my ear,
Either would my heart delight with;
'Tis myfelf that I muft fight with,
'Tis myfelf that I muft fear.

Antiftes.

Honour's here.

Ulyffes.

Thou fpeakeft true,
All things lie at honour's feet.

Circe.

Here is rapture.

Ulíses.
¡ Ay Circe bella,
Qué bien dices tú tambien !
Circe.
El gusto es dulce pasion.
Ulíses.
Razon tienes.
Antístes.
La victoria
Es mas aplauso, mas gloria.
Ulíses.
Tú tambien tienes razon.
Antístes.
Guerra y amor en rigor
Te llaman, miedos destierra.
Música (dentro).
Amor, amor !
Griegos (dentro).
Guerra, guerra !
Circe.
Quién ha vencido ?
Ulíses.
El amor ;
Que ¿ cómo pudiera ser,
Que otro afecto me venciera,
Donde tu hermosura viera ?
Esclavo tuyo he de ser.
No hay mas fama para mí
Que adorarte, no hay mas gloria
Que vivir en tu memoria.
Dichoso mil veces fui
El dia, que tu favor
Mereció mi voluntad.
Circe.
Venid todas, y cantad :
" El mayor encanto amor."—
Entra tú ; y vosotros, Griegos,
Mas pesares no me deis,
Y agradeced que no os veis,

Ulysses.
Circe sweet,
Ah ! how well thou speakest, too.
Circe.
Sweet is passion's rapturous bliss.
Ulysses.
Thou art right.
Antistes.
But far more glorious
Is the warrior's wreath victorious.
Ulysses.
Thou art also right in this.
Antistes.
War and love both call thee ; prove
Now thy wisdom,—hence, alarms !
Song (within).
Love, sweet love !
The Greeks (within).
To arms ! to arms !
Circe.
Which has conquer'd ?
Ulysses.
It is love ;
Since, what other power could have
Any chance of victory,
Thou in beauty standing by ?
From this hour I am thy slave ;
To adore thee be my fame,
All my glory, my reward,
But to live in thy regard.
O thrice-happy day ! that came
All my doubtings to remove,
Since it came thy love to bring.
Circe.
Come, my maidens, come and sing,
" The greatest of enchantments,
love ;"—
Enter thou ; and, O ye Greeks,
Interrupt our bliss no more,

Entre volcanes y fuegos,
De mi cólera abrafados.

Antiftes.

¡Ay de nofotros! que afi
Ya moriremos aqui
Cautivos y defterrados;
Sepulcro ferá efta tierra
De tanto griego valor. [*Vafe.*

Múfica.

¡El mayor encanto amor!
[*Vanfe todos cantando.*

En otra parte tocan armas, y dice ARSIDAS.

Arfidas (dentro).

Arma, arma! guerra, guerra!

Vuelve CIRCE *y todas las Damas.*

Circe.

¿Qué es efto, habiendo mandado
Yo, que temerofos callen
Los repetidos acentos
De baquetas y metales,
Otra vez ofais, villanos,
Otra vez ofais, cobardes,
Que oprimido el bronce gima,
Que herido fe queje el parche?

Sale FLERIDA.

Flérida.

No efte repetido acento,
Que con idiomas marciales,
Eftremeciendo los montes,
Titubear los ejes hace,
Cautela ha fido de Griegos;
Mas defdichas, mas pefares,
Mas penas, mas confufiones,

And be thankful that the roar
Of no red volcano breaks
Round you raging, through mine ire.

Antiftes.

Ah! unhappy we! fince here,
Exiled from our country dear,
Captives we muft all expire.
Land foredoom'd of fatal charms,
Grecian valour's grave to prove!
[*Exit.*

Song.

The greateft of enchantments, love!
[*Exeunt all, finging.*

In a third direction a martial charge is founded from within.

Arfidas (within).

War! war! to arms! to arms!

CIRCE, *with her train, returns.*

Circe.

How is this? when I commanded
That the trembling echoes, humbled,
Should no more repeat the rude notes
Of the drum-fticks and the trumpets;
Dare ye, once again, vile caitiffs,
Cowards, dare ye thus infult me,
Making the forced bronze-tubes groan,
And the wounded parchment mutter?

Enter FLERIDA.

Flerida.

No, this rude found now repeated,
Which, in martial idiom utter'd,
Makes the mighty mountains quiver,
And their deepeft caverns rumble,
Was not by the Greeks occafion'd;
Greater griefs, afflictions newer,
Added forrows, worfe confufions,

Mas tormentos y mas males
Son los que quieren los cielos,
Que eſtos aparatos cauſen.
Arſidas, que tantos dias
Fue de tu hermoſura amante,
A tus deſdenes quejoſo,
Ofendido á tus deſaires,
Deſde que ya enamorada
De Ulíſes te declaraſte,
Cuando de aquella cueſtion
Puſieron los rayos paces,
A ſu corte ſe fue, donde,
Queriendo el amor que paſen
De extremo á extremo ſus penas,
Que eſto en los hombres es fácil,
Amenazando eſtos montes
Viene, infeſtando eſos mares;
Y con razon, pues las ondas,
Gimiendo del peſo grave,
Con ambicion de peñaſcos
Blaſonan, cuando arrogantes
Ven por la campaña azul
De ſus ſalobres criſtales
Vagar un Volcan deſhecho,
Mover un Flegra portátil,
Correr un Etna movible,
E ir una Trinacria errante.
Líſidas, de mí ofendido,
Creyendo que yo mudable
Amaba á Ulíſes, (la cauſa
Con que yo lo fingí ſabes)
Le acompaña, porque aſi
Pretende de aqui ſacarme;
Que agravios de amor y zelos
No guardan reſpeto á nadie.
Yo lo ſé, porque ſentada
Sobre eſa punta, que hace
Corona al mar y á la tierra,
Arbitro de ondas y valles,

Countleſs ills and woes unnumber'd,
Are, ſo heaven has wiſh'd, the cauſes
Of the ſounds at which we ſhudder.
Arſidas, who was, thou knoweſt,
Long the lover of thy beauty,
By thy cold diſdainings wounded,
Anger'd by thy proud repulſes,
From the day that thou declared thee
Openly Ulyſſes' lover,
When the queſtion's doubtful iſſue
Cloſed in lightning and in thunder,
To his court went, where compelling
His late love to change with ſudden
Impulſe from one point to another
(Men find eaſy ſuch abruptneſs),
Now returns, theſe mountains threatening,
Comes oppreſſing theſe white ſurfs here;
And with reaſon, since the billows
Groaning 'neath ſo great a burthen,
Thinking that with rocks they wreſtle,
Proudly ruſh exulting up them,
They behold upon the cryſtal
Salt hills of their azure ſurface
Float along a looſed volcano,
Flit a Phlegra down the currents,
Haſten by a mobile Ætna,
A Trinacria through the ſurges.
Lyſidas, with me offended,
Thinking that my heart had ſuffer'd
Love-change for Ulyſſes (why
So I feign'd, thou knoweſt, that urged me)
Comes along with him, thus hoping
That from this he may abduct me;
Since nor love nor jealouſy
Show reſpect to aught that's human:—
This I know, becauſe when ſeated
On that point which crowns the furtheſt
Headland height o'er earth and water,

Ví, (como entre obſcuros lejos
De unos pintados celages,
Suelen pintarnos las ſombras,
Ya jardines, ya ciudades)
Una confuſa noticia,*
Que era, al perſpicaz exámen
De la viſta, neutral duda,
Mezcla de nubes y naves.
Cuando† al acercarſe al puerto
La grueſa armada que traen,
A los ſulcos de las proas
Rizarſe ví, y encreſparſe
Blanca eſpuma, que al azul
Camelote de aguas hace
Bella guarnicion de plata,
Que ſin que al dibujo guarde
El órden, es mas hermoſo,
Por ſer dibujo ſin arte.
Llegaron á nueſtro puerto,
Donde ſin faenas baten
Las blancas alas de lino,
Negándoſe al mar, ó al aire
Eſos peces, ſi ſon peces,
O eſas aves, ſi ſon aves.
Sin ſalva á tierra ſaltaron,
Y fueron en un inſtante
Griegos caballos, preñados
De aparatos militares,
Pues abortaron ſus vientres,
Siendo del agua Volcanes,
Iras y rayos, que luego
Fueron poblando la márgen.
Bien á los dos conocí,
Que armados á tierra ſalen,
Y en mal pronunciadas voces,
Que embarazó lo diſtante,

* Hartzenbuſch's edition reads *apariencia.*—Tr.

† Hartzenbuſch reads *luego.*—Tr.

Waves and valleys lying under,
Saw I, (as the far perſpectives
Of ſome painter's glorious ſunſets
Give us ſhadowy outlines, gleaming
Gardens here, and there dark turrets)—
A remarkable confuſion,
Which upon my ſight reſulted
In a ſplendid maze of mingled
Clouds and ſhips of lovelieſt colour.
When approach'd the great armada
To the port, I ſaw the ſurf there,
In the furrows of the prows,
Twiſt itſelf, and criſp, and curdle
Foam white fair, which on the azure
Camlet of the ſea made lovely
Broidery of netted ſilver,
Which without deſign reſulted
In that perfect grace, which nature
Ever without art produces.
Then our harbour having enter'd,
They, uncorded, let forth flutter
Their white wind-raiſed wings of linen,
Leaving ſea and ſky in utter
Doubt if the great keels were fiſhes,
Or the ſails the wings of birds were.
Giving no ſalute they leap'd forth
On the land; the ſhips grown ſubtle
Great Greek horſes, all with war-ſtores
Pregnant to the very gunnel:
For from out their wombs in birth-throes,
(Sea-borne forges they of Vulcan,)
Angry bolts were born, which peopled
All the ſhore round with their thunders.
Well I knew, of thoſe who leap'd forth
Arm'd on land there, two among them,
And in words caught indiſtinctly,
Which the diſtance half obſtructed,
Heard I Arſidas, who ſaid:—

Oí á Arſidas, que dijo:
Hoy deſta mágica acaben
Los encantos, y eſte monte,
Que es tiranizado Atlante
De Trinacria, á mi valor
Se poſtre.—Yo viendo el grande
Peligro, que te amenaza,
Volando vine á aviſarte.
Preven la deſenſa pues,
Si es que hay defenſa que baſte
A la ſangrienta venganza
De dos zeloſos amantes.

Circe.

¡ Calla, calla, no profigas!
Ni lleguen ecos marciales
A los oidos de Ulíſes.
Aqui tengo de dejarle
Sepultado en blando ſueño,
Porque el belicoſo alarde
No pueda de mi amor nunca
Dividirle, ni olvidarle;
Que yo con voſotras ſolas
Saldré á vencer arrogante.
Tú mi caudillo ſerás,
Y no temas, que te falten
Gentes; que aunque ſon tan pocos
Los ſoldados de mi parte,
Yo armadas hueſtes pondré
En las campañas del aire,
Que con tropas de caballos,
Con eſcuadrones de infantes,
Fantáſticamente lidien,
Y fingidamente marchen.
Y porque entre tantas ſombras
Vivas eſcuadras no falten,
Todas voſotras, armadas
Con eſcudos de diamante,
Galas deſnudad de Vénus,
Túnicas veſtid de Marte.

On this day at length is number'd
This magician's laſt enchantments;
And this mountain, this uſurper,
Which like Atlas lords Trinacria,
Shall beneath my valour crumble.
I perceiving the great danger
That thus threatens to engulf thee,
Flew to tell thee.—So get ready
All the aid that thou canſt muſter,
If aught aid can ſtop the bloody
Vengeance of two jealous lovers.

Circe.

Ceaſe, oh! ceaſe, proceed no more!
Nor let martial echoes thunder
In the cloſed ears of Ulyſſes;
Buried in a ſoothing ſlumber
Him I mean to leave here lying,
That again war's glorious hubbub
His remembrance, his affection,
Never from my love may ſunder.
I alone with you will go
This proud boaſter's pride to humble.
Thou my general wilt be;
Fear not that no troops will muſter
At thy call; for though few ſoldiers
Have I on my ſide to ſummon,
I can on the fields of air
Show arm'd hoſts in countleſs numbers,
Who in companies of horſe,
Who in ſquadrons of light foot-men,
Will fantaſtically fight,
Will in phantom files manœuvre;
And that thou may'ſt with theſe ſhadows
Lack not living hoſts among them,
All of you, my maidens, arm'd
With your dazzling diamond bucklers,
Doff the ſilken robes of Venus,
And put on Mars' martial tunics.

Caſandra.
Eſta vida, y eſte pecho
Te ofrezco yo de mi parte.
Clori.
Yo, que conozcan los hombres
Cuanto las mugeres valen.
Sirene.
Hoy el ſol ſerá teſtigo
De mi valor arrogante.
Tiſbe.
De nueſtro poder haré
Que el mundo ſe deſengañe.
Aſtrea.
A Pálas verás armada
Cada vez que me mirares.
Libia.
A mí á Vénus, pues verás
A mis pies rendido á Marte.
Circe.
Pues con eſa confianza,
Toca al arma.
Caſandra.
Suene el parche.
Clori.
Hiera la trompeta el eco.
Sirene.
El bronce oprimido brame.
Tiſbe.
El fuego reviente.
Aſtrea.
Sea
Toda Trinacria volcanes.
Libia.
El duro horror de las armas
Cielo, mar y tierra eſpante.
Flérida.
Y viva Circe, prodigio
Deſtos montes y eſtos mares.

Caſſandra.
I this life, this boſom offer
Thee on my part in thy trouble.
Chloris.
I that men may know how much
Woman's courage may be truſted.
Sirene.
On my valour will the ſun
Gaze to-day with looks of wonder.
Thiſbe.
Of our power the world no more
Shall make light, as is its cuſtom.
Aſtrea.
I a Pallas ſhall be thought,
Every time in arms I ſtruggle.
Libia.
I a Venus, ſince thou'lt ſee
Mars beneath my feet made ſubject.
Circe.
Thus then confident and bold
Sound the charge.
Caſſandra.
Ring out the trumpets.
Chloris.
Let the drums awake the echoes.
Sirene.
And the bugles blare and bluſter.
Thiſbe.
Let the fire burſt forth.
Aſtrea.
And be
All Trinacria but one furnace.
Libia.
At the horrid din of arms
Let heaven, earth, and ocean ſhudder.
Flerida.
And live Circe, of theſe ſeas,
Of theſe mountains, the fair wonder.

Circe.
Porque á los brazos de Ulíses,
Que en mudo letargo yace,
Vuelva rica de despojos,
Enamorada y constante. [*Vanse.*

Circe.
That she to Ulysses' arms—
Who lies there in silent numbness,
Still enamour'd and still constant—
May, enrich'd with spoils, return here.
[*Exeunt.*

MONTE.

Salen ARSÍDAS, LÍSIDAS *y Soldados.*

Arsidas.
Desde esta excelsa cumbre,
Que del sol se atrevió á tocar la lumbre,
Y altiva y eminente,
Coronada de rayos la alta frente,
Es immensa coluna
De ese cóncavo alcázar de la luna,
Entre celages de rubí y topacio
De Circe se descubre el real palacio.
¡ Ea pues, mis soldados,
Que valientes, intrépidos y osados,
En favor de los cielos
Manteneis la milicia de mis zelos !
Hoy este asombro muera,
Perezca hoy la memoria desta fiera,
Que á Trinacria estos campos tiraniza,
Siendo el Flegra su hoguera y su ceniza.
Libremos pues á tantos
Como tienen sus mágicos encantos
Presos aqui, y cautivos ;
Queden pues ó bien muertos, ó bien vivos.
Rescatemos valientes
Nuestra patria de tantos accidentes,
Y dejemos seguro este camino
Al náufrago piloto, al peregrino,
Que halló, cadáver de estas grutas hondas,
Mas tormenta en las peñas, que en las ondas,

A MOUNTAIN.

Enter ARSIDAS, LYSIDAS, *and Soldiers.*

Arsidas.
From this stupendous height,
Which dares to touch the sun's resplendent light,
And in its dazzling blaze
Crowns its proud forehead with the golden rays ;—
From this proud pillar-top
Which the fair moon's blue palace-dome doth prop,
'Twixt topaz clouds and ruby vistas we
The palace halls of Circe now may see.
Then on, brave soldiers ! bold,
Valiant, intrepid, resolute, enroll'd
By favour of the skies,
The avenging army of my jealousies !
To-day must die this terror of the earth,
This witch's memory fade as if she ne'er had birth ;
She who Trinacria tramples in the mire,
Its Phlegra she, its fount of ashes, smoke and fire.
This day we must set free
The many whom by cruel sorcery
She holds imprison'd here in piteous state,
Whom living we must loose, or dead avenge their fate.
Let us, brave comrades mine,

Cuando piſó por eſtos horizontes
Montes de agua y piélagos de montes.
Y tú, Líſidas fuerte,
A cuya voz ſe retiró la muerte,
Hoy á Flérida libra ſoberana
De la injuſta priſion de una tirana,
O véngate hoy en ella,
Si tus zelos te olvidan de querella.

Save now our country from ſuch plagues malign,
And leave this ſea-way clear
To ſhip-wreck'd pilot and lone mariner,
Who found, a cold corſe in theſe hollow caves,
More torment 'mid the rocks, than out upon the waves,
Though on this wild horizon his frail home
Had been high mountain waves and watery hills of foam.
And thou, brave Lyſidas, for whom
Death in indulgent mood re-oped the tomb,
Thou wilt to-day fair Flerida ſet free
From a dread tyrant's dread captivity,
Or elſe thy vengeance let her prove,
If in thy jealous rage thou canſt forget thy love.

Liſidas.

Arſidas, valeroſo
Príncipe de Trinacria, no zeloſo
Mi venganza prevengo;
Que no tengo los zelos que no tengo,
Porque ya ſé, que ha ſido
Un cauteloſo amor, amor fingido,
El que Flérida á Ulíſes le moſtraba,
Porque eſe Esfinge aſi ſe lo mandaba.
No zeloſo en efecto, enamorado
Sí, que vengo, atrevido y deſpechado
A reſcater á Flérida, que bella
Es de los cielos flor, del campo eſtrella.
Y aſi á tu lado juro
Por eſe hermoſo roſicler, que puro
Mirado, nos deſlumbra,
Y no mirado, á todos nos alumbra,
De no dejarte, haſta mirar poſtrada
Al fuego de tu enojo eſta encantada

Lyſidas.

Arſidas, valiant knight,
Trinacria's prince, no jealous torch doth light
My vengeful path to Circe's bower again,
For I no more, no more, can feel that bitter pain,
Knowing, as now I know,
'Twas falſe, feign'd love, 'twas love's deceptive ſhow
That to Ulyſſes Flerida diſplay'd—
The feint was order'd, and ſhe but obey'd.
'Tis not with jealouſy I come, but love,
Ardent, devoted, deſperate, to remove
From this foul ſpot fair Flerida, that fair
Flower of the faireſt field, and ſtar of cleareſt air;
And ſo, beſide thee now,

Selva de amor, donde, por mas efpanto,
Es el amor hoy fu mayor encanto,
Aunque en fus campos, que el Abril dibuja,
O brame el auftro, ó la arboleda cruja.

By that fair planet's rofy light I vow—
That planet which when feen ftrikes blind the fight,
And which unfeen ftill fills the world with light—
To leave thee not until thy wrathful mood
Strikes down each tree of this enchanted wood,
This bower of love,—where we to-day revere
Love, as the greateft of enchantments here,—
Like as when on the April-painted meads
The fouth-wind roars, the ftrong boughs bend like reeds.

Arfidas.
Guerra de amor y zelos
Pavor pondrá á los cielos.

Arfidas.
This war of love allied with jealoufy
Shall wake the fear, the wonder of the fky.

Voces dentro.
¡ Cierra, Trinacria, cierra ! [*Cajas.*

Voices within.
On! for Trinacria's right!

Lifidas.
Ya de allá nos refponden.

Lyfidas.
Yonder they anfwer.

Voces dentro.
Guerra, guerra !

Voices within.
To the fight, the fight!

Soldad.
¡ Ay, Arfidas, advierte,
Que á morir nos trajifte !

A Soldier.
Oh! hear me, Arfidas, oh! hear and ftay,
You lead us but to death here.

Arfidas.
De qué fuerte ?

Arfidas.
In what way?—

Soldad.
Dijifte, que no habia
Armas, ni gente en efta felva umbria,
Y apenas tus foldados
Han falido del mar, cuando embofcados
En efa felva vieron
Infantes y caballos, que falieron

Soldier.
You told us that we fhould
Nor men nor arms here meet within this fhadowy wood,
And fcarce your foldiers made
A landing from their fhips, when from an ambufcade

A defender la entrada
Del monte.

Arſidas.

No temais, no temais nada;
Que eſos monſtruos incultos
Son fantáſticas formas, que no bultos.
No hay que temer eſtragos,
Que ſus heridas ſolo ſon amagos;
Que tarde ejecutadas,
Se quedan en el aire ſeñaladas.

Líſidas.

Y tan cobardes fueron, [hirieron.
Que, amenazando ſiempre, nunca

Soldad.

¿Cómo, ſi ya, cauſando al ſol deſmayos,
Truenos abortan, y deſpiden rayos?

Arſidas.

Yo he de ſer el primero,
Que eſe pavor os quite; altivo y fiero
Penetraré la ſierra.

Líſidas.

Todos te ſeguiremos.

Todos.

Guerra, guerra!

Arſidas.

¡Ha cauteloſo Griego,
Sal á apagar retórico eſte fuego!

Salen Circe *y las mugeres con eſpadas.*

Circe.

No ſaldrá, ſino yo; que la memoria

Within the wood they ſaw
Horſemen and footmen to its outſkirts
draw,
The entrance to defend
That to the mountain leads.

Arſidas.

Fear naught, fear naught, my friend,
For all theſe monſtrous ſwarms
Are bodileſs ſhapes, are falſe fantaſtic
forms;
No need to fear ſuch foes
Whoſe very ſwords can deal but phan-
tom blows,
Which ſlowly dealt,
But by the yielding air are only felt.

Lyſidas.

And coward-like,
Who threaten ever, but who never ſtrike.

Soldier.

How, if already the ſcared ſunlight dies
And thunders rattle and the lightning
flies?

Arſidas.

I will be firſt this panic to ſubdue,
And with undaunted daring to burſt
through
This magic mountain's marge.

Lyſidas.

We all ſhall follow where you lead.

All.

Charge! charge!—

Arſidas.

Ha! wily Greek, [rhetoric!
Forth, and appeaſe this fire with all thy

Circe *and her women enter with drawn ſwords.*

Circe.

He comes not forth, but I; it were amiſs

No le ha de embarazar tan breve gloria.

Aſtrea.

Ninguno quede vivo.

Flérida.

Ni un amante, que vuelve vengativo
Sin zelos.

Liſidas.

Tú me ofendes, y yo te ofendo,
Que mas mi fama que tu amor pretendo.

Circe.

Segur de vueſtros cuellos
Hoy ſerán nueſtras armas. ¡ A ellos !

Todos.

¡ A ellos !

Arſidas.

En batalla tan dura
No atienda hoy el reſpeto á la hermoſura.
Preſto, Circe, ſerás tu mi trofeo.

Libia.

¡ O qué bonitamente lo peleo !

[*Daſe la batalla y retíranſe los hombres.*

To have his thoughts diſturb'd for glory ſuch as this.

Aſtrea.

Spare not their lives !

Flerida.

Not even a lover's, who for vengeance ſtrives,
Though jealouſy-cured.

Lyſidas.

Thou *me* doſt, and I thee offend,
For more than to thy love I to my fame pretend.

Circe.

Before the day is gone
Your necks ſhall ſtain our ſwords. On them !

All.

On ! on !

Arſidas.

In ſuch a battle and with ſuch a foe
Beauty to-day its homage muſt forego :
Soon, Circe, ſoon thy trophy crowns my might.

Libia.

Juſt look, how very prettily I fight.

[*The battle is joined and the men give way.*

Palacio de Circe.

Sale Lebrel, *y* Clarin *de mona.*

Lebrel.

Pues nos dejó Circe, y pues
A puerta cerrada eſtamos,
Y tan ſolos nos hallamos,
Tiempo, Doña Marta, es
De tomar una licion.
Ya la vuelta os enſeñé

Circe's Palace.

Enter Lebrel, *and* Clarin *as a monkey.*

Lebrel.

Now that Circe's gone, and we
Here are left, both you and I,
With cloſed doors, and no one by,
'Tis an opportunity
For a leſſon ; ſo, my pet,
As I lately taught you, tumble,

Del rodezno; cómo fue?
[*Voltea.*
¡Aſi bien, teneis razon!

Clarin.

¡Que aqueſto paſe por mí!
¡Y que en fin haya de ſer,
O voltear, ó no comer!
Deſdichado hablador fui.

Lebrel.

Ahora, Marta, ponte en pie.

Clarin.

Ello en fin no hay replicar,
O no comer, ó voltear. [*Voltea.*

Lebrel.

¡Lindamente, por mi fe!
Ahora, porque ſi yo
No tengo quien de veſtir
Me dé, uced me ha de ſervir;
Tome aqueſte eſpejo, y no
Le quiebre, porque es azar,
Y véngaſe tras mí en pie.

Clarin.

Qué cara tengo veré
De mona. Hay mayor peſar?
¡Válgame Júpiter ſanto,
Qué hocico!
[*En mirándoſe al eſpejo ſe le cae el veſtido de mona.*

Lebrel.

Quién aqui habló?

Clarin.

¿Quién ha de ſer, ſino yo?

Lebrel.

De verte, Clarin, me eſpanto.

Clarin.

Yo Clarin? muy bueno es eſo!
Mona ſoy.

Lebrel.

¿Dónde eſcondido?...

Try the wheel-trick—do not grumble—
[*Clarin tumbles.*
Pretty well, you'll do it yet.

Clarin.

What a fate is mine! thy laws
Nature thus to ſo maltreat—
I muſt tumble or not eat!
Wretched babbler that I was.

Lebrel.

Jocko, now on hands and feet.

Clarin.

All remonſtrance being paſt,
I muſt tumble or muſt faſt. [*Tumbles.*

Lebrel.

By my faith, you're quite complete!
Now, as here I hav'n't got
An attendant when I dreſs,
You your worſhip can't do leſs
Than be valet on the ſpot.
Take the glaſs, don't break it though,—
On your hind legs! that's the place.

Clarin.

Now at length my monkey face
I can have a peep at. Oh!
Holy Jove, above who eyes me,
What a ſnout!
[*At ſeeing himſelf in the mirror, he loſes the appearance of a monkey.*

Lebrel.

Who ſpeaks ſo nigh?

Clarin.

Why, who *could* it be, but I?

Lebrel.

Clarin here? you quite ſurpriſe me.

Clarin.

Clarin I? that's good of you!
I'm a monkey.

Lebrel.

Where were you hidden?....

Mas la mona ſe me ha ido.
Clarin.
Ya otra admiracion confieſo.
Lebrel.
¿Sabes por donde ſe fue
La mona, que aqui tenia?
Clarin.
Yo ſoy.
Lebrel.
Linda bobería!
Por la mona pregunté.
Clarin.
Pues yo ſoy.

Salen ANTÍSTES *y los Griegos con unas armas.*

Antíſtes.
Quién eſtá aqui?
Clarin.
Los dos.
Lebrel.
¡Que, porque vinieſe
Clarin, la mona ſe fueſe!
Tiempo y trabajo perdí.
Antíſtes.
Dime, Lebrel, ¿dónde eſtá . . . .
Lebrel.
La mona? No ſé, ay de mí!
Antíſtes.
Ulíſes? te digo.
Clarin.
Alli.

Deſcúbreſe un trono, donde eſtá ULÍSES *durmiendo.*

Antíſtes.
Entrar podeis todos ya;
Que pues aqui retirado
A Ulíſes Circe dejó,

But the monkey off has ſlidden.
Clarin.
This my wonder wakes anew.
Lebrel.
Did you ſee what way retired
The pet monkey that I had?
Clarin.
I am he.
Lebrel.
That's not ſo bad,—
'Twas for the monkey I inquired.
Clarin.
I am he, I ſay.

Enter ANTISTES, *and the* GREEKS *bearing pieces of armour.*

Antiſtes.
Who's here?
Clarin.
We two.
Lebrel.
Plague on't! for this flunky
Turning up, I've loſt my monkey—
Time and trouble too, I fear.
Antiſtes.
Do you know, Lebrel, where is . . . .?
Lebrel.
My poor monkey? no, ah! me.
Antiſtes.
Tut! I meant Ulyſſes.
Clarin.
See.

A throne is diſcovered, and on it ULYSSES *ſleeping.*

Antiſtes.
Softly tread this room of his:—
Since remote from any hum
Circe left Ulyſſes here,

Cuando al mar á ver ſalió
Las naves que habian llegado,
Eſte es el tiempo mejor,
Para vencer ſus extremos;
Y pueſto que no podemos
Aviſarle con rumor
De armas, hoy de Aquíles ſea
El arnes ſu trompa. Aqui
Le dejemos, porque aſi,
Cuando deſpierte, le vea.

Timántes.

Acuérdele mudo él
Las battallas, que venció,
Cuando en campaña ſe vió
Coronado de laurel,
Para que deſpertador
De tantos olvidos ſea.

Arquelao.

Quien no creyó la voz, crea
Las inſignias del valor.

[*Pónenle á los pies las armas.*

Polidoro.

Trofeos, que ſoberanos
Troya entre cenizas llora,
Y aun eſtais ſudando ahora
La ſangre de los Troyanos,
Volved por vos, y entre viles
Amores no os permitais
Empañar, pues aun guardais
El muerto calor de Aquíles.

[*Vanſe, y deſpierta* Ulíses.

Ulíſes.

Peſado letargo ha ſido
Eſte á que rendido eſtuve,
Ni bien vida, ni bien ſueño,
Sino letal peſadumbre
De los ſentidos, que torpes,
Ni deſcanſan, ni diſcurren,

When ſhe went to ſee anear
The great navy that had come,
'Tis the time to triumph o'er
Charms that ſo his ſoul have bow'd,
And ſince we are not allow'd
To adviſe him by the roar
Of the drums, his trumpet be
Now, Achilles' harneſs bright,—
Place it there within his ſight,
That when waking he may ſee.

Timantes.

Mute may it recall the round
Of the battles that he won,
Of the fields he ſtood upon,
With the victor laurel crown'd,
May it from deluſive charms,
Wake him ſoon to manlier deed.

Archelaus.

He who heeds no voice, may heed
The reproachful ruſt of arms.

[*They place the armour at his feet.*

Polydorus.

Trophies of a realm ſubdued,
Trophies Troy in aſhes weeps,
Since along your bright mail creeps
Still the ſweat of Trojan blood;
No baſe ſtain of low deſire
Let diſgraceful love fling o'er you,
Wake, by thoughts of him who bore
you,
Dead Achilles' martial fire.

[*Exeunt all.*

Ulyſſes (awaking.)

Lead-like lethargy, it ſurely
Muſt have been that I lay under,—
Neither wholly life, nor ſleeping,
But a dark lethean dulneſs
Of the ſenſes, which, grown torpid,
Neither moved, nor wholly ſlumber'd.

Crepúſculos ſon del alma,
Pues obran entre dos luces.
Quién eſtá aqui? Solo eſtoy.
¿Pues comó ſin Circe pude
Vivir un inſtante? Bien,
Que eſtaban ſin luz, preſumen
Mis ſentidos, pues ſin ſol
Aun todo el cielo no luce.
Circe! Circe! mi ſeñora!
¡Qué mal tanta auſencia ſuple
Tu memoria!—Mas qué veo?
El grabado arnes iluſtre
De Aquíles á mis pies yace,
Torpe, olvidado é inútil.
Bien eſtá á mis pies, porque
Rendido á mi amor ſe juzgue,
Y ſegunda vez en mí
Amor de Marte ſe burle.
Tarde, olvidado trofeo
Del valor, á darme acudes
Socorro contra mí miſmo;
Que aunque contra mí me ayudes,
Hoy colgado en eſte templo
Quedarás, donde ſepulten
Sus olvidos tus memorias.

El Eſpiritu de AQUÍLES, *deſde el centro de la tierra.*

Aquíles.
¡No le ofendas, no le injuries!
Ulíſes.
¿Qué voz es eſta, que en mí
Tan nuevo pavor infunde?
[*Tocan dentro cojas deſtempladas y una ſordina.*
¿A quién deſtempladas trompas,
Exequias ſiguen lúgubres?
¿Quién cauſa eſte efecto?

Twilights of the ſoul were they,
That 'twixt day and darkneſs ſtruggled.
Who is here? I am alone.
Ah! how can I live one flutter
Of the heart without my Circe?
Well my thoughts divined the murky
Dark near, ſince without the ſun
Heaven itſelf diſplays no luſtre.
Circe! Circe! my ſeñora,
For thy abſence, all I ſuffer
Memory poorly pays for. But,
What is this? the graved reſulgent
Armour of Achilles lieth
At my feet forgot, unuſed.
Rightly at my feet, becauſe
To my love it deems it ſubject,
And a ſecond time in me
Victor Love o'er Mars exulteth.
All too late, forgotten trophy
Of true valour, doſt thou come here
Succour 'gainſt myſelf to give me;
Since though 'gainſt myſelf thy ſuccour
Giv'ſt thou, in this fane ſuſpended
Must thou here remain, where buried
Shall thy memory be forgotten.

The ſhade of ACHILLES *from below.*

Achilles.
Mock them not; do not inſult them.
Ulyſſes.
Ah! what voice is this that makes me
In my inmoſt heart to ſhudder?
[*A mournful march of muffled drums and trumpets is heard from below.*
Ah! for whoſe ſad obſequies
Play theſe mournful drums and trumpets?
Who occaſions this?

Aquíles (*debajo de tierra*).

Quien
A ſus venganzas acude.

Ulíſes.

Si ojos tengo con què mire,
Si oidos tengo con que eſcuche,
En el centro de la tierra
Sonó la voz, y no ſufre
Ella aun de ſu grave faz
La arrugada peſadumbre;
Pues abre para quejarſe
Una boca, y de ella eſcupe
Pardas nubes de humo y fuego,
¿Cuando, contra la coſtumbre,
En el centro de la tierra
Forjan ſus rayos las nubes?

[*Abreſe una boca, y ſale fuego.*

A mas el aſombro paſa;
Triſte un monumento ſube
De ſu abiſmo, haciendo un caos
De vapores y viſlumbres.

Va ſubiendo un ſepulcro, y en él AQUÍLES, *cubierto de un velo.*

O tú, que en leves cenizas,.
Que aun el viento no ſacude,
En eſe ſepulcro yaces,
Quién eres?

Aquíles.

Porque no dudes
Quien ſoy, eſte negro velo
Corre, y mi aſpecto deſcubre.

[*Deſcúbrele* ULÍSES.

Conóceſme?

Ulíſes.

Si me deja
Eſpecies con que te juzgue
Lo pálido de tu faz,

Achilles (*from below*).

One who
To take ſtern revenge doth come here.

Ulyſſes.

If I can believe my eyes,
If my hearing can be truſted,
From the centre of the earth
Came that voice, the earth that ſuffers
Not upon its heavy face
Even the movement of a muſcle;
Since a mouth is open'd wide
For complaint, from which is ſputter'd
Denſeſt clouds of ſmoke and fire.
When, againſt all uſual cuſtom,
In the centre of the earth,
Have the clouds forged flaſhing thunders?

[*An abyſs opens from which fire burſts forth.*

Higher ſtill my terror riſes;
From the abyſs, a ſad ſepulchral
Tomb ariſes, making chaos [wreaths.
With its ſteams and glimmering dun-

A tomb ariſes from the abyſs, and in it is ACHILLES *covered with a veil.*

O dread ſhape, that in light aſhes,
Which not even the wind diſturbeth,
Lieſt in this ſepulchre,
Say, who art thou?

Achilles.

That all further
Doubt ſhould end, this black veil lift,
And my countenance diſcover.

[ULYSSES *raiſes the veil.*

Doſt thou know me?

Ulyſſes.

If I may
Truſt the teſts wherewith to judge the
Aſhy paleneſs of thy face,

Que no hay vista que no turbe,
Lo yerto de tu esqueleto.
Que aun desfigurado luce,
Aquíles, Aquíles eres.

Aquíles.

Su espíritu soy ilustre,
Que de los elisios campos,
Donde eterna mansion tuve,
Volví á pasar de Aqueronte
Las verdinegras y azules
Ondas, derretidas gomas
Del salitre y del azufre.
A cobrar vengo mis armas,
Porque el amor no las juzgue
Ya de su templo despojo,
Torpe, olividado é inútil;
Porque no quieren los dioses,
Que otro dueño las injurie,
Sino que en mi sepultura
A par de los siglos duren.
Y tú, afeminado Griego,
Que, entre las delicias dulces
Del amor, de negras sombras
Tantos esplendores cubres,
No entre amorosos encantos
Las tengas y las deslustres,
Sino rompiendo de amor
Las mágicas inquietudes,
Sal de Trinacria, y hollando
Al mar los vidrios azules,
A discrecion de los vientos
Sus pavimentos discurre;
Que en la curia de los dioses
Quieren, que otra vez los sulques,
Hasta que de mi sepulcro
Las muertas aras saludes,
Y en él esas armas cuelgues.
No lo ignores, no lo dudes,

Which no sight can see untroubled,
And thy stiffen'd skeleton,
Which, though maim'd, retains such lustre,
Thou Achilles art, Achilles.

Achilles.

I his spirit am, so bruited,
Who from the Elysian fields, my
Everlasting home and country,
Have pass'd through the green and azure
Waves of Acheron, thick gummy
Molten mires of fire and brimstone,
Pools of nitre and of sulphur,
To reclaim once more my arms,
So that Love may never judge them
Of his temple the proud spoil,
Idle, all forgot, and useless;
For the gods no longer wish
That another lord should rust them,
But that buried in my tomb
They should last while years are number'd.
And, O thou effeminate Greek,
Who, amid the soft indulgence
Of weak love, so many splendours
In thick ebon shades dost cover,—
Not in amorous enchantments
Shouldst thou let them lose their lustre,
But the magic-woven web
Of love's passionate joys and troubles
Breaking, fly Trinacria, and
Treading the sea's glass-blue surface,
At the winds' discretion scud
O'er its level lawns unruffled.
For it is the gods' decree
That once more your curved prow cuts them,
Till the funeral altars standing
By my far tomb thou salutest,

O harás, que un rayo, con voces
Que horrible un trueno pronuncie,
Segunda vez te lo mande,
Cuando en abortada lumbre
Desatadas sus cenizas,
Aun, antes que ardan, ahumen.
[*Húndese.*

Ulíses.

Espera, helado cadáver,
Que asombro y horror infundes,
Que yo postrada te doy
Palabra . . . . Todo se hunde.
Pesada imaginacion
Fue la que en mis sueños tuve;
Pero, aunque soñada, es bien
Que la crea, y no la dude.

Salen los Griegos.

Antístes.
Señor, qué es esto?
Timántes.
Que tienes?
Polidoro.
¿Qué accidente hay, que te turbe?
Arquelao.
¿De qué das voces al aire?
Floro.
¿Qué temor hay, que te ocupe?
Lebrel.
¡Que no parezca la mona,
Aunque todo el monte anduve!

Antístes.
De qué te asombras?
Clarin.
¿De qué
Te rezelas?

And in it these arms suspend.
Be not doubtful or reluctant,
If thou wouldst not that a flash,
Lightning-red, with voice of thunder,
This command should give once more,
When in the swift-born refulgence
Shall its scatter'd ashes steam,
Ere to burning dust they crumble.
[*He sinks down.*

Ulysses.

Stay, oh! stay, cold frozen corse,
Thou that with such fear dost stun me,
For my promise I now give thee
Prostrate here . . . . But all hath sunken.
Some oppressive fearful fancy
Was it that disturb'd my slumbers;
But although mere dreams, 'twere well
Not to doubt them, but to trust them.

Enter the Greeks.

Antistes.
What is this, my lord?
Timantes.
What wouldst thou?
Polydorus.
What hath happen'd, that disturbs thee?
Archelaus.
Why fill all the air with outcries?
Florus.
Whence this fear that so usurps thee?
Lebrel.
Though I've gone through all the moun-
tain,
Ah! I cannot meet my monkey!
Antistes.
What doth fright thee so?
Clarin.
At what
Dost thou shake?

Lebrel.
De quién huyes?
Ulises.
De mí mismo.
Antistes.
Pues ¿qué tienes?
Ulises.
Nada tengo, mucho tuve.
¡Ay amigos! tiempo es ya,
Que á los engaños me usurpe
Del mayor encanto, y hoy
El valor del amor triunfe.
¿Dónde está, dónde se ha ido
Circe?
Antistes.
A esa ribera acude,
Despues que aqui nos dejó,
A ver, qué bajeles surgen
A este golfo.
Ulises.
Pues en tanto
Que descuidada presume,
Que los encantos de amor
Firmes en mi pecho duren,
Por esta parte, que el mar
Siempre repetido surte
Altas montañas, de quien
Turbante han sido las nubes,
Salgamos, y por no hacer
Ruido, y que ella nos escuche,
No el bajel, sino el esquife
Tomemos, y en él . . . .
Antistes.
No dudes.
Ulises.
Huyamos de aqui; que hoy
Es huir accion ilustre,
Pues los encantos de amor

Lebrel.
From whom wouldst run here?
Ulysses.
From myself.
Antistes.
Oh! say, what hast thou . . .
Ulysses.
I had much, I now have nothing.
Ah! my friends, it now is time
To subdue the greatest, subtlest
Of enchantments, and this day
To crown valour love's triumpher.—
Where is she, say, where has gone
Circe?
Antistes.
To the shore she hurried,
When she left us here, to see
Whose the ships that in the gulf there
Had dropp'd anchor.
Ulysses.
Then while thus
She so carelessly presumeth
That the witchery of love
Still within my heart endureth,
By this path, to where the sea
Heaves incessantly and surges
Up the lofty mountains, whose
Heads the dark clouds crown with turbans,
Let us go, and for less noise,
Lest she hear and mar our purpose,
Not the vessel, but the boat
Let us take, and in it . . . .
Antistes.
Trust thee.
Ulysses.
Fly from here; for flight to-day
Is an act as brave as prudent,
Since the sorceries of love,

Los vence aquel que los huye.
Antiſtes.
Las lágrimas te reſpondan.
Ulíſes.
Hermoſa Juno, no culpes
El mayor encanto amor;
Pues, aunque tus flores tuve,
Pude vencer mil encantos,
Y aqueſte ſolo no pude.
Lebrel.
Al fin me voy ſin mi mona.
Clarin.
¿Que haſta ahora, que fui, dades?
[*Vanſe.*

He alone who flies, ſubdueth.
Antiſtes.
Let theſe tears of ours be anſwer.
Ulyſſes.
Lovely Juno, oh! excuſe the
Greateſt of enchantments, Love,
Since although thy flowers I flouriſh'd,
Which a thouſand ſpells could conquer,
This one only was above me.
Lebrel.
So in fine I loſe my monkey.
Clarin.
Doubt you ſtill 'twas I, you dullard?
[*Exeunt.*

ORILLAS DEL MAR, FRENTE AL PALACÍO DE CIRCE.

Salen, marchando, CIRCE *y ſus Damas, que traen preſos á* ARSIDAS *y* LÍSIDAS.

Circe.
Hagan ſalva á mis palacios
Los animados clarines,
Las cajas y las trompetas,
Porque ſus voces publiquen,
Que de Arſidas victorioſa
Hoy, y de Líſidas, Circe
Coronada de trofeos,
Vuelve á los brazos de Ulíſes.
Arſidas.
Bien, Circe, podré negarte,
Que valiente me venciſte,
Mágica no, que mis gentes
A tus apariencias rindes,
Pues huyeron de las hueſtes,
Que aparentemente finges.
Líſidas.
A ſacar de tu poder

THE SEA-SHORE IN FRONT OF CIRCE'S PALACE.

Enter CIRCE *and her ladies, marching with* ARSIDAS *and* LYSIDAS *as priſoners.*

Circe.
Hail my palace-walls, ye clarions,
With your proud notes wake its ſilence!
Drums and trumpets, with your powers
All the liſtening world enlighten,
That o'er Arſidas victorious,
And o'er Lyſidas, comes Circe
Back again, encrown'd with trophies,
To the fond arms of Ulyſſes!
Arſidas.
That 'twas valour that ſubdued me,
Circe, I could well deny thee,
That 'twas magic, no; my people,
By thy apparitions frighten'd,
Fled before the hoſts of phantoms
That thy ſubtle ſkill depicted.
Lyſidas.
To withdraw fair Flerida

A Flérida hermofa vine ;	From thy power came I hither ;
¿ Cómo pude defenderme,	How could I defend myfelf
Si ella mifma es quien me rinde ?	When 'twas fhe contended with me ?
Circe.	*Circe.*
Pues fi prefo eftás por ella,	If for her thou'rt here in chains,
Tambien por ella eftás libre.—	Then for her be free this inftant.
Ulífes, invicto Griego,	From thefe rich-rofed gardens fair,
Sal de efos ricos jardines,	Come, unvanquifh'd Greek! Ulyffes !
Porque de zelos y amor	And tread down the fallen pomps
Las caducas pompas pifes.	Love and jealoufy once lit here.
Advierte, que victoriofa,	See with what a victor air,
Llena de aplaufos infignes,	Led by plaufive trumps and timbrels,
Vuelvo á tus brazos, porque	I refeek thy arms, for only
Triunfe en ellos.—Mas ay trifte !	There I triumph ; but why thrills me
[*Suena un claron.*	[*A trumpet founds.*
¿ Qué baftarda trompa es efta,	So this boding bugle, this
Afpid de metal, que gime	Snake of metal, whofe throat hiffes
Al aire ?	On the air ?
Flérida.	*Flerida.*
En el mar, feñora,	From fea, Señora,
Sonó la voz.	Comes the found.
Libia.	*Libia.*
Y el efquife	And fee the fkiff there
De efe griego bajel, hecho	Of the Grecian veffel, making
Al mar, fus campañas mide.	From the fhore acrofs the ftill fea.
Aftrea.	*Aftrea.*
Ulífes defde él te habla;	And Ulyffes from it fpeaks ;
Efcucha lo que te dice.	Hearken to his words, oh ! liften.
Ulífes (*dentro*).	*Ulyffes* (*within*).
Afperos montes del Flegra,	Rugged mountains of wild Phlegra,
Cuya eminencia compite	Whofe exceffive heights are pitted
Con el cielo, pues fus puntas	'Gainft the fky, becaufe their proud peaks
Con las eftrellas fe miden,	With the ftars of Heaven are mingled,
Yo fui de vueftros venenos	I was o'er your many poifons
Triunfador, Tefeo felice	The triumpher, of your circled
Fui de vueftros laberintos,	Labyrinth the happy Thefeus,
Y Edipo de vueftra esfinge.	Œdipus of all your fphinxes ;
Del mayor encanto amor	From thy greateft of enchantments
La razon me facó libre,	Love, hath reafon me deliver'd,

Traſladando eſos palacios
A los campos de Anfitrite.

Voces (dentro).

Buen viage!

Flérida.

Buen viage,
Todos los vientos repiten.

Circe.

Eſcucha, tirano griego,
Eſpera, engañoſo Ulíſes,
Pues te habla, no cruel,
Sino enamorada Circe.
Cuando victorioſa yo
Triunfos arraſtro, que piſes,
¿Quieres, que vencida llore?
¿Quieres, que me queje humilde?
Eſcucha!—Mas ¡ay triſte!
No llore quien te pierde, ni ſuſpire,
Si te dan, para hacer mejor camino,
Agua mis ojos, viento mis ſuſpiros.

Flérida.

Señora, en vano te quejas;
Que ſordo el ingrato Ulíſes,
Deſbocado bruto, corre
A vela y remo el eſquiſe.

Libia.

Ya, perdiéndoſe de viſta,
Un atomo es inviſible.

Aſtrea.

Y ya entre el agua y las nubes
Un pájaro apenas finge.

Circe.

Ya eſtás, Arſidas, vengado.
Pero mal dije, mal dije;

All your palaces exchanging
For the fields of Amphitrite.

Voices within.

Pleaſant voyage!

Flerida.

Pleaſant voyage
All the winds appear to wiſh them.

Circe.

Liſten, liſten, tyrant Greek!
Stay, deceitful, falſe Ulyſſes,
Since 'tis not the cruel queen
Calls thee, but the love-lorn Circe.
When, that thou might'ſt tread them down,
Triumphs for thy feet I bring thee,
Wouldſt thou, conquering, I ſhould weep,
Wouldſt thou weakly I ſhould whimper?
Hear me!—But, O bitter woe!
She muſt not weep or ſigh from whom thou flieſt,
If ſhe muſt give thee for thy ſpeedier flight,
Water her eyes, and wind the ſobs ſhe ſigheth.

Flerida.

Vainly, lady, thou lamenteſt,
Since the deaf ingrate Ulyſſes
Flies with rudder and with ſail
On his ſhip as on a ſwift ſteed.

Libia.

Almoſt loſt to ſight, 'tis now
To the ſmalleſt atom dwindled.

Aſtrea.

And betwixt the wave and cloud
Like a tiny ſea-bird wingeth.

Circe.

Arſidas, thou art avenged;
But my words are falſe and idle,—

Que nunca ſe venga un noble
En mirar un infelice.
Si lo eres, eſe acero
En mi roja ſangre tiñe;
Que no es venganza, piedad
Sí, darle la muerte á un triſte.
Y ſea antes que traſpueſto
Eſe neblí, que deſcribe
Las ondas, eſe delfin,
Que el campo del aire mide,
Eſe caballo, que corre,
Eſe eſcollo, que ſe rige,
Eſe peñaſco, que nada,
Se eſconda, y no ſe diviſe;
Porque, perdido de viſta,
Tardará tu acero inſigne,
Y no ſerá meneſter
Mas muerte, que no ſeguirle.
¡Eſcucha! Mas ¡ay triſte!
No llore quien te pierde, ni ſuſpire,
Pues te dan, para hacer mejor camino,
Agua mis ojos, viento mis ſuſpiros.—
¿Mas qué me quejo á los cielos?
¿No ſoy la mágica Circe?
¿No puedo tomar venganza
En quien me ofende y me rinde?
Alterados eſtos mares
A ſer pedazos aſpiren
De los cielos; que ſi lleva,
Porque de encantos ſe libre,
El ramillete de Juno,
Que trajo del cielo Iris,
No de tormentas del mar
Le librarán ſus matices.
Llamas las ondas arrojen,
Fuego las aguas eſpiren.
[*Sale fuego del agua.*
Arda el azul pavimento,
Y ſus campañas turquíes

True hearts ne'er can vengeance find
In the ſight of one afflicted.
If thou art ſo, take this ſword,
And with my red heart's blood tinge it,
Since to kill a wretch like me
Is not vengeance, but true pity:
And do this, or ere, faſt fading,
Yon fleet falcon, that ſwift ſwimmeth
Ocean's waves, yon white-wing'd dolphin,
'Mid the fields of air uplifted,
Yonder ſea-ſteed gently flowing,
Yonder rudder'd rock that drifteth,
Yonder looſen'd cliff that floateth,
Undeſcried is wholly hidden;
For when it is loſt to ſight,
Then too late will fall thy ſwift ſteel,
Since no other death I'll need;
Then the thought I can't go with him.
Hear me! But, O bitter woe!
She muſt not weep or ſigh from whom thou flieſt,
If ſhe muſt give thee for thy ſpeedier flight,
Water her eyes, and wind the ſobs ſhe ſigheth.
But why wail thus to the ſkies,
Am I not the ſorcereſs Circe?
Cannot I take vengeance on
Him who wrongs me? who afflicts me?
Let the rouſed-up ſeas aſpire,
As it were, to be the ſplinters
Of the broken heavens: and though
He that charm againſt bewitchments
Bears—the beauteous flowers of Juno,
Which from heaven were brought by Iris,—
From the tempeſts of the ſea
Him ſhall not their tints deliver;
Flame, be darted from the billows,

Miefes de rayos parezcan,
Que cañas de fuego vibren,
A ver, fi hay deidad, que tanta
Tormenta le facilite.

Serénafe el mar, y fale por él, en un carro triunfal tirado de dos delfines, GALATEA, *y al rededor muchos Tritones y Sirenas con inftrumentos.*

Galatea.
Sí habrá, y quien, fereno el mar,
Manfo, quieto y apacible,
Le dé pafo en fus esferas.

Circe.
¿Quién eres tú, que faliste
De efas húmidas alcobas
En triunfal carro fublime,
A ferenar de mi enojo
Las iras defapacibles?

Galatea.
Yo, que en efte hermofo carro,
A quien tiran dos delfines,
De Sirenas y Tritones
Tan acompañada vine,
Galatea foy, de Dóris
Hija, y de Nereo, invencible
Dios marino, y la que amante
De Acis, jóven infelice,
Murió á los bárbaros zelos
De Polifemo, terrible
Monftruo, que el tálamo dulce
De nueftras bodas felices
Cubrió de un peñafco, que hoy
Túmulo es, que nos aflige:

Fire, from out the waves be fpirted;
[*Fire rifes from the water.*
Let the azure pavement burn,
And its plains of turquoife gliften,
Like a harveft field of lightning,
Vibrating innumerous fire-ftems,
To find out if any goddefs
Can fo great a ftorm extinguifh.

The fea grows ferene, and upon it GALATEA *is feen advancing in a triumphal car drawn by two dolphins, and furrounded by many Tritons and Sirens bearing mufical inftruments.*

Galatea.
There is one, who fmooths the fea
To a peaceful path of filver
For his paffage through its fpheres.

Circe.
Who art thou that hath arifen
From the deep fea's damp receffes,
In triumphal chariot driven,
To appeafe the unappeafèd
Anger of the wrath I've kindled?

Galatea.
I, who in this beauteous car,
Which two dolphins move fo lightly,
Come accompanied and circled
By the Tritons and the Sirens,
Galatea am, the daughter
Of fair Doris, and the mighty
Sea-god Nereus, and the loved once
Of young Acis, haplefs ftripling,
Victim of the jealous fury
Of wild Polyphemus, grimmeft
Of all monfters, who the fweet bed
Of the happy vows we plighted
Cover'd with a rock, which ever
Like a dark tomb o'er us rifes,

Cuya pirámide, cuanta
Sangre de los dos exprime,
Criſtal es, que deſatado
Nueſtro fin llorando dice.
Deſte rúſtico jayan
Vengada me dejó Ulíſes,
A cuya cauſa mi voz
Al amparo ſuyo aſiſte;
Y pidiendo á las deidades
De Neptuno y de Anfitrite,
Que ſerenaſen los mares,
Y que ſus claros viriles
Eſpejos fueſen del ſol,
Mientras los Griegos los piſen.
Como á Ninfa de ſus ondas,
Que diſcurra me permiten
El mar, apagando cuanto
Fuego en él introdujiſte;
Y aſi ondas de plata y vidrio
Veloz mi carro deſcribe,
Haciendo á ſu hermoſa eſpuma,
Que á las rodadas sútiles,
O como plata ſe entorchen,
O como vidrio ſe ricen.

Circe.

Si deidad eres del mar,
Cuando en él mis fuerzas quites,
No en la tierra; y ſi no puedo
Vengarme en quien huye libre,
En mí podré. Eſtos palacios,
Que mágico el arte finge,
Deſvanecidos en polvo,
Sola una voz los derribe.
Su hermoſa fábrica caiga
Deſhecha, rota y humilde;
Sean páramo de nieve
Sus montes y ſus jardines.
Un Mongibelo ſuceda
En ſu lugar, que vomite

Preſs'd beneath whoſe pyramid
All the blood that from us trickles,—
So to weep our tragic end—
Turns to cryſtal murmuring ripples.
'Gainſt this ruſtic giant rude
Vengeance gave to me Ulyſſes,
On account of which my voice
In his cauſe has been uplifted,
Aſking of the deities
Neptune and fair Amphitrite,
That they would make ſmooth the ſeas,
And that they, tranſlucent mirrors,
Should outſpread them for the ſun,
While the Greek ſhip ſail'd amidſt them.
I, as being a ſea-nymph born,
Am to run their realm permitted,
In the ſea the fire appeaſing,
Which your vengeful anger flings here;
And my ſwift car thus o'er-rideth,
Sparkling waves of glaſs and ſilver,
Making with its beauteous foam
'Neath its wheels the waves to gliſten,
Now in curling wreaths of glaſs,
Now in ſilvery twine entwiſted.

Circe.

If thou'rt of the ſea a goddeſs,
Thou may'ſt of my might deprive me
There, but not on land; if vengeance
I can't have on him who flies me,
On myſelf I can. This palace,
Which by magic art I builded,
Let it vaniſh into duſt,
Let a ſingle word, to ſhivers
Shake this beauteous fabric down,
Ruin'd, broken, rent, made little.
O'er its mountains and its gardens
Let the dreary ſnow be drifted,
And where now it ſtands in beauty,
Be a wild volcano kindled,

Fuego, que á la luna abrafe,
Entre humo, que al fol eclipfe.

[*Húndefe el palacio de Circe, y aparece un volcan, arrojando llamas.*

Aftrea.

¡ Qué confufion tan notable!

Libia.

¡ O qué afombro tan terrible!

Flérida.

Huyamos, Libia! [*Vafe.*

Libia.

Huye, Aftrea! [*Vafe.*

Aftrea.

¿ Dónde eftar podemos libres? [*Vafe.*

Circe.

Cuantos efpíritus tuve
Prefos, fujetos y humildes,
Inficionando los aires,
Huyan á fu centro horrible.
Y yo, pues de mis encantos
A faber que es mayor vine
El amor, pues el amor,
A quien no rindieron, rinde,
Muera tambien, y fuceda
A mi fin la noche trifte. [*Húndefe.*

Galatea.

Pues feguro el mar por donde
Venturofo corre Ulífes,
Tormentas vé de la tierra,
El mar con fieftas publique
Su vencimiento, y haciendo
Regocijos y feftines,
Sus Tritones y Sirenas
Lazos formen apacibles;
Pues fue el agua tan dichofa,
En efta noche felice,

Belching fire, the pale moon burning,
And with fmoke the fea eclipfing.

[*The palace of Circe finks into the earth, and a volcano rifes in its place, darting out flames.*

Aftrea.

O confufion fo unequall'd!

Libia.

O the horror fo terrific!

Flerida.

Libia, fly! [*Exit.*

Libia.

Oh! fly, Aftrea! [*Exit.*

Aftrea.

Where for fafety? fay, oh! whither? [*Exit.*

Circe.

All the fpirits that I held
Captive, fubject to my fway, and willing,
Flying on the poifon'd air,
Seek the horrid homes that hide them.
And fince I of my enchantments
Have now come to know the chief is
Love, fince love it was that conquer'd
Him, whom all the reft left victor,
Let me alfo die, and let
Mournful night's dark gloom engird me.
[*She finks down.*

Galatea.

Since the fea, upon whofe breaft
Flies the fortunate Ulyffes,
Views unmoved the ftorms of land,
Let it now in joy and mirth here
Publifh to the world his triumph,
And its Tritons and its Sirens,
Making *fêtes* and glad rejoicings,
Dance in many mazes mingled;
And fince on this happy night
Has the water been permitted

Que mereció ſer teatro
De ſoles, á quien humilde
El Poeta, entre otras honras,
Perdon de las faltas pide.
[*Hiciéron un bailete Tritones y Sirenas.*

The proud theatre to be
Of two ſuns, the Poet wiſhes
Humbly, 'mid his other honours,
For his faults to aſk forgiveneſs.
[*The ſcene cloſes with a Ballet of Tritons and Sirens.*

THE SORCERIES OF SIN.

AN AUTO.

FROM THE SPANISH OF CALDERON.

INTRODUCTION.

THE *Sorceries of Sin* is the only attempt that has ever been made in Engliſh to preſent even one of Calderon's *Autos* in its integrity. Indeed, with the exception of the ſcenes introduced into Dean Trench's analyſis of *The Great Theatre of the World*, not a ſingle line of theſe remarkable dramas has ever previouſly been preſented in Engliſh verſe. Writers in Reviews and Magazines have occaſionally drawn attention to a few of the ſecular dramas of Calderon; but the *Autos*, the moſt wonderful of all his productions, and the only ones (with but two exceptions) which the great poet himſelf thought worthy of his reviſion,* have been paſſed over, I may ſay, in almoſt utter ſilence.† One of them has been admirably ana-

* Vera Taſſis mentions that Calderon corrected the proofs of the two dramas which he allowed to be printed in the forty-ſixth volume of the *Comedias de Varios Autores*. A ſmall number out of one hundred and twenty. The *Autos* which he prepared for the preſs are contained in the volume of 1690 alluded to in the text.

† Even German enthuſiaſm, which has done ſo much for the *Comedias* of Calderon, has ſhrunk from the difficult taſk of dealing with the *Autos*. I know of but two writers who have given a tranſlation of any of them. The firſt is J. F. von Eichendorff, who publiſhed eleven of them in his *Geiſtliche Schauſpiele von Don Pedro Calderon de la Barca*, Stuttgart, 1846-53. The other is Ludwig Braunfels, who publiſhed two little volumes of tranſlations from Lope de Vega, Tirſo de Molina and Calderon, at Frankfort-on-the-Main in 1856. The ſecond volume contains the Auto *La Cena de Balthaſar*, previouſly tranſlated by Eichendorff in the original *aſonantes*, which Braunfels

lyſed in proſe by Mr. Ticknor ;* another in the Rambler :† two or three have been meagrely and frigidly condenſed into a few lines by Southey ;‡ and Siſmondi, who condeſcended only to read one of them out of ſeventy three, has favoured us with an outline of that one, which is characterized by his uſual want of ſympathy or appreciation. This neglect, perhaps, is not to be wondered at, conſidering how very ſlight, after all, if we take into account their number and variety, has been the notice which his ſecular dramas have as yet received from Britiſh writers. Though it is not at all improbable, that, had the ſame attention, ſuch as it is, been devoted to the *Autos*, which has been given to the *Comedias*, a far greater amount of curioſity and intereſt would be felt towards Calderon than any preſentation of his merely ſecular dramas has yet ſucceeded in awakening. This opinion, expreſſed in different language in the introductory remarks which I prefixed to *The Sorceries of Sin* as originally publiſhed in the Atlantis,§ has received the ſtrongeſt confirmation from an obſervation of Mr. Ticknor's, contained in a letter which he had the kindneſs to addreſs to me ſhortly after the appearance of *The Sorceries of Sin* in the ſcientific and literary journal to which I have alluded. Contraſting my former labours upon Calderon with my later, and encouraging me to proceed in the new path, Mr. Ticknor ſays :—" With the two volumes of your tranſlations from Calderon's plays, which you publiſhed in 1853, I have been familiar from their firſt appearance, and very thankful that you ventured on the bold undertaking. But this verſion of the *Encantos*

---

rejects as being unſuited to the genius even of the German language. *Los Encantos de la Culpa* is tranſlated by Eichendorff under the title *Der Sünde Zauberei*, in the ſecond volume (p. 315) of his work. The German tranſlations of the *Comedias* are numerous. I have in my own poſſeſſion excellent ones by Auguſtus Schlegel, Schach the hiſtorian, Gries, Malſburg, Martin, Barman, Schmid, Schumacher, and others.

* *The Divine Orpheus*. Hiſtory of Spaniſh Literature, v. ii. p. 323.

† *Poiſon and Antidote*, Rambler, Dec. 1855.

‡ Common Place Book, ſecond ſeries, p. 253.

§ No. IV. July, 1859.

de la Culpa, with its *aſonantes*, is much more intereſting as a work of art, and more important. Allow me, then, to expreſs the hope that you will go on and tranſlate more of the *Autos*. Nothing can, I think, give a clearer idea of what is moſt characteriſtic in Spaniſh literature, or give foreigners a more juſt idea of its peculiar power." This important teſtimony to the attractiveneſs of the *Autos* in themſelves, and to a certain ſucceſs which has attended my attempt to transfer one of them, with its peculiar and varied verſification, into Engliſh, I confeſs I print here with great, and, I think, not unjuſtifiable pride. Though the time and labour neceſſary to complete the long dramas contained in this volume have not left me leiſure to include another *Auto* in this collection, I truſt that what is here preſented, by its ſtrict and rigid adherence to thoſe principles of tranſlation which in the ſmaller piece have obtained the approval of ſo eminent an authority, will ſhow how highly I value it, and how earneſtly I have again ſtruggled to deſerve it.

The preciſe time at which the firſt volume of the *Autos* was publiſhed appears to be a matter of ſome uncertainty. But two collected editions have been made in Spain, one in 1717, in ſix volumes, 4to., the other in 1759-60, alſo in 4to. On the title-pages of both editions they are called *Obras Poſthumas*, and are repreſented as being then firſt publiſhed. This is true no doubt of the greater number of them, the manuſcripts of all having been preſerved in the archives of the corporation of Madrid, whoſe property, for the purpoſes of the Corpus Chriſti feſtivities, they were. This property the municipality parted with on the 31ſt of May, 1717, to Don Pedro de Pando y Mier, for the ſum of ſixteen thouſand reals, and it was by him that the firſt collection was made.* Although the preface which Calderon prepared himſelf for the firſt volume of the

* The *Autos* have never been republiſhed out of Spain. The edition of Keil contains only the vague alluſion of Vera Taſſis as to their number. In Spain itſelf they have not yet been included in the valuable *Biblioteca de Autores Eſpañoles* ſtill in courſe of publication, though promiſed by Señor Hartzenbuſch in the preface to his edition of the *Comedias*, (p. xx.) and more recently by Don Juſto de Sancha in the notice prefixed

Autos is given in the two editions above mentioned, the volume itſelf is not alluded to, and ſeems to be unknown in Spain, if I may judge from the ſilence obſerved towards it in one of the lateſt publiſhed volumes of the *Biblioteca de Autores Eſpañoles*,* where the uſual ſtatement is made of the *Autos* being *firſt* publiſhed in 1717. Having picked up a few years ago, on a Dublin book-ſtall, a volume of the *Autos* publiſhed in 1690,† I took the liberty, in my paper in the Atlantis, of calling the attention of Mr. Ticknor to the fact, he having ſtated, in his Hiſtory of Spaniſh Literature (v. ii. p. 319, *note* 25), that " the *Autos*, being the property of the city of Madrid, and annually repreſented, were not permitted to be printed for a long time (Lara Prólogo). They were firſt publiſhed in 1717, in 6 volumes, 4to., and they fill the ſame number of volumes in the edition of 1759-60, 4to." This correction, if I may call it ſo, I made with very great diffidence and deference, and I was relieved beyond meaſure at finding Mr. Ticknor not only received my obſervations with indulgence, but favoured me with the following moſt intereſting and valuable information upon the ſubject :—

" What you ſay of the confuſion that you find in my notice of the firſt publication of the Autos is partly true. When I wrote my Hiſtory of Spaniſh Literature, I had not ſeen the twelve Autos publiſhed in 1690 from a MS. that ſeems to have been prepared by Calderon as early as

to his *Romancero y Cancionero Sagrados*, Madrid, 1855, p. vi. If well edited, this volume would form one of the moſt intereſting of the ſeries. The date " 31ſt of May, 1717," in the text, I have taken from the work referred to in the next note. Mr. Ticknor, in his letter, gives the date, 31*ſt of March*, 1716. The name of the aſſignee of the copyright in that work is given *Prado* (inſtead of *Pando*) y Mier. The correct name is ſupplied in Mr. Ticknor's letter, and is found at the bottom of the fly-leaf of each volume of the edition of 1759-60, containing the *Fee de erratas*.

* *Dramaticos Poſteriores a Lope de Vega*, t. i. Note to *Chronological Catalogue of Dramatic Authors from Calderon to Canizares*, p. xxxvii.

† *Autos Sacramentales Alegoricos y Hiſtoriales. Dedicados al Patriarca San Juan de Dios, compueſtos por Don Pedro Calderon de la Barca, &c.* En Madrid: por Juan Garcia Infanzon, año 1690.

1676; but a few years ago, at Florence, I picked up a copy, together with a copy of the Comedias publifhed by Vera Taffis in nine volumes between 1683 and 1694. From thefe fources and from odd volumes of the Comedias *de Diferentes Autores*, going back to 1633, and the volumes publifhed by Calderon's brother Jofeph, I intend to give as good an account as I can of the firft editions, whether fpurious or genuine, of all Calderon's dramas, religious and fecular, in the third American edition of my Hiftory, now in the prefs. Of courfe, I fhall ufe in it what Hartzenbufch has fo well done.

"But there ftill remains fome obfcurity about the matter..... When Calderon, in July, 1680, gave the Duke de Veraguas the lift of his dramas, which was publifhed in the *Obelifco* of Lara in 1683, the twelve Autos are marked as *imprefos*. But I know of no edition of them earlier than that of 1690, where they all appear, but *in a different order* from the one to which they ftand in the lift, which is, after all, the true foundation for all difcuffions about Calderon's dramas. It is plain, that, when he collected them for publication, he had the purpofe of making more than one volume. The prefatory matter fhows this, as you have well obferved. But I know of nothing of the fort, except the volume of 1690, until the 31ft of March, 1716, when the City of Madrid—Como legataria del Doctor D. Pedro Calderon de la Barca—gave or fold the right of printing them *all* to Pedro de Pando y Mier, after which everything is plain. Now can you give me any indication of the publication of any of Calderon's Autos earlier than the laft date, except that of the twelve in 1690? If you can you will add another obligation to the many I owe you already.

"My only conjecture in relation to the matter is, that the twelve *Autos* of 1690 were *printed* in 1676; but that the prefatory matter in the firft four leaves was not printed until the volume was *publifhed* in 1690, where the title-page fhows that no fubfequent volume was likely to be added; the city of Madrid having then the right of property in them, which it did not part with until nineteen years later. But I do not much rely on this. Calderon was very loofe in his ftatements about his dramas and his unwillingnefs to have them publifhed."

The information afked for by Mr. Ticknor, in the above valuable bibliographical note, it is fcarcely neceffary to fay I was unable to fupply; and to the few obfervations I ventured to make upon the fubject, Mr. Ticknor was good enough to refer in a fubfequent letter which he favoured me with, a paffage from which I here fubjoin, as all that is likely to be ever known about the matter.

"The queftion of the firft publication of the *Autos* is, as you fay, a puzzling one, and I think will never be fettled to abfolute certainty. I rely little on Lara's Obelifco Funebre, becaufe there are certainly feveral grofs miftakes in it. Calderon's ftatements, too, I have found are not always to be trufted, and as for Taffas, aprobaciones &c., I have many times had as much trouble with them in other cafes as in this. My general impreffion, therefore, is that the Autos of 1690 were the firft publifhed, and that nothing was done earlier except to prepare them for the prefs, and get the needful permiffions to print them, beginning this work in 1676."

An allufion has been made in one of the notes to the *Catalogo Cronologicoy Alfabetico* by Don Ramon de Mefonero Romanos (prefixed to his *Dramaticos Pofteriores a Lope de Vega*, t. I. pp. xxxvii. to liii.) of dramas and dramatifts in Spain from 1635 to 1740. The number of Calderon's *Comedias* fet down in this lift is 126, which includes thofe dramas in which Calderon was affifted by other poets, as well as thofe of which no copies are now known to exift; among others the *Don Quixote de la Mancha*, the lofs of which is fo much to be regretted. The names of 84 *Autos* are given, being eleven more than the number contained in the fix quarto volumes of 1717 or 1759-60, which I have mentioned as being but 73. There is certainly fome confufion in this lift, which contains the names of fourteen *Autos* not to be found in the fix quartos juft alluded to, omits two which thofe volumes contain, and alters the names of two others, if, indeed, thefe laft are not different *Autos* altogether.

Among the *new Autos* is one called *Devocion de la Cruz*, which muft not be confounded with the terrible tragedy of that name which Bouterwek fo ftrangely miftook for an *Auto*, as mentioned in the introduction to my tranflation of *The Devotion of the Crofs* in this volume. Another is called *Cruz en la Sepultura*, the very name under which *The Devotion of the Crofs* was firft publifhed in the edition of Huefca, 1633, as fully defcribed in the fame introduction. The expectation of new treafure, however, which this lift awakens adds greatly to the anxiety which Spanifh fcholars feel for the long-promifed republication of them in the *Library of Spanifh Authors.*

It only remains for me to add that my reafon for felecting *Los Encantos de la Culpa* in preference to others of at leaft equal, if not fuperior, brilliancy, was its connection with *El Mayor Encanto Amor*, and the intereft I felt, and which I am fure others will feel, at tracing the ingenuity and marvellous frefhnefs with which Calderon takes up the fame theme, which one would think he had exhaufted in the longer drama, and reprefenting it anew in a more wonderful and original manner than at firft. The remarks of Dean Trench on this fubject, in his admirable effay on the genius of Calderon, are fo appofite, that I make no fcruple of transferring them here:—

"The manner in which Calderon ufes the Greek Mythology is exceedingly interefting. He was gifted with an eye fingularly open for the true religious element, which, however overlaid and debafed, is yet to be detected in all inferior forms of religion. Thefe religions were to him the veftibules through which the nations had been guided till they reached the temple of the abfolute religion, where God is worfhipped in Chrift. The reaching out and feeling after an unknown truth, of which he detected fomething in the fun-worfhip of the Peruvians,* he

* See his *Daybreak in Copacabana.*

recognized far more diſtinctly in the more human, and therefore more divine, mythology and religion of ancient Greece. It may be that the genuine Caſtilian alienation from the Jew, which was not wanting in him, may in part have been at work when he extols, as he often loves to do, the ſuperior readineſs of the Gentile world, as contraſted with the Jewiſh church, to receive the proffered ſalvation, its greater receptivity of the truth. But whether this may have had any ſhare in the matter or not, it is a theme to which he is conſtantly in theſe *Autos* recurring, and which he loves under the moſt various aſpects to preſent. And generally he took a manifeſt delight in finding or making a deeper meaning for the legends and tales of the claſſical world, ſeeing in them the ſymbols and unconſcious prophecies of Chriſtian truth. He had no miſgivings, therefore, but that theſe would yield themſelves freely to be moulded by his hands. He felt that in employing them he would not be drawing down the ſacred into the region of the profane; but elevating that which had been profaned into its own proper region and place. Theſe legends of heathen antiquity ſupply the allegorical ſubſtratum for ſeveral of his *Autos*. Now it is *The True God Pan*, or Perſeus reſcuing Andromeda, or Theſeus deſtroying the Labyrinth, or Ulyſſes defying the Enchantments of Circe, or the exquiſite mythus of Cupid and Pſyche. Each in turn ſupplies him with ſome new poetical aſpect under which to contemplate the very higheſt truth of all." *

* *Life's a Dream: The Great Theatre of the World.* From the Spaniſh of Calderon. With an Eſſay on his Life and Genius. By Richard Chenevix Trench. London, 1856, p. 96.

PERSONS REPRESENTED.

El Hombre.	The Man.
La Culpa.	Sin.
La Lascivia.*	Voluptuousness.*
La Lisonja.	Flattery.
El Entendimiento.	The Understanding.
La Penitencia.	Penance.
El Olfato.	The Smell.
El Oído.	The Hearing.
El Tacto.	The Touch.
El Gusto.	The Taste.
La Vista.	The Sight.
Músicos.	*Musicians.*
Acompanamiento.	*Chorus, &c.*

* This character, though taking a part in the *Auto,* is not included in the list of *Personas* in the edition of 1759-60, from which I print.

AUTO SACRAMENTAL ALEGORICO,

INTITULADO

LOS ENCANTOS DE LA CULPA.

Suena un Clarin, y se descubre una Nave, y en ella el Hombre *el* Entendimiento, *y los* Cinco Sentidos.

El Entendimiento.

N la anchurosa Plaza
Del mar del Mundo, oy hombre te amenaza
Gran tormenta.

El Oído.

Yo he sido
De tus cinco sentidos el Oido,
Y assi el primero siento
Bramar las ondas, y gemir el viento.

La Vista.

Yo, que he sido la Vista,
Que al Sol los rayos perspicáz conquista,
Desde lexos diviso
Uno, y otro uracán, á cuyo viso
En esta cristalina
Campaña te previene fatál ruina.

El Tacto.

El Tacto soy, á horrores te provoco,
Pues yá cercanos los peligros toco.

THE SACRAMENTAL ALLEGORICAL AUTO,

ENTITLED

THE SORCERIES OF SIN.

A Trumpet ſounds, and a Ship is diſcovered at ſea. In it are the MAN, *the* UNDERSTANDING, *and the* FIVE SENSES.

The Underſtanding.

UPON the boundleſs plain of the world's wide ſea,
O Man! this day doth darkly threaten thee
A mighty tempeſt.

The Hearing.

I who am the Hearing
'Mong thy five Senſes call'd, perceive the nearing
Of the impending ſtorm; to me is known
Firſt when the waves grow hoarſe and winds begin to groan.

The Sight.

I who am call'd the Sight—
Swift victor of the great Sun's golden light,—
With power to look between
Each whirlwind wild that breaks the blue ſerene,
Foreſeeing, can behold the coming woe
That on this cryſtal plain this day thou'rt doom'd to know.

The Touch.

The Touch am I, harrowing thy ſoul ſo much,
That dangers cloſing round thee ſeem to touch.

El Olfato.
El Olfato te dice, que ſe crea
El humedo vapor de la maréa.
El Guſto.
Yo en trance tan injuſto,
Con ſer el Guſto, eſtoy aqui ſin guſto.
El Oído.
Gran tormenta corremos.
El Entendimiento.
En el Mar de la vida nos perdémos.

El Tacto.
Larga aquella mayor.
El Olfato.
Iza el Trinquete.
El Guſto.
A la Triza.
El Oído.
A la Eſcolta.*
La Viſta.
Al Chafaldete.
El Entendimiento.
En alterados hielos
Corre tormenta el hombre.
Todos.
Piedad, Cielos!
El Hombre.
En el Texto Sagrado,
Quantas veces las aguas ſe han nombrado,
Tantos doctos Varones
Las ſuelen traducir tribulaciones,
Con que la humana vida
Navega zozobrada, y ſumergida.
El Hombre ſoy, á aſtucias inclinado,
Y por ſerlo, oy Ulíſes me ha nombrado,
Que en Griego decir quiere
Cauteloſo: y aſſi, quien oy quiſiere

* Should obviouſly be *Eſcota.*

The Smell.

Smell, too, proclaims how near doth ruin glide,
Even by the humid vapours of the tide.

The Taſte.

For ſuch a tumult of the ſea and ſky
No taſte I feel, though Taſte itſelf am I.

The Hearing.

We run before the wind.

The Underſtanding.

Storm-toſt,
Upon the ſea of life our bark is loſt.

The Touch.

Looſen the mainſheet!

The Smell.

Hoiſt the foreſail, ho!

The Taſte.

To the cable!

The Hearing.

To the tack-rope!

The Sight.

Let the clew-lines go!

The Underſtanding.

Over the waves by mighty tempeſts driven,
Man ſtruggles on.

All.

Have pity, gracious Heaven!

The Man.

In the ſacred text do we
Find frequent mention of the waves of the ſea,
Which learnèd doctors all tranſlate
The tribulations of this mortal ſtate,
Through which in ſtormy ſtrife
Struggles ſubmerged and toſt the bark of human life.
I then am Man, to craft and cunning prone,
And therefore by Ulyſſes' name am known,
As if a Grecian ſynonym it were
For cautious ſenſe; therefore if any here
Wiſh to track well the ſtraits my fate goes through,
Let him Ulyſſes' ſtory keep in view:

Correr las lineas de la ſuerte mia,
De Ulíſes ſiga en mí la Alegoría :
Y los que en una parte
Me llamaron viador, viendo mi arte,
Y en otra navegante, que el camino
Del Mar diſcurro ſiempre peregrino,
Dando ocaſion á que ningun viviente
Se admire de peligro tan urgente :
Y aſsi nadie ſe eſpante,
Que Ulíſes peregrino, y navegante,
Con inquietud violenta,
Corra tanta tormenta,
Confuſos, y perdidos
En mis tribulaciones mis ſentidos.

El Oído.

Solo ſe eſcuchan en la ſelva fria
Ráfagas, que nos dán por travesía.

La Viſta.

Solo ſe vén en eſſos orizontes
Montes, que ſe deſhacen ſobre montes.

El Tacto.

Solo ſe tocan ondas, con quien ſube
El mar, que nace mar, á morir nube.

El Olfato.

Uno ſon yá los dos azules velos.

El Guſto.

Qué nos vamos á pique.

Todos.

Piedad, Cielos !

El Entendimiento.

Si los llamais, ſerenidades crea
Vueſtro temor cobarde, y que no ſea
Eſte Baxél, que en pielagos ſe mueve,
Sepulcro de criſtal, tumba de nieve,
Que el Cielo, á humildes voces ſiempre abierto,
Al naufragio Piloto es felíz Puerto.

El Guſto.

Acordemonos dél, aora que eſtamos
En rieſgo los que el Mundo navegamos.

Then thofe who ca!l me at one part
Of my courfe a wayfarer, feeing my art,
A mariner at another, day by day
Pilgrim-like treading over the fea's falt way,
Will wonder not at th' extremity
Of danger, which none living 'fcaped but he;
And thus without a fear,
A pilgrim and a voyager,
You may behold Ulyffes braving
The fea's unreft, the tempeft's raving,—
See him in me confufed and loft,
And by my Senfes girded like a hoft.

The Hearing.

The wild gufts on this frozen foreftry
Of mafts fide-ftriking lift alone to thee.

The Sight.

Nought can be feen on the horizon wild,
But mountains upon yielding mountains piled.

The Touch.

Nought can be touch'd but waves, if waves they be
Which die in the air a cloud, though born a fea.

The Smell.

Commingled are their veil's deep azure dyes.

The Tafte.

We ftrike! we fink!

All.

Have pity, O ye fkies!

The Underftanding.

If upon Heaven you call, your prayers, though weak,
Will of themfelves create the calm we feek,
Bringing this bark, which through the waves doth go,
A cryftal fepulchre, a tomb of fnow,
Safe to that holy haven it lays bare
To fhipwreck'd pilot's eyes—fo ftrong is humble prayer.

The Tafte.

Oh! may it grant it foon, for here are we
Toft in extremeft rifk upon the world's wide fea.

El Entendimiento.

Dadle voces en tales desconsuelos,
Pues él siempre responde.

Todos.

Piedad, Cielos!

El Oïdo.

Yá escucho, que se llena
De paz la vaga habitacion serena.

El Gusto.

Y el Mar tranquilo, yá con ira suma
No riñe, sino juega con la espuma.

El Entendimiento.

Todo el ayre es cambiantes, y reflexos.

La Vista.

Todo es serenidad, y yá no lexos,
Antes que todos miro
Cumbres, que tocan al azul Zafiro,
Del Mar burlando la sañuda guerra.

El Entendimiento.

Zelages se descubren: tierra, tierra.

El Hombre.

Prudente Entendimiento,
Piloto, que al govierno estás atento
De aquesta humana Nave,
Que nadar, y bolar á un tiempo sabe,
Siendo en mansiones de atomos de espumas,
Sin escamas Delfin, Cisne sin plumas,
Pón la Proa en aquella
Montaña, en quien la mas luciente Estrella
Peligra, pues su cumbre
Es en donde se roba al Sol la lumbre:
Y assi sus puertas inconstantes cierra
A este humano Baxél.

Todos.

A tierra, á tierra.

Desembarcan, y desaparece la Nave.

El Hombre.

Humanos sentidos mios,

The Underſtanding.

In ſuch affliction let its vault be riven
Still with your cries, 'twill anſwer.

All.

Save us, Heaven.

The Hearing

Already calm comes on, the wild winds ceaſe,
And o'er our heaving home glides the ſoft breath of peace.

The Taſte.

The ſea grows tranquil—ſmoothly ſilver'd o'er,
It plays with the foam with which it fought before.

The Underſtanding:

Bright grows the air with many a changeful hue.

The Sight.

All grows ſerene, and lo! not far I view—
I firſt of all—the bare
Peaks of tall hills, which touch the azure air,
Now mocking the far wave-war on the ſtrand.

The Underſtanding.

Now the clouds part—it is the land! the land!

The Man.

O prudent pilot Underſtanding!
Thou who haſt been ſo long commanding
This bark of human life, this boat,
That at the ſelf-ſame time can fly or float,
Being upon the foam-flakes it reſts on,
A ſcaleleſs dolphin, and a plumeleſs ſwan,
Beneath yon mountain turn its prow,
Beneath yon peak which on its brow
Wears a ſtar of brighteſt ray—
That point whoſe light is filch'd even from the God of Day—
There where it ſeems to ſtretch a curvèd hand
To claſp this human bark.

All.

To land! to land!

[*All diſembark and the veſſel diſappears.*

The Man.

Human Senſes mine, my vaſſals,

Vaſſallos, que componeis
La Republica del Hombre,
Que mundo pequeño es.
Generoſo Entendimiento,
Piloto de eſſe Baxél,
Que ſobre el campo del mar
Monſtruo ſe alimenta, pues
Quanto bate el viento es ave,
Quanto baña el agua es pez.
Compañeros de mi vida,
Dexad el mar, no porque
Nueſtra peregrinacion
En la tierra, que aora veís,
Aya de ceſſar, ſupueſto
Que ſiempre tengo de ſer
Yo Peregrino del Mar,
Y de la Tierra tambien:
Dexad fiada eſſa Nave
A la diſcrecion cruel
De un embate, y otro embate,
De un baybén, y otro baybén.
Seguramente amarrada
Con las Ancoras eſté,
Que de quien Piloto ha ſido
El Entendimiento, aunque
Aora le dexe, quizá
Le avré meneſter deſpues:
Y entremos á examinar
Eſtos montes, que han de ſer
Puerto de nueſtra fortuna.

Who together all compoſe*
Man's Republic, he a little
World himſelf, as all do know.
Generous Underſtanding, thou
Pilot of this myſtic boat,
Changeful monſter, paſturing well
Over the ſea-way, ſwift or ſlow,—
Being a bird when winds it play'd
with,
Being a fiſh when ſeas waſh'd o'er.
Ye, companions of my life,
Leave the ſea, but not therefóre
Think that our long wandering ceaſes
In the land that you behold—
Since ſtill moving onward ever
Muſt my fate be, I ſuppoſe—
Over the earth to move a pilgrim—
Over the ſea likewiſe to go:—
Leave this bark awhile entruſted
To the cruel care and cold
Of waves daſhing wildly together,
Of foam writhing in hoſtile foam,
But let anchors firm and ſtrong
Safely ſtill the veſſel hold,
For the pilot Underſtanding,
Though he leaves her for the ſhore,
May perchance again require her:—
Let us enter now, and go
Curious through theſe hills which
Heaven
Gives our fortunes as their port.

* The metre changes here to one which is ſeldom found in Calderon's ſecular dramas, but frequently in the Autos. It is a *ſingle* aſonante vowel rhyme in the laſt ſyllable of each alternate line, which, as in the more uſual *double* aſonantes, is kept up through the entire ſcene. It appears to be the oldeſt form of the aſonante, being found in the earlieſt primitive ballads, ſuch as that of *Vergilios*, of *Count Arnaldos*, of *The Infanta of France*, &c. (See Duran's *Romancero General*, Madrid, 1849, t. i. p. 151.) In the original of this ſcene, the vowel uſed is *e*, which is an effective one in Spaniſh; for this, which is comparatively weak in Engliſh, I have ſubſtituted the ſtronger *o*. The laſt ſcene of *The Devotion of the Croſs* is in this *ſingle* aſonante vowel rhyme.

El Gusto.
Qué tierra es esta?
El Tacto.
No sé;
Mas quiera el Cielo que sea
Tiro, para que aya en él
Olandas, sedas, y ropas,
Donde regalado esté
Mi tacto.
El Olfato.
¿Mejor no fuera,
Que fuera á tanta altivéz
La gran India de Sabá,
Donde huviera para oler
Yo, suavissimas Aromas?
El Oído.
Ninguno ha pedido bien,
Pedid la India Oriental,
Porque habitan su vergél
Dulces Aves, cuyos cantos
Sonora musica dén,
Que regalen mis oídos.
La Vista.
¿Necios sois, pues no quereis
Que sea Tiro, y que aya aqui
Oro, y diamantes, en que
Mi vista halle mas reflexos,
Que el Sol en su rosicler?

El Gusto.
Mal aveis deseado todos
En no desear, y creer,
Que sea la Tierra de Egypto
Essa tierra, para que
En ella hallémos las ollas,
Que en ella déxo Moysés,
Pues no ay en el Mundo gusto
Sin comer, y sin beber.

The Taste.
What land's this?
The Touch.
I cannot say.
Heaven but grant 'tis Tyre: if so
I shall find abundant here—
Silks, fine linen, purple robes,
Things my touch delights to feel.

The Smell.
Were it not better then to hope
That 'twill prove some Arab plain—
Some Sabæan scented shore,
Where the sweetest odours may
Glad the happier sense I own?—
The Hearing.
No one yet has wish'd aright:
Wish the land through which we roam
May be beauteous eastern Ind,
In whose vocal bowers and groves
Sweet birds' songs may fill my ears
With melodious music tones.
The Sight.
Idle are your wishes all,
Since you wish not for the zone
Where the diamonds glisten bright
And the land is rich with gold:
Sweeter to the sight are gems
Than the morn on roses throned.
The Taste.
Badly have you all desired
In not wishing this alone,—
That this land should prove to be
Egypt's comfortable coasts,
Where perchance we'll find the flesh-pots
Left by Moses long ago,
Since the world hath little better
Than good drink and meat to show.

El Entendimiento.
¡Qué como humanos ſentidos
Todos deſeado aveis
Hallar cada uno el objeto,
Que mas conviene á ſu ſér!
¿No fuera mejor que fuera
La toſca Tebayda, en quien
La penitencia ſe hallára,
Riyendoſe del poder
De las Cortes populoſas,
Pueſto que tan cierto es,
Que ſin pena de eſta vida
No aya en la eterna placer?

El Hombre.
¡Y qué como Entendimiento
Has hablado tú! ¿Qué eſtés
Siempre aconſejando penas
A mis ſentidos? ¿No vés,
Que ſon ſentidos humanos,
Y que al ſin es meneſter
Alivios, que los diviertan
De las fatigas en que
Han nacido?

El Entendimiento.
¿Cómo tú,
Siendo ſu Señor, y Rey,
Buelves por ellos? ¿Yá olvidas
Aquel paſſado baybén
De la fortuna, en quien viſte
La Troya del Mundo arder,
De adonde te ſaqué yo?
¿Yá te olvidas, que deſpues
En una tormenta viſte
Tus ſentidos padecer
Con tantas tribulaciones?
¿Yá no te acuerdas de que
El Cielo te libró de ellas?

The Underſtanding.
Human Senſes, oh! how each,
Each and all are prompt and prone
To deſire this land may offer
What its inſtinct longs for moſt!
Were it not better that it prove
The Thebais wild and lone,
Deſerts where pale Penance may
Trample down the pride of courts—
Since there's nought more ſure than this—
We through temporal pain alone
Can expect th' eternal bliſs?

The Man.
Why for ever words of woe
Speak'ſt thou, Underſtanding, thus?
Why for ever ſhadows throw
On the path my Senſes take?
Doſt thou not their nature know,
That they're human, and require
Something ſoothing to conſole—
Something ſweet to eaſe the pangs
That from birth-time they have known?

The Underſtanding.
Canſt thou ſpeak in their defence,
Thou who art their King and Lord?
Can it be thou haſt forgot
That late peril ſcarcely flown,
When from out the world's dread Troy
Wrapp'd in ſinful flames, alone
Thou wert reſcued, and by me?—
Haſt thou too forgot the roar
Of the wild waves, and the plight
Of thy ſenſes ſuffering ſore,
And that Heaven it was that drew
Them and thee from their control?

El Gusto.
No tienes que responder,
Yo responderé por tí.
Prudentissima vejez,
Que aunque somos de una edad,
Solo tú cano te vés,
Porque te ha hecho tu podrida
Condicion encanecer:
¿Aora sabes tú, que el hombre,
Quando en peligro se vé
De la enfermedad prolija,
Del enemigo cruel,
De la perdida de hacienda,
De la esperanza del bien,
Solo se acuerda del Cielo,
Y que se olvida despues,
Que lo uno esté mejorado,
U essotro alcanzado esté?

El Entendimiento.
Essa ingratitud le pienso
Quitar yo, que aqueste fue
Del Entendimiento oficio.

El Hombre.
Mi Gusto os ha dicho bien:
Sentidos, seguid al Gusto,
Y no arguyais mas con él,
Sino esta tierra á que avemos
Llegado, á reconocer
Entrad. Pues eres la Vista,
Delante de todos vé,
Mira si acaso descubres
Poblacion. Tú, que eres fiel,
Oído, mira si oyes
Voces, que noticia dén
De gente, ó ganado. Tú,
Del suavissimo placer

*The Taste.**
Do not *thou* reply: to *me*
Leave the answer and the tone.—
O thou cautious eld and wise,
Thou whose hair is white and hoar,
Thou alone of all our band,
Though thine age is not more old—
'Tis thy colder constitution
Doubtless caps thy head with snow,—
Hast thou yet to know that Man,
When some peril he beholds,
When some tedious sickness threatens,
Or some more malicious foe,
Or the loss of worldly wealth,
Or perchance the hope of gold,
Only then remembers Heaven,
And remembers it no more,
When his health he hath recover'd,
Or hath reach'd the wish'd-for goal?

The Understanding.
Be it mine, O Man, to free thee
From ingratitude so low,—
'Tis thy Understanding's duty.

The Man.
Taste, thy words are wise and bold:—
Follow Taste, my Senses all,
And with *him* dispute no more,—
But this land to reconnoitre,
On whose bosom we are thrown,
Enter now: since thou, O Sight,
Seest many a mile before,
Look if thou, by any chance,
Canst the dwellers here behold.
Hearing, thou my faithful friend,
List if thou canst catch the tones
Of human voices borne afar,
Or the pasturing herd's deep low.

* *To the Man.*

Con que eſſas flores reſpiran
El raſtro ſigue con él.
Mira ſi puedes topar
Algun blando lecho en quien
Deſcanſe. Y tú, Guſto, al fin,
Mira ſi hallas que comer,
Y todos buſcad delicias
Para mí.

El Entendimiento.

Aunque deſee,
Que halles, penitencia, yendo
A eſſo, la Culpa hallaréis.

La Viſta.

Yo veré ſi ay publacion. [*Vaſe.*

El Hombre.

Y yo me quedo ſin vér.

El Oído.

Yo eſcucharé ſi oygo voces. [*Vaſe.*

El Hombre.

Yo, auſente tú, nada oiré.

El Tacto.

Yo, ſi ay lecho en quien deſcanſes.

El Hombre. [*Vaſe.*

Yá yo no le he meneſter.

El Olfato.

Yo, ſi hallo blandos aromas. [*Vaſe.*

El Hombre.

Yá no tienes para qué.

El Guſto.

Yo, ſi hallo dulces manjares. [*Vaſe.*

El Hombre.

Aora no quiero comer,
Porque mientras vais voſotros
El Mundo á reconocer,
Al pie de eſte Cyprés quedo
Echado á dormir.

[*Echaſe al pie de un Cyprés.*

Thou whoſe rapture riſes ſweet
From each ſcented flower that blows,
Follow too the track with them :—
Some ſoft bed for my repoſe
Thou by gentle preſſure find,—
And the taſk, O Taſte, I'll throw
Upon thee of finding food.
All on ſeparate miſſions go,
Seeking ſweet delights for me.

The Underſtanding.

By another path I hoped
Thou wouldſt Penance find: purſuing
That, thou'lt find Sin's ſyren door.

The Sight.

I depart to look for people. [*Exit.*

The Man.

Blind I ſtay, ſince Sight hath flown.

The Hearing.

I to liſt if ſounds can reach me. [*Exit.*

The Man.

Since thou'rt gone, I hear no more.

The Touch.

I a bed in which to reſt thee. [*Exit.*

The Man.

None I need now for repoſe.

The Smell.

I to find delicious odours. [*Exit.*

The Man.

Now they're naught, how ſweet they
blow.

The Taſte.

I ſweet ſavoury food to ſeek for. [*Exit.*

The Man.

Now the thoughts of food I loathe.
Wherefore, whilſt you all depart
To explore this land unknown,
I, in ſleep, my weary body
At this cypreſs' foot ſhall throw.

[*He lies down.*

El Entendimiento.

Qué bien,
Para dormir, los ſentidos
Apartas de tí; pues es
Cierto, que queda ſin ellos
El que duerme: y qué bien fue
Cyprés el Arbol, que aqui
Tomaſte para tí, pues
Viene á ſer Arbol de muerte,
De quien el ſueño tambien
Es ſombra; y aunque dorados
Los ricos Catres eſtén,
En que deſcanſen los hombres,
Deſde el mendígo, haſta el Rey,
Aunque ſean de otras maderas,
Son Arboles de Cyprés.
Quedó el hombre ſin ſentido,
Y durmió; ¿ yá qué he de hacer?
Que aunque potencia del alma
Soy, y ella, que mortal no es,
Dormir no puede, eſte tiempo
Que yáze el hombre, tambien
Eſtoy yo ſin diſcurrir,
Sin percibir, ni entender.
Vaga mi imaginacion
Confuſas viſiones vé;
Y todo es tiniebla, y ſombras
Para mí el Mundo, porque
Sin los ſentidos no puedo
Actos de razon hacer:
Seguirélos, pues ſin mí
Se queda el hombre la vez
Que duerme, y que ſepultado
Temporal cadaver es. [*Vaſe.*

El Hombre.

Ay de mí! peſado ſueño,
No tanto me aflijas, ten
La violencia de las ſombras.
¿ Qué es lo que mis ojos vén

The Underſtanding.

Yes; 'tis right that thou ſhouldſt ſleep,
Since apart from thee, there prone,
Are thy Senſes; for 'tis certain
That the man who ſleeps doth hold
Them no longer in his keeping:
And the tree thou ſleep'ſt below,
Rightly hath thy choice ſelected,
Since the cypreſs long hath grown
Death's eſpecial tree; and ſleep
Is death's ſhadow as we know.
Thus though weary man may ſlumber
In rich couches gilded o'er,
Call the wood of which they're made
What you pleaſe, to king and clown
Cypreſs is it all the while.
Here then Man, by ſleep o'erthrown,
Lies inſenſate: this being ſo,
What remains for me to do?
Since although I am the ſoul's
Manifeſted power, and *that*
Deathleſs ſpark no ſleep can know,
Still while man thus lies, am I
Likewiſe left without diſcourſe,
Powerleſs to perceive or think.
Now my ſantaſy beholds
Viſions all confuſed and dim,
Darkneſs o'er the world is thrown,
Since without the Senſes, I
Loſe all reaſon and control:
I ſhall follow them, ſince Man,
While his eyes in ſleep are cloſed,
Without *me* remains, and buried
Thus, is for the while a corſe. [*Exit.*

The Man (aſleep).

Woe is me! oppreſſive dream,
Pain me not ſo much! withhold
Theſe thy ſhadows' violent rage.
What is this my eyes behold,

Sin viſta? Mas digo mal,
Que mis ſentidos cobré;
Si bien informes, y brutos,
En el punto que llegué
A vér eſtos fieros monſtruos,
Que me quieren deſhacer;
Me paſma advertir, que quando
Eſperaba, que cruel
Cada uno cebaſſe en mí,
Todos ſe echan á mis pies;
Por ſeñas dicen, que huya,
Que los quiero conocer
Parece; deſeſperados
Se entran al Monte otra vez.
Qué es eſto, Cielos!

Al irſe ſale el ENTENDIMIENTO *como aſſombrado.*

El Entendimiento.

Eſcucha,
Ulíſes, yo lo diré,
Que aunque eſtás aora incapáz
De ſentir, tocar, y vér,
Porque brutos tus ſentidos,
Y entorpecidos ſe vén,
Por los vicios, á que tú
Los diſte licencia; bien
Me entiendes: mas los del alma
Fuerza es que velando eſtén.
Apenas fuimos, Ulíſes,
Vagando aqueſte Orizonte
Tus compañeros, del Monte
Penetrando los Paíſes,
Quando un Palacio eminente

Though my ſight is gone?—Ah me!
Badly muſt my thoughts be told
Till my ſenſes I recover.
But I ſeem to ſee a ſwarm
Of miſshapen beaſts approach me,
Bent on draining my heart's gore.
When their cruel fangs my fear
Seems to faſten round my throat,
At my feet I ſee them kneeling
With ſubmiſſive reverence low:
They by ſigns appear to ſay,
Fly! oh! fly this fatal ſhore!
Then when they perceive that I
This their hidden meaning know,
In deſpair they all re-enter
The wild mountain waſte once more.
What is this? O Heavens!

As he ſtarts up, the UNDERSTANDING *enters amazed.*

The Underſtanding.

Ulyſſes,
Hear me, and thou ſoon art told.
For although thou haſt not now
Power to ſee, or ſeel, or hold,
Since thy Senſes have become
Torpid, brutaliſed, o'erthrown
By the vices that thou gav'ſt them
Leave to ſeek, yet ſtill I know
Thou canſt underſtand my meaning
Through the ſoul's inſtinctive force.*
Scarce had we, Ulyſſes, gone
This wild mountain's ſummit over,
Hope, ſome fair fields to diſcover,
Thy companions leading on,
When our ſight beheld with wonder

* The alternate vowel monorhymes terminate here, and the metre changes to the full conſonant rhyme as in the text.

Nueſtra viſta deſcubrió,
Cuya eminencia tocó
A las nubes con la frente.
Llegamos á ſus umbrales,
Y aviendo llegado á ellos,
En dos Eſquadrones bellos
De hermoſuras celeſtiales,
Vimos ſalirnos á hacer
Fieſtas á nueſtra fortuna,
Con varias muſicas una
Hermoſiſſima muger.
De paſſo la repetí
Nueſtra peregrinacion,
Que el uſo de la razon
Siempre me ha tocado á mí.
Ella, afablemente humana,
Dulcemente liſonjera,
A entender nos dió, que era
De eſtos Campos la Diana.
Mas yo, como Entendimiento
Soy, y á mi divino ſér
Siempre le toca tener
Natural conocimiento,
Conocí al inſtante, que era
La Culpa fiera, y cruel,
Que á habitar en un Verjél
Fue deſde la edad primera.
Aqui damas ſuyas ſon
Los vicios con que ella lidia,
Laſcivia, Gula, y Embidia,
Liſonja, y Murmuracion.
Mandonos agaſſajar
De eſtas damas, y ellas luego
Al mandato, ſi no al ruego,
Quiſieron executar:
Y con vicioſos placeres
Al momento nos brindaron;
Tus ſentidos, que ſe hallaron
Servidos yá de mugeres

A proud palace rich and fair,
For whoſe lofty roofs the air
Bade the gold clouds part aſunder.
We its beauteous threſholds nearing,
Reach'd them, and beheld, delighted,
Two fair ſquadrons diſunited
Of celeſtial nymphs appearing,
And with ſmiling looks of human
Sympathy for our diſtreſſes—
Muſic mingling its careſſes—
After them one beauteous woman.
Of our perils on the ſea,
Of our journeyings ending never,
Brief I ſpoke, ſince Reaſon ever
Throws that duty upon me.
Then her voice ſo ſoftly bland,
Yielding ſwift to pity's law,
Let us know, in her we ſaw
The Diana of this land.
I, the Underſtanding, who
To that part which is divine
Add a wit ſo keen and fine,
By my natural inſtinct knew
She was Sin, that fierce and fell
Monſter full of ravening rage,
She who when of earlieſt age
In a garden loved to dwell,
And her dames, to whoſe addreſs
All her wiles entruſteth ſhe,
Are Envy, Calumny, Gluttony,
Flattery, and Voluptuouſneſs.
Theſe, her ladies, then ſhe bade
To regale us,—a beheſt
Scarcely needed; the requeſt
Seem'd to make them but too glad,
Since upon the inſtant they
Flung their vicious wiles around them,
And thy Senſes, who thus found them
Served in this ſeductive way

Tan hermoſas, y tan bellas,
Sin vér que el Entendimiento
Alli ſe hallaba, al momento
Se conformaron con ellas.
La Embidia, que es toda enojos
Del bien que en los otros vé,
Viendo á la Viſta, porque
La Embidia, al fin, toda es ojos.
La Laſcivia, que ſe ofrece
En los alhagos cruel,
Brindó al Tacto, porque él
Las blanduras apetece.
La Murmuracion, que es quien
Lo malo vé, y no lo bueno,
Brindó al Olfato, que lleno
De eſte defecto le vén.
Solo por eſſo le igualo
Con cauſa al murmurador,
Que no alaba lo mejor,
Y hace lo malo mas malo.
La Gula al Guſto brindó,
Probarlo no es meneſter ;
Porque bien ſe dexa vér,
Que el Guſto á la Gula amó.
La Liſonja, mortal fiera
De las Cortes, al Oído
Brindó, que él objeto ha ſido
De toda voz liſonjera.
La Sobervia, con intento
De que el veneno que eſconde
Paſſaſſe á mí, porque es donde
Peligra el Entendimiento,
Me brindó ; mas ſin el fruto,
Que de mí eſtaba eſperando,
Por ſaber yo, que en pecando
Se convierte el hombre en bruto.
David lo diga, que atento
Eſte ſentir en él hallo,
Que el que peca es un cavallo,

By ſuch lovely ladies fair,
(Neither wiſhing nor demanding
Aid from me, the Underſtanding),
Yielded all, without a care.
Envy, who with agonies
Sees another's merit ſhine,
Pledged the Sight, becauſe in fine
Envy is herſelf all eyes.
Wantonneſs, that ever were
Cruel moſt when moſt careſſing,
Tempted Touch by her addreſſing,
Since he loves ſoft lures like her.
Calumny that doth reject
Good for bad, and falſe for true,
Smell ſelected, ſince he too
Labours 'neath the ſame defect :
If on this account alone,
He with Calumny ſhould mate,
That he ne'er doth celebrate
The better and the worſe makes known.
Gluttony the Taſte allured,
Little proof this needs from me,
Since that Taſte loves Gluttony
All the world is well aſſured.
Flattery was Hearing's choice,—
Flattery, that mortal peſt,
Known to courts, where he's the queſt
Of each falſe and flattering voice.
Pride, with full intent that I
Should her hidden poiſon drink,
(Underſtanding, Danger's brink
Neareth, when that nymph is nigh),
Came and pledged me, but the fruit
Hoped for ſo, ſhe fail'd in winning,
Since I know that man, by ſinning
Is tranſmuted to a brute.
David's ſong the ſinner tells,
If in ſin perſiſteth he,
Comes a beaſt of earth to be,

En quien no ay entendimiento.
Y ſue aſſi, que como fueron
Bebiendo, todos mudados
En fieras, y transformados
En varias formas ſe vieron.
Mas atencion deſde aqui,
Hombre, te pide mi acento;
Eſcucha á tu entendimiento,
Que es el que te habla.

El Hombre.

Dí.

El Entendimiento.

La Viſta, en Tigre cruel
Fue de la Embidia deſpojos,
Que eſte animal todo es ojos,
Bien lo publica ſu piel
Manchada de ellos; y quando
No baſte eſto, baſtará,
Que el Tigre muerte ſe dá,
Si oye múſica, rabiando.
Y el embidioſo, en ſus penas
Se dá muerte cada dia,
Si oye la dulce harmonia
Que hacen las dichas agenas.
El Tacto, que fue el objeto
Que á la Laſcivia creyó,
En Oſſo ſe convirtió,
Que eſte animal, imperfecto.
Sin forma, y ſin ojos nace:
Y el Apetito, á creer llego,
Que nace ſin forma, y ciego,
Pues tantos errores hace.
El Guſto (gloton hambriento)
En un bruto inmundo fue
Transformado; eſto porque
Solo á ſu comida atento
Vive, ſin que de ſu pecho
El hombre ſervicio adquiera,
Pues ha meneſter que muera

In whoſe ſoul no reaſon dwells.
Thus it was, as each, the bowl
Drank of poiſon'd bliſs deranged,
Quick to grovelling beaſts they changed,
Reft of ſenſe, of ſhape, of ſoul.
Thy attention, O thou weak
Man! my voice is ſtill demanding;
Liſten to thy Underſtanding,
Who doth ſpeak to thee.

The Man.

Still ſpeak.

The Underſtanding.

Sight, a tiger fierce did grow.
He, the keen-eyed Envy's prize,
Since an animal all eyes,
As its ſpotted ſkin doth ſhow,
Is the tiger, and we may
This additional reaſon add,
That the tiger dieth mad,
If he hears ſweet muſic play.
Thus the envious man doth feel
Every day the pangs of death,
If he heareth rumour's breath
Sweetly ſpeak another's weal.
Touch, that ſoon became the thrall
Of Deſire's laſcivious air,
Was transform'd into a bear—
An imperfect animal,
At its birth unform'd and blind—
As is Appetite, that makes,
Therefore, all its dread miſtakes
Sightleſs, formleſs, undefined.
Taſte, the hungry glutton, grew
Eaſily a filthy ſwine—
It a beaſt that doth incline
But to eat and eat anew,—
Long delaying to conduce
To man's benefit thereby,
Since 'tis needful he muſt die

Para ſerle de provecho.
El Olfato, que entregado
Se vió á la murmuracion,
Se convirtió en un Leon,
Que es quien rugidos ha dado.
Y finalmente, el Oído,
Que falſedades creyó
Liſonjeras, ſe miró
En Camaleon convertido:
Y el bruto, que vivir quiere
Del viento ſolo fiado,
Es el mas vivo traſlado
De la liſonja en que muere.

El Hombre.

Docto Entendimiento mio
En gran peligro me veo,
A mis ſentidos deſeo
Reſcatar con mi alvedrio,
Para vivir, pues que yo
No puedo de aqui auſentarme,
Que no tengo de dexarme
Compañeros, que me dió
Mi miſma naturaleza.
Y ſupueſto que perdidos
Todos mis cinco ſentidos
Eſtán en eſta aſpereza
De la culpa, entrar intento
A libertarlos, porque
Bien de la empreſſa ſaldré,
Si voy con mi Entendimiento.

El Entendimiento.

Pues que conmigo has de ir
A cobrarlos, ha de ſer
Con tres coſas que has de hacer.
Primeramente, pedir
Al Cielo perdon de que
Tan mal los aconſejaſte,
Que al rieſgo los entregaſte.
Otra, confeſſar que fue

Ere he turns to any uſe.
Calumny, that had thrown out
Lures to Smell, converted him
Into a lion, gaunt and grim,
Who, loud roaring, roams about.
Laſtly, Hearing, that had grown
But to live on what it heard,
Truſting every idle word,
Changed to a chameleon;
Since the being that but needs
For its life the air, be ſure
Is a lively portraiture
Of the ſenſe that Flattery feeds.

The Man.

O my guide in every ill!
'Mid the riſks that round me hover,
I my Senſes would recover
By the ranſom of my will,
If 'twere but to live, ſince I
Have no power by flight to ſave me,
If all thoſe whom Nature gave me,
As companions, forth not fly
With me from this fatal coaſt.
And ſuppoſing that within
This enchanted wild of ſin
My five Senſes may be loſt,
Still I'll enter, notwithſtanding,
Them to free, becauſe I know
I to victory muſt go,
Going with my Underſtanding.

The Underſtanding.

Since then to this dangerous taſk,
Led by me, you mean to run,
There are three things to be done.
In the firſt place, you muſt aſk
Heaven to pardon the expreſs
Sanction and unwiſe advice
Given by you, that they to Vice
Should entruſt them: next, confeſs

Tuya la culpa que ha avido,
Aunque ellos fueron, Ulíſes,
Los que entregarſe quiſieron.
Y otra, averſe arrepentido.

El Hombre.

Digo, que pido perdon
Del mal exemplo, (ay de mí!)
Que á mis ſentidos les dí:
Digo, que hago confeſſion
De la culpa que he tenido
De que ſe ayan entregado
A las manos del pecado,
Y que voy arrepentido.

Tocan Chirimías, y deſcubreſe un Arco Iris en un Carro, y en él la PENITENCIA, *y canta la Múſica.*

La Múſica.

Yá que el Hombre confieſſa ſu culpa,
Y arrepentido me pide perdon,
(O Penitencia!) pues eres el Iris,
Acude bolando á darle favor.

Penitencia.

Yá corro veloz
En el arco de Paz, en quien haces
Las amiſtades del hombre, y de Dios.

El Hombre.

¿Qué múſica tan ſonora
Es la que oímos los dos?

El Entendimiento.

Auxilio es que te dá Dios.

El Hombre.

¿Y aquel bello Arco, que aora
Sobre las nubes ſe aſſienta?

El Entendimiento.

Arco es, que la Paz abona,

That the fault was thine that caſt
Them into the ſnares of ſin,
They not loath to enter in,—
Let repentance be the laſt.

The Man.

I declare, for ſuch tranſgreſſion,
For the bad example given
To my Senſes, I aſk Heaven
To forgive me: next, confeſſion
For the fault, by whoſe event
Into Sin's foul hands they fell,
I declare aloud as well:
And that truly I repent.

There is a peal of Clarions, and a Rainbow appears; beneath it is a Chariot, and in it is PENANCE; *the Muſic ſings.*

The Muſic.

Now that Man his ſinful fault confeſſes,
And repenting aſks to be forgiven,
Fly, O Penance! fly, celeſtial Iris,
Grace to grant him once again from Heaven!

Penance.

Yes, adown the ſky,
On the arch of Peace I fly—
On the arch whoſe myſtic ſpan
Amity proclaims 'twixt God and man.

The Man.

Ah! that muſic ſo ſonorous
Which we hear, what may it be?—

The Underſtanding.

God's aſſiſtance aiding thee.

The Man.

And that beauteous Bow, that o'er us
Reſts on clouds its radiant form?

The Underſtanding.

Is the Bow that bringeth Peace—

Y que yá cessó pregona
El rigor de la tormenta.
Dios le puso por señal
De Paz entre si, y el hombre,
Y assi el verle no te assombre.
El Hombre.
¿Y la Ninfa Celestial,
Quién es, que saberlo espero?
El Entendimiento.
La Iris, Embaxatriz
Mas solicita, y felíz
Del Jupiter verdadero,
La que á los hombres embia
A consolar su dolencia.
El Hombre.
Pues quién es?
El Entendimiento.
La Penitencia;
Bien que en esta alegoría
Probado está con decir,
Que es la que con dulce nombre
Se pone entre Dios, y el hombre.

El Hombre.
Su voz bolvamos á oír.
La Música.
Pues el hombre confiessa, &c.
Penitencia.
Yá corro veloz, &c.
Christiano Ulíses, tus voces
En el Empyreo se oyeron,
Que ellas hasta él subir saben
Por las Escalas del viento.
Y viendo, que tus sentidos
Tan postrados, y deshechos
De la culpa están, y que es

Is the Bow that maketh ceafe
All the rigour of the ftorm.
God has placed it as a fign—
Peaceful fign—'twixt him and thee:
Therefore, Man, rejoice and fee.
The Man.
And the heavenly nymph divine,
Who is fhe? oh! make her known!
The Underftanding.
Iris, the Embaffadrefs,
Who with happy hafte doth prefs
Downward from the true Jove's throne,
Bears her hither, to confole
Man in all his mifery.
The Man.
And her name?—
The Underftanding.
Is Penance: fee
How this allegoric whole
Proves what has been faid before,—
She it is who comes in Heaven's high plan,
Mediating betwixt God and man.
The Man.
Let us hear her voice once more.
The Mufic.
Now that man, &c.
Penance.
Yes, adown the fky, &c.
Chriftian-born Ulyffes, higher
Than the heavens were heard thy accents,*
They well knowing how to climb there
By the wind's invifible ladder,
When, beholding that thy Senfes
Were by fin o'erthrown and fcatter'd,

* The afonante vowels in the original are, *e*, *o*, as in Vient*o*, Oy*e*r*o*n, &c.; for thefe I have fubftituted, in this fcene, *a*, *e*, as in *a*cc*e*nts, l*a*dd*e*r, ench*a*nt*e*d, &c.

El reſcatarlos tu intento,
El gran Jupiter me embia
Con auxilios, y conſuelos
A tí, para que la Culpa
Con ſus hechizos ſobervios
No pueda dañarte, y puedas
Tú poſtrarlos, y vencerlos.
Aqueſtas flores te traygo,

[*Dale un Ramillete de flores.*
Que es un Ramillete bello
De virtudes matizadas
Con la Sangre de un Cordero,
De quien Ara fue cruenta
La Inmenſa crueldad de un Leño.
En virtud de ſus virtudes
Poſtrar podrás ſus venenos,
Que no tendrán fuerza alguna
En tocandolas á ellos.
Toma, y á Dios: y no temas
Que me auſente, aunque me auſento,
Porque ſiempre que me llames,
Verás, que á tus voces buelvo.

Ella, y Múſica.
Corriendo veloz
En el arco de Paz, en quien hace
Las amiſtades del hombre, y de Dios.

[*Tocan Chirimías, y deſaparece el Arco.*

El Hombre.
Iris bello, hermoſa Ninfa,
No deſvanezcas tan preſto
Tanta multitud de Eſtrellas,
Tanta copia de Luzeros.

El Entendimiento
Rayo de Luz, que has corrido
Por las Campañas del viento,
Señal de Paz, que á Moyſés

And that thy intention is
For their reſcue to do battle,—
Me, to aid thee and to counſel,
Hath the mighty Jove deſpatchèd,
That from all Sin's proud bewitchments
Should to thee no evil happen;
And that thou may'ſt wholly conquer
And undo her worſt enchantments,
Take theſe flowers that I bring thee.

[*Lets fall a bunch of flowers.*
Beauteous bunch of flowers, all dappled
O'er with virtues from the life-blood
Of a Lamb, whoſe crimſon altar
Was a tree's unmeaſured hardneſs,
By whoſe myſtic aid thou mayeſt
All her poiſon'd ſnares down trample;
Touch them but with this—that moment
Shall they loſe all power to harm thee—
Take it, and adieu! Thou need'ſt not
Fear my abſence; for, though abſent,
Ever when thou calleſt on me
Thou ſhalt ſee that I will anſwer.

Penance and Muſic together.
Yes, along the ſky,
On the arch of Peace I fly—
On the arch whoſe myſtic ſpan
Amity proclaims 'twixt God and man.

[*While the Clarions play, the Rainbow and Penance diſappear.*

The Man.
Beauteous Iris, lovely nymph,
Do not hide in ſuch ſwift darkneſs
Such a hoſt of ſtarry ſplendours—
Such a crowd of meteor flaſhes.

The Underſtanding.
Ray of light, that through the windſwept
Plains of azure Heaven hath darted—

Dios ſeñaló en el Deſierto :

El Hombre.

Tente, aguarda.

El Entendimiento.

Eſcucha, eſpera.

El Hombre.

Fueſe, dexandome impreſſo
Un renglon de tres colores
En el Papel de los Cielos.
¡ Ay Entendimiento mio,
Dichoſo ſoy, pues que tengo
Con que vencer los encantos
De eſta Circe !

El Entendimiento.

Alza del ſuelo
Eſſas flores.

El Hombre.

Ay de mí!

El Entendimiento.

Qué ſientes ?

El Hombre.

Herirme ſiento
Con ſus eſpinas. [*Alza las flores.*

El Entendimiento.

Las flores
De la penitencia, es cierto
Que aſperas ſon al principio,
Quanto ſon fragrantes luego.

El Hombre.

Eſpinas de mi pecado,
Con temor á alzaros llego.
Vamos, que aunque mis ſentidos
Eſtén cautivos, y preſos
De ſu belliſſimo encanto,
Aſſi libertad pretendo.

El Entendimiento.

No tienes que ir á buſcarla,

Sign of peace, which in the deſert
God to Moſes indicated—

The Man.

Stay ! detain thee !

The Underſtanding.

Liſten ! wait !

The Man.

She is gone, but in her paſſage
Leaving me a line of greeting
Writ in triple-hued enamel,
On the ſkies cerulean paper,—
Underſtanding mine, how happy
Am I in a power poſſeſſing
Of ſubduing the enchantments
Of this Circe !

The Underſtanding.

From the ground
Raiſe the flowers.

The Man (in doing ſo).

Oh !

The Underſtanding.

What ſmarts thee ?

The Man.

By the ſharp thorns round theſe roſes
I am wounded.

The Underſtanding.

Yes ; the ſharpneſs
Of the penitential flowers
Is the firſt thing felt, but after,
Nought but their delicious fragrance.

The Man.

Ah ! with fear I ſtoop to handle
Ye, the ſharp thorns of my ſin.
Let us on ! for though this faſtneſs
Keeps my captive Senſes chain'd,
Spell-bound by ſuch ſweet enchantment,
Still I hope to liberate them.

The Underſtanding.

Then to meet with the enchantreſs,

Que ella á bufcarte á efte puefto
Ha falido, con las voces
De mufìcas, é Inftrumentos.

Salen la Lascivia, *y la* Culpa *detrás de todos, y traen una Salvilla, un Vafo de plata, y otra una Toalla al Hombro.*

La Múfica.

En hora dichofa venga
A eftos Jardines amenos
El Peregrino del Mar,
Donde halle feguro Puerto.

La Culpa.

En hora dichofa venga,
Digan los dulces acentos,
Una, y mil veces, fin que
Nada les ufurpe el eco,
Vandolero de los Ayres,
Que fe queda con los medios.
En hora dichofa venga
El hombre, que por fus hechos
Es affunto de la fama
Por fu valor, y fu ingenio,
Donde tengan fus fortunas
Dulce Patria, amado centro,
Noble afylo, illuftre amparo,
Blando albergue, y felíz Puerto.
Apenas fupe, inconftante
Huefped de dos Elementos,
Que fobre tribulaciones
Baten las olas, furgiendo
Yá los embates del Mar,
Yá las rafagas del Viento.
Apenas fupe, Señor,
Oy de vueftros compañeros,
(A quien yá en Palacios mios
Bien agaffajados tengo)

Thou no farther need'ft to go,
Since to meet thee fhe advances.
See, fhe comes with fongs and mufic,
And her firen train, to charm thee!

Enter Sin, *followed by* Voluptuousness, Flattery, *and others.* Voluptuousness *bears a falver, on which is a filver goblet, and* Flattery *a napkin.*

The Mufic.

Happy, happy, be the hour
That to thefe delicious gardens
Comes the Pilgrim of the Sea,
In a fafe port happily landed.

Sin.

Happy be the hour he cometh!
Sing again in fofteft accents—
Once, a thoufand times repeat it—
So that Echo, the freehanded
Robber of the air, may filch not
From the found his ufual largefs.
Happy be the hour that cometh
Here the man to whom is granted,
For his wit and worth in warfare,
Fame the proudeft and the ampleft:
Here, wherein a home and country
Now his happier fate imparteth,—
A proud fhelter—a high fafeguard—
A foft reft—a happy haven.
Scarcely had I heard, O ever
Changeful gueft of air and water,
Of two elements the victor,
Since on troublous billows wafted,
Now the rude fea's rage thou curbeft—
Now the wild wind's mightier mad- [nefs:—
Scarcely had I heard, my lord,
From thy comrades, whom my palace
Entertaineth now and welcomes
In obedience to my mandate,—

Que erais el valiente Ulíſes,
Que quiere decir en Griego
Hombre ingenioſo (que al fin
No ay ſin, cautelas ingenio)
Que de la Troya del Mundo
Huyendo venís al fuego,
A quien vos miſmo en vos miſmo
Alimentais en incendios,
Quando á recibiros ſalgo
Con todo eſſe Coro bello
De mis damas, celebrando
Tan noble recibimiento.
Llegad todas á ſus plantas,
Y con corteſes feſtejos
Le ſaludad; y porque
El que en el Mar tanto tiempo
Fluctuó golfos de penas
En pielagos de tormentos,
Es la ſed la que le aflije;
Mas á quién no admira eſto,
Que ſiendo el Mar todo agua,
Tenga á ſu hueſped ſediento?
Brindadle con eſſe Nectar,
Que eſtá de dulzuras lleno,
En tanto que en mis Palacios
Mas regalos le prevengo.

La Laſcivia.

Bebe, Señor, el ſabroſo
Licor que yo te preſento.

El Entendimiento.

¡Ay de tí, ſi le bebieres,
Que todo es laſcivo fuego!
Qué haces?

El Hombre.

Para reſiſtirme
Conmigo meſmo peleo.

El Entendimiento.

¿No le bebas, yá no ſabes
Que es toſigo, y es veneno?

That thou wert the brave Ulyſſes,
Which doth mean in Grecian parlance,
An aſtute-ſoul'd man (aſtuteneſs
Being, as 'twere, a twin with talent),
Who from flaming Troy eſcaping,
Hither to a fire haſt wander'd,
Which within thyſelf thou feedeſt,
From internal quenchleſs aſhes,—
When I hurried to receive thee
With this beauteous choir of damſels,
Celebrating with due honour
Such a noble ſtranger's advent.
At his feet then lowly kneeling,
Welcome in the coſtlieſt manner
His arrival, and, becauſe
He who in the ſea has tarried
Such a length of time, exchanging
Gulfs of gloom for waves of ſaltneſs,
Was by thirſt afflicted moſtly—
Strange, the ſea, which is all water,
That it ſhould its gueſts leave thirſty,
And the liquid ſtore ſo ample!—
Pledge him with this honey'd nectar
Sweeten'd by celeſtial ſavours,
While within my palace yonder
Are prepared more feſtive banquets.

Voluptuouſneſs.

Drink, my lord, the ſweetly-ſavour'd
Liquor, which I dare to hand thee.

The Underſtanding.

Woe to thee, if thou doſt drink it!
Liquid luſt-fire fills that chalice!
What then wilt thou do?

The Man.

I ſtruggle
With myſelf in ſelf-fought battle!—

The Underſtanding.

Drink it not: the draught concealeth
Poiſon deadlier than the adder.

El Hombre.
Sí, Entendimiento, y tu aviſo
Ha llegado á muy buen tiempo.
Eſtoy cobarde, eſtoy mudo,
Tanto al cortés cumplimiento,
Que debo á vueſtra beldad,
Y á vueſtra hermoſura debo;
Que aunque retorico fui,
Al miraros enmudezco:
En fé de lo qual, el nectar
Con que me brindais acepto;
Mas por no ſer deſcortes
Haré la ſalva primero
Con eſtas flores, que no
Se atreven á ſer groſſeros
Tanto mis labios, que lleguen
Sin aqueſſe cumplimiento.
[*Toca el Vaſo en el Ramillete, y ſale Fuego.*

La Laſcivia.
Ay de mí! El Fuego que avia
En eſte Vaſo encubierto
Rebentó.

El Hombre.
Es verdad, que mal
Arde encendido tu fuego,
Vil Laſcivia.

La Laſcivia.
Ay infelíz!

La Culpa.
Mortales furias!

El Hombre.
Qué es eſto?

La Culpa.
Saber oy, que deſvanezcas
Mis encantos.

El Hombre.
Sí, que aviendo

The Man.
Yes, my Underſtanding, yes: [*Aſide.*
Timely come thy words to warn me:—
I am timid, I am mute, [*To Sin.*
Thinking of the courteous favour
Which I owe to thy perfections,
Which I owe thy beauty, lady.
For, though ſkill'd in ſpeech were I,
Dumb I'd grow in gazing at thee:—
Therefore I thy proffer'd nectar
Take, and thus by taking thank thee;
But, that I may not be wholly
Wanting in more courteous manner,
I ſhall firſt ſalute and touch it
With theſe flowers, the groſſer advent
Of my lips preſuming only
Such ſweet tribute to come after.
[*He dips the noſegay in the golet from which fire iſſues.*

Voluptuouſneſs.
Woe is me! the ſecret fire
Which within this cup I ſcatter'd
Has burſt forth.

The Man.
'Tis true, for hard
Is't to hide the fire thou wakeſt,
Vile Voluptuouſneſs.

Voluptuouſneſs.
Ah! me,
Woe the day!—

Sin.
My fury mads me!

The Man.
Why, O Sin?

Sin.
For now I know
You have conquer'd my enchantments.

The Man.
Yes, for having ventured hither

Llegado aqui accompañado
De mi noble entendimiento,
Aunque llegué ſin ſentidos,
Porque tú me los has preſo,
Con eſte ramo ſabré
Deſvanecer tus intentos,
Porque es el ramo de Iris,
Que eſtá de virtudes lleno.

La Culpa.

Ay infelice de mí!
¿Aviendo volado el fuego
De la mina, que ocultaba
Entre liſonja mi pecho,
Cómo ſoy yo, cómo ſoy
La que me abraſo? Qué es eſto?
¿Tú eres quien la mina enciende,
Y ſoy yo quien la rebiento?

El Hombre.

Sí, que ſabiendo que eres
Horror de aqueſtos Deſiertos,
Y Circe de eſtas Montañas,
Que quiere decir en Griego
Maleficioſa Hechicera,
A darte la muerte vengo,
Y á reſcatar mis ſentidos
De la priſion de tus hierros.
[*Saca la Daga.*

La Culpa.

Ten la Daga; eſpera, aguarda,
No manches tan noble acero
En mí, que ſoy inmortal,
Y yá ſin morir me has muerto.
Yo bolveré tus ſentidos
A ſu ſér, porque viniendo
Armado de las virtudes,
Que dió tu arrepentimiento,
No tengo yo poder, no,
Para guardarlos mas tiempo.

Companied and happily guarded
By my noble Underſtanding,
Though I come here in the abſence
Of my Senſes, ſtill kept captive
By thy wiles, to me is granted
Power to fruſtrate thy intentions
By this little branch I carry—
Wonder-working branch of Iris—
Full of virtues and of marvels.

Sin.

Ah! unhappy me! the fire
Having from the mine departed,
Which beneath fair Flattery's ſeeming
Hid my heart within its caverns!
How am I? Oh! how am I
Still its victim? How does't happen
That the mine for *thee* enkindled,
Burſts 'neath *me* and leaves me blaſted?

The Man.

Thus; no ſooner had I heard
That thou wert the ſhame and ſcandal
Of theſe deſerts, the dread Circe
Of theſe mountains, the enchantreſs
That thy Grecian name expreſſes,
Than I came here to deſpatch thee,
And to liberate my Senſes
From the priſon of thy ſhackles.
[*Draws his dagger.*

Sin.

Hold thy hand! Oh! do not thou
Stain the bright ſteel of thy dagger
With the blood of an immortal.
Deathleſs though I be, thou ſtabbeſt
Deep enough without ſuch aidance.
Back, the Senſes thou demandeſt
I ſhall give thee, ſince beholding
That thy penitence hath arm'd thee
So with virtues, I no longer [them.
Have the ſtrength or power to guard

Oído, que oíſte liſonjas,
Que tu dulce encanto fueron,
Por quien te tuvo trocado
En Camaleon tu afećto.

Sale el Oído *como aſſombrado.*

El Oído.

¿ De qué letargo tan dulce
A eſta nueva voz deſpierto ?

La Culpa.

Olfato murmurador
De lo malo, y de lo bueno,
Que fuiſte Leon, que diſte
Dañado olor con tu aliento.

Sale el Olfato *aſſombrado.*

El Olfato.

¡ O nunca yo deſpertara
De tan regalado ſueño !

La Culpa.

Tacto, que laſcivamente
Empleado en tus deſeos
Oſſo fuiſte, pues que nace
Sin forma, ſin viſta, y cuerpo.

Sale el Tacto *aſſombrado.*

El Tacto.

¡ Qué á mi peſar me levanto
De tan regalado lecho !

La Culpa.

Viſta, que manchado Tigre
Has pacido eſte Deſierto,
Pues embidioſo eres ojos
Que ſientes bienes agenos.

Sale la Vista *como aſſombrado.*

La Viſta.

¿ Si noche han de ſer los mios,
De qué ſirve lo que veo ?

Hearing ! thou to whom light words
Were a ſource of ſweet enchantment,
On account of which defećt
A chameleon's ſhape I gave thee !

Enter the Hearing, *amazed.*

The Hearing.

Ah ! from ſuch ſweet lethargy
Muſt I at this new voice waken ?

Sin.

Smell ! that libelleſt in turn
Equally all forms of matter,
Thou a lion late, whoſe breath
Fetid odours round thee ſcatter'd !

Enter the Smell, *amazed.*

The Smell.

Ah ! that I had never woken
From a ſleep by dreams ſo gladden'd !

Sin.

Touch ! that, by thy low deſires
Wholly occupied and trammell'd,
Wert a bear, ſince it is born
Sightleſs, formleſs, and unſhapen !

Enter the Touch, *amazed.*

The Touch.

Oh ! the ſorrow ! to ariſe
From a bed ſo ſoftly padded !

Sin.

Sight ! that in theſe deſerts here
Liveſt like a ſpotted panther,
Fleck'd with envious eyes to ſee
Aught of alien good that happens !

Enter the Sight, *amazed.*

The Sight.

Of what ſervice are mine eyes,
If I'm doom'd to dwell in darkneſs?

La Culpa.

Guſto, que animal inmundo
Eres, porque ſiempre hambriento
Solo en eſta vida cuidas
De ſuſtentarte á tí meſmo.

Sale el Gusto *aſſombrado.*

El Guſto.

Que era un gran puerco ſoñaba,
Nadie que ay que creer en ſueños
Diga, ó ſi diga, pues oy
Lo ſoy dormido, y deſpierto.

La Culpa.

Yá eſtán aqui tus ſentidos,
Yá á tu poder te los buelvo.
Idos, que en mí no durais
Sino ſolamente el tiempo
Que tarda en venir el hombre
Por voſotros ; pues es cierto,
Que eſtá en ſu mano el cobraros,
Como en ſu mano el perderos.

El Entendimiento.

No eſperas mas, vén á eſte
Baxél de tu Entendimiento.

El Oído.

¿ Dónde hemos de ir tan aprieſſa ?
¿ Apenas llegado avemos
A eſtos Palacios, y yá
Nos quieres auſentar de ellos ?

La Viſta.

¿ Adónde quieres llevarnos
Por eſſe Mar padeciendo ?

El Olfato.

Dexa que de las paſſadas
Fortunas nos reparemos.

El Guſto.

Dexame, Señor, que ſea
Puerco otro poco de tiempo,
Pues no ay mas ſeguridad

Sin.

Taſte ! that art a beaſt unclean,
Since with hunger never ſated,
The ſole thought of thy exiſtence
Is how beſt to feed and fatten !

Enter the Taste, *amazed.*

The Taſte.

What a hog I dream'd I was !
Dreams are fables though, what matter ?
Waking or aſleep by me
Is the ſelf-ſame part enacted.

Sin.

See, thy Senſes all are here :
Back into thy power I hand them.
Go ! your ſtay with *me* endured
Only for the time your maſter,
Man, delay'd to come and claim you,
Since 'tis certain power is granted
Not alone to man to loſe you,
But to regain you when you're abſent.

The Underſtanding.

Stay no longer here, but come
To my bark in which we landed.

The Hearing.

Whither ſhould we go ſo quickly ?
Scarce have we the beauteous gardens
Of this friendly palace enter'd,
And already we're debarr'd them.

The Sight.

Wouldſt thou bring us back to ſea,
There to ſuffer new diſaſters ?

The Smell.

Let us here recruit our ſtrength
After all the ills we've maſter'd.

The Taſte.

Let me be a hog, I pray,
Once again, good ſir, I aſk thee,
Since of all the lives I know

En el Mundo, que ſer puerco.
El Entendimiento.
En fin, ſois brutos, ſentidos,
Tan brutos, que holgais de ſerlo.
El Guſto.
¿No ſabemos quan bueno es
Eſtár comiendo, y gruñendo?
El Entendimiento.
¿Vamos, qué eſperes, Ulíſes?
El Hombre.
Vamos, pero no tan preſto,
Porque de aver viſto aqui
Mis ſentidos mal contentos
De dexar eſtas delicias,
No ſé (ay de mí!) lo que ſiento.
El Entendimiento.
Yo te llevaré por fuerza.
El Hombre.
No harás tal, que tu conſejo
Arraſtrarme no podrá,
Moverme sí, yá lo has hecho:
Vé á prevenir el Baxél,
Pues Piloto eres.
El Entendimiento.
Yá buelvo. [*Vaſe.*

El Hombre.
Por poder mas libremente
Vér eſta Deidad, le auſento
De mí aqueſte breve inſtante
Sin temor de ſus preceptos.—
La Culpa (aparte).
Aora podré hablarle, pues
Apartó ſu entendimiento.
Ya Ulíſes, que victorioſo
Te miras de mí, bolviendo
De eſſas incultas Montañas
Coronado de troſeos,
No tan preſto al Mar te entregues

A hog's life is the moſt happy.
The Underſtanding.
Ah! ſo brutiſh are the Senſes,
To be brutes appears to glad them!
The Taſte.
Have we not found out how pleaſant
'Tis to eat and grunt untrammell'd?
The Underſtanding.
Come, Ulyſſes, why delay?
The Man.
Let us go,—but ſtill there's ample
Time to ſpare, for ſince I ſee
How my Senſes are diſtracted
At abandoning theſe pleaſures,
Ah! I know not how I falter.
The Underſtanding.
I muſt drag you hence by force.
The Man.
Ah! by force you cannot drag me,
But by counſel you may lead:
Even already you attract me;
Go, prepare the bark, for you
Are the pilot.
The Underſtanding.
Yes, with gladneſs
To return here. [*Exit.*
The Man (aſide).
That this goddeſs
I may ſee with freer glances,
Undeterr'd by his ſuggeſtions,
I have thus contrived his abſence.
Sin (aſide).
I can tempt him now, ſince his
Underſtanding hath departed.
O Ulyſſes! crown'd with trophies,
Vanquiſher of my enchantments,
Flying from this lonely iſland,
From its mountains and moraſſes,
Do not truſt thyſelf ſo quickly

En eſſe inconſtante leño,
Que el Mar da la Vida ſurca,
Amenazado de rieſgos.
Mira alterados los Mares,
Que con veloz movimiento
En pyramides de eſpumas,
Son Alcazares de hielo.
Dexa que el Mar ſe ſerene ;
Y pues te miras exempto
De la Magia de mi encanto,
En fé de eſſe ramo bello,
Que te dió la Iris, no quieras
Bolverte al afán tan preſto :
Deſcanſa en mi albergue oy,
Que mañana ſerá tiempo
Para dexar eſtos Montes
De tantas delicias llenos.
¿ Qué prieſſa te corre aora
De auſentarte ; y mas ſabiendo,
Que yo, cada vez que quieras
Ir, detenerte no puedo ?
Entra en mis ricos Palacios,
Donde ſon divertimientos
Todas ſus ocupaciones
Para el aplicado Ingenio.
Verás mis grandes Eſtudios,
Mis admirables portentos
Examinaras, tocando
De mi Ciencia los efectos.
¿ Por qué pienſas que me llaman
La Circe de eſtos Deſiertos ?
Porque Ciencias prohibidas,
Que ſon Leyes que yo tengo,
Con mis eſtudios alcanzo,
Con mis vigilias aprendo.
Verás apagado el Sol,
Solo á un ſoplo de mi aliento ;
Pues en la luciente edad,
El dia yo le obſcurezco :

To the wild and dangerous vaſtneſs
Of the ſea of life, to plough it
In a frail bark ſo unſtable.
See ! its mighty breaſt upheaving,
In its rapid movement ſparkles
Now as pyramids of cryſtal,
Now as ſnow-embattled caſtles.
Wait the wild turmoil's abating,
Wait until the ſea grows calmer ;
And ſince thou haſt been exempted
From the ſpell of my enchantment
By the gift that Iris gave thee,—
By that budding beauteous branchlet,—
Oh ! return not back ſo quickly
To its dangers and diſaſters :
Reſt thee in my houſe to-day ;
In the morning will be ample
Time for thee to fly theſe mountains
And theſe joy-enfolding gardens.
Why ſo ſwiftly fly for ſafety,
Knowing well thou art ſo guarded,
That whenever thou wouldſt leave me
I am powerleſs to withſtand thee ?—
Enter then my dazzling palace,
Where an intellectual banquet,
Graced by gladneſs and enjoyment,
Waits upon thy welcome advent.
Thou wilt ſee my deep reſearches,—
Thou my wonders wilt examine,—
All the ſecrets of my ſcience
Will be bared to give thee anſwer.
Wherefore, thinkeſt thou, the Circe
Of theſe deſert waſtes they call me ?
'Tis becauſe forbidden knowledge
(*That* ſole law I leave untrampled)
I, by application, reach to,—
I, by mighty ſtudies, maſter.
By a breath from out my lips,
Thou wilt ſee the ſunlight blacken'd,

Bien digo, la ſombra ſoy, [*Aparte.*
David lo dixo en un Verſo.
Verás, á ſolo una linea,
Que corran mis penſamientos,
Deſclavadas las Eſtrellas
Del octavo Firmamento:
Y es verdad, pues tercer parte
[*Aparte.*
De ellas aparté del Cielo.
La Nigromancía verás
Executada, ſaliendo,
A mi conjuro obedientes,
De ſus ſepulcros los muertos.
Cadaver es el que peca, [*Aparte.*
Pues me obedece, no miento.
La grande Chiromancía
Verás, quando en vivo fuego,
En los papeles del humo
Caracteres de luz leo.
¿ Qué fuego no enciendo yo ?
[*Aparte.*
No es engaño, pues le enciendo.
Titubear verás caducos
Uno, y otro Polo, haciendo
Que deſplomados ſe caygan
Sobre todo el Univerſo.
No ſerá la vez primera, [*Aparte.*
Que yo eſtremecí ſu Imperio.
El idioma de las aves
Verás, que yo ſola entiendo,
Siendo el canto vaticinio,
Y ſiendo el graznido aguero,
De las flores te leerá
Eſtos eſcritos quadernos,
Donde la naturaleza
Eſcrivió raros myſterios.
A todas horas tendrás
Dulces muſicas, oyendo
Suaves cantos de las aves,

Since in all its perfect prime,
Can I the bright noon-day darken ;
I may ſay ſo, ſince a ſhadow [*Aſide.*
David calls me in the Pſalter.—
Thou wilt ſee that my mere thought,
Even my wiſh in ſilence wafted,
From the Heaven beyond the ſeventh
Will the mighty ſtars unfaſten.
True, a third of Heaven's bright hoſt
[*Aſide.*
Thus my primal fall brought after.—
Necromancy ſhalt thou ſee,
Tried and teſted to the fartheſt ;—
So that, yielding to my ſpells,
From their graves the dead will an-
ſwer :—
Yes ; for dead in ſin is he [*Aſide.*
Who doth yield to my advances.—
Pyromancy, too, will ſhow thee
How upon the red flames' ſparkles,
How upon the curling ſmoke-wreaths,
Knowledge there inſcribed I gather :
I deceive not here—the fire [*Aſide.*
Lit by me doth ever crackle.—
Thou wilt ſee the poles of Heaven
Tremble at my dread commandments,
As if down about to fall
On the world's diſturbèd axes :—
Not the firſt time will it be [*Aſide.*
That its kingdom I have ſhaken.—
All the language of the birds
Wilt thou learn, by *me* ſole maſter'd—
Both their ſweet prophetic warble
And their harſher augural cackle.
On the flowers, too, wilt thou read,
As upon illumined parchment,
Written characters revealing
Nature's myſteries and marvels.
Every moment wilt thou have

De los hombres dulces verſos,
Sabroſiſimos manjares
Te ſervirán con aſſeo
Tal, que el Olfato, y el Guſto
Se eſten liſongeando á un tiempo.
La viſta divertirás
En eſſos jardines bellos,
Que ſon nueſtros paraíſos,
De varias delícias llenos.
Dormirás en regalada
Cama, donde el Tacto atento
A tu deſcanſo, en muilidas
Flores, tendrá blando lecho.
A todas horas tendrás
Damas, que te eſtén ſirviendo,
Que, como ſoy en comun
La Culpa, conmigo tengo
Y en particular á todas
Las que ſe precian de ſerlo.
[*Vá dexando caer el* HOMBRE *las Flores del Ramillete poco á poco.*
Y ſobre todo tendrás
Los regalos de mi pecho,
Las caricias de mis brazos,
Los alhagos de mi afecto,
Las finezas de mi amor,
La verdad de mi deſeo,
La atencion de mi alvedrio,
De mi vida el rendimiento:
Y finalmente, delicias,
Guſtos, regalos, contentos,
Placeres, dichas, favores,
Muſicas, bayles, y juegos.

El Hombre (*aparte*).
No ſé qué he de reſponder,
Porque divertido, oyendo

Sweeteſt ſtrains to greet and glad thee,—
Now the nightingale's lone ditty,
Now the poet's lovelier anthem.
Food the daintieſt ſhall be ſpread
For thee with ſuch nice exactneſs,
So that ſmell and taſte together
Shall at once thy ſenſes flatter.
Thy enraptured ſight ſhall revel
In theſe ſweet delicious gardens,
Which to us are bowers of Eden,
Full of every form of gladneſs.
In a ſoft bed ſhalt thou ſleep,
Where the Touch, that looketh after
Thy repoſe, on downieſt flower-leaves
Shall outſpread thy pleaſant pallet.
Lovely ladies every hour
Shall their various ſervice grant thee,
Whom, as Sin ſupreme, I keep
Here at once my ſlaves and partners,
Specially all thoſe who are
To my ſervice ſelf-attracted.
[*During the latter part of this addreſs, the* MAN *has let fall the flowers of his noſegay one by one.*
But, above all other joys,
Wilt thou have my heart's free largeſs,
The delight of my embraces,
The ſweet proof of my attachment,
All the fondneſs of my love,
All the truth deſire implanteth,
The devotion of my will;
Of my life the ſweet enthralment:
In a word, delicious joys,
Raptures, raviſhments, entrancements,
Pleaſures, bliſſes, fondeſt favours—
Sports and plays, and ſongs and dances.

The Man (*aſide*).
Ah! I know not what to ſay!
Ah! I know not what to anſwer!

La retorica ſuave
De ſu voz, fui deſhaciendo
El Ramo de las Virtudes,
Que deſperdiciadas veo,
Y ajadas entre mis manos;
¿Pero qué mucho, ſi advierto,
Que para que ella me hablaſſe
Aparté mi Entendimiento?
Sin él hablaré. Gallarda
Circe, á tus voces atento,
De mí me olvido, y yá ſolo
De tu hermoſura me acuerdo.
A tus Palacios me guia,
Porque ſer tu hueſped quiero
Deſde oy, eſtimando humilde
Tan corteſes cumplimientos.

La Culpa.

Vencí. La Muſica buelva
A repetir ſus acentos;
Y eſſos gallardos Palacios,
Que eſtán en el duro centro
Del Monte, ſus puertas abran,
Que vá gran hueſped á ellos.
[*Deſcubreſe un Palacio muy viſtoſo.*

El Oído

Al Entendimiento aguarda
Antes, Señor, que entres dentro,
Porque ſepas donde eſtás.

El Hombre.

Para qué? pues es tan cierto
Que no entrára, ſi ſupiera
(Ay de mí!) mi Entendimiento.

El Guſto.

Dices bien, vamos ſin él;
¿Para qué acá le querémos,
Que es un Miniſtro canſado,

Since, oblivious of myſelf,
Liſtening to her ſweet-toned accents,
I have been, ah me! deſtroying
All the beauty of this branchlet.
Wither'd in my hand it lies,
At my feet its leaves lie ſcatter'd.
But what wonder, when I think,
In my Underſtanding's abſence
Has ſhe ſpoken to me thus?
Thus without him, then, I anſwer:—
Circe fair, in mute attention
I unto thy ſweet voice hearken,
Self-forgetting, loſt in dreaming,
By thy wondrous beauty dazzled.
Lead me to thy long'd-for palace;
As thy gueſt, thy ſlave command me;
Let my humble acquieſcence
For thy courteſy thus thank thee.

Sin.

I have conquer'd!—once again,
Muſic, ſing your ſweeteſt accents,
And my beauteous palace home,
Which amid theſe mountains ſtandeth,
Open wide your dazzling doors
For the great gueſt who advanceth.
[*A magnificent palace appears.*

The Hearing.

Oh! my lord, before thou goeſt
Where thou know'ſt not what may happen,
Here await thy Underſtanding.

The Man.

Wherefore? ſince if thus I acted,
Ah! I know to well that *he*
Ne'er would ſanction my advances.

The Taſte.

Right! without him let us go:—
What's the uſe of being ſaddled
With a pig and pleaſure-hating

Todo limpio, y nada puerco?

Múſica.

En hora dichoſa venga
A eſtos jardines amenos
El Peregrino del Mar,
Donde halle ſeguro puerto.

Vanſe, dadas las manos, y ſale el ENTENDIMIENTO.

El Entendimiento.

Hombre, eſpera, eſcucha, aguarda,
No entres en eſſe ſobervio
Alcazar, porque no ſabes
Los peligros que eſtán dentro.
Mas ay de mí! con las voces,
Que le han tenido ſuſpenſo,
No me oye: ¡ Qué bien (ay triſte !)
Se echa de vér, pues pudieron
Los alhagos de la Culpa,
Los hechizos, y venenos
Moverle, que me tenía
Retirado! porque es cierto
Que á tenerme á mí conſigo,
No ſe rindiera tan preſto.

Sale la PENITENCIA.

La Penitencia.

¿ Entendimiento, qué voces
Son eſtas que dás al viento?

El Entendimiento.

Laſtimas ſon de aver dado
Mala cuenta de un ſugeto
Que Dios me entregó: Oy el Hombre
Me ha dexado, de mí huyendo
Se ha entrado en eſſe Palacio,
Poblado de Encantamientos.
Las Virtudes que adquirió,
Con un arrepentimiento

Cool cantankerous old carper?—

The Muſic.

Happy, happy be the hour
That to theſe delicious gardens
Comes the Pilgrim of the ſea
In a ſafe port happily landed!

Exeunt all hand in hand. The UNDERSTANDING *enters from the oppoſite ſide.*

The Underſtanding.

Hear! weak Man, oh! liſten! ſtay!
Enter not that pride-built caſtle,
Since thou knoweſt not the quickſands
On whoſe dangerous top it ſtandeth:
But, ah me! their flattering ſongs
Keep his ſenſes ſo abſtracted,
That he hears me not! How ſoon
Can it now be ſeen, O ſadneſs!
That the luſtful lures of ſin,
That her philtres and enchantments
Have the power to overwhelm him
In his Underſtanding's abſence,
Since with *me*, he would not have
His conſent ſo freely granted.

Enter PENANCE.

Penance.

Why theſe outcries, Underſtanding,
That thou to the winds imparteſt?

The Underſtanding.

Wailings are they for diſcharging
Towards my human ward ſo badly
Duties truſted me by God.
Man has left me, hath departed,
Fled me but juſt now, and enter'd
This enchantment-peopled palace;
All the virtues which by thee
Were to him repentant granted,

Que tuvo, deſperdiciadas
En el ayre las encuentro.

La Penitencia (*mira á las Flores*).

Pues yo las recogeré,
Guardandolas para el tiempo
Que arrepentido me buſque,
De ſu culpa, y de ſu yerro.

El Entendimiento.

Sin mí eſtá, que no eſtuviera,
Connigo (ay de mí !) tan ciego,
Que ſe olvidára de tí.

La Penitencia.

Darte yo una induſtria quiero,
Para ſacarle de aqueſſe
Encanto ; toca en ſu pecho
Al arma, pues eſcuchando
Eſte belicoſo eſtruendo,
(Haciendole de sí miſmo
Siempre mortales acuerdos)
Verás, que con tal temor
Creera advertido, y atento
A ſu Entendimiento, donde
Eſtá ſin Entendimiento.

Salen la CULPA, *y el* HOMBRE, *y los* SENTIDOS, *y canta la Múſica.*

La Múſica.

Compitiendo con las ſelvas,
Donde las flores madrugan,
Los paxaros en el viento
Forman Abriles de plumas.

La Culpa.

Vén por aqueſtos jardines,
Adonde critica, y culta
La naturaleza, ha hecho,

As I enter'd here, I found
By the wanton breezes ſcatter'd.

Penance (*ſeeing them on the ground*).

I ſhall re-collect them all,
And preſerve them 'till he aſk me
For them once again, when he
Feels repentant for his lapſes.

The Underſtanding.

Ah ! without me is he now !
With me never had ſuch hardneſs
Steel'd his heart forgetting *thee !*

Penance.

I ſhall ſhow thee in what manner
Thou may'ſt yet perchance releaſe him
From the chains of this enchantment.
Touch the key-note of his ſoul,—
Sound to arms ! the martial clatter
(For of death and deathfulleſt omens
Ever breathes the call to battle !)
Soon will wake him from the ſtupor
That his memory now doth darken :—
Then he will attend to *thee,*
Now without thee he advanceth.

Enter SIN, *the* MAN, *and the* SENSES ; *the Muſic ſings.*

The Muſic.

With the bloſſom'd boughs competing,
When the ſweet flowers riſe from ſlumber,*
Birds an April of the air
Faſhion with their painted plumage.

Sin.

Come unto theſe gardens fair,
Where rich Nature's careful culture
With her beds and myrtle buds

* In this ſcene the aſonante vowels of the original are, *u, a:* in the tranſlation, *u, e,* or their equivalents in ſound, are uſed.

Entre jardines, y murtas,
Alardes de ſus primores,
Pues ſu varia compoſtura
Academia es, donde el Mayo
De un año para otro eſtudia.

El Hombre.

Tan hermoſa es eſta eſtancia,
Que el miſmo Sol que la alumbra,
Su esfera dexára, á precio
De que fuera esfera ſuya.
Digalo el Cielo, que al vér
Las flores que la dibujan,
Arreboló las Eſtrellas,
Porque compitan las unas
Con las otras: Y aſſi, eſtán
Deſde la tiniebla obſcura,
Haſta la luciente Aurora,
Eſſas Eſtrellas ceruleas,
Donde en brazos de la noche
Duermen las esferas mudas,

El, y Múſica.

Compitiendo con las ſelvas,
Donde las flores madrugan.

La Culpa.

Todo el jardin es delicias;
No ay planta, no ay hoja alguna,
Que verde aroma, los mas
Blandos perfumes no ſupla.
Y porque Viſta, y Olfato
La pompa no ſe atribuyan
Para sí ſolos, objetos
Son del Oído las puras
Fuentes, ſiendo en el ruido,
Compás que á coros ſe eſcucha,
Apacibles porque parlan,
Y alegres porque murmuran.
Embidioſo todo viento,
Al ver por la tierra, en una

Maketh ſuch a dazzling muſter,
That united they appear
Like a fair collegiate ſtructure,
Whither comes the young-eyed May,
Year by year, an eager ſtudent.

The Man.

Yes, ſo lovely is this place,
That the ſun that flames refulgent
Would his own bright ſphere abandon
For the fairer flower-ſphere under;
And the Heavens, the flowers beholding
Radiant in their roſy cluſters,
Would paint red their own pale ſtars,
That with theſe they might be number'd.
Thus it is from evening's grey
To the morn's glad gleams of umber,
Theſe cerulean ſtars appear,
Twinkling each with trembling luſtre,
When within the arms of Night
Sleep the ſilent ſpheres of Summer,

He and the Muſic together.

With the bloſſom'd boughs competing,
When the ſweet flowers riſe from ſlumber.

Sin.

All the garden is one joy:
Not a plant that here hath budded,
Not a leaf but breathes from out it
Fragrance that no tongue can utter:
And that Sight and Smell ſhould boaſt not,
That this Eden hath reſulted
Solely from their aidance, liſt!
Limpid fountains, leap and bubble,
Breaking with melodious beat
Songs whoſe never-ceaſing burden
Seemeth ſad when moſt they laugh,
Mirthful moſt when moſt they murmur.
And the envious Nymph of Air,

Primavera ſolamente,
Tantas Primaveras juntas,
De otras flores ſe ha poblado,
Que aladas ſus golfos ſurcan,
Siendo ramilletes vivos:
Y aſſi, quanto entre eſta ſuma
Deydad, las flores, y fuentes
De la tierra, con induſtria,
Paxaros forman de roſas,
Por igualar ſu hermoſura:

Ella, y Múſica.

Los paxaros en el viento
Forman Abriles de plumas.

La Múſica.

De una belleza engañados,
Por Aurora la ſaludan,
Y viendo ſus bellos ojos,
Quedan vanos de ſu culpa.

El Hombre.

Toda eſſa belleza, toda
Eſſa varia compoſtura
De vientos, y quadros, que
Emulos ſiempre ſe uſurpan
La alabanza, dignamente
Sus trofeos aſſegura,
Quando al ſaludar tu viſta
A todas horas te juzga
Aurora de eſſas Montañas,
Haciendo que ſe confundan
En los tormentos del dia
Salpicadas las purpureas
Hojas; pues aunque haya Aves,
Y flores del dia en la cuna,
Bebiendo á la Aurora el llanto,
Que cendales de oro enjuga,
El verte ſegunda vez,

Seeing earth ſo richly ſtudded
With the flowers of many ſprings,
Join'd in *this* that is the youngeſt,
Has unto her azure plains
Flowers of other kinds conducted,
Which, upborn on myriad wings,
Living noſegays float and flutter.
And as earth's young goddeſs fair
With her flowers and founts conſtructeth
Spring's ſweet Paradiſe below,
So the other in her upper
Beauteous realm of birds makes roſes
Rivalling the rich ones under:

She and the Muſic together.

Birds an April of the air
Faſhion with their painted plumage.

The Muſic.

By her lovelineſs deceived,
For Aurora they ſalute her,
And beholding her bright eyes,
Love the ſweet miſtake they ſuffer.

The Man.

All this fair variety,
All this lovelineſs that ſurgeth
Up from billowy buds of bloom,
By the wandering zephyrs ruffled,
All this realm of ſpring, whoſe crown
Earth and ſky in turn uſurpeth,
When it looks upon thy face,
Every moment doth it judge thee
The Aurora of theſe hills,
Blending hours that erſt were ſunder'd,
Streaking in the noontide's glow
All the leaves with roſeate purple,
So that birds and flowers that drank
Morning's pearly tears unnumber'd
Round the cradle of the day,
Tears that from her eyes ſhe bruſhes
With the golden-threaded clouds,

Con nueva ſalva ſegunda :

El, y Múſica.
De tu belleza engañados
Por Aurora la ſaludan.
La Culpa.
Culpa fuera de las aves,
Y las flores, porque nunca
Para equivocar deydades
Hallar pudieran diſculpa.

El Hombre.
Si es culpa, ó acierto, no
Es juſto que yo lo arguya ;
Pero bien ſé, que mi amor
Oy de ſu parte aſſegura ;
Que aunque culpa decir ſea,
Que por Aurora te anuncian
Flores, y aves ; ni las aves,
Ni las flores ſe diſculpan
De eſſa culpa, porque antes
Sé, que con cauſa mas juſta,
El, y Múſica.
En viendo tus bellos ojos,
Quedan vanos de ſu culpa.
El Guſto.
Yá que me ha tocado á mí,
(Que en efecto ſoy la Gula)
Preveniros las viandas,
En cuya alegre dulzura,
Quanto corre, nada, y buela
Regiſtro entre mil dulzuras
Su ſabor, deſnudo yá
De piel, de eſcama, y de pluma,
Mirad adonde quereis
Comer oy.
La Liſonja.
Sea con una

Seeing on the horizon under
Thee ariſe a ſecond time,
Hail thee with new matin muſic ;
He and the Muſic together.
By thy lovelineſs deceived
For Aurora they ſalute thee.
Sin.
This were wrong in bird and flower.
Bird and flower are both excuſeleſs
For confounding goddeſſes,
Whom their ſeparate ſhapes have ſunder'd.
The Man.
If 'tis right or no, the point
It were wrong I argued further.
This though know I well, my love
Is of *one* thing well aſſurèd,—
That, although 'twere wrong to ſay
That the flowers and birds misjudge thee
For Aurora, bird and flower
Would not wiſh to be excusèd
For that fault, ſince they, I feel,
Acting with impulſive juſtneſs—
He and the Muſic together.
In beholding thy bright eyes,
Love the ſweet miſtake they ſuffer.
The Taſte.
Now ſince it devolves on me
(I who am thy Taſte), the duty
Of providing for thy need
Viands cull'd from out the number
Of the things that ſwim or fly,
Or poſſeſs the earth's green ſurface,
'Mid whoſe thouſand varied forms,
Stript of ſkin, of ſcale, and plumage,
I their hidden ſavours ſeize,—
Think where art thou to have ſupper ?
Flattery.
Here, with all due ſervice fair,

Ceremonia liſongera.

El Guſto.

La Liſonja es muy aſtuta,
Pues que ſabe ſembrar meſas
Tan candidas, y purpureas.

Sale por debaxo del Tablado una Meſa con muchas viandas, y ſientaſe la CULPA, *y* ULÍSES, *y los demás ſirven, y los* SENTIDOS *ſe ſient an en el ſuelo.*

La Culpa.

Sientate, y todos
Os ſentad en la verdura
De eſſas flores.

La Laſcivia.

Pues yo quiero
Que no todas ſe atribuyan
Las finezas, ſin que á mi
El Hueſped me deba una.
Aquella letra cantad,
Que yo hice.

El Hombre.

Pues ſi es tuya
Será amoroſa.

La Laſcivia.

Sí es.

El Hombre.

No ay Dama aqui, que no acuda
A un Sentido.

El Guſto.

Si ſeñor,
Pero victor.

El Hombre.

Quién?

El Guſto.

La Gula.

Let it on the ſpot be uſher'd.

The Taſte.

What a clever laſs is this!
Since with ſkill as ſharp as ſudden
Tables o'er the ground ſhe ſcatters
Gleaming all with plate and purple.

A table ſumptuouſly provided with viands riſes from beneath. SIN *and* ULYSSES *place themſelves at the table, the* SENSES *on the ground: all are waited on by the others.*

Sin.

Sit, Ulyſſes, at my ſide:—
On the ſoft and verdurous turf here
Let the reſt recline.

Voluptuouſneſs.

Since I
Would not that our gueſt ſhould number
Every courteſy as thine,
One on my part thou wilt ſuffer:
Sing that little canzonet
Made by me.

The Man.

Its gentle burden
Muſt be love, if thine it be.

Voluptuouſneſs.

So it is.

The Man.

Each Senſe is ſuited
With a ſeparate lady.

The Taſte.

Yes;
But there's one deſerves a bumper.

The Man.

Who is ſhe?

The Taſte.

Intemperance.

La Música.

Si quereis gozar florida
Edad entre dulce ſuerte,
Olvidate de la muerte,
Y acuerdate de la vida.

Tocan Caxas, y alborotanſe todos, y dicen dentro el ENTENDIMIENTO, *y la* PENITENCIA.

La Culpa.

No canteis mas; ¿ qué atrevida
Voz nueſtros guſtos divierte ?

El Entendimiento.

Ulíſes, Capitan fuerte,
Si quieres dicha crecida.

La Penitencia.

Olvidate de la vida.

El Entendimiento.

Y acuerdate de la muerte.

La Culpa.

¿ Quién, con tanto atrevimiento,
Trueca el guſto en confuſion ?

El Hombre.

Circe, las que eſcuchas ſon
Voces de mi Entendimiento,
El me ha llamado, é intento
Reſponderle.

La Culpa.

De él te olvida.

El Hombre.

Suelta.

La Culpa.

Es accion atrevida.
Cantad, porque no ſe aſſombre
De oír aquella voz el Hombre.

La Música.

Acuerdate de la vida.

The Muſic.

Wouldſt thou, Man, to rapture give
Life's young hours that flower and fly,
Oh ! forget that thou muſt die !
And but think that thou doſt live !

A ſound of drums and voices is heard from within : all ſtart with ſurpriſe. The UNDERSTANDING *and* PENANCE *anſwer from within.*

Sin.

Ceaſe the ſong ! What voice doth ſtrive
Thus to mar our joy thereby ?

The Underſtanding.

Valiant ſoldier ! from on high
Wouldſt thou laſting bliſs receive ?

Penance.

Oh ! forget that thou doſt live !

The Underſtanding.

And remember thou muſt die !

Sin.

Who is this whoſe bold voice breaketh
Rudely on my ſtartled ear ?

The Man.

'Tis my inner voice you hear—
'Tis my Underſtanding ſpeaketh ;
Him my anſwering conſcience ſeeketh.

Sin.

Heed him not, no anſwer give.

The Man.

Let me go.

Sin.

Thou goeſt to grieve.
Sing once more, leſt Man ſhould hear
That myſterious voice ſevere.

The Muſic.

Oh ! remember thou doſt live !

El Hombre.
Sí haré, que bien larga es:
Y despues tendré lugar
Para sentir, y llorar,
Pues me bastará despues:
A tus brazos buelvo, pues,
Dulce dueño.
La Culpa.
Feliz suerte!
El Hombre.
Tu hermusura me divierte;
Contigo usano me nombre;
No quiero mas dicha.
El Entendimiento.
Hombre,
Acuerdate de la muerte.
[*Suena Caxa.*
El Hombre.
¡Fuerza es que me acuerde (ay triste!)
Quando mi afecto se mueve
De que es tan caduca, y breve,
Que en un instante consiste!
Entendimiento, que hiciste
En mí tal efecto, advierte,
Que yá voy á obedecerte.
La Culpa.
Vuestra voz su passo impida.
La Música.
Acuerdate de la vida.
El Entendimiento.
Acuerdate de la muerte.
[*Suena Caxa.*
El Hombre.
Aqui me están alhagando
Gusto, placer, y contento,
Quando alli mi Entendimiento
Al arma me está tocando.
La Culpa.
Qué dudas?

The Man.
Be it so: the days extend;
Life is long and full of joy:—
For contrition and annoy
Time enough ere comes the end.
To thine arms, then, dearest friend,
To thine arms once more I fly.
Sin.
Happy fate!
The Man.
Felicity
Is it but thy face to see:
Greater bliss there cannot be.
The Understanding.
Man! remember thou must die!
[*Drums sound.*

The Man.
Oh! the woe, to be compell'd
This to think of even in bliss—
Rapture, oh! how fleet it is,
Flying ere it scarce is held:—
Understanding mine, impell'd
By thy low voice whispering nigh,—
See! at thy behest I fly!
Sin.
Song, arrest the fugitive.
The Music.
Oh! remember thou dost live!
The Understanding.
Oh! remember thou must die!
[*Drums sound.*
The Man.
Here enjoyment round me draws
Nets of bliss, whose woof enthrals me:
There my Understanding calls me
To comply with valour's laws.
Sin.
Canst thou waver?

El Entendimiento.
Qué eſtás penſando?
La Culpa.
No de eſſa voz confundida
Tu memoria eſté afligida.
El Entendimiento.
En aqueſte encanto advierte:
Acuerdate de la muerte.
La Múſica.
Acuerdate de la vida.
El Hombre.
En dos mitades eſtoy
Partido, (paſſion tyrana!)
Entre el horror de mañana,
A la ventura de oy;
A aquel ſigo, y á eſte voy;
Y uno, y otro en mal tan fuerte,
O me aflige, ó me divierte:
¿Qual ha de ſer preferida
De mis glorias?
La Múſica.
Vida, vida.
El Hombre.
De mis penas?
El Entendimiento.
Muerte, muerte.
Y aunque me la dén á mí [*Sale.*
Los encantos de eſta fiera,
He de entrar, porque no fuera
Entendimiento, ſi aqui
Temiera morir: ¿aſſi,
Ulíſes, te has olvidado
De tí miſmo? ¿Aſſi entregado
A unos placeres fingidos,
Que ſin mí, y con tus ſentidos
Aqui vives engañado?

La Culpa.
¿Eſtará (dime) mejor,

The Underſtanding.
Canſt thou pauſe?
Sin.
Oh! no more attention give
To that voice, but bliſs receive!
The Underſtanding.
Think, 'mid all this witchery—
Think that thou art doom'd to die.
The Muſic.
Only think that thou doſt live.
The Man.
Oh! to which, torn heart, give way—
Preſent bliſs or future ſorrow,
Or the anguiſh of to-morrow,
Or the rapture of to-day?—
This I follow, that obey.
Wiſh the gladneſs, yet would fly
All the grief that comes thereby:—
Oh! to which the preference give?—
Which for my joy?
The Muſic.
That thou doſt live!—
The Man.
Which for my pain?
The Underſtanding.
That thou muſt die!—
Yes; and though that fate be mine,
[*He enters.*
By this monſter's ſorceries ſlain,
Here I enter: ſince 'tis plain,
I were not myſelf, or thine
God-given guide, ſhould I reſign
Death itſelf defending thee:
Haſt thou loſt all memory
Of thyſelf? that thus, Ulyſſes,
Thou wouldſt live in phantom bliſſes
Here with thy ſenſes, without *me?*
Sin.
Were it better, then, that he,

Creído de tu prudencia,
Allá con la Penitencia,
Adonde todo es horror,
Todo trifteza, y pavor,
Que aqui, donde le divierte
Tanta gloria?

El Entendimiento.

Sí, fi advierte,
Que aquefta gloria es fingida.

La Culpa.

Cantad, cantad.

La Múfica.

Vida, vida.

El Entendimiento.

Tocad, tocad: muerte, muerte.

El Hombre.

Dices bien, á tí te creen
Los influxos de mi eftrella.

La Culpa.

Pues dexafme?

El Hombre.

¿Ay Culpa bella,
Que tú tambien dices bien?

El Entendimiento.

Valor mis voces te dén.

La Culpa.

Muevate el verme rendida.

El Entendimiento.

Nada el feguirme te impida:
Tocad.

La Culpa.

Cantad.

El Hombre.

Pena fuerte!

La Múfica.

Vida, vida.

El Entendimiento.

Muerte, muerte.

Following thy advice, fhould go,
Penance led, where all is woe,
All is grief and mifery,
Than remain contentedly
Here, where on his every figh
Pleafure waits?

The Underftanding.

Undoubtedly,
If he knows fhe nought can give.

Sin.

Sing! fing!

The Mufic.

'Tis fweet to live!

The Underftanding.

Peal! peal! Man needs muft die!

The Man.

True! oh true! my ftar to thee
Yields, oh voice! that fpeaks within.

Sin.

Canft thou leave me?

The Man.

Beauteous Sin,
Ah! thy voice, too, moveth me.

The Underftanding.

May my voice thy foul's ftrength be!

Sin.

May my tears thy love revive!

The Underftanding.

Follow me, be ftrong and ftrive;
Drums, rebeat.

Sin.

Sing fweet!

The Man.

I try
Suffering's depths!

The Mufic.

To live!

The Underftanding.

To die!

(*Dentro La Penitencia*).
Muerte, muerte.
La Múſica.
Vida, vida.
El Entendimiento.
Eſte es bien perecedero.
La Culpa.
Aquella es pena cruel.
El Entendimiento.
Por eſſo eſpera laurél.
La Culpa.
Goza tu vida primero.
El Entendimiento.
Mira que es encanto fiero.
La Culpa.
Mira que es tormento fuerte.
El Entendimiento.
En que eres mortal advierte.
La Culpa.
No te acuerdes de eſſo, no.
La Múſica.
Vida.
La Penitencia.
Muerte.
Los dos.
Quién venció?
El Hombre.
La memoria de la muerte.
La Culpa.
¿Qué importa que aya vencido,
Si eſcaparte no podrás
De mí? En mi poder eſtás,
Sin reſervarte un ſentido.
Las flores que avia texido
La Penitencia, que eran
Las virtudes que pudieran
Salvarte, yá las perdiſte,
Tú miſmo las deſhiciſte;
¿Pues qué alivio de mí eſperan

Penance (*within*).
To die! to die!
The Muſic.
To live! to live!
The Underſtanding.
Life is but a dying day.
Sin.
Death, a pang that ſtrikes thee down.
The Underſtanding.
But it gives the laurel crown.
Sin.
Life enjoy though, while you may.
The Underſtanding.
Life's a dream that fades away.
Sin.
Death's a pain that all would fly.
The Underſtanding.
Think thy final hour draws nigh.
Sin.
Think not ſo till life be done.
The Muſic.
Life!
Penance (*within*).
Death!
The two.
Say which has won?
The Man.
The remembrance I muſt die.
Sin.
What imports it thus the gaining
Barren victory, if thou art
Powerleſs to eſcape my art?
Thou, with not a ſenſe remaining:
Since the potent flowers diſdaining,
Woven for thee by Heaven's hoſt,
Which the hands of Penance gave thee,
Virtues were they which could ſave thee,
Thou haſt ſcatter'd, thou haſt loſt;
Wherefore, therefore, canſt thou boaſt

Oy tus anſias?

El Entendimiento.

No te dé
Aqueſſo deſconfianza,
Tén en el Cielo eſperanza,
Que es columna de la Fé.
Eſſas virtudes, yo ſé,
Que quando mas divertido
Las avias eſparcido,
Para guardarlas llegó
A recogerlas . . . .

La Culpa.

Quién?

Sale la PENITENCIA.

La Penitencia.

Yo,
Que el Arco de paz he ſido,
Que ſi oy en Carro Triunfal
Me llegas á vér ſentada,
Subſtituyendo Doſél
De oro, de purpura, y nacar,
Es, porque á triunfar de tí
Vengo, que quando me llama
Del hombre el Entendimiento,
No puedo yo hacerle falta.
Las virtudes, que ſin él
Deſperdició ſu ignorancia,
Yo recogí; pues es cierto,
Que ſi ſe adquieren en Gracia,
Siempre que buelva por ellas,
En depoſito las halla.
Y para que el Hombre vea,
Que ſolas á vencer baſtan
Tus Encantos, oy verás
Todas aqueſtas viandas,

Thou art free from me to-day?

The Underſtanding.

Do not, therefore, Man, miſtruſt thee,
Hope in Heaven, to *that* entruſt thee—
Hope, the Faith's beſt prop and ſtay,
All thoſe virtues flown away,
Scatter'd in thy wantonneſs—
One, I know, doth hither preſs
To reſtore them; from the ſky
Comes ſhe hither now.

Sin.

Who?

PENANCE *enters.*

Penance.

I,
Erſt who wore the rainbow's dreſs:
Who if in a car triumphal
Thou to-day behold'ſt me ſeated*
'Neath a canopy, wherein
Purple, pearl, and gold are blended,
'Tis becauſe I come to triumph
Over thee, for whenſoever
Calleth me Man's Underſtanding,
Never is the call neglected.
All the virtues which he ſquander'd
In his ignorance, demented,
I have here re-gather'd, ſince
Certain 'tis that when preſented
By the hand of Grace they've been,
He who turneth back repentant
Ever findeth them again,
Safely guarded and preſervèd.
And that Man may know that they
Can alone thy ſorceries render

* The metre in the original changes to aſonante alternate vowel rhymes in *a, a*. For theſe I have ſubſtituted correſponding ones in *e, e*.

Del viento desvanecidas,
En humo, en polvo, y en nada,
Mostrando con este exemplo
Lo que son glorias humanas,
Pues el Manjar solamente,
Que es eterno, es el del alma:
Este es el Pan Soberano,
Que veis yá sobre esta Tabla:
La Penitencia os le ofrece,
Que sin ella (cosa es clara)
Que verle no merecia
El hombre con glorias tantas.
Sentidos esto no es Pan,
Sino mas noble substancia:
Carne, y Sangre es, porque huyendo
Las especies, que aí estaban,
Los accidentes no mas
Quedaron en Hostia blanca.

La Culpa.

¿ Como quieres que te crean
Los Sentidos con quien hablas,
Si todos conocerán
Que los ofendes, y agravias?
¿ Llega, Olfato, llega á oler
Esse Pan: en él qué hallas,
Pan, ó Carne?

Van llegando los Sentidos.

El Olfato.

De Pan es
El olor.

La Culpa.

¿ Llega, qué aguardas,
Gusto?

El Gusto.

Este gusto es de Pan.

Powerless, thou wilt now behold
All the viands here collected
Vanish into air, and leave
Nought behind to tell their presence:
Showing thus how human glory
Is as false as evanescent;
Since the only food that lasteth
Is the food for souls intended—
Is the eternal Bread of Life
Which now fills this table's centre.
It is Penance that presents it,
Since without her (nought more certain)
Man deserveth not to witness
So much glory manifested.
Yet, ye Senses, 'tis not Bread,
But a substance most transcendent:
It is Flesh and Blood; because,
When the substance is dissever'd
From the species, the White Host then
But the accidents preserveth.

Sin.

How canst thou expect to gain
Credence from thy outraged Senses,
When they come to understand
How you wrong them and offend them?
Smell, come here, and with thy sense
Test this bread, this substance,—tell me,
Is it bread or flesh?

The Senses *approach.*

The Smell.

Its smell
Is the smell of bread.

Sin.

Taste, enter;
Try it thou.

The Taste.

Its taste is plainly
That of bread.

La Culpa.
¿ Llega, Tacto, qué te efpantas,
Dí lo que tocas?
El Tacto.
Pan toco.
La Culpa.
¿ Vifta, á vér qué es lo que alcanzas?
La Vifta.
Pan folamente.
La Culpa.
Tú, Oído,
Rompe effa Forma, que llama
Carne la Fé, y Penitencia,
Y luego las defengaña
Al ruido de la fraccion:
¿ Qué refpondes?
El Oído.
Culpa ingrata,
Aunque la fraccion fe efcucha
Ruido de Pan, cofa es clara,
Que en fé de la Penitencia,
A quien digo que la llaman
Carne, por Carne la creo,
Pues que ella lo diga bafta.
El Entendimiento.
Effa razon me cautiva.
La Penitencia.
¿ Ea, Hombre, pues qué aguardas?
Cautivo tu Entendimiento
Eftá yá de la Fé Santa
Por el Oído, á la Nave
De la Iglefia Soberana
Buelve, y dexa de la Culpa
Las delicias momentaneas.
Ulífes cautivo ha fido
De efta Circe injufta, y falfa:
Huye, pues, de fus encantos,

Sin.
Touch, come, why tremble?
Say what's this thou toucheft?
The Touch.
Bread.
Sin.
Sight, declare what thou difcerneft
In this object?
The Sight.
Bread alone.
Sin.
Hearing, thou, too, break in pieces
This material, which, as flefh,
Faith proclaims, and Penance preacheth;
Let the fraction, by its noife,
Of their error undeceive them:
Say, is it fo?
The Hearing.
Ungrateful Sin,
Though the noife in truth refembles
That of bread when broken, yet
Faith and Penance teach us better
It is flefh, and what *they* call it
I believe: that Faith afferteth
Aught, is proof enough thereof.
The Underftanding.
This one reafon brings contentment
Unto me.
Penance.
O Man! why linger?
Now that Hearing hath firm-fetter'd
To the Faith thy Underftanding,
Quick, regain the faving veffel
Of the fovereign Church, and leave
Sin's fo briefly fweet exceffes.
Thou, Ulyffes, Circe's flave,
Fly this falfe and fleeting revel,
Since, how great her power may be,
Greater is the power of Heaven,

Yá que eſtos ſecretos hallas
En el Jupiter Divino,
Quien ſus encantos deſhagan.

El Hombre.

Dices bien, Entendimiento,
De aquí mis Sentidos ſaca.

Todos.

Vamos al Baxél, que aqui
Todo es ſombras, y fantaſmas.

La Culpa.

¿Qué importa, (ay de mí!) qué importa,
Que aſſi de mí poder ſalgas,
Si mis Encantos ſabrán
Seguirte por donde vayas?
Yo ſabre alterar las ondas.

La Penitencia.

Y yo ſabré ſerenarlas.

Tocan Clarines, y deſcubreſe la Nave, y todos ſe meten dentro.

La Culpa.

¿Tribulaciones no ſon
En la Eſcritura las aguas?
Luego á padecer le llevas
Trabajos, afanés, y anſias.

La Penitencia.

Sí; pero eſtos ſon regalos,
Con que mas merito alcanza.

Dentro todos.

Buen viage, buen viage.

La Culpa.

Aqueſſas voces me matan.

El Hombre.

Circe cruel, pues que ſupe
Vencer prodigioſas Magias,
Quedate, donde te ſirva
De monumento tu Alcazar.

And the true Jove's mightier magic
Will thy virtuous purpoſe ſtrengthen.

The Man.

Yes, thou'rt right, O Underſtanding!
Lead in ſafety hence my Senſes.

All.

Let us to our ſhip; for here
All is ſhadowy and unſettled.

Sin.

What imports it—woe is me!—
What imports it that my ſceptre
Thus you ſeem to 'ſcape from, ſince
My enchantments will attend ye?
I ſhall rouſe the waves to madneſs.

Penance.

I ſhall follow and appeaſe them.

Trumpets peal. The ſhip is diſcovered, and all go on board.

Sin.

Does not Holy Writ compare
Waves with woes that life engenders?
Thither then ye go to ſuffer
Toils, diſcomforts, and diſtreſſes.

Penance.

Yes, but theſe prove pleaſures when
They to greater favour lead them.

All (within).

Happy voyage! happy voyage!

Sin.

Oh! with rage theſe cries o'erwhelm me!

The Man.

Cruel Circe, now that all—
All thy wondrous wiles have ended,
Drag thy palace o'er thy head,
As thy monument and emblem.

La Culpa.
Ondas, que tanto Baxél
Sufris ſobre las eſpaldas,
En vueſtros ſenos de nieve
Le dad ſepulcro de plata.

La Penitencia.
Ondas ſerenas, al blando
Movimiento de las aguas,
Porque vueſtros pavimentos
No ſean montes, ſino alcazar.

La Culpa.
Vientos que ſoplais del Norte
No le ſaqueis de Trinacria,
Y chocad, caſcado el pino,
En aquellas peñas altas.

La Penitencia.
Notos, que venís del Auſtro,
Soplad con ſuaves auras,
Porque haſta el Puerto de Hoſtia
Oy á ſalvamento ſalga.

El Entendimiento.
Buen viage nos prometen
Las ſeñas de la bonanza.

La Culpa.
Haced, vicios, que velamen
Todo pedazos ſe haga,
Y buelto el Barco, ſea tumba
Con piramides, y jarcias.

El Hombre.
Haced, Virtudes, que rompa
La quilla ſuave, y blanda,
Encreſpando las eſpumas
Vidrios de nieve, y de plata.

Todos.
Buen viage, buen viage,
Que vientos, y ondas amaynan.

El Hombre.
Circe, poco tus Encantos

Sin.
Waves, that on your foam-white ſhoulders
Bear the weight of ſuch a veſſel,
Give it ſwift a ſilver tomb
In your boſom's ſnowy centres.

Penance.
Halcyon waves, with ſilent ſwell,
Roll your waters ſmooth and level;
Like the bright floor of a palace,
Let your azure hills extend them.

Sin.
Winds, that from the black north blow,
Waft it not to ſeas ſerener,
But upon Trinacrian rocks
Daſh its broken hull to pieces.

Penance.
Airs, that float from ſouthern ſkies,
Gently breathe with favouring breezes,
That it may the happy haven
Of the Hoſt in ſafety enter.

The Underſtanding.
Friends, a proſperous voyage promiſe
All the ſigns of ſettled weather.

Sin.
Vices, tear the canvas down,
Rend the rifled ſails in pieces,
Let the obeliſcal maſts
Make the hull a tomb reſemble.

The Man.
Virtues, for its curvèd keel
Make the ſea-way ſmooth and ſettled,
Send its prow ſwift-gliding through
Silvery foam, a ſnow-ſcaled ſerpent.

All.
Happy voyage! happy voyage!
Sing the winds and waves together.

The Man.
Circe, now thy ſorceries vile

Han podido, pues me ſaca
(Ay de mí !) la Iris Divina,
Coronado de eſperanzas.

La Penitencia.

Circe, yá ſu Entendimiento
Va con él : poco las trazas
De tu Magia te han valido.

La Culpa.

Llena eſtoy de pena, y rabia :
¿ Si yo ſoy vivora, cómo
No me rompo las entrañas ?
¿ Si ſoy aſpid, cómo oy
Mi veneno no me mata ?
Pedazos del corazon
Me arrancaré con mis anſias
Para tirarlos al Cielo :
¿ Mas á mí, qué me acobarda ?
Si en la Nave de la Igleſia
Huyes de mí, ſabré darla
Tormentas que la zozobren ;
Mas ay de mí ! que ya es vana
Mi Ciencia, pues que la veo
Navegar con tal bonanza :
Falten todos mis Sentidos,
Pues que yá poder me falta.

[*Suena Terremoto, y la ruido ſe bunde el Palacio.*

Confundanſe los Palacios,
Y bolviendoſe montañas
Obſcuras, no viva en ellas
Sino yo, porque me ſaca
A quien encantado tuve
La Penitencia Sagrada,
En virtud de aquel Divino
Manjar, que dá por Vianda.

Todos.

A cuyo grande milagro

Harm me not, ſince from thy meſhes
Faith, the heavenly Iris, leads me
With Hope's glory round my temples.

Penance.

Circe, now that as his guide
See his Underſtanding wendeth,
Little can thy ſorceries wound him.

Sin.

Rage and anguiſh overwhelm me !
If I am a viper, ſay
Why, O heart ! doſt thou not ſever ?
If I am an aſp, oh ! why
Does not my own poiſon end me ?
In my anguiſh I will tear
Out my heart in purple pieces
But to daſh them in Heaven's face.
Wherefore, though, ſhould fear unnerve me ?
If thou flieſt from me thus
In the Church's ſaving veſſel,
Know, my ſtorms can overwhelm it.
Idle boaſt ! for all is ended,—
All my ſcience now is o'er,
Since the ſhip ſails on ſo ſteady :
All my ſenſes leave me too,
Since my magic power hath left me !

[*The ſound of an earthquake is heard, and the palace diſappears.*

Palaces ſink down in ruin,
And the dark hills that upheld them,
Reappear in all their wildneſs—
I ſole dweller in the deſert :
For from me hath holy Penance
Him releaſed, whom charm'd I held here,
By the virtue this divineſt
Bread, this heavenly food, poſſeſſes.

All.

Let this mightieſt miracle

El Mundo mil Fieſtas haga,
Principalmente Madrid,
Noble corazon de Eſpaña,
Que en celebrar á Dios Fieſta
Con la opinion ſe levanta.

Con eſta repeticion, y al ſon de las Chirimías, ſe dá FIN AL AUTO.

Over all the world be fêted,
Specially within Madrid,
City where Spain's proud heart ſwelleth,
Which, in honouring God's Body,
Takes the foremoſt place for ever.

With a repetition of this, and to the ſound of clarions, THE AUTO CONCLUDES.

THE DEVOTION OF THE CROSS.

FROM THE SPANISH OF CALDERON.

INTRODUCTION.

L*A Devocion de la Cruz* was firſt printed at Hueſca, in 1634, in the twenty-eighth volume of the collection devoted to the dramatic works of various authors.* In the Introduction to *Love the Greateſt Enchantment*, I have already deſcribed this exceedingly rare collection, and enumerated the very few volumes of it that are now known to exiſt. The volume which contains *La Devocion de la Cruz*, under the name of *La Cruz en la Sepultura*, contains alſo another of Calderon's dramas, *Amor*, *Honor y Poder*, under the leſs conciſe title of *La Induſtria contra el Poder*, *y el Honor contra la Fuerza*, and both are ſtrangely attributed to Lope de Vega. *La Cruz en la Sepultura* is deſcribed as differing occaſionally from *La Devocion de la Cruz*, as ordinarily printed, and contains three characters and one entire ſcene which are not to be found in any of the editions of the drama publiſhed under that title. The *names* I have introduced, between brackets, into the liſt of *Perſons repreſented*, and the *ſcene*, ſimilarly marked, I have tranſlated at the proper place. Conſidering the power exhibited in this "wonderful and terrible drama," as

* *Parte Veinte y Ocho de Comedias de Varios Autores.* En Hueſca, por Pedro Bluſon, impreſor de la Univerſidad, año de 1634. A coſta de Pedro Eſcuer, mercader de libros. Señor Hartzenbuſch mentions his having ſeen *La Cruz en la Sepultura* printed as a ſeparate play, but without date, place, or name of printer. See his *Prologo*, t. I. p. xv. and his liſt of *Ediciones Conſultadas*, t. IV. pp. 654 and 659.

it has been well called by a diſtinguiſhed living writer,* and the celebrity which it has obtained in foreign countries, moſt readers will be ſurpriſed to learn that it was one of the earlieſt productions of Calderon; written probably during his reſidence at the Univerſity of Salamanca, which he left at nineteen, but certainly, as it is ſtated, before 1620, when he had only completed his twentieth year.† Like moſt young dramatic writers, he appears to have freely made uſe of the labours of his predeceſſors; and the following dramas are ſuppoſed to have had very conſiderable influence upon him, both in the conception and working out of *The Devotion of the Croſs*. The firſt of theſe is *La Fundacion de la Orden de la nueſtra Señora de la Merced*, by the Canon Tarrega, which is given in the exceedingly ſcarce volume of Valencian Dramatiſts, publiſhed at Valencia in 1616, a copy of which I poſſeſs.‡ Another is Tirſo de Molina's *El Condenado por Deſconfiado*, the *Enrico* of which ſingularly reſembles, both in his crimes and his love of relating them,§ the *Euſebio* of *The Devotion of the Croſs*, the *Ludovico Enio* of *The Purgatory of St. Patrick*, and other of Calderon's heroes of a ſimilar ſtamp. Mira de Meſcua's *El Eſclavo del Demonio* is, however, the play to which Calderon

* The Rev. Chenevix Trench, Dean of Weſtminſter. See his *Life's a Dream*, &c. p. 69. London, 1856.

† "*La Devocion de la Cruz.* Eſcrita antes del año 1620, cenſurada ya para la impreſion en 3 de Abril de 1633." See CORRECCIONES at the end of *Comedias* de ALARCON; Madrid, 1852.

‡ *Norte de la Poeſia Eſpañola*, &c. Año 1616; con privilegio. Impreſo en Valencia; en la Impreſion de Felipe Mey. This and a preceding volume, *Doce Comedias famoſas de cuatro Poetas naturales de la inſigne y coronado Ciudad de Valencia*, año 1609, are among the ſcarceſt of Spaniſh books, no copy being known to exiſt in any of the pubilc or private libraries of Madrid, or perhaps of all Spain, as Señor Ramon de Meſoneros Romanos ſays, except that in the library of the Queen at Madrid, from which he has made his extracts in the firſt volume of his *Dramaticos Contemporaneos a Lope de Vega*; Madrid, 1857. See his *Diſcurſo Preliminar*, pp. xii. and xxi.

§ See *Comedias Eſcogidas* de Fray Gabriel Tellez (el Maeſtro Tirſo de Molina); Madrid, 1850, p. 189.

is more directly indebted, he having not only imitated the general action of that drama, but having transferred, according to Tieck, ſeveral paſſages of it, almoſt verbatim, to his own pages.* *The Devotion of the Croſs* has been admirably tranſlated into German by Auguſt Wilhelm von Schlegel, as has alſo *El Mayor Encanto Amor*, of which, in the preceding pages, a tranſlation has been given. In Engliſh and French literature few writers have ever referred to Calderon without praiſing the poetical power and beauty of this drama, and condemning it as "the very ſublime of antinomianiſm." Like many other celebrated literary works, however, it has been more frequently referred to than read, and many writers have, either through careleſſneſs or wilful hoſtility, needleſsly miſrepreſented and exaggerated its defects.† Among critics who ſeem to have been actuated by the latter ſpirit muſt be placed Siſmondi, whoſe analyſis of *The Devotion of the Croſs* is more than uſually inaccurate and unfair. One would think that there are crimes enough, either referred to or committed, in this drama, without the neceſſity of adding to them; and yet, by direct aſſertion and inſinuation, he leaves on the mind of the reader a horrible impreſſion of the almoſt unutterable criminality of the two principal characters, which, if true, would of courſe render it unfit to be read, enacted, and, I need ſcarcely ſay, tranſlated. The ſubject is difficult to be alluded to; and yet, in juſtice to a great poet, whoſe defects, whatever they may have been, were certainly not thoſe which might be

* See Schack's *Geſchichte der dramatiſchen Literatur und Kunſt in Spanien*, b. iii. p. 55.

† In deſcribing the claſs of dramas to which *The Devotion of the Croſs* belongs, it is ſingular that Bouterwek ſhould have fallen into the miſtake of calling it an *Auto;* thereby leaving us to infer that he did not underſtand the marked and impaſſible diſtance that ſeparates a religious *Drama* (*Comedia*) of Calderon, or any other Spaniſh poet, from an *Auto. The Sorceries of Sin* in this volume will give the reader ſome idea of what an *Auto* is, and how impoſſible it is to confound it with a *Drama* in the ordinary ſenſe, even when dealing with ſpiritual or religious ſubjects or things. Mr. Longfellow has fallen into the ſame miſtake as Bouterwek, in his deſcription of this drama. See the chapter on *The Devotional Poetry of Spain*, in his *Outre Mer*.

inferred from the ſelection of ſuch topics as thoſe alluded to, I cannot avoid it altogether. Siſmondi, in ſpeaking of this drama, calls the hero, Euſebio, "an inceſtuous brigand;" and, as if this were not enough, adds, further on, the phraſe, "His ſiſter, Julia, *who is alſo his miſtreſs*,"* &c. Now for the ſhocking aſſertion contained in theſe two quotations there is not the ſlighteſt ſhadow of foundation. No criminal intercourſe whatever exiſts between the hero and heroine of this terrible tragedy (how prevented the reader will learn in the powerful ſcene, which, however faintly interpreted, muſt rivet his attention), and the unſuſpected relationſhip which exiſts between them is never known to one of the parties until his laſt moments, and to the other until after the death of her brother. How differently does another diſtinguiſhed French writer allude to this ſubject. With the beautiful paſſage to which I refer, I ſhall leave the drama in the hands of the reader. "On devine ſans peine," ſays M. Philaréte Chaſles, "que Julia eſt la ſœur d'Euſebe; et cette invention dramatique augmentant d'intenſité irait coudoyer l'horrible et l'inſoutenable, ſi Calderon n'était doué de ce vrai genie dont l'eſſence eſt pure. Nous allons le voir, dans une occaſion ſi difficile, retrouver la moralité qui lui eſt propre, la ſublime pudeur qui ne l'abandonne jamais. Ses ailes blanches et vierges trempent dans l'orage ſans ſe flétrir, et effleurent la foudre ſans ſe bruler."†

With regard to the locality in which the action of this ſingular drama is ſuppoſed to take place, it may be right to add a few words. Neither in this, nor in any of the other dramas of Calderon, as given to us in the ordinary editions,‡ is the *ſcene* ever mentioned, nor any of the uſual aids

* *Literature of the South of Europe*. I quote from Bohn's tranſlation, v. II. p. 379, not having the original by me. Mr. Lewes, with equal inaccuracy, alſo adds the crime alluded to in the text to the category of Euſebio's offences. See his *Spaniſh Drama;* London, 1846, p. 110.

† *Etudes ſur l'Eſpagne*, par M. Philaréte Chaſles; Paris, 1847, p. 55.

‡ A remark which may be applied not only to all the Spaniſh editions prior to that

to the reader's imagination ſupplied, ſuch as we generally find in the dramatic literature of other countries. In the early Engliſh drama, a board with the name of a town written upon it was ſufficient for the lively imagination of the audience to waſt the ſpectators from London to York, or from Venice to Verona. But in the Spaniſh plays, as *printed*, this ſignpoſt information is wanting, and the reader is obliged to infer the ſcene of the event from the language of the characters engaged. This want, with many others, is ſupplied in the edition of Señor Hartzenbuſch, as well as in ſuch German and French tranſlations as I have ſeen. In the preſent inſtance "Sena" is the centre round which all the action of the drama revolves. Señor Hartzenbuſch prints the word "Sena" as in the text, leaving it doubtful whether he underſtands it to mean Siena in Italy, or one of the three ſmall towns in Spain that are called Sena. M. Damas Hinard, in his proſe verſion of this play,* mentions two of theſe, one in Aragon, the other in Leon, and is uncertain which of them to decide on. A third, near Santander, might be added, which, if we are to look at all in Spain for the locality, might be more likely, as the ſea is mentioned more than once, as being in the neighbourhood of "the mountain," which is the ſcene of ſo many wonders. This, however, would not be ſufficient to decide the queſtion, becauſe in matters of geographical preciſion Calderon was as careleſs as Greene in his *Pandoſto*, or Shakeſpeare in his *Winter's Tale*. But it ſeems to me that, notwithſtanding the ſtrong Spaniſh colouring of the entire landſcape, the rude croſſes, the *bandoleros*, and the *ſierras*, Siena in Italy muſt be conſidered the centre round which all this wild and imaginary ſcenery lies, Sena being the ancient Latin name of Siena, which Calderon probably adopted. If proof were wanting, the facts of the ſtory, either alluded to

of Señor Hartzenbuſch's, but to all the foreign reprints that I have ſeen, including thoſe of Ochoa (Paris, 1847), and of Keil (Leipzic, 1827-30).

* *Chefs-d'œuvre de Théâtre Eſpagnol:* Calderon, 1re ſérie; Paris, 1841, p. 148, *note*.

or enacted, would be sufficient:—the mission of Curcio from the Republic to the Pope; the journeying to and from Rome by Alberto, bishop of Trent; his professorship in the University of Bologna; and, lastly, the account which the Genoese painter gives of himself, in the scene taken from the Huesca edition of *La Cruz en la Sepultura*, of his bringing to Florence a painting ordered by one of his patrons there. Schlegel, in his *Die Andacht zum Kreuze*, adopts Siena without any remark, as does the writer of the very accurate paper on *The Devotion of the Cross* in Blackwood,* and as most other English writers have done who have alluded to this play.

* Blackwood's Magazine, vol. xviii. p. 83. July, 1825.

PERSONS REPRESENTED.

EUSEBIO.	EUSEBIO.
CURCIO, *viejo.*	CURCIO.
LISARDO.	LISARDO, *his ſon.*
OCTAVIO.	OCTAVIO, *in Curcio's ſervice.*
ALBERTO, *viejo.*	ALBERTO, *an aged prieſt, biſhop of Trent.*
GIL, *villano gracioſo.*	GIL, *a peaſant.*
BRAS, TIRSO, TORIBIO, } *villanos.*	TIRSO, BRAS, TORIBIO, } *peaſants.*
CELIO, RICARDO, } *bandoleros.*	CELIO, RICARDO, } *bandits.*
[UN PINTOR.	[A PAINTER.
UN POETA.	A POET.
UN ASTROLOGO.]*	AN ASTROLOGER.]*
JULIA, *dama.*	JULIA, *Curcio's daughter.*
ARMINDA, *criada.*	ARMINDA, *her attendant.*
CHILINDRINA.	CHILLINDRINA, *a follower of the bandits.*
MENGA, *villana gracioſa.*	MENGA, *Gil's wife.*
Bandoleros y Villanos.	*Bandits and Peaſants.*
Soldados.	*Soldiers.*

SCENE, *Siena and its Neighbourhood.*

* From the edition of Hueſca, 1634.

THE DEVOTION OF THE CROSS.

JORNADA I.

ARBOLEDA IMMEDIATA A UN CAMINO QUE SE DIRIGE A SENA.

Dicen dentro MENGA *y* GIL.

Menga.
VERÁ por dó va la burra.

Gil.
Jo dimuño; jo mohina.

Menga.
Ya verá por do camina:
Arre acá.

Gil.
¡El diabro te aburra!
¿No hay quién una cola tenga,
Pudiendo tenella mil?

[*Salen los dos.*

Menga.
¡Buena hacienda has hecho, Gil!

Gil.
¡Buena hacienda has hecho, Menga,
Pues tú la culpa tuviste!

ACT I.

A WILD WOODY MOUNTAIN DISTRICT, NOT FAR FROM THE HIGH ROAD TO SIENA.

MENGA *and* GIL *behind the Scenes.*

Menga.
SEE! the aſs is going to turn her!

Gil.
Yo, dolt's dam! yo, devil's daughter!

Menga.
There, ſhe's ſtuck! you ſhould have caught her;
Yo! geho!

Gil.
The devil burn her!
Had ſhe fifty tails to tickle,
All were vain againſt her will.

[*They enter.*

Menga.
What a fix we're in, friend Gil!

Gil.
What the devil of a pickle!
All through fault of yours, I'm thinking,

Que como ibas caballera,
Que en el hoyo ſe metiera,
Al oido la dijiſte,
Por hacerme regañar.

Menga.

Por verme caer á mí,
Se lo dijiſte, eſo sí.

Gil.

¿ Cómo la hemos de ſacar ?

Menga.

¿ Pues en el lodo la dejas ?

Gil.

No puede mi fuerza ſola.

Menga.

Yo tiraré de la cola,
Tira tú de las orejas.

Gil.

Mejor remedio ſeria
Hacer el que aprovechó
A un coche, que ſe ataſcó
En la corte eſotro dia.
Eſte coche, Dios delante,
Que arraſtrado de dos potros,
Parecia entre los otros
Pobre coche vergonzante.
Y por maldicion muy cierta
De ſus padres (hado eſquivo !)
Iba de eſtribo en eſtribo,
Ya que no de puerta en puerta ;
En un arroyo ataſcado,
Con ruegos el caballero,
Con azotes el cochero,
Ya por fuerza, ya por grado,
Ya por guſto, ya por miedo,
Que ſalieſen procuraban :
Por recio que lo mandaban,
Mi coche quedo que quedo.
Viendo que no importan nada
Cuantos remedios hicieron,

Since, my Menga, ſince you rode her,
You it muſt have been who ſhow'd her
Juſt the very ſpot to ſink in ;—
'Tis to vex me that you teaze her.

Menga.

Since ſhe threw me o'er her ſhoulder,
You it muſt have been who told her.

Gil.

But the queſtion, How releaſe her ?

Menga.

In the mud wouldſt leave her here ?

Gil.

All my ſtrength, as nought, avails her.

Menga.

I can pull her by the tail, ſir ;
You can pull her by the ear.

Gil.

No, I think a better way,
And a quicker to revive her,
Is to do, as did the driver
Of a coach the other day.
This ſame coach, the execration
Of the ſtreets, in ſlow approaches
Slunk beſide the other coaches,
Like a ſhabby poor relation ;
Or for ſome deep grief it bore,
(Who or what its grief can ſmother ?)
Went from one ſide to the other,
'Stead of *on* from door to door :—
In the kennel now 'tis ſtuck,
How the knight within doth growl !
Some try fair means, ſome try foul,
Coachee laſhes, footmen chuck,
Cuſhions fly to make it lighter,
All is noiſe and cries and worrit ;
But the more they ſtrive to ſtir it,
Seems my coach to ſtick the tighter.
Seeing thus 'twere beſt to parley,
Coachee takes the beſt of courſes,

Delante el coche puſieron
Un harnero de cebada.
Los caballos, por comer,
De tal manera tiraron,
Que toſieron y arrancaron;
Y eſto podemos hacer.

Menga.

¡Que nunca valen dos cuartos
Tus cuentos!

Gil.

Menga, yo ſiento
Ver un animal hambriento,
Donde hay animales hartos.

Menga.

Voy al camino á mirar
Si paſa de nueſtra aldea
Gente, cualquiera que ſea,
Porque te venga á ayudar,
Pues te das tan pocas mañas.

Gil.

¿Vuelves, Menga, á tu porfía?

Menga.

¡Ay burra del alma mia! [*Vaſe.*

Gil.

¡Ay burra de mis entrañas!
Tú fuiſte la mas honrada
Burra de toda la aldea;
Que no ha habido quien te vea
Nunca mal acompañada.
No eres nada callejera;
De mijor gana te eſtabas
En tu peſebre, que andabas,
Cuando te llevaban fuera.

And before the half-ſtarved horſes
Holds outſtretch'd a ſieve of barley;—
The poor ſtarvelings ſeek to ſwallow,
So they tug with might and main,
Drag the coach from out the drain,
And the example we may follow.*

Menga.

Tales like this you've now related
Ar'n't two farthings worth.

Gil.

O'ercaſt
Am I, ſeeing one beaſt *faſt*,
Where ſtand two quite ſatiated.

Menga.

I will to the road, the diſtance
Iſn't far, to ſee ſome neighbour
Paſſing to his daily labour,
Who will come to give aſſiſtance:
Since 'tis little zeal you ſhow.

Gil.

Menga mine, your wrath control.

Menga.

Oh! dear donkey of my ſoul! [*Exit.*

Gil.

Donkey of my bowels, oh!
Thou that wert the moſt reſpected
Donkey of our village green,
Thou that never yet haſt been
In bad company detected;
Thou that gadded not about,
But preferr'd domeſtic quiet,—
A ſnug manger and good diet—
To the joys of going out:

* Sydney Smith, in his amuſing lecture "On the Conduct of the Underſtanding," condemning what he calls "the foppery of univerſality" in one's ſtudies, ſays whimſically, that "he would exact of a young man a pledge never to read Lope de Vega!" Fortunately he does not include or exclude Calderon, who in this little ſtory happens to have anticipated the witty canon in the anecdote which he tells us of himſelf and his horſe "Calamity."—See *Life of* SYDNEY SMITH *by* LADY HOLLAND.

Pues ¿altanera y liviana?
Bien me atrevo á jurar yo,
Que ningun burro la vió
Aſomada á la ventana.
Yo ſé que no merecia
Su lengua deſdicha tal;
Pues jamas para habrar mal
Dijo: Aqueſta boca es mia.
Pues como á ella la ſobre
De lo que comiendo eſtá,
Luego al punto ſe lo da
A alguna borrica pobre.
[*Ruido dentro.*
Mas ¿qué ruido es eſte? Alli
De dos caballos ſe apean
Dos hombres, y hácia mí vienen,
Deſpues que atados los dejan.
¡Deſcoloridos, y al campo
De mañana¡ Coſa es cierta,
Que comen barro, ó eſtán
Opilados. Mas ¿ſi fueran
Bandoleros? ¡Aqui es ello!
Pero lo que fuere ſea,
Aqui me eſcondo; que andan,
Que corren, que ſalen, que entran.
[*Eſcóndeſe.*

Salen LISARDO *y* EUSEBIO.

Liſardo.

No paſemos adelante,
Porque eſta eſtancia encubierta
Y apartada del camino,
Es para mi intento buena.
Sacad, Euſebio, la eſpada;
Que yo, de aqueſta manera,
A los hombres como vos

Though thou'rt ſkittiſh, may be vain,
Yet I'll ſwear it, notwithſtanding,
No one ever ſaw you ſtanding,
Ogling at the window-pane.
True, that honeſt tongue of thine
Is a little rough, no matter,
You ſpeak truly, and don't flatter,
When you ſay, This voice is mine.
And you're generous, too, the graſs
Which your maw declines receiving,
I have often ſeen you leaving
To ſome poor and hungrier aſs.*
[*A noiſe within.*
But what noiſe is this? Oh! yonder
I behold two men who've ridden
Hard here, tie their panting horſes
To the trees, and wander hither;—
Pale! and in the fields ſo early!
Oh! 'tis plain they've got green ſickneſs.
Should they prove, though, bandoleros!
'Gad! that were a pretty buſineſs!—
Be they who they may, 'tis better
That I hide me here a little.
Here they come; they reach, they enter,
Ere I've ſcarcely time to fix me.
[*He conceals himſelf.*

Enter LISARDO *and* EUSEBIO.

Liſardo.

Let us then proceed no farther,
Since this thorny-tangled thicket,
Screen'd and ſever'd from the highway,
For my object is well fitted.
Draw then, draw your ſword, Euſebio,
As I mine, for thus ſuccinctly
Do I challenge men like you

* The humour of this addreſs will not unpleaſantly recall Goldſmith's "Elegy on the glory of her Sex, Mrs. Mary Blaize."

Saco á reñir.

Euſebio.

Aunque tenga
Baſtante cauſa en haber
Llegado al campo, quiſiera
Saber lo que á vos os mueve.
Decid, Liſardo, la queja,
Que de mí teneis.

Liſardo.

Son tantas,
Que falta voz á la lengua,
Razones á la razon,
Y al ſufrimiento paciencia.
Quiſiera, Euſebio, callarlas,
Y aun olvidarlas quiſiera;
Porque cuando ſe repiten,
Hacen de nuevo la ofenſa.
¿Conoceis eſtos papeles?

Euſebio.

Arrojadlos en la tierra,
Y los alzaré.

Liſardo.

Tomad.
Qué os ſuſpendeis? qué os altera?

Euſebio.

Mal haya el hombre, mal haya
Mil veces aquel, que entrega
Sus ſecretos á un papel;
Porque es diſparada piedra,
Que ſe ſabe quien la tira,
Y no ſe ſabe á quien llega.

Liſardo.

¿Habéiſlos ya conocido?

Euſebio.

Todos eſtán de mi letra,
Que no la puedo negar.

Liſardo.

Pues yo ſoy Liſardo, en Sena,

To the combat.

Euſebio.

Though ſufficient
Cauſe have I in having come
To the field here, yet my wiſhes
Are to know what thus has moved you.
Say, Liſardo, ſay what hidden
Charge againſt me have you?

Liſardo.

I
Have ſo many, that to hint them
Would my tongue want words, my
reaſon
Utterance, and all patience quit me.
I, Euſebio, would in ſilence,
Nay, in dark oblivion ſink them,
Since an inſult when repeated
Is a ſecond time committed.
Do you recognize theſe papers?

Euſebio.

Throw them down, and I will lift them
From the ground.

Liſardo.

They're *there* then, take them:—
Why thus tremble? Why thus ſhiver?

Euſebio.

Woe unto the man! a thouſand
Woes to him, who hath committed
His heart's ſecrets to a letter!
'Tis a random ſtone, a miſſile,
Which the hand that flings it knoweth,
But is ignorant whom it hitteth.

Liſardo.

Have you ſcrutiniſed them fully?

Euſebio.

That theſe letters were all written
By my hand, I muſt acknowledge.

Liſardo.

Well, Siena is my birth-place,

Hijo de Lifardo Curcio.
Bien excufadas grandezas
De mi padre confumieron
En breve tiempo la hacienda,
Que los fuyos le dejaron ;
Que no fabe cuánto yerra
Quien, por excefivos gaftos,
Pobres á fus hijos deja.
Pero la necefidad,
Aunque ultraje la nobleza,
No excufa de obligaciones
A los que nacen con ellas.
Julia pues, (¡ faben los cielos,
Cuanto el nombrarla me pefa !)
O no fupo confervarlàs,
O no llegó á conocerlas.
Pero al fin, Julia es mi hermana ;
¡ Pluguiera á Dios no lo fuera !
Y advertid, que no fe firven
Las mujeres de fus prendas
Con amorofos papeles,
Con razones lifonjeras,
Con ilícitos recados,
Ni con infames terceras.
No os culpo en el todo á vos ;
Que yo confiefo, que hiciera
Lo mifmo, á darme una dama
Para fervirla licencia ;
Pero cúlpos en la parte
De fer mi amigo, y en efta
Con mas culpa os comprehende
La culpa que tuvo ella.
Si mi hermana os agradó
Para mujer (que no era
Pofible, ni yo lo creo
Que os atreviérais á verla
Con otro fin, ni aun con efte ;
Pues ¡ vive Dios ! que quifiera
Antes, que con vos cafada,

And my fire Lifardo Curcio.
The unfparing, the unftinted
Habits of my father wafted
Soon the wealth to him tranfmitted
By more prudent predeceffors;
Ignorant how much he finneth,
Who by wild and wafteful outlay
Maketh paupers of his children.
But although neceffity
May a noble name disfigure,
It exempts not from their duties
Thofe whofe birth is burthen'd with
them.
Julia then . . . . (ah me! Heaven knows
How to name her name afflicts me!)
Knew not rightly to obferve them,
Or not knowing them could omit them.
But ftill Julia (would to God
That fhe were not!) is my fifter,
And you know, when wooing women
Of her rank, 'tis not permitted
To indite perfuafive flatteries,
To addrefs love-laden billets,
To fend meffages in fecret,
And hire go-betweens to bring them.
I for this don't wholly blame you,
Since I will confefs, in this way
Would I act too, if a lady
Leave to woo her would but give me;
But I blame you, from the fact of
Being my friend, and fo, from *this*, fee
How through you the fault is doubled,
That by her has been committed.
If my fifter pleafed your fancy
As a wife (I cannot bring me
To believe it poffible,
That you ever hoped to win her
Otherwife, or even as this;
Since, as God lives! I would wifh her,

Mirarla á mis manos muerta):
En fin, ſi vos la elegíſteis
Para mujer, juſto fuera
Deſcubrir vueſtros deſeos
A mi padre, antes que á ella.
Eſte era término juſto,
Y entonces mi padre viera,
Si le eſtaba bien el darla,
Que pienſo que no os la diera;
Porque un caballero pobre,
Cuando en coſas como eſtas
No puede medir iguales
La calidad y la hacienda,
Por no deſlucir ſu ſangre
Con una hija doncella,
Hace ſagrado un convento;
Que es delito la pobreza.
Aqueſte á Julia mi hermana
Con tanta priſa la eſpera,
Que mañana ha de ſer monja,
Por voluntad, ó por fuerza.
Y porque no ſerá bien,
Que una religioſa tenga
Prendas de tan loco amor,
Y de voluntad tan necia,
A vueſtras manos las vuelvo,
Con reſolucion tan ciega,
Que no ſolo he de quitarlas,
Mas tambien la cauſa dellas.
Sacad la eſpada, y aqui
El uno de los dos muera;
Vos, porque no la ſirvais,
O yo, porque no lo vea.

Euſebio.

Tened, Liſardo, la eſpada,
Y pues yo he tenido flema
Para oir deſprecios mios,

Ere with you I ſaw her married,
Dead, although my own hands kill'd her):
In a word, if you ſelected
Her to be your wife, 'twere fitteſt
That, before herſelf, my father
Were acquainted with your wiſhes.
That were the correct proceeding.
Then my father would conſider
If 'twere right to give her to you,
And I think he would not give her;
For a gentleman grown poor,
When a caſe like this ariſes,
If he finds he cannot equal
Fortune with his rank's requirements,
Leſt through an unmarried daughter
On his blood ſhould fall defilement,
Seeks the ſafeguard of a convent;
Such a crime is want of riches.
This fate now ſo ſoon awaiteth
Upon Julia, on my ſiſter,
That ſhe muſt the veil to-morrow
Take, though force control her wiſhes!
And becauſe it were not right
That a novice ſhould have with her
Proofs of ſuch a fooliſh paſſion,
And of a deſire ſo ſilly,
I return them to your hands,
With a blind reſolve and fixèd,
To deſtroy not only them,
But the very hand that writ them.
Draw then, draw your ſword, for now
Either of us twain muſt die here;
You, that you may ceaſe your ſervice,
I, that ſervice not to witneſs.

Euſebio.

Sheathe your ſword awhile, Liſardo,
And ſince I have deign'd to liſten
With ſuch phlegm to my diſpraiſes,

Eſcuchadme la reſpueſta;
Y aunque el diſcurſo ſea largo
De mi ſuceſo, y parezca
Que, eſtando ſolos los dos,
Es demaſiada paciencia,
Pues que ya es fuerza reñir,
Y morir el uno es fuerza;
Por ſi los cielos permiten,
Que yo el infelice ſea,
Oid prodigios que admiran,
Y maravillas que elevan;
Que no es bien, que con mi muerte
Eterno ſilencio tengan.
Yo no ſé quien fue mi padre;
Pero ſé, que la primera
Cuna fué el pie de una Cruz,
Y el primer lecho una piedra.
Raro fué mi nacimiento,
Segun los paſtores cuentan,
Que deſta ſuerte me hallaron
En la falda de eſas ſierras.
Tres dias, dicen, que oyeron
Mi llanto, y que á la aſpereza,
Donde eſtaba, no llegaron
Por el temor de las fieras,
Sin que alguna me ofendieſe:
Pero ¿quién duda que era
Por reſpeto de la Cruz,
Que tenia en mi defenſa?
Hallóme un paſtor, que acaſo
Buſcó una perdida oveja
En la aſpereza del monte,
Y trayéndome á la aldea
De Euſebio, que no ſin cauſa
Eſtaba entónces en ella.
Le contó mi prodigioſo
Nacimiento, y la clemencia
Del cielo aſiſtió á la ſuya.
Mandó en fin, que me trajeran

Hear the anſwer that I give them:—
And although my life's ſtrange ſtory
May ſeem long, and the recital
Out of reaſonable patience
Weary you, we ſtanding pitted
Breaſt to breaſt thus for the combat,
In which one of us muſt die here,
And leſt Heaven perchance permitteth
Me to be the hapleſs victim,
Hear the wonders moſt aſtounding,
Hear the marvels moſt ſurpriſing,
Which 'twere wrong my death ſhould
hide here
In its everlaſting ſilence.
Who my father was I know not;
But I know this, I, an infant,
Had a croſs's foot for cradle,
And a hard ſtone for my firſt bed.
Strange my birth, and ſtrange the ſtory
Which the ſhepherds oft recited,
Who had found me thus abandon'd
In a gorge of theſe wild hills here.
For three days, they ſaid, they heard me
Crying, but to reach the cliffs where
I was placed they could not venture,
Through the terror of the wild beaſts,
One of whom nor hurt nor touch'd me;
Who can doubt through certain inſtincts
Of reſpect unto the Croſs
Which in my defence ſtood nigh me?
There by accident, a ſhepherd,
Seeking a loſt lamb, deſcried me
In the wildneſs of the mountain,
And who brought me to the village
Of Euſebio, who had cauſe then
Doubtleſs to be dwelling in it.
Him he told of my prodigious
Birth, and pitying Heaven aſſiſted
By its own, to wake his pity.

A ſu caſa, y como á hijo
Me dió la crianza en ella.
Euſebio ſoy de la Cruz,
Por ſu nombre, y por aquella,
Que fue mi primera guia,
Y fue mi guarda primera.
Tomé por guſto las armas,
Por paſatiempo las letras;
Murió Euſebio, y yo quedé
Heredero de ſu hacienda.
Si fue prodigioſo el parto,
No lo fue menos la eſtrella,
Que enemiga me amenaza,
Y piadoſa me reſerva.
Tierno infante era en los brazos
Del ama, cuando mi fiera
Condicion, bárbara en todo,
Dió de ſus rigores mueſtra;
Pues con ſolas las encías,
No ſin diabólica fuerza,
Partí el pecho de quien tuve
El dulce alimento; y ella,
Del dolor deſeſperada,
Y de la cólera ciega,
En un pozo me arrojó,
Sin que ninguno ſupiera
De mí. Oyéndome reir,
Bajáron á él, y cuentan,
Que eſtaba ſobre las aguas,
Y que con las manos tiernas
Tenia una Cruz formada,
Y ſobre los labios pueſta.
Un dia que ſe abraſaba
La caſa, y la llama fiera
Cerraba el paſo á la huida,
Y á la ſalida la puerta,
Entre las llamas eſtuve
Libre, ſin que me ofendieran:
Y advertí deſpues, dudando

Finally he bade them bring me
To his houſe, and as his ſon
To be rear'd, and cared, and chriſten'd.
Thus, Euſebio of the Croſs
Am I call'd; a name that mingles
His with that one which to me
Was my guide firſt, and my firſt friend.
Arms I took to as a paſſion,
As a paſtime books enticed me.
Then Euſebio died, and left me
The ſole heir of all his riches.
If my birth was ſo prodigious,
Nothing leſs ſo was my life's ſtar,—
Now a threat'ning foe to fright me,
Now a pitying friend to guide me.
Still a tender infant, lying
In my nurſe's arms, my wicked
Nature, which was wholly ſavage,
Gave a ſample of its wildneſs;
Since but with my gums, their weakneſs
By a demon's power aſſiſted,
I cut through the tender boſom
Out from which my ſweet food trickled:—
She, made deſperate by the anguiſh,
And by ſudden anger blinded,
Down into a deep well threw me,
Unperceived by any witneſs.
Thence my laugh being heard, they ventured
To the bottom, and the finders
Said they found me on the water,
And that with my little fingers
I a natural Croſs had faſhion'd,
And had placed it on my lips there.
On a certain day when fire had
Seized our dwelling, and the wild flame
Barr'd all entrance or all exit
From the outſide or the inner,

Que haya en el fuego clemencia,
Que era dia de la Cruz.
Tres luſtros contaba apenas,
Cuando por el mar fui á Roma,
Y en una brava tormenta,
Deſeſperada mi nave
Chocó en una oculta peña,
En pedazos dividida,
Por los coſtados abierta:
Abrazado de un madero
Salí venturoſo á tierra,
Y eſte madero tenia
Forma de Cruz. Por las ſierras
De eſos montes caminaba
Con otro hombre, y en la ſenda
Que dos caminos partia,
Una Cruz eſtaba pueſta.
En tanto que me quedé,
Haciendo oracion en ella,
Se adelantó el compañero;
Y deſpues dándome prieſa
Para alcanzarle, le hallé
Muerto á las manos ſangrientas
De bandoleros. Un dia,
Riñendo en una pendencia,
De una eſtocada caí,
Sin que hicieſe reſiſtencia,
En la tierra; y cuando todos
Penſaron hallarla ajena
De remedio, ſolo hallaron
Señal de la punta fiera
En una Cruz que traia
Al cuello, que en mi defenſa
Recibió el golpe. Cazando
Una vez por la aſpereza
Deſte monte, ſe cubrío
El cielo de nubes negras,
Y publicando con truenos
Al mundo eſpantoſa guerra,

I among the flames was able
To paſs free, untouch'd, uninjured;
And 'twas thought of then, while wonder
At the fire's forbearance fill'd them,
That it was the Day of the Croſs!
Scarce three luſtres had I circled,
When by ſea to Rome I journey'd;
And a wild ſtorm having riſen,
Drove my hapleſs bark with fury
On a ſharp rock lying hidden;
And the open bulwarks parting,
Soon the veſſel broke in ſplinters;—
I, a paſſing plank embracing,
Safely to the ſhore was drifted!
And this plank, I found, was faſhion'd
Like a Croſs. Among the ridges
Of theſe mountains once I travell'd
With a friend, and in the middle
Of the path where two roads parted
Was a ruſtic Croſs uplifted;
To recite a prayer before it
While I ſtay'd behind a little,
My companion ſtill went forward;
And when uſing double quickneſs
To o'ertake him, dead I found him,
By the red hands of banditti
Foully murder'd. I one day
Mix'd up in a feud, was ſmitten
By the ſharp ſtroke of a dagger,
So that down I fell reſiſtleſs
On the ground, and when all round me
Reckon'd that my wound admitted
Of no help, they could but only
Find a ſlight mark of the fierce ſteel
On a Croſs I wore ſuſpended
From my neck, and which was dinted
Thus in my defence. When hunting
Once amid the rougheſt diſtrict
Of this mountain, heaven had cover'd

Lanzas arrojaba en agua,
Balas diſparaba en piedras.
Todos hicieron las hojas
Contra las nubes defenſa,
Siendo ya tiendas de campo
Las mas ocultas malezas;
Y un rayo, que fue en el viento
Caliginoſo cometa,
Volvió en ceniza á los dos
Que de mí eſtaban mas cerca.
Ciego, turbado y confuſo
Vuelvo á mirar lo que era,
Y hallé á mi lado una Cruz,
Que yo pienſo que es la meſma,
Que aſiſtió á mi nacimiento,
Y la que yo tengo impreſa
En los pechos; pues los cielos
Me han ſeñalado con ella,
Para públicos efectos
De alguna cauſa ſecreta.
Pero aunque no ſé quien ſoy,
Tal eſpíritu me alienta,
Tal inclinacion me anima,
Y tal ánimo me fuerza,
Que por mí me da valor
Para que á Julia merezca;
Porque no es mas la heredada,
Que la adquirida nobleza.
Eſte ſoy, y aunque conozco
La razon, y aunque pudiera
Dar ſatisfaccion baſtante
A vueſtro agravio, me ciega
Tanto la paſion de veros
Hablando de eſa manera,
Que ni os quiero dar diſculpa,
Ni os quiero admitir la queja;
Y pues quereis eſtorbar,
Que yo ſu marido ſea;
Aunque ſu caſa la guarde,

Itſelf o'er with black clouds thickly,
And in thunder-claps proclaiming
'Gainſt the world a war terrific,
Shot its bullets in the hail-ſtones,
In the rain its lances tilted.
We all flying from the cloud-guſts,
Shelter ſought beneath the thick leaves,
Where, like tents of an encampment,
Arch'd the thickets dark and prickly;
When a bolt, that on the ſwift wind
Like a vaporous comet glitter'd,
Into aſhes burn'd the two
Who were ſtanding cloſe beſide me!
Blind, diſtracted, in confuſion
Round I turn'd to ſee what hid me,
And I then perceived a Croſs,—
It the ſame, in my opinion,
Which ſtood o'er me on my birth-day,
And of which I bear the impreſs
On my breaſt; ſince Heaven hath mark'd me
With that ſymbol's myſtic image,
Thus to publiſh the effects
Of a cauſe that yet lies hidden.
Thus though ignorant who I am,
Such a ſpirit doth incite me,
Such an impulſe animates me,
Such a glow of courage fires me,
That I feel I'm not unworthy
To love Julia, and to win her;
Since nobility is equal
Whether ſelf-born or tranſmitted.
This I am, and though the reaſon
I well know, and though ſufficient
Satisfaction I could make you
For your wrong, ſuch paſſion blinds me,
Seeing that you have adreſs'd me
In a way ſo cold and ſlighting,
That I'll neither make excuſes,

Aunque un convento la tenga,
De mí no ha de eſtar ſegura ;
Y la que no ha ſido buena
Para mujer, lo ſerá
Para dama ; aſi deſea
Deſeſperado mi amor,
Y ofendida mi paciencia,
Caſtigar vueſtro deſprecio,
Y ſatisfacer mi afrenta.

Liſardo.

Euſebio, donde el acero
Ha de hablar, calle la lengua.

[*Sacan las eſpadas y riñen, y* LISARDO *cae en el ſuelo, y procurando levantarſe, torna á caer.*

¡ Herido eſtoy !

Euſebio.

¿ Y no muerto ?

Liſardo.

No, que en los brazos me queda
Aliento para . . . . ¡ Ay de mí !
Faltó á mis plantas la tierra.

Euſebio.

Y falte á tu voz la vida.

Liſardo.

No me permitas que muera
Sin confeſion.

Euſebio.

¡ Muere, infame !

Liſardo.

No me mates, por aquella
Cruz en que Criſto murió.

Euſebio.

Aqueſa voz te defienda

Nor admit the quarrel right here ;
And ſince my deſire of being
Married to her you would hinder,
Though her father's houſe ſhould guard her,
Though a convent's walls may hide her,
Neither ſhall enſure her ſafety ;
She, too good to be permitted
To become my wife, ſhall ſerve me
As a miſtreſs :—thus deſireth
The deſpair of my affection,
Thus my patience now extinguiſh'd,
To chaſtiſe your proud deſpiſal,
And my honour's ſtain outwipe here.

Liſardo.

When the ſword can ſpeak, Euſebio,
Let the tongue at leaſt be ſilent.

[*They draw and fight.*

Ah ! I'm wounded ! [*He falls.*

Euſebio.

And not dead ?

Liſardo.

No ! for in theſe arms ſurviveth
Strength enough . . . . But woe is me,
'Neath my feet the firm earth ſinketh !

Euſebio.

And in life's laſt gaſp thy voice ſinks.

Liſardo.

Oh ! allow me not unſhriven
Here to die !

Euſebio.

Die ! miſcreant, villain !

Liſardo.

I implore you not to kill me,
By the Croſs on which Chriſt ſuffer'd.

Euſebio.

Ah ! that ſolemn word unfits me

De la muerte. Alza del ſuelo;
Que cuando por ella ruegas,
Falta rigor á la ira,
Y falta á los brazos fuerza.
Alza del ſuelo.

Liſardo.

No puedo;
Porque ya en mi ſangre envuelta
Voy deſpreciando la vida,
Y el alma pienſo que eſpera
A ſalir, porque entre tantas
No ſabe cual es la puerta.

Euſebio.

Pues fíate de mis brazos,
Y anímate; que aqui cerca
De unos penitentes monjes
Hay una ermita pequeña,
Donde podrás confeſarte,
Si vivo á ſus puertas llegas.

Liſardo.

Pues yo te doy mi palabra,
Por eſa piedad que mueſtras,
Que ſi yo merezco verme
En la divina preſencia
De Dios, pediré que tú
Sin confeſarte no mueras.

[*Llévale* EUSEBIO *en brazos.*

Gil.

¡Han viſto lo que le debe!
La caridad eſtá buena;
Pero yo ſe la perdono.
¡Matarle, y llevarle á cueſtas!

Salen BRAS, TIRSO, MENGA *y* TORIBIO.

Toribio.

¿Aqui dices que quedaba?

Menga.

Aqui ſe quedó con ella.

For the death-ſtroke. Riſe, Liſardo,
Since when you through it aſk pity,
From my arm the ſtrength departeth,
From my anger flies its rigour.
Riſe, then, from the ground.

Liſardo.

I cannot;
For already the red river
Of my life is paſt all ſtaying,
And I think the ſoul but lingers
To go forth, becauſe it knows not
Which, 'mid many, is the right door.

Euſebio.

Then entruſt thee to my arms,
And take courage; for hard by here
Stands the little hermitage
Of ſome penitential friars,
Where thou may'ſt confeſs, if haply
Thou to reach their doors ſurviveſt.

Liſardo.

For the pity thou doſt ſhow me,
I my ſolemn promiſe give thee,
That if e'er to God's divineſt
Preſence I ſhall be admitted,
I ſhall aſk for thee the grace
Likewiſe not to die unſhriven.

[EUSEBIO *carries him out in his arms.*

Gil.

Whoe'er ſaw the like of this?
Charity in faith's a fine thing;
But I'll rather you'd excuſe me:—
Firſt to kill him, then to lift him!

Enter MENGA, BRAS, TIRSO, *and* TORIBIO.

Toribio.

Was it here you ſaid he waited?

Menga.

Here it was I left him with her.

Tirſo.
Mírale alli embeleſado.
Menga.
Gil, ¿qué mirabas?
Gil.
¡Ay Menga!
Tirſo.
¿Qué te ha ſucedido?
Gil.
¡Ay Tirſo!
Toribio.
¿Qué viſte? Danos reſpueſta.
Gil.
¡Ay Toribio!
Bras.
Di, ¿qué tienes,
Gil, ó de qué te lamentas?
Gil.
¡Ay Bras, ay amigos mios!
No lo ſé mas que una beſtia:
Matóle, y cargó con él,
Sin duda á ſalar le lleva.
Menga.
¿Quién le mató?
Gil.
¿Que ſé yo?
Tirſo.
¿Quién murió?
Gil.
No ſé quien era.
Toribio.
¿Quién cargó?
Gil.
¿Que ſé yo quien?
Bras.
¿Y quién le llevó?
Gil.
Quien quiera.

Tirſo.
See him, how he ſtares and gapes there.
Menga.
What do you gaze at, Gil?
Gil.
Ah, Menga!
Tirſo.
What has happen'd to you?
Gil.
Ah, Tirſo!
Toribio.
What have you ſeen? come, tell us quickly.
Gil.
Ah, Toribio!
Bras.
Say, what ails you,
Gil, or wherefore do you ſigh ſo?
Gil.
Ah! friend Bras, ah! all my neighbours,
Aſs that I am, I know not *why* ſo:
Him he kill'd, and raiſed and carried
Off, I hav'n't a doubt, to pickle.
Menga.
Who was it kill'd him?
Gil.
How do *I* know?
Tirſo.
Who was kill'd?
Gil.
I know not either.
Toribio.
Who raiſed him up?
Gil.
How know I who did?
Bras.
Who carried him off?
Gil.
Whoe'er you like then:

Pero porque lo ſepais,
Venid todos.

Tirſo.

¿Do nos llevas?

Gil.

No lo ſé; pero venid,
Que los dos van aqui cerca.

[*Vanſe todos.*

SALA EN CASA DE CURCIO, EN SENA.

Salen JULIA *y* ARMINDA.

Julia.

Déjame, Arminda, llorar
Una libertad perdida,
Pues donde acaba la vida,
Tambien acaba el peſar.
¿Nunca has viſto de una fuente
Bajar un arroyo manſo,
Siendo apacible deſcanſo
El valle de ſu corriente;
Y cuando le juzgan falto
De fuerza las flores bellas,
Paſa por encima dellas,
Rompiendo por lo mas alto?
Pues mis penas, mis enojos
La miſma experiencia han hecho;
Detuviéronſe en el pecho,
Y ſalieron por los ojos.
Deja que llore el rigor
De un padre.

Arminda.

Señora, advierte . . .

Julia.

¿Qué mas venturoſa ſuerte
Hay, que morir de dolor?
Pena que deja vencida
La vida, ſer gloria ordena;

But to find out all about it
Come with me.

Tirſo.

But where will you bring us?

Gil.

I don't know, but come along
For the two are not far diſtant.

[*Exeunt.*

A ROOM IN CURCIO'S HOUSE AT SIENA.

Enter JULIA *and* ARMINDA.

Julia.

Let me weep, my faithful friend,
Liberty's laſt hope that leaves me,
Since till death's cold hand relieves me,
Can my ſorrow have no end.
Haſt thou ne'er, its fount outgrowing,
Seen a gentle ſtreamlet fleeing,
Its ſmooth peaceful pathway being
The ſweet valley of its flowing;
And when all the lovely flowers
Think it ſcarce has ſtrength to move them,
Lo! the pent-up ſtream above them
Sweeps their lovelieſt from the bowers?—
This, whereby the fair flower dies,
Have my pains, my griefs effected:
In my breaſt they were collected,
And they burſt forth from mine eyes.
Let me weep the cruelty
Of a father.

Arminda.

Lady, ſee . . . .

Julia.

But what happier deſtiny
Is there, than of grief to die?
Pain that, victor of the ſtrife,
Conquers life is a glorious fate,—

Que no es muy grande la pena,
Que no acaba con la vida.

Arminda.

¿ Qué novedad obligó
Tu llanto ?

Julia.

¡ Ay, Arminda mia !
Cuantos papeles tenia
De Eufebio, Lifardo halló
En mi efcritorio.

Arminda.

¿ Pues él
Supo que eftaban alli ?

Julia.

Como aquefo contra mí
Hará mi eftrella cruel.
Yo, (¡ ay de mi !) cuando le via
El cuidado con que andaba,
Penfé que lo fofpechaba,
Pero no que lo fabia.
Llegó á mí defcolorido,
Y entre apacible y airado,
Me dijo, que habia jugado,
Arminda, y que habia perdido;
Que una joya le preftafe
Para volver á jugar.
Por prefto que la iba á dar,
No aguardó á que la facafe :
Tomó él la llave, y abrió
Con una cólera inquieta,
Y en la primera naveta
Los papeles encontró.
Miróme y volvió á cerrar.
Y fin decir nada (¡ ay Dios !)
Bufcó á mi padre, y los dos
(¿ Quién duda es para tratar
Mi muerte ?) gran rato hablaron
Cerrados en fu apofento;
Salieron, y hácia el convento

Since the pain cannot be great,
Unto which fuccumbs not life.

Arminda.

But what *new* grief is the ground
Of thefe tears ?

Julia.

Arminda mine,
Of Eufebio, every line,
By Lifardo has been found
In my efcritoir.

Arminda.

Did hé
Know that they were there conceal'd ?

Julia.

This my cruel ftar reveal'd
Shining balefully on mé;
I (ah me!) becaufe he grew,
Plainly, hourly, more dejected,
Thought indeed that he fufpected,
But I did not think he knew.
Thus he came, his hair was toft,
Pale his cheek, his eye betray'd
Peace and wrath, he faid he play'd
Deep and long, that he had loft;
Luck was bad, and, to retrieve it,
Afk'd me for fome trinkets' loan,
Which to give I would have flown
Had he waited to receive it;
But he, with an angry air,
Seized the key, unlock'd the drawer,
And within the efcritoir
Found Eufebio's letters there.
Coldly eyeing me, he ftraight
Lock'd the drawer, faid naught, withdrew
(God!) to feek my fire, the two,
(Oh! who doubts that the debate
Turn'd up on my death ?) difcourfe
Held there long within his room,

Los dos ſus paſos guiaron,
Segun Octavio me dijo.
Y ſi lo que eſtá tratado
Ya mi padre ha efectuado,
Con juſta cauſa me aflijo;
Porque ſi de aqueſta ſuerte,
Que olvide á Euſebio, deſea,
Antes que monja me vea,
Yo miſma me daré muerte.

Sale EUSEBIO.

Euſebio (*aparte*).
Ninguno tan atrevido,
Si no tan deſeſperado,
Viene á tomar por ſagrado
La caſa del ofendido.
Antes que ſepa la muerte
De Liſardo Julia bella,
Hablar quiſiera con ella,
Porque á mi tirana ſuerte
Algun remedio conſigo,
Si, ignorado mi rigor,
Puede obligarla el amor
A que ſe vaya conmigo;
Y cuando llegue á ſaber
De Liſardo el hado injuſto,
Hará de la fuerza guſto,
Mirándoſe en mi poder.—
Hermoſa Julia.

Julia.
¿Qué es eſto?
¿Tú en eſta caſa?

Euſebio.
El rigor
De mi deſdicha, y tu amor
En tal peligro me ha pueſto.

Then came forth, and through the gloom
To the convent bent their courſe,
As Octavio has told me.
If then what was there projected
By my father is effected,
Juſtly you in tears behold me;
For if thus he ſeeks to try
From Euſebio's love to free me,
Ere a nun he lives to ſee me,
By my own hands ſhall I die.

EUSEBIO *enters unſeen.*

Euſebio (*aſide*).
No one ever dared before,
Deſperate though his caſe might be,
Thus to fly for ſanctuary
To the injured party's door;
But my urgent fate compels me,
Ere Liſardo's death be known,
Ere fair Julia's love be grown
Into hate and ſhe repels me,
Quickly to anticipate
Rapid rumour's dread revealings,
And by both our mutual feelings
Urge her to embrace my fate,
And to fly with me this hour:—
Then, although his death muſt pain her,
She will feel ſhe muſt reſtrain her,
Seeing that ſhe's in my power:—
[*He advances.*
Beauteous Julia!

Julia.
Can it be
Thou art in this houſe?

Euſebio.
To prove
My misfortune and thy love,
I have run this riſk for thee.

Julia.
Pues ¿ cómo has entrado aqui,
Y emprendes tan loco extremo?
Eusebio.
Como la muerte no temo.
Julia.
¿ Qué es lo que intentas así?
Eusebio.
Hoy obligarte deseo,
Julia, porque agradecida
Des á mi amor nueva vida,
Nueva gloria á mi deseo.
Yo he sabido cuanto ofende
A tu padre mi cuidado,
Que á su noticia ha llegado
Nuestro amor, y que pretende
Que tú recibas mañana
El estado que desea,
Para que mi dicha sea,
Como mi esperanza, vana.
Si ha sido gusto, si ha sido
Amor el que me has mostrado,
Si es verdad que me has amado,
Si es cierto que me has querido,
Vente conmigo; pues ves
Que no tiene resistencia
De tu padre la obediencia,
Deja tu casa; y despues
Que habrá mil remedios piensa;
Pues ya en mi poder, es justo
Que haga de la fuerza gusto,
Y obligacion de la ofensa.
Villas tengo en que guardarte,
Gente con que defenderte,
Hacienda para ofrecerte,
Y un alma para adorarte.
Si darme vida deseas,
Si es verdadero tu amor,
Atrévete, ó el dolor

Julia.
Oh! why hast thou ventured here,
Such a wild attempt to try?
Eusebio.
I am not afraid to die.
Julia.
What's thy object?—O my fear!
Eusebio.
Julia, I have grown ambitious
That this happy day at length
Should my love give newer strength,
Newer glory to my wishes.
I have learn'd how much offended
Is your father by my suit,
That to him has come the bruit
Of our love, that 'tis intended,
Ere shall come to-morrow's e'en,
Thou a state of life must take,
Which, he thinks, my bliss will make
Vain as all my hopes have been.
If with favour thou hast heard me
Speak my love, nor yet reproved me,
If 'tis certain thou hast loved me,
If 'tis true thou hast preferr'd me,
Come then with me: since 'tis plain
Thou canst never make resistance
To thy father's strong persistence,
Leave thy house; thy strength will gain
Thousand aids when thou art hence;
When thou'rt in my power 'twill be
Best to yield to fate's decree,
And to pardon the offence.
Villas have I to rise o'er thee,
Vassals have I to defend thee,
Wealth and all its aids to tend thee,
And a true heart to adore thee.
Wouldst thou stay this life nigh fled,
Dost thou worth a true love deem me,
Dare this step, or thou wilt see me

Hará que mi muerte veas.

Julia.

Oye, Euſebio.

Arminda.

Mi ſeñor
Viene, ſeñora.

Julia.

Ay de mí!

Euſebio.

¿ Pudiera hallar contra mí
La fortuna mas rigor ?

Julia.

¿ Podrá ſalir ?

Arminda.

No es poſible
Que ſe vaya ; porque ya
Llamando á la puerta eſtá.

Julia.

¡ Grave mal !

Euſebio.

¡ Pena terrible !
¿ Qué haré ?

Julia.

Eſconderte es forzoſo.

Euſebio.

¿ Dónde ?

Julia.

En aqueſe apoſento.

Arminda.

Preſto, que ſus paſos ſiento.

[*Eſcóndeſe* Eusebio.

Sale Curcio.

Curcio.

Hija, ſi por el dichoſo
Eſtado, que tú codicias,
Y que ya ſeguro tienes,
No das á mis parabienes
La vida y alma en albricias,

Slain by grief, here lying dead.

Julia.

Oh ! Euſebio, hear . . . .

Arminda.

My maſter
Comes, ſeñora.

Julia.

Woe is me !

Euſebio.

Oh ! with what perſiſtency
Fortune dogs me with diſaſter !

Julia.

Can he not go forth ?

Arminda.

'Tis vain
To attempt it ; 'tis too late,
For he's calling at the gate.

Julia.

Dread miſchance !

Euſebio.

Terrific pain !
What remains ?

Julia.

Concealment ſolely.

Euſebio.

Where ?

Julia.

Within this chamber here.

Arminda.

Quick ! his ſteps are drawing near.

[Eusebio *conceals himſelf.*

Enter Curcio.

Curcio.

Daughter, if for that moſt holy
State thou long'ſt for, that calm goal
Which now crowns thy expectations,
Thou, as my beſt gratulations,
Yield'ſt not up thy heart and ſoul,

Del deſeo que he tenido
No agradeces el cuidado.
Todo queda efectuado,
Y todo tan prevenido,
Que ſolo falta ponerte
La mas bizarra y hermoſa,
Para ſer de Criſto eſpoſa;
Mira ¡ que dichoſa ſuerte!
Hoy aventajas á todas
Cuantas ſe ven envidiar,
Pues te verán celebrar
Aqueſtas divinas bodas.
¿ Qué dices?

Julia (*aparte*).

¿ Qué puedo hacer?

Euſebio (*aparte*).

Yo me doy la muerte aqui,
Si ella le dice que sí.

Julia.

No ſé como reſponder.— [*Aparte.*
Bien, ſeñor, la autoridad
De padre, que es preferida,
Imperio tiene en la vida;
Pero no en la libertad.
¿ Pues, que ſupiera antes yo
Tu intento, no fuera bien?
¿ Y que tú, ſeñor, tambien
Supieras mi guſto?

Curcio.

No;
Que ſola mi voluntad,
En lo juſto, ó en lo injuſto,
Has de tener tú por guſto.

Julia.

Solo tiene libertad
Un hijo para eſcoger
Eſtado; que el hado impío
No fuerza el libre albedrío.

Then my zeal will be derided,
By thy ingrate heart eluded.
Everything has been concluded,
I have everything provided;
There's but one thing to await,
In a rich robe to be clothèd
As Chriſt's veſtal bride betrothèd;
See now, what a happy fate!
All the friends thy feaſt invites
Will be envious of thy mating,
Since they'll ſee thee celebrating
Theſe divineſt marriage rites.
What then ſay'ſt thou?

Julia (*aſide*).

Woe the day!

Euſebio (*aſide*).

Here I'll give myſelf my death
If the fatal "Yes" ſhe ſaith.

Julia.

(Ah! I know not what to ſay!)
[*Aſide.*
Though a ſire's authority
So endow'd, ſo richly riſe,
Hath dominion over life,
It hath none o'er liberty.
Wer't not right that I ſhould know
Earlier what thou tell'ſt me now?
Wer't not proper, too, that thou
Knew my wiſhes likewiſe?

Curcio.

No;
For my will alone ſhould be
Ever ſacred in thy ſight,
Be the matter wrong or right.

Julia.

Sir, the only liberty
That a child has is to chooſe
In the world its fitting ſtate;
This no law or impious fate

Déjame penſar y ver
De eſpacio eſo ; y no te eſpante
Ver que término te pida ;
Que el eſtado de una vida
No ſe toma en un inſtante.

Curcio.

Baſta que yo lo he mirado,
Y yo por tí he dado el sí.

Julia.

Pues ſi tú vives por mí,
Toma tambien por mí eſtado.

Curcio.

¡Calla, infame! ¡calla, loca!
Que haré de aqueſe cabello
Un lazo para tu cuello,
O ſacaré de tu boca
Con mis manos la atrevida
Lengua, que de oir me ofendo.

Julia.

La libertad te defiendo,
Señor, pero no la vida.
Acaba ſu curſo triſte,
Y acabará tu peſar;
Que mal te puedo negar
La vida que tú me diſte.
La libertad, que me dió
El cielo, es la que te niego.

Curcio.

En eſte punto á creer llego
Lo que el alma ſoſpechó,
Que no fue buena tu madre,
Y manchó mi honor alguno ;
Pues hoy tu error importuno
Ofende el honor de un padre,
A quien el ſol no igualó
En reſplandor y belleza,
Sangre, honor, luſtre y nobleza.

Julia.

Eſo no he entendido yo,

E'er ſhould hinder or refuſe.
Let me think awhile, nor fear
For this pauſe to be petition'd,
For a moment's inſufficient
To decide a life's career.

Curcio.

'Tis enough that I've decided,
And have given the "Yes" for thee.

Julia.

Since my life thou liv'ſt for me,
Take the ſtate, too, thou'ſt provided.

Curcio.

Silence, rebel! ſilence, fool!
Leſt around thy neck I twine
Laſſo-like thoſe locks of thine,
Or permit my hands to pull
Out thy tongue, that like a knife
Cuts me to the heart to hear.

Julia.

'Tis the freedom I hold dear
I defend, but not the life:—
Finiſh its unhappy courſe,
And thy grief conclude thereby,
Since 'twere ſinful to deny
That to thee who art its ſource ;
What I wiſh to have reſpected
Is my freedom—Heaven's ſole gift.

Curcio.

Now aſſurance doth uplift
Doubt from that I've long ſuſpected,
That my wife, your mother rather,
Stain'd my life's elſe ſpotleſs mirror,
Since to day thy obſtinate error
Wounds the honour of a father,
Who hath not the ſun for equal,
In its light and lovelineſs,
For blood, birth, and nobleneſs.

Julia.

Ere I ſpeak, I wait the ſequel,

Por eſo no he reſpondido.
Curcio.
Arminda, ſalte allá fuera.—
[*Vaſe* ARMINDA.
Y ya que mi pena fiera
Tantos años he tenido
Secreta, de mis enojos
La ciega paſion obliga
A que la lengua te diga
Lo que te han dicho los ojos.
La Señoría de Sena,
Por dar á mi ſangre fama,
En ſu nombre me envió
A dar la obediencia al Papa
Urbano Tercio. Tu madre,
Que con opinion de ſanta
Fue en Sena comun ejemplo
De las matronas romanas,
Y aun de las nueſtras, (no ſé
Como mi lengua la agravia;
Mas, ¡ay infelice! tanto
La ſatisfaccion engaña)
En Sena quedó, y yo eſtuve
En Roma con la embajada
Ocho meſes; porque entonces
Por concierto ſe trataba,
Que eſta Señoría fueſe
Del Pontífice; Dios haga
Lo que á ſu eſtado convenga,
Que aqui importa poco, ó nada.
Volví á Sena, y hallé en ella . . . .
(Aqui el aliento me falta,
Aqui la lengua enmudece,
Y aqui el ánimo deſmaya)
Hallé (¡ay injuſto temor!)
A tu madre tan preñada,
Que para el infeliz parto,
Cumplia las nueve faltas.
Ya me habia prevenido

As thy meaning is not clear.
Curcio.
Wait without, Arminda, go!
[*Exit* ARMINDA.
Seeing that my bitter woe,
Which I've held ſo many a year
Hidden, from its centre flies,
And by paſſion render'd bold,
Makes thee by the tongue be told
What's been told thee by the eyes.
This proud ſeigniory Siena,
To my blood to add new honour,
Sent me once to pay obedience,
In its name, unto the Pontiff,
The third Urban; and thy mother,
Who, reputed and acknowledged
As a ſaint, was through Siena
Thought the univerſal model,
The bright copy and exemplar,
Of all matrons, of the Roman,
And even of our own: (I know not
How my tongue can dare to wrong her,
But alas! the ſatisfaction
That ſeems fair deceives too often!)
She remain'd behind; I tarried
Eight months at the ſacred college
With the embaſſy, at that time
The idea being in progreſs
'Bout the giving of Siena
To the Pontiff, which ſame project
May God ſettle as beſeems him!
For 'tis here of ſlight importance.
On returning home, I found her . . . .
(Here the breath doth fail my body,
Here my tongue grows mute in ſilence,
Here my frighten'd courage falters,)
Found her . . . (hence, O coward fear!)
In her pregnancy ſo forward,
That for her unhappy burden

Por ſus mentiroſas cartas
Eſta deſdicha, diciendo,
Que, cuando me fui, quedaba
Con ſoſpecha; y yo la tuve
De mi deſhonra tan clara,
Que diſcurriendo mi agravio,
Imaginé mi deſgracia.
No digo que verdad ſea;
Mas quien tiene ſangre hidalga
No ha de aguardar á creer,
Que el imaginar le baſta.
¿Qué importa que un noble ſea
Deſdichado, (¡oh ley tirana
De honor! ¡oh bárbara fuero
Del mundo!) ſi la ignorancia
Le diſculpa? Mienten, mienten
Las leyes; porque no alcanza
Los miſterios al efecto
Quien no previene la cauſa.
¿Qué ley culpa á un inocente?
¿Qué opinion á un libre agravia?
Miente otra vez; que no es
Deſhonra, ſino deſgracia.
¡Bueno es, que en leyes de honor
Le comprenda tanta infamia
Al Mercurio que le roba,
Como al Argos que le guarda!
¿Qué deja el mundo, qué deja,
Si aſi al inocente infama,
De deſhonra, para aquel
Que lo ſabe y que lo calla?
Yo entre tantos penſamientos,
Yo entre confuſiones tantas,
Ni ví regalo en la meſa,
Ni hice deſcanſo en la cama.
Tan deſabrido conmigo
Eſtuve, que me trataba
Como ajeno el corazon,
Y como á tirano el alma.

She her nine months had accompliſh'd;
She already had forewarn'd me,
In falſe lines of ſeeming fondneſs,
Of this great misfortune, ſaying,
When I left her, that the proſpect
Seem'd moſt likely: and ſo patent
Thought I then was my diſhonour,
That, deep brooding on my inſult,
I imagined my misfortune:
That 'twas real I aſſert not,
Since what man whoſe blood is noble
Waits for proof, when 'tis ſufficient
To imagine it as proven?
What imports it that a noble
Is unhappy (oh! deſpotic
Law of honour! oh! ſtern edict
Of the world!) when want of knowledge
Exculpates him? Lying, lying
Laws are they, becauſe the mortal
Should be blamed not for the iſſues
Who the cauſe hath not foreboded.
What law proves the innocent guilty?
Blameleſs, what opinion wrongs them?
Lying laws once more: for then 'twere
Not diſhonour but misfortune.
Is it right, by the laws of honour,
That an equal infamy follows
Him, the Argus who doth guard it,
And the Mercury who robs it?
I, involved in ſuch dark fancies,
I, in ſuch a maze involvèd,
Found no ſolace at the table,
No repoſe upon the ſoft bed.
And I grew ſo diſcontented
With myſelf ſoon, that my cold heart
Came to treat me as a ſtranger,
And my ſoul as not its owner.
And though many a time I reaſon'd
With myſelf, and well-nigh proved her

Y aunque á veces discurria
En su abono, y aunque hallaba
Verisímil la disculpa,
Pudo en mí tanto la instancia
Del temer que me ofendia,
Que con saber que fue casta,
Tomé de mis pensamientos,
No de sus culpas, venganza.
Y porque con mas secreto
Fuese, previne una caza
Fingida, porque á un zeloso
Ficciones solo le agradan.
Al monte fui, y cuando todos
Entretenidos estaban
En su alegre regocijo,
Con amorosas palabras,
(¡ Qué bien las dice quien miente !
¡ Qué bien las cree quien ama !)
Llevé á Rosmira, tu madre,
Por una senda apartada
Del camino, y divertida
Llegó á una secreta estancia
Deste monte, á cuyo albergue
El sol ignoró la entrada;
Porque se la defendian
Rústicamente enlazadas,
Por no decir que amorosas,
Arboles, hojas y ramas.
Aqui pues, adonde apenas
Huella imprimió mortal planta,
Solos los dos . . . .

Sale Arminda.

Arminda.

Si el valor,
Que el noble pecho acompaña,
Señor, y si la experiencia,
Que te han dado honrosas canas,
En la desdicha presente

Innocent, I still was haunted
With the fear she might have wrong'd me.
And though thus with full assurance
She was chaste, I yet resolvèd
To avenge not her offences
But the dark thoughts that engross'd me.
And more secretly and safely
That this should be done, I order'd
A fictitious hunt, for fictions
Are the jealous man's sole comfort.
We departed to the mountain,
And while all our friends disported
In the joyous recreation,
I, with words of amorous fondness,
(Ah ! how easily by falsehood
Can such treacheries be spoken !
Ah ! how easily be trusted
By the fond heart of a lover !)
Led thy mother, led Rosmira,
By a path, that, through the copses
Winding, from the roadway brought us
To a lone and distant corner
Of the mountain, to whose entrance
Scarce the sun reveal'd a portal,
It was so completely hidden
By the rustic running over,
Not to say the amorous twining
Of leaves, trees, and thorns, and roses.
Here, then, here, where human footstep
Scarce was planted till that moment,
We two only . . . .

Enter Arminda.

Arminda.

If the firmness
Which to noble breasts belongeth,
If, sir, the dear-bought experience
Which has given thee honour'd hoar hairs,

No te niega ó no te falta,
Exámen ſerá el valor
De tu ánimo.

Curcio.
¿Qué cauſa
Te obliga á que aſi interrumpas
Mi razon?

Arminda.
Señor . . . .

Curcio.
Acaba;
Que mas la duda me ofende.

Julia.
¿Por qué te ſuſpendes? Habla.

Arminda.
No quiſiera ſer la voz
De mi pena y tu deſgracia.

Curcio.
No temas decirla tú,
Pues yo no temo eſcucharla.

Arminda.
A Líſardo, mi ſeñor . . . .

Euſebio.
Eſto ſolo me faltaba.

Arminda.
Bañado en ſu ſangre traen
En una ſilla por andas
Cuatro rúſticos paſtores,
Muerto (¡ay Dios!) á puñaladas;
Mas ya á tu preſencia llega:
No le veas.

Curcio.
¡Cielos, tantas
Penas para un deſdichado!
¡Ay de mí!

In the preſence of this ſorrow
Fail thee not nor fly thee wholly,
It will be the teſt and trial
Of thy ſtrength of mind.

Curcio.
What object
Forces thee to interrupt me
Thus unſummon'd?

Arminda.
Sir . . . .

Curcio.
Say ſhortly
What it is, for doubt is worſe ſtill.

Julia.
Speak! Why pauſe thus? What doth ſtop thee?

Arminda.
That I may not be the voice
Of my pain, and thy misfortune.

Curcio.
Be not thou afraid to tell
What I fear not to have told me.

Arminda.
Sir, oh! ſir, thy ſon Liſardo . . . .

Euſebio (at the ſide).
This remain'd to overthrow me!

Arminda.
Bathèd in his blood, and lying
On a litter ſtretch'd, is borne here
By four ruſtic ſhepherd ſwains,
Dead (O God!) from cuts and ſword-ſtabs;
But already he is here:—
Look not on him.

Curcio.
Heavens! what torments
Numberleſs for one poor wretch here!
Woe is me!—

Salen los Villanos con LISARDO *muerto en una ſilla.*

Julia.

Pues ¿ qué inhumana
Fuerza enſangrentó la ira
En ſu pecho ? ¿ qué tirana
Mano ſe bañó en mi ſangre,
Contra ſu inocencia airada ?
¡ Ay de mí !

Arminda.

Mira, ſeñora . . . .

Bras.

No llegues á verle.

Curcio.

Aparta.

Tirſo.

Detente, ſeñor.

Curcio.

Amigos,
No puede ſufrirlo el alma.
Dejadme ver eſe cadáver frio,
Depóſito infeliz de heladas venas,
Ruina del tiempo, eſtrago del impío
Hado, teatro funeſto de mis penas.
¿ Qué tirano rigor (¡ ay hijo mio !)
Trágico monumento en las arenas
Conſtruyó, porque hicieſe en quejas vanas
Mortaja triſte de mis blancas canas ?
¡ Ay amigos ! decid ; ¿quién fue homicida
De un hijo, en cuya vida yo animaba ?

Enter GIL, MENGA, BRAS, TORIBIO, *and others, bearing a bier, upon which is the body of* LISARDO.

Julia.

Unpitying monſter,
Who art thou whoſe wrath is written
Blood-red on this breaſt? What horrid
Hand is bathèd in my heart's blood ?
Anger'd by his innocence only ?
Woe is me !

Arminda.

Reflect, ſeñora . . . .

Bras.

Come not nearer !

Curcio.

Hence ! nor ſtop me.

Tirſo.

Do hold back, ſir.

Curcio.

Friends, my heart
Leaves me powerleſs to withhold me.
Let me behold this corſe, ſo coldly lying,
The ſad depoſit now of frozen veins—
Ruin of time, dead fruit of fate undying,
The fatal theatre of all my pains.
What tyrant wrath, a demon's wrath outvying,
Raiſed, O my ſon, upon theſe crimſon'd plains,
This tragic pile, o'er which in ſorrow bow'd
My white hairs ſtreaming ſerve thee as a ſhroud ?
Tell me, my friends, what hand to mercy ſteel'd
Slew this dear ſon, in whom my life's blood lay ?

Menga.
Gil lo dirá; que, al verle dar la herida,
Oculto entre unos árboles eſtaba.

Curcio.
Di, amigo, di, ¿quién me quitó eſta vida?

Gil.
Yo ſolo ſé, que Euſebio ſe llamaba,
Cuando con él reñia.

Curcio.
¿Hay mas deſhonra?
Euſebio me ha quitado vida y honra.
Diſculpa ahora tú de ſus crueles
[*A Julia.*
Deſeos la ambicion; di que concibe
Caſto amor, pues, á falta de papeles,
Laſcivos guſtos con tu ſangre eſcribe.

Julia.
Señor . . . .

Curcio.
No me reſpondas como ſueles;
A tomar hoy eſtado te apercibe,
O apercibe tambien á tu hermoſura
Con Liſardo temprana ſepultura.
Los dos á un tiempo el ſentimiento eſquivo
En eſte dia ſepultar concierta,
El muerto al mundo, en mi memoria vivo,

Menga.
Gil, who was preſent, 'mong ſome trees conceal'd,
Saw him fall wounded in a deſperate fray.

Curcio.
Say, who was he who ſent him unanneal'd
Before his God, and ſnatch'd from me to-day
My life's beſt life?

Gil.
But this alone I know,
He call'd himſelf, I think, Euſebio.

Curcio.
Euſebio! thus my honour and my life
He robs relentleſs in his ſateleſs mood!
[*To Julia.*
Excuſe him, prithee, thou his would-be wife;
Say the chaſte eagerneſs with which he wooed
Cauſed the ſlight error that produced this ſtrife,
He wanted ink, and ſo he wrote in blood!

Julia.
Oh! ſir . . . .

Curcio.
Reply not in thy uſual way;
Hear my commands and ſtudy to obey.
Prepare to-day to ſeek the cloiſter's gloom,
Or elſe prepare in beauteous death to lie
With young Liſardo in his early tomb:
At one ſad moment both my children die;
Both ſhare the ſame and yet a different doom;

Tú, viva al mundo, en mi memoria muerta.
Y en tanto que el entierro os apercibo,
Porque no huyas, cerraré eſta puerta.
Queda con él, porque de aqueſa ſuerte
Lecciones al morir te dé ſu muerte.

[*Vanſe todos, y queda* Julia *en medio de* Lisardo *y* Eusebio, *que ſale por otra puerta.*

Julia.

Mil veces procuro hablarte,
Tirano Euſebio, y mil veces
El alma duda, el aliento
Falta, y la lengua enmudece.
No ſé, no ſé como pueda
Hablar; porque á un tiempo vienen
Envueltas iras piadoſas
Entre piedades crueles.
Quiſiera cerrar los ojos
A aqueſta ſangre inocente,
Que eſtá pidiendo venganza,
Deſperdiciando claveles:

Both leave me lone, and yet how differently,—
One lives in memory, though his ſoul has fled,
And one, though living, ſeems to me as dead.
Here, by thy brother's bloody bier, think o'er
The choice I give thee; think what thou haſt done;
Look on theſe tears and on that innocent gore,—
A ſire diſhonour'd and a murder'd ſon!
Thou canſt not fly, for I ſhall lock this door.
Here I ſhall leave thee by this couch alone;
Look on this pallid form that here doth lie,
And learn from it the way that thou ſhalt die.

[*Exeunt all but* Julia, *who ſtands in the middle of the ſtage, between the dead body of* Lisardo *and* Eusebio, *who comes forth from his place of concealment.*

Julia.

I attempt a thouſand times,
Dread Euſebio, to addreſs thee,
And a thouſand times my breath
Fails me, and my tongue is fetter'd.
Ah! I know not, know not how
To addreſs thee, ſince together
Pious anger ſteels my heart,
And unnatural pity melts me.
I would wiſh to cloſe mine eyes
To this innocent blood here preſent,
Which, in aſking vengeance, ſheds
Purple pinks o'er all this death-bed:

Y quiſiera hallar diſculpa
En las lágrimas que viertes ;
Que al fin heridas y ojos
Son bocas que nunca mienten.
Y en una mano el amor,
Y en otra el rigor preſente,
A un miſmo tiempo quiſiera
Caſtigarte y defenderte.
Y entre ciegas confuſiones
De penſamientos tan fuertes
La clemencia me combate,
Y el ſentimiento me vence.
¿ Deſta ſuerte ſolicitas
Obligarme ? ¿ deſta ſuerte,
Euſebio, en vez de finezas,
Con crueldades me pretendes ?
Cuando de mi boda el dia
Reſuelta eſperaba, ¿ quieres
Que, en vez de apacibles bodas,
Triſtes obſequias celebre ?
Cuando por tu guſto era
A mi padre inobediente,
¿ Lutos funeſtos me das,
En vez de galas alegres ?
Cuando, arrieſgando mi vida,
Hice poſible el quererte,
¿ En vez de tálamo (¡ ay cielos !)
Un ſepulcro me previenes ?
Y cuando mi mano ofrezco,
Deſpreciando inconvenientes
De honor, ¿ la tuya bañada
En mi ſangre me la ofreces ?
¿ Qué guſto tendré en tus brazos,
Si para llegar á verme,
Dando vida á nueſtro amor,
Voy tropezando en la muerte ?
¿ Qué dirá el mundo de mí,
Sabiendo que tengo ſiempre,
Si no preſente el agravio,

And I would find ſome excuſe
In the tears I ſee thou ſheddeſt :
Since but tears and eyes alone
Are the mouths that lie not ever.
Thus on one hand here is love,
And on the other is reſentment,
And I would at one time wiſh
Both to puniſh and defend thee ;
And amid the wild confuſion
Of the paſſionate thoughts that preſs me,
Now with clemency contend,
Now to ſterner duty nerve me.
Is it in this way, Euſebio,
Thou wouldſt ſhow thy wiſh to ſerve me ?
Is it in this way thou giv'ſt me
Cruelties and not careſſes ?
When reſolved, my marriage day
I awaited, wouldſt thou let me,
'Stead of peaceful bridal feaſts,
Celebrate but ſad interments ?
When I was, to make thee happy,
To my father diſobedient,
Wouldſt thou give me mourning robes
In the place of gala dreſſes ?
When at riſk of life I made it
Poſſible perchance to wed thee,
Is it not a bride-bed, (heavens !)
But a tomb thou wouldſt preſent me ?
When I offer thee my hand,
Scorning all the fears ſuggeſted
By my honour, thine deep-dyed
In my blood thou wouldſt extend me !
In thine arms what bliſs were mine,
If to reach them I beheld me
Giving life unto our love,
Struggling with death's hand that led me ?
What would ſay the world of me,
Knowing that I kept for ever,
If not preſent, the deep wrong,

Quien le cometió preſente?
Pues cuando quiera el olvido
Sepultarle, ſolo el verte
Entre mis brazos ſerá
Memoria con que me acuerde.
Yo entonces, yo, aunque te adore,
Los amoroſos placeres
Trocaré en iras, pidiendo
Venganzas; pues ¿cómo quieres
Que viva ſujeta un alma
A efectos tan diferentes,
Que eſté eſperando el caſtigo,
Y deſeando que no llegue?
Baſta, por lo que te quiſe,
Perdonarte, ſin que eſperes
Verme en tu vida, ni hablarme.
Eſa ventana, que tiene
Salida al jardin, podrá
Darte paſo; por ahí puedes
Eſcaparte; huye el peligro,
Porque, ſi mi padre viene,
No te halle aqui. Vete, Euſebio,
Y mira que no te acuerdes
De mí; que hoy me pierdes tú,
Porque quiſiſte perderme.
Vete, y vive tan dichoſo,
Que tengas felicemente
Bienes, ſin que á los peſares
Pagues penſion de los bienes.
Que yo haré para mi vida
Una celda priſion breve,
Si no ſepulcro, pues ya
Mi padre enterrarme quiere.
Allí lloraré deſdichas
De un hado tan inclemente,
De una fortuna tan fiera,
De una inclinacion tan fuerte,
De un planeta tan opueſto,
De una eſtrella tan rebelde,

The wrong-doer ever preſent?
Since if in forgetfulneſs
I would hide it, but to ſee thee
In my arms alone would be
A dread memory and remembrance.
I then, I, though I adore thee,
Will love's joys ſo ſweet and tender
Change to anger, ſternly calling
For revenge; ſince wouldſt thou, tell me,
Have a ſoul live on and be
To ſuch different moods ſubjected,
As to hope the chaſtiſement
And yet wiſh it not effected?
'Tis enough that I forgive thee,
Since I loved thee: but hope never
In your life-time to ſpeak with me,
Or to ſee me. Look, this trellis,
Opening on the garden, gives thee
A free exit: fly the peril,
That when back returns my father,
Here he find thee not. In mercy
Go, Euſebio, and no thought have
More of me; to-day for ever
Haſt thou loſt me. Since, to loſe me,
Thus for ever thou preferreſt.
Go, then, go, and live ſo happy,
So ſerenely be poſſeſſor
Of life's bleſſings, as to pay not
Sorrow's toll for being bleſſèd.
I ſhall make my narrow cell
As a life-long priſon ſerve me,
If not as a grave; my father
So deſiring to inter me:
There I'll weep o'er the misfortunes
Of a hard fate ſo inclement,
Of a fortune ſo ungenial,
Of a liking ſo exceſſive,
Of a ſtar ſo unpropitious,
Of a planet ſo averted,

De un amor tan deſdichado,
De una mano tan aleve,
Que me ha quitado la vida,
Y no me ha dado la muerte,
Porque entre tantos peſares,
Siempre viva, y muera ſiempre.

Euſebio.

Si acaſo mas que tus voces
Son ya tus manos crueles
Para tomar la venganza,
Rendido á tus pies me tienes.
Preſo me trae mi delito,
Tu amor es la cárcel fuerte,
Las cadenas ſon mis yerros,
Priſiones que el alma teme,
Verdugo es mi penſamiento;
Si ſon tus ojos los jueces,
Y ellos me dan la ſentencia,
Por fuerza ſerá de muerte.
Mas dirá entonces la fama
En ſu pregon: "eſte muere,
Porque quiſo;" pues que ſolo
Es mi delito quererte.
No pienſo darte diſculpa;
No parezca que la tiene
Tan grande error, ſolo quiero
Que me mates y te vengues.
Toma eſta daga, y con ella
Rompe un pecho que te ofende,
Saca un alma que te adora,
Y tu miſma ſangre vierte.
Y ſi no quieres matarme,
Para que á vengarſe llegue
Tu padre, diré que eſtoy
En tu apoſento.

Julia.

¡Detente!
Y por última razon,

Of a life's love ſo unhappy,
Of a hand whoſe treacherous ſternneſs
Takes away my life indeed;
Yet my death doth not preſent me,
Since I muſt amid ſuch ſorrows
Live for ever, die for ever.

Euſebio.

If by any chance thy hands
Can more cruelly avenge thee
Than already have thy words,
At thy feet, ſee, I ſurrender.
Here my crime has led me captive,
Love for thee is my ſtrong cell here,
Mine own failings are my chains,
Bonds at which the ſcared ſoul trembles;
The ſtern headſman is my thought:
If the judges are preſented
By thine eyes, my doom muſt be
Death, if they pronounce the ſentence.
But then Fame, my fate proclaiming,
Will declare, "This man met death here
For his love"—becauſe in loving
Thee alone have I offended.
I attempt not to excuſe me,—
Vain, it ſeems, would ſuch attempt be,
For ſo great a fault: I only
Wiſh thou'dſt kill me, and avenge thee.
Take this dagger, and with it
Pierce a boſom that offends thee,
Break a fond heart that adores thee,
And in mine thine own blood ſhed
here.
If to kill me thou declineſt,
That thy father for his vengeance
May return, I'll ſay I'm hid here
In thy chamber.

Julia.

Oh! arreſt thee!
Stay! and as the laſt requeſt

Que he de hablarte eternamente,
Has de hacer lo que te digo.

Eusebio.

Yo lo concedo.

Julia.

Pues vete
Adonde guardes tu vida;
Hacienda tienes, y gente
Que te podrá defender.

Eusebio.

Mejor será que yo quede
Sin ella; porque si vivo,
Será imposible que deje
De adorarte, y no has de estar,
Aunque un convento te encierre,
Segura.

Julia.

Guárdate tú;
Que yo sabré defenderme.

Eusebio.

¿Volveré yo á verte?

Julia.

No.

Eusebio.

¿No hay remedio?

Julia.

No le esperes.

Eusebio.

¿Que al fin me aborreces ya?

Julia.

Haré por aborrecerte.

Eusebio.

¿Olvidarásme?

Julia.

No sé.

Eusebio.

¿Veréte yo?

Julia.

Eternamente.

I may make of thee for ever,
Grant the favour that I ask thee.

Eusebio.

I concede it.

Julia.

Flee, oh! flee hence,
Where thou may'st preserve thy life:
Thou hast property and people
Who for thy defence are able.

Eusebio.

It were better that I stay'd here
Without *it:* for if I live,
From adoring thee I never
Can desist; nor shalt thou be
Safe, although a convent's shelter
Seem to guard thee.

Julia.

Guard thou thee;
I shall know how to defend me.

Eusebio.

Once more shall I see thee?

Julia.

No.

Eusebio.

No resource?

Julia.

Do not expect it.

Eusebio.

Am I then detested so?

Julia.

I have reason to detest thee.

Eusebio.

Wilt forget me?

Julia.

I don't know.

Eusebio.

Shall I see thee?

Julia.

Never, never.

Eusebio.
Pues ¿aquel pasado amor . . . . ?
Julia.
Pues ¿esta sangre presente . . . . ?
La puerta abren; vete, Eusebio.
Eusebio.
Iré por obedecerte.
¡Que no he de volverte á ver!
Julia.
¡Que no has de volver á verme!
[*Suena ruido, vanse los dos, cada uno por su parte, y entran el cuerpo algunos criados.*

Eusebio.
What then of our fond love past?—
Julia.
What then of this red blood present?—
Lo! the door! Eusebio, fly!
Eusebio.
I shall go, but through obedience:—
Oh! to see thee never more!
Julia.
Oh! that thou no more must see me!
[*A noise is heard outside; they go out at opposite doors, and servants enter and remove the body.*

JORNADA II.

Monte.

Disparan dentro un arcabuz, y salen Ricardo, Celio *y* Eusebio *en trage de bandoleros, con arcabuces.*

Ricardo.

PASÓ el plomo violento
Su pecho.

Celio.

Y hace el golpe mas sangriento,
Que con su sangre la tragedia imprima
En tierna flor.

Eusebio.

Ponle una Cruz encima,
Y perdónele Dios.

ACT II.

The Mountain. A rude Cross at one side, with several others in the distance.*

A shot is heard within: enter Ricardo, Celio, *and* Eusebio, *dressed as bandits, and armed with arquebuses.*

Ricardo.

THAT ball of wingèd lead
Pass'd through his breast.

Celio.

And made a wound so red,
That the sad tale o'er all the tender moss
Is writ in blood.

Eusebio.

Put over him a cross,
And God be merciful to his soul.

---

* M. Philarète Chasles greatly assists the imagination in its efforts to realize the externals of this scene:—

" Dans une gorge de montagne, au sein d'une solitude âpre et sauvage, loin de tous les chemins fréquentés, au milieu de rocs bronzés par la pluie, jaunis sous le soleil, et de grands blocs de pierre superposés, aux arêtes aigués qui se dessinent durement à l'horizon, il y a une grande croix, formée de deux débris de chêne que l'outil du charpentier n'a pas même equarrés. C'est un de ces paysages aux couleurs tranchées, aux lignes aigués, qui s'accordent avec toutes les pensées terribles, et toutes les fureurs de l'âme. Là doivent se réfugier les *bandoleros;* là des ennemis acharnés doivent commencer et finir un combat mortel.

" C'est là aussi que Calderon place ses acteurs."—*Etudes sur l'Espagne,* p. 43.

Ricardo.
Las devociones
Nunca faltan del todo á los ladrones.

[*Vanſe* RICARDO *y* CELIO.

Euſebio.
Y pues mis hados fieros
Me traen á capitan de bandoleros,
Llegarán mis delitos
A ſer, como mis penas, infinitos.
Como ſi diera muerte
A Liſardo á traicion, de aqueſta ſuerte
Mi patria me perſigue,
Porque ſu furia y mi deſpecho obligue
A que guarde una vida,
Siendo de tantas bárbaro homicida.
Mi hacienda me han quitado,
Mis villas confiſcado,
Y á tanto rigor llegan,
Que el ſuſtento me niegan.
No toque paſagero
El término del monte, ſi primero
No rinde hacienda y vida.

Salen RICARDO *y Bandoleros con* ALBERTO.

Ricardo.
Llegando á ver la boca de la herida,
Eſcucha, Capitan, el mas extraño
Suceſo.

Euſebio.
Ya deſeo el deſengaño.

Ricardo.
Hallé el plomo deſhecho
En eſte libro que tenia en el pecho,
Sin haber penetrado,
Y al caminante ſolo deſmayado:

Ricardo.
Right notions,
Thieves though we be, we've got of our devotions.

[*Exeunt* RICARDO *and* CELIO.

Euſebio.
Since then by fate's command
I now am captain of a robber-band,
Be my offences from this day
Great as my griefs, and infinite as they.
Treating Liſardo's death as if it were
By treachery cauſed and not in duel fair,
My country ſo purſued me with its hate,
So great its fury, and my wrath ſo great,
I was compell'd, a barbarous murderer grown,
Full many a life to take to ſave my own.
My property they ſequeſtrated,
My villas all they confiſcated,—
Their rigour ſo increaſed, that they
My very means of ſuſtenance took away;
Therefore no traveller more
Shall paſs the mountain's boundary before
Money and life he yield me on the ſpot.

Enter RICARDO *and bandits leading in* ALBERTO.

Ricardo.
Going to ſee the place where he was ſhot,—
Oh! liſten, captain, nothing has come near it
For downright wonder.

Euſebio.
Then I wiſh to hear it.

Ricardo.
I found the bullet preſs'd
Againſt this book he carried in his breaſt;
The book unpierced, his breaſt without a wound,

Vesle aqui sano y bueno.

Eusebio.

De espanto estoy, y admiraciones lleno.
¿ Quién eres, venerable
Caduco, á quien los cielos admirable
Han hecho con prodigio milagroso ?

Alberto.

Yo soy, o Capitan, el mas dichoso
De cuantos hombres hay ; que he merecido
Ser Sacerdote indigno, y he leido
En Bolonia sagrada Teología
Cuarenta y cuatro años con desvelo ;
Dióme su Santidad, por este zelo,
De Trento el Obispado,
Premiando mis estudios ; y admirado
Yo de ver, que tenia
Cuenta te tantas almas,
Y que apenas la daba de la mia,
Los laureles dejé, dejé las palmas,
Y huyendo sus engaños,
Vengo á buscar seguros desengaños
En estas soledades,
Donde viven desnudas las verdades.
Paso á Roma, á que el Papa me conceda
Licencia, Capitan, para que pueda
Fundar un órden santo de eremitas.
Mas tu saña atrevida
Quita el hilo á mi suerte y á la vida.

For the scared traveller had only swoon'd ;—
Here see him safe and sound once more.

Eusebio.

Terror and wonder thrill me to the core !—
Who art thou, venerable sage,
Whom Heaven hath made the wonder of the age,
Working for thee a miracle so great ?

Alberto.

I am, O captain, the most fortunate
Of all mankind, although in worth the least,
Since I have merited to be a priest.
For four-and-forty years I read with care
Sacred theology from Bologna's chair.
His Holiness, for all the years thus spent,
Gave me the Bishopric of Trent,
Rewarding thus my studious zeal long shown ;
But I afraid, from conscious qualms,
To account for others' souls that scarce can save mine own,
Fled its laurels, fled its palms,
And the world's deceits rejecting,
Sought securer peace, selecting
These remote and lonely dells,
Where nought but naked truth austerely dwells.
I was going to Rome, with hope
Of obtaining licence from the Pope
To found, O captain, 'mid these heights,
A holy order of lone eremites,
When thy rage so desperate
Sever'd my thread of life, and changed my fate.

Eusebio.
¿ Qué libro es este, di ?

Alberto.
Este es el fruto,
Que rinde á mis estudios el tributo
De tantos años.

Eusebio.
¿ Qué es lo que contiene ?

Alberto.
El trata del orígen verdadero
De aquel divino y celestial madero,
En que animoso y fuerte,
Muriendo, triunfó Cristo de la muerte.
El libro, en fin, se llama
" Milagros de la Cruz."

Eusebio.
¡ Qué bien la llama
De aquel plomo inclemente,
Mas que la cera, se mostró obediente !
¡ Pluguiera á Dios, mi mano
Antes, que blanco su papel hiciera
De aquel golpe tirano,
Entre su fuego ardiera !
Lleva ropa y dinero
Y la vida, solo este libro quiero ;
Y vosotros salidle acompañando,
Hasta dejarle libre.

Alberto.
Iré rogando
Al Señor, te dé luz para que veas
El error en que vives.

Eusebio.
Tell me, what book is this ?

Alberto.
It is the fruit
Which many a year's hard study in pursuit
Of truth has given me.

Eusebio.
What does it contain ?

Alberto.
It treats of the true history
Of that divine and holy tree
On which by yielding up his mighty breath
Christ died, and, dying, triumph'd over death.
The book is call'd by the appropriate name,
" The Miracles of the Cross."

Eusebio.
How well the flame
Of the fierce bullet knew what to obey,
When, soft as wax, the stubborn lead gave way !
Oh ! would to God ! that ere my hand's wild rage
Had dared to do a deed so dire,
As to deface this spotless page
By that rude shot, 'twere burn'd in its own fire !
Keep thou thy money, life, and dress,
This book alone is all I would possess :
Do you, my comrades, guide him on his way
Till you can set him free.

Alberto.
And I shall pray,
Each step I take, that God may thee inspire

Eufebio.
Si defeas
Mi bien, pídele á Dios, que no permita
Muera fin confefion.

Alberto.
Yo te prometo,
Seré miniftro en tan piadofo efeto,
Y te doy mi palabra,
(Tanto en mi pecho tu clemencia labra)
Que fi me llamas en cualquiera parte,
Dejaré mi defierto,
Por ir á confefarte:
Un Sacerdote foy, mi nombre Alberto.

Eufebio.
¿Tal palabra me das?

Alberto.
Y la confiefo
Con la mano.

Eufebio.
Otra vez tus plantas befo.
[*Vafe* Alberto *con* Ricardo *y los Bandoleros.*

Sale Chilindrina.

Chilindrina.
Hafta venir á hablarte,
El monte atravefé de parte á parte.

Eufebio.
Qué hay, amigo?

Chilindrina.
Dos nuevas harto malas.

Eufebio.
A mi temor el fentimiento igualas.
Qué fon?

To know thy finful life.

Eufebio.
Doft thou defire
My welfare? Then afk God that I may not
Without confeffion die.

Alberto.
I promife thee
Thy helper in that pious wifh to be;
Yes, I pledge to thee my word,
(So much thy clemency my heart hath ftirr'd,)
That in whatever place thou wilt addrefs me,
In my defert I fhall own thy claim,
And haften to confefs thee:
I am a prieft, Alberto is my name.

Eufebio.
Thy word doft give me?

Alberto.
Let my hand repeat
The promife thus.

Eufebio.
Once more I kifs thy feet.
[Alberto *is led out by* Ricardo *and the other bandits.*

Enter Chillindrina.

Chillindrina.
Up this wild mountain's fteep acclivity
I've roam'd through every part to fpeak with thee.

Eufebio.
What brings thee, friend?

Chillindrina.
Two bits of evil news.

Eufebio.
Terror and grief my feelings interfufe:
What are they?

Chilindrina.

Es la primera,
(Decirla no quiſiera)
Que al padre de Liſardo
Han dado . . . .

Euſebio.

Acaba, que el efecto aguardo.

Chilindrina.

Comiſion de prenderte ó de matarte.

Euſebio.

Eſotra nueva temo
Mas, porque en un confuſo extremo
Al corazon parece que camina
Toda el alma, adivina
De algun future daño.
¿ Qué ha ſucedido ?

Chilindrina.

A Julia . . . .

Euſebio.

No me engaño
En prevenir triſtezas,
Si para ver mi mal, por Julia empiezas.
¿ Julia no me dijiſte ?
Pues eſo baſta para verme triſte.
¡ Mal haya amen la riguroſa eſtrella,
Que me obligó á querella !
En fin, Julia . . . . proſigue.

Chilindrina.

En un convento
Seglar eſtá.

Chillindrina.

The firſt is,
(I would that I had not to tell thee this,)
Unto Liſardo's father by the ſtate
Is given . . . .

Euſebio.

Conclude, the whole reſult I wait.

Chillindrina.

Commiſſion or to ſeize thee or to ſlay thee.

Euſebio.

Thy ſecond news I fear
More than the firſt; becauſe, on ſtretch to hear,
My troubled ſoul flies to my trembling heart
Confuſed, diſturb'd, divining that thou art
The bearer of bad tidings of worſe pain:
What then has happen'd ?

Chillindrina.

Julia . . . .

Euſebio.

Not in vain
My boding ſorrows whiſper'd from within,—
If thou haſt evil news, with Julia thou'lt begin:
Saidſt thou not Julia? more thou need'ſt not add,
For that is quite enough to make me ſad.
Accursèd be the baneful ſtar above her
That forces me to love her!
Julia in fine . . . . proceed.

Chillindrina.

Is by her friends
Placed in a convent.

Eusebio.
¡ Ya falta el sufrimiento !
¡ Que el cielo me castigue
Con tan grandes venganzas
De perdidos deseos,
De muertas esperanzas,
Que de los mismos cielos,
Por quien me deja, vengo á tener zelos !
Mas ya tan atrevido,
Que viviendo matando,
Me sustento robando,
No puedo ser peor de lo que he sido :
Despéñese el intento,
Pues ya se ha despeñado el pensamiento.
Llama á Celio y Ricardo. (Amando muero !)

Chilindrina.
Voy por ellos. [*Vase.*

Eusebio.
Ve, y diles, que aqui espero.—
Asaltaré el convento que la guarda.
Ningun grave castigo me acobarda ;
Que por verme señor de su hermosura,
Tirano amor me fuerza
A acometer la fuerza,
A romper la clausura,
Y á violar el sagrado ;
Que ya del todo estoy desesperado.
Pues si no me pusiera
Amor en tales puntos,
Solamente lo hiciera
Por cometer tantos delitos juntos.

Eusebio.
My endurance ends !
Oh ! that Heaven should have decreed
Its vengeful bolts to launch at me so fast !
My lost desires—
My hopes all past—
And now the heaven she leaves me for requires
I should be jealous even of heaven at last.
But so bold am I, so changed my mien,
Who in murder can disport me,
Who by robbing can support me,
Worse I cannot be than I have been.
Let then the daring deed be wrought,
In fact, since I have dared it in my thought :
Call Celio and Ricardo. (Ah ! love leads me to my bier !)

Chillindrina.
I go to call them. [*Exit.*

Eusebio.
Go, and say I wait them here.—
I shall scale the convent that doth hold her,
No fear shall fright me, till these arms enfold her ;
Since to see me master of her charms
Tyrant love's tumultuous course
Forces me to trust to force ;
To fill her cloister with alarms,
To violate a consecrated place,
Since desperate have I grown and lost to every grace ;
Though if love that brings me to it
Were not enough to make this deed be done,
I for this alone would do it,
That all possible crimes I might commit [in one.

Salen Gil *y* Menga.

Menga.
¡Mas que encontramos con él,
Segun mezquina nací!

Gil.
¿Menga, yo no voy aqui?
No temas ese cruel
Capitan de buñuleros,
Ni el hallarlo te alborote,
Que honda llevo yo, y garrote.

Menga.
Temo, Gil, sus hechos fieros;
Si no, á Silvia á mirar ponte,
Cuando aqui la acometió;
Que doncella al monte entró,
Y dueña salió del monte,
Que no es peligro pequeño.

Gil.
Conmigo fuera cruel,
Que tambien entro doncel,
Y pudiera salir dueño.

[*Reparan en* Eusebio.

Menga.
¡Ah señor! que va perdido,
Que anda Eusebio por aqui.

Gil.
No eche, señor, por ahí.

Eusebio (*aparte*).
Estos no me han conocido,
Y quiero disimular.

Gil.
¿Quiere que aquese ladron
Le mate?

Eusebio (*aparte*).
Villanos son.—

¿Con qué podré yo pagar
Este aviso?

Enter Gil *and* Menga.

Menga.
But if we should meet him here!
Born to all bad luck am I!

Gil.
Don't you see that I am by,
Menga mine? So do not fear
This bold captain of banditti,
This cantankerous curmudgeon,
While I carry sling and bludgeon.

Menga.
Ah! I fear, and more's the pity,
Left, like Silvia, such another
Trick in my case should be play'd,
Who to the mountain came a maid,
And went out of the mount a mother;
'Tis no trifling risk to run.

Gil.
Mine will be the danger rather
To come out, perchance, a father,
Having gone in but a son.

[*They perceive* Eusebio.

Menga.
Ah! sir, you are lost! this spot
Is Eusebio's haunt, they say.

Gil.
Do not venture, sir, that way.

Eusebio (*aside*).
It is plain they know me not:
I'll dissemble in their presence.

Gil.
Would you have the robber slay you?
Stop, sir!

Eusebio.
How can I repay you
[*aside.*
For this good advice? (But peasants
Are they).

Gil.
Con huir.
De efe bellaco.
Menga.
Si os coge,
Señor, aunque no le enoje
Ni vueftro hacer, ni decir,
Luego os matará; y creed,
Que con poner, tras la ofenfa,
Una Cruz encima, pienfa,
Que os hace mucha merced.

Salen RICARDO *y* CELIO.

Ricardo.
¿Dónde le dejafte?
Celio.
Aqui.
Gil.
Es un ladron, no le efperes.
Ricardo.
Eufebio, ¿qué es lo que quieres?
Gil.
¿Eufebio le llamó?
Menga.
Sí.
Eufebio.
Yo foy Eufebio; ¿qué os mueve
Contra mí? ¿No hay quien refponda?
Menga.
Gil, ¿tienes garrote y honda?
Gil.
Tengo el diabro que te lleve.
Celio.
Por los apacibles llanos,
Que hace del monte la falda,
A quien guarda el mar la efpalda,
Ví un efcuadron de villanos,
Que armado contra tí viene,
Y pienfo que fe avecina;

Gil.
Juft by fimply flying
From the rafcal.
Menga.
If he catch you,
In a moment he'll difpatch you,
Though you ne'er, his temper trying,
Wrong'd him, or provoked his flaver
By a word or deed. When dead
He'll a crofs place at your head,
Thinking he confers a favour.

Enter RICARDO *and* CELIO.

Ricardo.
Here you left him?
Celio.
Here, I fay.
Gil (to Eufebio).
Quick! don't wait the robber, go!
Ricardo.
What's your wifh, Eufebio!
Gil.
Eufebio did he call him?
Menga.
Yea.
Eufebio.
That's my name: what ails you? pooh!
In a moment why fo ftill?
Menga.
Where's the fling and bludgeon, Gil?
Gil.
Where's the devil except in you?
Celio.
Where the peaceful vales expand
At this mountain's foot, that fwelleth
O'er the fea which it expelleth,
I have feen a fhepherd band
Coming in a well-arm'd crowd,
Seeking thee, nor long it tarries,

Que aſi Curcio determina
La venganza que previene.
Mira qué pienſas hacer;
Junta tu gente, y partamos.

Euſebio.

Mejor es que ahora huyamos;
Que eſta noche hay mas que hacer.
Venid conmigo los dos,
De quien juſtamente fio
La opinion y el honor mio.

Ricardo.

Muy bien puedes; que por Dios,
Que he de morir á tu lado.

Euſebio.

Villanos, vida teneis,
Solo porque le lleveis
A mi enemigo un recado.
Decid á Curcio, que yo
Con tanta gente atrevida
Solo defiendo la vida,
Pero que le buſco no.
Y que no tiene ocaſion
De buſcarme deſta ſuerte,
Pues no dí á Liſardo muerte
Con engaño, ó con traicion.
Cuerpo á cuerpo le maté,
Sin ventaja conocida,
Y antes de acabar la vida
En mis brazos le llevé
Adonde ſe confeſó,
Digna accion para eſtimarſe;
Mas que ſi quiere vengarſe,
Que he de defenderme yo.—

[*A los Bandoleros.*

Y ahora, porque no vean
Aqueſtos por donde vamos,
Atadlos entre eſtos ramos:
Vendados ſus ojos ſean,
Porque no aviſen.

Since 'tis here: thus Curcio carries
Out the vengeance he hath vow'd.
Think now what is beſt to do,
Summon all the troop and try . . . .

Euſebio.

It is beſt that now we fly,
Since to-night there's much to do.
Come with me, ye two, whom I
With a confidence ſo juſt
Honour and my fame entruſt.

Ricardo.

So you may, for we would die
At your ſide our zeal to ſhow.

Euſebio.

Peaſants, know I let you live
But for this, that you may give
A brief meſſage to my foe;
This from me to Curcio ſpeak:—
With the brave bands that attend me
I will for my life defend me;
But that his I do not ſeek.
And that he hath got no reaſon
For purſuing me in this way,
Since if I his ſon did ſlay
'Twas not foully or by treaſon;
Arm'd as he I ſtood before him,
Vantage none on either ſide.
True, he fell, but, ere he died,
In theſe very arms I bore him
Where his ſins he might confeſs,
Act more worthy praiſe than blame;
But if vengeance be his aim,
I'll defend me ne'ertheleſs.

[*To the Robbers.*

Now that theſe two may not ſee
By what road our troop is wending,
Tie them to theſe boughs here bending;
Let their eyes, too, bandaged be,
That they may not tell aught.

Ricardo.
Aqui
Hay cordel.
Celio.
Pues llega presto.
Gil.
De San Sebastian me han puesto.
Menga.
De San Sebastiana á mí.
Mas ate cuanto quisiere,
Señor, como no me mate.
Gil.
Oye, señor, no me ate,
Y puto sea yo, si huyere.
Jura tú, Menga, tambien
Este mismo juramento.
Celio.
Ya estan atados.
Eusebio.
Mi intento
Se va ejecutando bien;
La noche amenaza obscura,
Tendiendo su negro velo.
Julia, aunque te guarde el cielo,
He de gozar tu hermosura.
[*Vanse los Bandoleros, dejando á* GIL *y* MENGA *atados.*
Gil.
¿Quién habrá que ahora nos vea,
Menga, aunque caro nos cueste,
Que no diga, que es aqueste
Peralvillo de la aldea?
Menga.
Vete llegando hácia aqui,

Ricardo.
Try
This good cord, 'twill do.
Celio.
Make fast then.
Gil.
See me tied like Saint Sebastian!
Menga.
Saint Sebastiana am I.
Tightly as you like, sir, tie,
Only don't quite crucify me.
Gil.
Ah! sir, listen, do not tie me,
And I'll swear I will not fly:
Menga, too, will swear pell-mell
All the oaths that you can mention.
Celio.
Now they're fasten'd.
Eusebio.
My intention
Has been carried out right well.
Now night threatens, and its sooty
Veil draws o'er the face of even.
Julia, spite of hell or heaven,
Soon I shall possess thy beauty.
[*The Bandits depart, leaving* GIL *and* MENGA *tied.*
Gil.
Who that saw us to this willow
Tied here, Menga, wouldn't say,
Here's a pair condemn'd to-day
By the parish Peralvillo?*
Menga.
Gil, as I can't get near *you*,

* Peralvillo is the name of a small town near Ciudad-Rodrigo, where the archers of the Holy Brotherhood were accustomed to execute without trial all criminals found in the act of committing their offences. From this circumstance, very rapid justice in Spain went by the name of *La justice de Peralvillo.*—M. DAMAS-HINARD.

Perhaps "Lynch Law" would best express its meaning in English.—TR.

Gil; que yo no puedo andar.

Gil.

Menga, venme á deſatar,
Y te deſataré á tí
Luego al punto.

Menga.

Ven primero
Tú, que ya eſtás importuno.

Gil.

¿Es decir, que vendrá alguno?
Pondré que falta un arriero,
Las tres ánades cantando,
Un caminante pidiendo,
Un eſtudiante comiendo,
Una ſantera rezando,
Hoy en aqueſte camino,
Lo que á ninguno faltó:
Mas la culpa tengo yo.

Una voz (dentro).

Hácia eſta parte imagino
Que oigo voces; llegad preſto.

Gil.

Señor, en buena hora acuda
A deſatar una duda
En que ha rato que eſtoy pueſto.

Menga.

Si acaſo buſcais, ſeñor,
Por el monte algun cordel,
Yo os puedo ſervir con él.

Gil.

Eſte es mas gordo y mejor.

Menga.

Yo, por ſer muger, eſpero
Remedio en las anſias mias.

Gil.

No repare en cortesías,
Desáteme á mí primero.

You come here, now don't deny me.

Gil.

Menga, come here and untie me,
And I'll then untie you too,
In a twinkling.

Menga.

Come you firſt,
Since you are ſo *haſty*, you know.

Gil.

Come, come, anyone, high or low!
Would to God that at the worſt
Some gay muleteer loud trolling
A light lilt, ſome nun her pſalms,
Some poor ſcholar aſking alms,
Some foot-traveller ſlowly ſtrolling,
Would but take this road to-day,
So that help may fail not wholly!—
Oh! my looſe tongue and my folly!

A voice within.

It appears to me this way
Voices I can hear, quick! ſee!

Gil.

At a lucky time, Sir Traveller,
Have you come to be th'unraveller
Of this knotty point for me.

Menga.

If you're ſeeking, ſir, along
This wild road a rope to tie you,
I'm the one that can ſupply you.

Gil.

Mine is better and more ſtrong.

Menga.

As a woman, from my pains
I ſhould firſt deliver'd be.

Gil.

Oh! a fig for courteſy!
Looſe me firſt, ſir, from my chains.

Salen Curcio, Octavio, Tirso, Bras, *y soldados.*

Tirso.
Hácia aquesta parte suena
La voz.

Gil.
¡ Qué te quemas !

Tirso.
Gil,
¿ Qué es esto ?

Gil.
El diabro es sútil ;
Desata, Tirso, y mi pena
Te diré despues.

Curcio.
¿ Qué es esto ?

Gil.
Venga en buen hora, señor,
A castigar un traidor.

Curcio.
¿ Quién desta suerte os ha puesto ?

Gil.
¿ Quién ? Eusebio, que en efeto
Dice : . . . . Pero ¿ qué se yo
Lo que dice ? El nos dejó
Aqui en semejante aprieto.

Tirso.
No llores pues, que no ha estado
Hoy muy poco liberal
Contigo.

Bras.
No lo ha hecho mal,
Pues á Menga te ha dejado.

Gil.
¡ Ay Tirso ! no lloro yo,

Enter Curcio, Octavio, Tirso, Bras, *and others.*

Tirso.
From this place doth sound again
That same voice.

Gil.
You burn.*

Tirso.
How ? why ?
What's this, Gil ?

Gil.
The devil is sly :—
Loose me first, and I'll explain
All about it.

Curcio.
What's this ? say.

Gil.
Sure you're sent, sir, by the skies
A vile traitor to chastise.

Curcio.
Who has tied you in this way ?

Gil.
Who ? Eusebio : and the scamp
Said . . . . but hang me ! if I know
What he said ; he left us, though,
Tied up tight here with the cramp.

Tirso.
Well, don't cry ! 'twas well to find him
Act so generously, Gil,
Towards you to-day.

Bras.
He meant no ill,
Menga to have left behind him.

Gil.
Ah ! I do not shed a tear,

* Gil, who it is to be recollected is the *gracioso* or buffoon of the drama, treats the advancing party as if they were playing the game of hide-and-seek, and makes use of the exclamation generally employed to attract or divert the attention of the seeker.—M. Damas-Hinard.

Porque piadoſo no fue.
Tirſo.
Pues ¿por qué lloras?
Gil.
¿Por qué?
Porque á Menga me dejó:
La de Anton llevó, y al cabo
De ſeis, que no parecia,
Halló á ſu muger un dia;
Hicimos un baile bravo
De hallazgo, y gaſtó cien reales.

Bras.
¿Bártolo no ſe caſó
Con Catalina, y parió
A ſeis meſes no cabales?
Y andaba con gran placer
Diciendo: ¡Si tú le vieſes!
Lo que otra hace en nueve meſes,
Hace en cinco mi muger.

Tirſo.
Ello, no hay honra ſegura.
Curcio.
¿Que eſto llegue á eſcuchar yo
Deſte tirano? ¿quién vió
Tan notable deſventura?
Menga.
Como deſtruirle pienſa;
Que haſta las miſmas mugeres
Tomaremos, ſi tú quieres,
Las armas para ſu ofenſa.
Gil.
Que aqui acude es lo mas cierto;
Y toda eſta proceſion
De Cruces que miras, ſon,
Señor, por hombres que ha muerto.

Tirſo, for his illiberality.
Tirſo.
Why then weep?
Gil.
For the fatality
Of his *leaving* her with me here.
Anton's bride when he took away,
Six days long ſhe was out of our ſight,
On the ſeventh ſhe came to light;—
Oh! what a feaſt we had that day
On the hundred reals ſhe brought in her pocket!
Bras.
Yes, and didn't Bartolo wed
Catalina, and waſn't ſhe brought to bed
In ſix months of a boy, and didn't he rock it,
Feeling the happieſt man alive,
And telling his friends triumphantly, too,
What takes other women nine months to do
Mine is able to do in five?
Tirſo.
Honour's nothing in his ſight.
Curcio.
Still am I condemn'd to hear
Of this villain's vile career?—
Oh! my wretched, wretched plight!
Menga.
Think this monſter of ſeduction
How to capture, how to kill.
Even the women, if you will,
All will arm for his deſtruction.
Gil.
That we're on his track is plain,
For theſe croſſes, far projected
O'er the horizon, are erected
O'er the men that he hath ſlain.

Octavio.
Es aqui lo mas ſecreto
De todo el monte.
Curcio (*aparte*).
Y aqui
Fue ¡ cielos ! donde yo ví
Aquel milagroſo efeto
De inocencia y caſtidad,
Cuya beldad atrevido
Tantas veces he ofendido
Con dudas, ſiendo verdad
Un milagro tan patente.
Octavio.
Señor, ¿ qué nueva paſion
Cauſa tu imaginacion ?
Curcio.
Rigores, que el alma ſiente,
Son, Octavio ; y mis enojos,
Para publicar mi mengua,
Como los niego á la lengua,
Me van ſaliendo á los ojos.
Haz, Octavio, que me deje
Solo eſa gente que ſigo,
Porque aqui de mí y conmigo
Hoy á los cielos me queje.
Octavio.
Ea, ſoldados, deſpejad.
Bras.
¿ Qué decis ?
Tirſo.
¿ Qué pretendeis ?
Gil.
Deſpiojad,* ¿ no lo entendeis ?
Que nos vamos á eſpulgar.
[*Vanſe todos, menos* Curcio.
Curcio.
¿ A quién no habrá ſucedido

Octavio.
'Tis the moſt ſecluded ſpot
Of the mountain.
Curcio (*aſide*).
And 'twas here,
Heavens ! I ſaw with awe and fear
That ſtupendous wonder wrought
By the power of two magicians—
Innocence and Chaſtity—
Beauteous guardian powers by me
Wrong'd ſo oft through vile ſuſpicions
Of one fair as ſhe was pure.
Octavio.
Ah ! ſir, what new form of pain
Thus diſturbs your mind again ?
Curcio.
'Tis a pain no time can cure ;
'Tis a grief that *will* ariſe ;
'Tis a pang whoſe hidden cauſe,
Though to tell the tongue may pauſe,
Muſt be ſpoken by the eyes.
Lead aſide, O friend ! the train
Of my followers ; in this lonely
Spot, and to the high heavens only,
Of me, *to* me, would I plain.
Octavio.
Lads, our leader reſt allows ye.
Bras.
How allows ye ?
Tirſo.
What's that, pray ?
Gil.
Don't you ſee, as plain as day,
That he ſays to us, Lads, all louſe ye ?*
[*Exeunt all but* Curcio.
Curcio.
Doth it happen not in ſorrow,

* This coarſe pleaſantry of miſtaking the word *deſpejad* for *deſpiojad* I have ventured to imitate.

Tal vez, lleno de peſares,
Deſcanſar conſigo á ſolas,
Por no deſcubrirſe á nadie?
Yo á quien tantos penſamientos
A un tiempo afligen, que hacen
Con lágrimas y ſuſpiros
Competencia al mar y al aire,
Compañero de mí miſmo
En las mudas ſoledades,
Con la penſion de mis bienes
Quiero divertir mis males.
Ni las aves, ni las fuentes
Sean teſtigos baſtantes;
Que al fin las fuentes murmuran,
Y tienen lengua las aves.
No quiero mas compañía,
Que aqueſtos rúſticos ſauces;
Pues quien eſcucha, y no aprende,
Será fuerza que no hable.
Teatro eſte monte fue
Del ſuceſo mas notable,
Que entre prodigios de zelos
Cuentan las antigüedades
De una inocente verdad.
Pero ¿ quién podrá librarſe
De ſoſpechas, en quien ſon
Mentiroſas las verdades?
Muerte de amor ſon los zelos,
Que no perdonan á nadie,
Ni por humilde le dejan,
Ni le reſpetan por grave.
Aqui pues, donde yo digo,
Roſmira y yo . . . De acordarme,
No es mucho que el alma tiemble,
No es mucho que la voz falte;
Que no hay flor, que no me aſombre,
No hay hoja, que no me eſpante,
No hay piedra, que no me admire,
Tronco, que no me acobarde,

When the heart is full of ſadneſs,
That one ſeeketh ſelf-communion
Rather than confide in any?
I, afflicted at one moment
By the numerous thoughts that wrack me,
With my ſighing and my weeping
Rivalling the air and water,
I, companion of myſelf,
'Mid theſe wilds that no voice gladdens,
Seek to while away my ſorrows,
Thinking of the joys departed.
I would have nor birds nor fountains
Witneſſes of this ſelf-parley,—
For in fine the fountains murmur,
And the birds have tongues that warble;
I would only be companion'd
By theſe rough and ruſtling alders:
For who hears and underſtands not
Cannot ſpeak of aught that paſſes.
This wild mountain was the ſcene
Of a more ſurpriſing marvel
Than antiquity relateth,
All through jealouſy's ſtrange annals,
Of an innocent woman's truth.
Ah! but who can break the ſhackles
Of ſuſpicions, which to truths
Give the very air of falſeneſs?
Jealouſy is the death of love.
No love lives while that plague laſteth,
Nor the lowly is paſs'd over,
Nor the lofty left unblaſted.
Here then, here, where I am ſpeaking,
I Roſmira led . . . . What marvel
That the thought doth make me ſhudder,
That the memory makes me falter!
Since there's not a flower but frights me,
Not a leaf but makes me ſtartle,
Not a ſtone I ſee but ſhocks me,
Not a tree-trunk but unmans me,

Peñafco, que no me oprima,
Monte, que no me amenace;
Porque todos fon teftigos
De una hazaña tan infame.
Saqué al fin la efpada, y ella,
Sin temerme y fin turbarfe,
Porque en riefgos de honor* nunca
" El inocente es cobarde:
Efpofo, dijo, detente;
No digo que no me mates,
Si es tu gufto, ¿porque yo
Cómo he de poder negarte
La mifma vida que es tuya?
Solo te pido, que antes
Me digas por lo que muero;
Y déjame que te abrace."
Yo la dije: " En tus entrañas,
Como la víbora, traes
A quien te ha de dar la muerte.
Indicio ha fido baftante
El parto infame que efperas:
Mas no le verás, que antes,
Dándote muerte, feré
Verdugo tuyo y de un ángel."
" Si acafo," me dijo entonces,
" Si acafo, efpofo, llegafte
A creer flaquezas mias,
Jufto ferá que me mates.
Mas á efta Cruz abrazada,
A efta que eftaba delante,
Profiguió, doy por teftigo,
De que no fupe agraviarte,
Ni ofenderte; que ella fola
Será jufto que me ampare."
Bien quifiera entonces yo,
Arrepentido, arrojarme
A fus pies, porque fe via
Su inocencia en fu femblante.

* Hartzenbufch reads "*amor.*"

Not a rock but feems to crufh me,
Not a mountain but o'erhangs me;
Since they all have been fpectators
Of fo infamous an act here.
I my fword drew, and fhe fhowing
Fear nor trouble in her manner,
Since in rifks of love and honour
Innocence is ne'er faint-hearted,—
" Hold!" fhe faid, " oh! hold, my
husband!
'Tis not for my life I afk thee,
Take it, if thou fo art minded,
Since I can't refufe to grant thee
That which is thine own already;
What I afk thee for, is rather
To fay *why* I die, then let me
Die, but die in thy embraces."
I replied, " Within thy body,
Like the viper, thou doft carry
That which is thine own deftruction,
Proved enough by that unhappy
Birth of fhame that thou awaiteft;
But that birth fhall never happen,
For in killing thee my vengeance
Seals thine own fate and an angel's."
" If by any chance, my hufband,—
If by any chance," fhe anfwer'd,
" Thou my frailty canft believe in,
It is juft that thou fhouldft ftab me;
But I call this crofs to witnefs,"
(Then, as now, the one here planted),
" This that I embrace, that never
Have I thought to wrong or harm thee
In thine honour, and I truft me
To its faving power to guard me."
I would then have almoft wifh'd,
In repentance, to have caft me
At her feet, her innocence
Shining in her eyes' pure glances.

El que una traicion intenta
Antes mire lo que hace ;
Porque una vez declarado,
Aunque procure enmendarſe,
Por decir que tuvo cauſa,
Lo ha de llevar adelante.
Yo pues, no porque dudaba
Ser la diſculpa baſtante,
Sino porque mi delito
Mas amparado quedaſe,
El brazo levanté airado,
Tirando por varias partes
Mil heridas ; pero ſolo
Las ejecuté en el aire.
Por muerta al pie de la Cruz
Quedó, y queriendo eſcaparme,
A caſa llegué, y halléla
Con mas belleza que ſale
El alba, cuando en ſus brazos
Nos preſenta el ſol infante.
Ella en ſus brazos tenia
A Julia, divina imágen
De hermoſura y diſcrecion :
(¿ Qué gloria pudo igualarſe
A la mia ?) que ſu parto
Habia ſido aquella tarde
Al miſmo pie de la Cruz ;
Y por divinas ſeñales,
Con que al mundo deſcubria
Dios un milagro tan grande,
La niña que habia parido,
Dichoſa con ſeñas tales,
Tenia en el pecho una Cruz,
Labrada de fuego y ſangre.
Pero ¡ ay ! que tanta ventura
Templaba el que ſe quedaſe
Otra criatura en el monte ;
Que ella, entre penas tan graves,
Sintió haber parido dos ;

He who treachery meditateth
Well at firſt ſhould weigh the matter :
For if once it is outſpoken,
Though he'd have it countermanded,
From his having own'd a cauſe,
To the cloſe it muſt be acted.
I then, not becauſe I thought her
Exculpation leſs than ample,
But becauſe ſome palliation
Wiſh'd I for my guilty madneſs,
Raiſed my angry arm, inflicting,
In a wild and furious manner,
Many a death-wound; but I dealt them
Only on the air that parted :—
At the foot of the Croſs, for dead,
She remain'd, and I, diſtracted,
Flying thence, went home, and found her
Lovelier than in golden gladneſs
When day dawns, and, in its arms
Bearing the infant ſun, advances.
For within her arms ſhe held
Julia, image and example
Of all heavenly grace and beauty ;
(Oh ! what rapture could be balanced
Againſt mine then !) the birth having
On that very evening happen'd
At the foot of that ſame Croſs.
And for proofs divinely patent,
By whoſe means would God diſcover
To the world ſo great a marvel,
On the new-born baby's boſom,
Happy to be thus ſo mark'd there,
Was a Croſs of blood and fire
Work'd in wonderful enamel.
But, alas ! what moderated
So much joy was, that an after
Child was left upon the mountain.
Since ſhe, in her painful travail,

Y yo entonces . . . .

Sale Octavio.

Octavio.

Por el valle
Atraviesa un escuadron
De bandoleros; y antes
Que cierre la noche triste,
Será bien, señor, que bajes
A buscarlos, no obscurezca;
Porque ellos el monte saben,
Y nosotros no.

Curcio.

Pues junta
La gente vaya adelante;
Que no hay gloria para mí,
Hasta llegar á vengarme. [*Vanse.*

Vista exterior de un Convento.

Salen Eusebio, Ricardo *y* Celio *con una escala.*

Ricardo.

Llega con silencio, y pon
A esa parte las escalas.

Eusebio.

Icaro seré sin alas,
Sin fuego seré Faeton:
Escalar al sol intento,
Y si me quiere ayudar
La luz, tengo de pasar
Mas allá del firmamento.
Amor ser tirano enseña.—
En subiendo yo, quitad
Esa escala, y esperad,
Hasta que os haga una seña.
Quien subiendo se despeña,

Felt she had given birth to two.
And I then . . . .

Enter Octavio.

Octavio.

Along the valley
Winds its devious way a squadron
Of banditti; and, ere darkness
In the night's sad gloom enfolds it,
It were well, sir, that you hasten'd
Down to seek them, lest you lose them:
For they know the mountain-passes,
And we know them not.

Curcio.

Combined,
Let our people all advance then;
Since no rest can I enjoy
Till my heart's revenge is granted.
[*Exeunt.*

Outside a Convent at Night.

Enter Eusebio, Ricardo, *and* Celio *with a scaling-ladder.*

Ricardo.

Silently tread; a little nigher:—
Here fix the ladder with the slings.

Eusebio.

Icarus I'll be without his wings,
Phaëton without his fire;
I intend to scale the sun,
If then I would have its light
Aid me in my daring flight;
Mount I must till heaven is won,—
Tyrant love, watch over all!—
When I enter, from the grating
Take the ladder, and be waiting
Hereabouts until I call.—
Though proud Phaëton may fall,

Suba hoy, y baje oſendido,
En cenizas convertido;
Que la pena del bajar,
No ſerá parte á quitar
La gloria de haber ſubido.

Ricardo.

¿Qué eſperas?

Celio.

Pues ¿qué rigor
Tu altivo orgullo embaraza?

Euſebio.

¿No veis como me amenaza
Un vivo fuego?

Ricardo.

Señor,
Fantaſmas ſon del temor.

Euſebio.

¿Yo temor?

Celio.

Sube.

Euſebio.

Ya llego,
Aunque á tantos rayos ciego,
Por las llamas he de entrar;
Que no lo podrá eſtorbar
De todo el infierno el fuego.

[*Sube y entra.*

Celio.

Ya entró.

Ricardo.

Alguna fantasía
De ſu miſmo horror fundada,
En la idea acreditada,
O alguna iluſion ſeria.

Celio.

Quita la eſcala.

Ricardo.

Haſta el dia
Aqui le hemos de eſperar.

Dazzled by the light ſurpriſing,
In his aſhes agoniſing,
Still the pain of falling down
Cannot take away the crown,
Or the glory of the riſing.

Ricardo.

What delays thee?

Celio.

Say, what here
Can impede thy haughty aim?

Euſebio.

Saw you not a living flame
Flaſh before my eyes?

Ricardo.

A mere
Phantaſy it was of fear.

Euſebio.

I to fear?

Celio.

Then up!

Euſebio.

Although
Lightnings blind me, I ſhall go:
Through the very flames I'll enter;
Powerleſs now as a preventer
Were the infernal fire below.

[*He aſcends and enters.*

Celio.

Now he's in.

Ricardo.

Some phantaſy
On its in-born horror founded—
Of ideal fears compounded,—
Some illuſion it muſt be.

Celio.

Take the ladder down.

Ricardo.

Here we
Muſt remain till morning's prime.

Celio.
Atrevimiento fue entrar,
Aunque yo de mejor gana
Me fuera con mi villana ;
Mas despues habrá lugar. [*Vanse.*

CELDA DE JULIA.

Sale EUSEBIO.

Eusebio.
Por todo el convento he andado
Sin ser de nadie sentido,
Y por cuanto he discurrido,
De mi destino guiado,
A mil celdas he llegado
De religiosas, que abiertas
Tienen las estrechas puertas,
Y en ninguna á Julia ví.
¿ Dónde me llevais asi,
Esperanzas siempre inciertas ?
¡ Qué horror ! ¡ qué silencio mudo !
¡ Qué obscuridad tan funesta !
Luz hay aqui ; celda es esta,
Y en ella Julia. ¿ Qué dudo ?
[*Corre una cortina, y ve á* JULIA *durmiendo.*
¿ Tan poco el valor ayudo,
Que ahora en hablarla tardo ?
Qué es lo que espero ? qué aguardo ?
Mas con impulso dudoso,
Si me animo temeroso,
Animoso me acobardo.
Mas belleza la humildad
Deste trage la asegura ;
Que en la muger la hermosura
Es la misma honestidad.
Su peregrina beldad,
De mi torpe amor objeto,

Celio.
'Twas a daring thing to climb,—
Though the hours I'd rather pass
With my own dear village lass,—
Better luck another time ! [*Exeunt.*

THE CORRIDOR OUTSIDE THE CELL OF JULIA.

Enter EUSEBIO.

Eusebio.
All through the convent I have glided
Unperceived by any mortal,
And my path through porch and portal
By my destiny seems guided.
To a thousand cells, divided
By their narrow open doors,
Have I come on the corridors,
And have Julia seen in none.
Whither would ye lead me on,
Hopes that seek but phantom shores ?
Oh ! what silent horror's here !
Oh ! what darkness here doth dwell !
There's a light within this cell ;
Julia's in it ! Why this fear ?
[*Draws a curtain, and* JULIA *is seen asleep.*
Does my courage disappear ?
Is't so slight, that I delay
Now to advance ? Why pause ? Why stay ?
By an impulse to and fro,
Trembling, I a boldness show,
Bold, a coward's heart betray.
Lovelier in the humbleness
Of this dress she seems to me,
For with women modesty
Is in itself a comeliness.
Her surpassing loveliness,

Hace en mí mayor efeto ;
Que á un tiempo á mi amor incito
Con la hermoſura apetito,
Con la honeſtidad reſpeto.
! Julia ! ¡ ah Julia !

Julia.
Quién me nombra ?
Mas ¡ cielos ! ¿ qué es lo que veo ?
¿ Eres ſombra del deſeo,
O del penſamiento ſombra ?

Euſebio.
¿ Tanto el mirarme te aſombra ?

Julia.
¿ Pues quién habrá que no intente
Huir de tí ?

Euſebio.
Julia, detente.

Julia.
¿ Qué quieres, forma fingida,
De la idea repetida,
Sola á la viſta aparente ?
¿ Eres, para pena mia,
Voz de la imaginacion ?
¿ Retrato de la iluſion ?
¿ Cuerpo de la fantasía ?
¿ Fantaſma en la noche fria ?

Euſebio.
Julia, eſcucha, Euſebio ſoy,
Que vivo á tus pies eſtoy ;
Que ſi el penſamiento fuera,
Siempre contigo eſtuviera.

Julia.
Deſengañándome voy
Con oirte, y conſidero,
Que mi recato ofendido
Mas te quiſiera fingido,
Euſebio, que verdadero,

Which I ſeek, unawed, uncheck'd,
Moves me with a twin effect ;
At one time it doth incite,
By its beauty, appetite,
By its modeſty, reſpect.
Julia ! Julia !

Julia (awaking).
Who doth call me ?—
But, O heavens ! what's this I ſee ?
Art thou deſire's dread phantaſy ?
Art thou a dream that doth enthral me ?

Euſebio.
Does my preſence ſo appal thee ?

Julia.
Who would not in dread diſmay
Fly from thee ?

Euſebio.
Ah ! Julia, ſtay !

Julia.
What's thy wiſh, fictitious form,
Spectre that no life doth warm,
Sight-born ſhape, what wouldſt thou ? ſay.
Art thou, for my puniſhment,
The expreſſion of my thought ?
Image by illuſion wrought ?
Phantaſy's embodiment ?
Phantom on the cold night ſent ?

Euſebio.
Thine Euſebio am I, ſweet,
Living, lying at thy feet.
For if I thy thought could be,
I for ever were with thee.

Julia.
The deluſion, the deceit,
Liſtening thee, I'm labouring through,
And I think that my pride-pain'd
Honour would prefer the feign'd,
Falſe Euſebio, than the true,

Donde yo llorando muero,
Donde yo vivo penando.
¿Qué quieres? ¡eſtoy temblando!
¿Qué buſcas? ¡eſtoy muriendo!
¿Qué emprendes? ¡eſtoy temiendo!
¿Qué intentas? ¡eſtoy dudando!
¿Cómo has llegado haſta aqui?

Euſebio.

Todo es extremos amor,
Y mi pena y tu rigor
Hoy han de triunfar de mí.
Haſta verte aqui, ſufrí
Con eſperanza ſegura;
Pero viendo tu hermoſura
Perdida, he atropellado
El reſpeto del ſagrado,
Y la ley de la clauſura.
De lo cierto, ó de lo injuſto
Los dos la culpa tenemos,
Y en mí vienen dos extremos,
Que ſon la fuerza y el guſto.
No puede darle diſguſto
Al cielo mi pretenſion;
Antes deſta ejecucion,
Caſada eras en ſecreto,
Y no cabe en un ſugeto
Matrimonio y religion.

Julia.

No niego el lazo amoroſo,
Que hizo con felicidades
Unir á dos voluntades,
Que fue ſu efecto forzoſo,
Que te llamé amado eſpoſo;
Y que todo eſo fue aſi,
Confieſo; pero ya aqui,
Con voto de religioſa,
A Criſto de ſer ſu eſpoſa
Mano y palabra le dí.
Ya ſoy ſuya, ¿qué me quieres?

Here, where weeping I renew
Every day a living death.
What's your wiſh? I gaſp for breath!
What's your object! Ah! I die!
What's your aim? an aſpen I!
What's your end? doubt anſwereth.
Here why have you dared to be?

Euſebio.

'Tis but love's inſenſate daring,
Thy diſdain and my deſpairing,
That have triumph'd over me.
Till I ſaw thee here, thy free
State my love with fond hopes fed;
But, beholding thee as dead,
Loſt to me, the cloiſter's law,
This aſylum's ſacred awe,
Have I cruſh'd beneath my tread.
Be the act unjuſt, or juſt,
We muſt bear the blame united.
By two powers am I incited—
Violence and pleaſure's luſt.
In the ſight of Heaven diſguſt
My pretenſions cannot rouſe,
Since at heart thou wert my ſpouſe
Ere thou cam'ſt this ſtep to take,
And one tongue ſhould never make
Marriage and monaſtic vows.

Julia.

I deny not the ſweet bond
That in happieſt uniſon
Join'd two ſeparate wills in one;
Nay, that, 'neath love's magic wand,
I beſtow'd on thee the fond,
Sweet name of huſband,—I confeſs
All this is true; but ne'ertheleſs,
By a holier law invited,
Have I hand and promiſe plighted
Here to wear Chriſt's bridal dreſs;
I am His: what wouldſt thou? Go!

Vete, porque el mundo aſombres,
Donde mates á los hombres,
Donde fuerces las mugeres.
Vete, Euſebio; ya no eſperes
Fruto de tu loco amor;
Para que te cauſe horror,
Que eſtoy en ſagrado, pienſa.

Euſebio.

Cuanto es mayor tu defenſa,
Es mi apetito mayor.
Ya las paredes ſalté
Del convento, ya te ví;
No es amor quien vive en mí,
Cauſa mas oculta fue.
Cumple mi guſto, ó diré,
Que tú miſma me has llamado,
Que me has tenido encerrado
En tu celda muchos dias:
Y pues las deſdichas mias
Me tienen deſeſperado,
Daré voces: Sepan . . . .

Julia.

Tente,
Euſebio, mira . . . . (¡ay de mí!)
Paſos ſiento por aqui,
Al coro atravieſa gente.
¡Cielos, no ſé lo que intente!
Cierra eſa celda, y en ella
Eſtarás, pues atropella
Un temor á otro temor.

Euſebio.

¡Qué poderoſo es mi amor!

Julia.

¡Qué riguroſa es mi eſtrella! [*Vanſe.*

Where with fear the world thou filleſt,
Where unhappy men thou killeſt,
Where thou work'ſt weak women's woe.
Go! nor hope, Euſebio,
Thy inſenſate love's fruition,—
Think with horror and contrition
Of this ſacred place, and fly me.

Euſebio.

Ah! the more thou doſt deny me,
Greater grows my love's ambition.
I have ſcaled the walls, my way
Through the convent led to thee;
Love no more impelleth me—
I ſome ſubtler law obey.
Grant my wiſh, or I ſhall ſay,
That I came by thee here bidden;
That thou here haſt kept me hidden
In thy cell for many days;
And, ſince my misfortunes craze
This poor brain, deſpairing, chidden,
I ſhall cry out: Know . . . .

Julia.

Oh, ſtay!
Hold, Euſebio! . . . (woe is me!)
For the nuns' ſteps, audibly,
To the choir approach this way.
Heavens! I know not what to ſay:—
Cloſe the cell—the entrance bar—
Here remain: ſince oft a far
Worſe fear doth a leſs remove.

Euſebio.

Oh! how powerful is my love!

Julia.

Oh! how rigorous is my ſtar!
[*Scene cloſes.*

VISTA EXTERIOR DEL CONVENTO.

Salen RICARDO *y* CELIO.

Ricardo.
Ya ſon las tres, mucho tarda.
Celio.
El que goza ſu ventura,
Ricardo, en la noche obſcura,
Nunca el claro ſol aguarda.
Yo apueſto que le parece,
Que nunca el ſol madrugó
Tanto, y que hoy apreſuró
Su curſo.
Ricardo.
Siempre amanece
Mas temprano á quien deſea,
Pero al que goza mas tarde.
Celio.
No creas, que al ſol aguarde,
Que en el oriente ſe vea.
Ricardo.
Dos horas ſon ya.
Celio.
No creo,
Que Euſebio lo diga.
Ricardo.
Es juſto;
Porque al fin ſon de ſu guſto
Las horas de tu deſeo.
Celio.
¿No ſabes lo que he llegado
Hoy, Ricardo, á ſoſpechar?
Que Julia le envió á llamar.
Ricardo.
Pues ſi no fuera llamado,
¿Quién á eſcalar ſe atreviera
Un convento?

OUTSIDE THE CONVENT.

Enter RICARDO *and* CELIO.

Ricardo.
'Tis three o'clock; he tarries late.
Celio.
He for whom the dark night flies
With love's planet in its ſkies,
Ne'er the ſun's clear beams need wait.
I'll be bound, to him it ſeems
That the ſun gets up to-day
Far too ſoon, his golden way
Thus foreſtalling.
Ricardo.
Yes, it beams
Ever early for deſire,
Ever late when love is bleſt.
Celio.
Do not think, though, he will reſt
In there till the eaſt's on fire.
Ricardo.
Two hours gone.
Celio.
I would admire,
If he thinks ſo.
Ricardo.
You are right,
For the hours of his delight
Are the hours of your deſire.
Celio.
Do you know, that the ſuſpicion
I have form'd, Ricardo, is
'Tis the lady's wiſh, not his?
Ricardo.
If he had not got permiſſion,
Who is there that thus would dare
Convent walls to ſcale?

Celio.
¿No has ſentido,
Ricardo, á eſta parte ruido?
Ricardo.
Sí.
Celio.
Pues llega la eſcalera.

Salen por lo alto Julia *y* Eusebio.

Euſebio.
Déjame, muger.
Julia.
¿Pues cuando
Vencida de tus deſeos,
Movida de tus ſuſpiros,
Obligada de tus ruegos,
De tu llanto agradecida,
Dos veces á Dios ofendo,
Como á Dios, y como á eſpoſo,
Mis brazos dejas, haciendo
Sin eſperanzas deſdenes,
Y ſin poſeſion deſprecios?
¿Dónde vas?
Euſebio.
Muger, qué intentas?
Déjame, que voy huyendo
De tus brazos, porque he viſto
No ſé qué deidad en ellos.
Llamas arrojan tus ojos,
Tus ſuſpiros ſon de fuego,
Un volcan cada razon,
Un rayo cada cabello,
Cada palabra es mi muerte,
Cada regalo un infierno:
Tantos temores me cauſa
La Cruz, que he viſto en tu pecho;
Señal prodigioſa ha ſido,
Y no permitan los cielos,

Celio.
Doſt hear
Sounds, Ricardo, drawing near?
Ricardo.
Yes.
Celio.
Then place the ladder there.

Julia *and* Eusebio *appear at the window.*

Euſebio.
Leave me, woman.
Julia.
How? when I,
By thy fond deſirings conquer'd,
Moved to pity by thy ſighings,
By thy warm entreaties ſoften'd,
Doubly have diſpleaſed the Godhead,
As my God and my eſpouſèd;
Flying from theſe arms that lock'd thee,
Doſt thou without hope diſdain me,
And without poſſeſſion ſcorn me?
Whither goeſt thou?

Euſebio.
Woman, leave me,
For I fly thoſe arms that fold me,
Having ſeen but now within them
Some, I know not what, God's token;
In each glance a flame is darted,
In each ſigh a fire outbloweth,
A volcano every accent,
Lightning every fair treſs golden,
In each word my death is mutter'd,
At each fond careſs hell opens;
So much fear that Croſs hath cauſed me
Which thy breaſt reveal'd and ſhow'd me:
Sign prodigious! ſacred ſymbol!

Que, aunque tanto los ofenda,
Pierda á la Cruz el reſpeto.
Pues ſi la hago teſtigo
De las culpas que cometo,
¿Con qué vergüenza deſpues
Llamarla en mi ayuda puedo?
Quédate en tu religion,
Julia, yo no te deſprecio,
Que mas ahora te adoro.

Julia.
Eſcucha, detente, Euſebio.

Euſebio.
Eſta es la eſcala.

Julia.
Detente,
O llévame allá.

Euſebio.
No puedo, [*Baja.*
Pues que, ſin gozar la gloria
Que tanto eſperé, te dejo.
Válgame el cielo! caí. [*Cae.*

Ricardo.
Qué ha ſido?

Euſebio.
¿No veis el viento
Poblado de ardientes rayos?
¿No mirais ſangriento el cielo,
Que todo ſobre mí viene?
¿Dónde eſtar ſeguro puedo,
Si airado el cielo ſe mueſtra?
Divina Cruz, yo os prometo,
Y os hago ſolemne voto
Con cuantas cláuſulas puedo,
De en cualquier parte que os vea,
Las rodillas por el ſuelo,
Rezar un Ave Maria.

And the heavens allow me nowhere,
Though I ſo offend, to fail in
Reverence for a ſign ſo holy.
Since if I a witneſs make it
Of the crimes I dare each moment,
With what ſhame would I hereafter,
In my hour of need, invoke it?
Stay, then, Julia, in religion;
Ah! indeed I do not ſcorn thee,
I adore thee more than ever.

Julia.
Oh! Euſebio, hear me! hold thee!

Euſebio.
Here's the ladder.

Julia.
Oh! remain,
Or elſe take me with you.

Euſebio.
Hopeleſs [*He deſcends.*
Is it; no; I leave thee here
With my ſo long-ſigh'd-for glory
Unenjoy'd. But, heavens! I fall.
[*He falls.*

Ricardo.
What has happen'd?

Euſebio.
See you nowhere
Red bolts peopling all the night wind?
Do you not behold the gory
Heavens that open to o'erwhelm me?
Where can I be ſafe, if o'er me
Heaven diſplays its awful anger?
Thee, O Croſs divine, I promiſe,
And a ſolemn vow I make thee,
With all ſtrictneſs of devotement,
Whereſoe'er I ſee thee ſtanding,
Kneeling on the ground before thee,
To recite then a Hail Mary!

[*Levántase, y vanse los tres, dejando la escala puesta.*

Julia.

Turbada y confusa quedo.
¿ Aquetas fueron, ingrato,
Las firmezas ? ¿ Estos fueron
Los extremos de tu amor ?
¿ O son de mi amor extremos ?
Hasta vencerme á tu gusto,
Con amenazas, con ruegos,
Aqui amante, alli tirano,
Porfiaste ; pero luego
Que de tu gusto y mi pena
Pudiste llamarte dueño,
Antes de vencer huiste.
¿ Quién, sino tú, venció huyendo ?
¡ Muerta soy, cielos piadosos !
¿ Por qué introdujo venenos
Naturaleza, si habia,
Para dar muerte, desprecios ?
Ellos me quitan la vida ;
Pues que con nuevo tormento
Lo que me desprecia busco.
¿ Quién vió tan dudoso efecto
De amor ? Cuando me rogaba
Con mil lágrimas Eusebio,
Le dejaba ; pero ahora,
Porque él me deja, le ruego.
Tales somos las mugeres,
Que contra nuestros deseos,
Aun no queremos dar gusto
Con lo mismo que queremos.
Ninguno nos quiera bien,
Si pretende alcanzar premio ;
Que queridas despreciamos,
Y aborrecidas queremos.
No siento que no me quiera,
Solo que me deje siento.
Por aqui cayó, tras él

[*He arises, and the three go out, leaving the ladder in its place.*

Julia (at the window).

In confusion I am lost here.
Was this then, O thou ungrateful !
Thy fix'd purpose ? This the whole, then,
Of thy love's excess ? Or is it
Mine own love's excess absorbs me ?
Till you conquer'd me to yield you
All your wish, by threats, by softness,
Now a lover, now a tyrant,
You persisted ; but, when wholly
Of your joy and of my sorrow
You could call yourself the owner,
You before the victory fled me ;
Who but you e'er fled that conquer'd ?
Ah ! I die ! ye pitying heavens !
Why has Nature's hand concocted
Poisons, when contempt she nurtures,
Which to kill is far more potent ?
It is *that* that takes my life :
Since, to add unto my torment,
That which shuns me I must seek.
Such effects of love, what mortal
Ever saw ? For when Eusebio
Ask'd me, in all forms of fondness,
Even with tears, I scorn'd him ; now
Him I ask, because he scorns me.
Such the nature of us women,
That against what most we covet,
We even would not wish to please
With what would delight our ownselves.
No one loves us well who seems
To over-value what he hopeth :
For when we are loved, we scorn,
When we're scorn'd, our love is strongest.
Me, his want of love moves not,
'Tis his leaving me that moves me.

Me arrojaré. ¿ Mas qué es esto ?
¿ Esta no es escala ? Sí.
¡ Qué terrible pensamiento !
Detente, imaginacion,
No me despeñes ; que creo,
Que si llego á consentir,
A hacer el delito llego.
¿ No saltó Eusebio por mí
Las paredes del convento ?
¿ No me holgué de verle yo
En tantos peligros puesto
Por mi causa ? ¿ pues qué dudo ?
¿ Qué me acobardo ? ¿ qué temo ?
Lo mismo haré yo en salir,
Que él en entrar ; si es lo mesmo,
Tambien se holgará de verme
Por su causa en tales riesgos.
Ya por haber consentido,
La misma culpa merezco ;
¿ Pues si es tan grande el pecado,
Por qué el gusto ha de ser menos ?
¿ Si consentí, y me dejó
Dios de su mano, no puedo
De una culpa, que es tan grande
Tener perdon ? ¿ pues qué espero ?
[*Baja por la escala.*
Al mundo, al honor, á Dios
Hallo perdido el respeto,
Cuando á ceguedad tan grande
Vendados los ojos vuelvo.
Demonio soy que he caido
Despeñado deste cielo,
Pues sin tener esperanza
De subir, no me arrepiento.
Ya estoy fuera de sagrado,
Y de la noche el silencio
Con su obscuridad me tiene
Cubierta de horror y miedo.
Tan deslumbrada camino,

Here he fell, then after him
Shall I throw me. But what holds here ?
Is not this the ladder ? Yes.
What a dreadful thought comes o'er me !
Stay, imagination, stay ;
Whelm me not, for faith has told me
That, when I consent in thought,
I commit the crime that moment.
Was it not for me Eusebio
Scaled the steep walls of my convent ?
Did I not feel pleased to see him
Running so much risk to show me
His regard ? Then what doth fright me ?
What doth cow me ? Why thus ponder ?
I will do the same in leaving,
As in entering, he ; if so then,
He too will be pleased to see me,
For his sake, like risks encounter.
By consenting, I already
With an equal guilt am loaded ;
If the sin has been committed,
Why not with the joy console me ?
If I've given consent, and God
Flings me from his hand, 'tis hopeless,
For a crime so great, to expect
Pardon ; then why wait ? What holds me ? [*She descends the ladder.*
For the world, for God, for honour,
All respect I find I've lost here,
When I turn my hooded eyes
Round upon this darksome prospect ;
I'm a demon that has fallen
From this heaven serene and spotless,
Since, all hope being gone, to rise there
No repentant instinct prompts me.
I am out of sanctuary,
And the silent night involves me,
With its darkness, in a net-work

Que en las tinieblas tropiezo,
Y aun no caigo en mi pecado.
¿Dónde voy? ¿qué hago? ¿qué intento?
Con la muda confuſion
De tantos horrores temo,
Que ſe me altera la ſangre,
Que ſe me eriza el cabello.
Turbada la fantasía,
En el aire forma cuerpos,
Y ſentencias contra mí
Pronuncia la voz del eco.
El delito, que antes era
Quien me animaba ſoberbio,
Es quien me acobarda ahora.
Apenas las plantas puedo
Mover, que el miſmo temor
Grillos á mis pies ha pueſto.
Sobre mis hombros parece
Que carga un prolijo peſo,
Que me oprime, y toda yo
Eſtoy cubierta de hielo.
No quiero paſar de aqui,
Quiero volverme al convento,
Donde de aqueſte pecado
Alcance perdon; pues creo
De la clemencia divina,
Que no hay luces en el cielo,
Que no hay en el mar arenas,
No hay átomos en el viento,
Que, ſumados todos juntos,
No ſean número pequeño
De los pecados que ſabe
Dios perdonar. Paſos ſiento,
A eſta parte me retiro
En tanto que paſan; luego
Subiré, ſin que me vean.

[*Retiraſe.*

Of intenſeſt fear and horror.
So bereft of light I wander,
That, at every ſtep I totter,
Stray from all things but my ſin.
Whither go I? With what object?
I am fearful, in the ſilent
Throng of horrors that enfold me,
That my hair will ſtand on end ſoon,
That my heart's blood will be frozen.
On the air perturbèd fancy
Phantoms and ſtrange ſpectres formeth;
And, in ſentencing me, ſounds
Echo's voice auſtere and ſolemn:
The offence, which was erewhile
That which ſo my pride embolden'd,
Makes a coward of me now.
I can ſcarcely move my footſteps,
Scarce can drag my feet, for fear
Hangs its heavy fetters on them.
An oppreſſive weight appears
To be placed upon my ſhoulders,
Which doth weigh me down; and I
All with ice am cover'd over.
No! I will not further go,
I will back unto my convent.
Where for this ſin I may aſk
Pardon, ſince ſuch faith I foſter
In the clemency divine,
That the ſtars that light heaven yonder,
That the ſands upon the ſhore,
That the atoms of the mote-beams,
All together join'd, would be,
I believe, but a faint token
Of the number of the ſins
God can pardon.—Steps approach here!
I ſhall to this ſide retire
Until they have paſs'd and gone hence;
Then I ſhall aſcend unſeen.

[*Retires.*

Salen RICARDO *y* CELIO.

Ricardo.

Con el eſpanto de Euſebio
Aqui ſe quedó la eſcala,
Y ahora por ella vuelvo,
No aclare el dia, y la vean
A eſta pared.

[*Quitan la eſcala y vanſe, y* JULIA *llega donde eſtaba la eſcala.*

Julia.

Ya ſe fueron;
Ahora podré ſubir,
Sin que me ſientan. Qué es eſto?
¿No es aqueſta la pared
De la eſcala? Pero creo,
Que hácia eſtotra parte eſtá.
Ni aqui tampoco eſtá. Cielos!
¿Cómo he de ſubir ſin ella?
Mas ya mi deſdicha entiendo;
Deſta ſuerte me negais
La entrada vueſtra, pues creo,
Que, cuando quiero ſubir
Arrepentida, no puedo.
Pues ſi ya me habeis negado
Vueſtra clemencia, mis hechos
De muger deſeſperada
Darán aſombros al cielo,
Darán eſpantos al mundo,
Admiracion á los tiempos,
Horror al miſmo pecado,
Y terror al miſmo infierno.

Enter RICARDO *and* CELIO.

Ricardo.

In Euſebio's fright, forgotten
Here the ladder has remain'd;
And to take it, I now come here,
Leſt at dawn of day they ſee it
On this wall.

[*Exeunt, taking the ladder.* JULIA *returns to the place where it ſtood.*

Julia.

They've gone: now ſoftly,
Unperceived I may aſcend.
How is this, though? Is it not here,
In this part of the wall, the ladder
Stood this moment? In this other
Place, I think, then it muſt be:—
No, nor here 'tis. Heavens above me!
How can I aſcend without it?
Ah! I now know my misfortune;
In this way you would all entrance
Bar againſt me, ſince it ſhows me
That when I would wiſh, repentant,
To aſcend, the attempt were hopeleſs.
Since then you have thus denied me
Your ſoft clemency, the bold deeds
Of a woman's deſperation,
Shall the heavens ſcare that behold them,
Make the world that ſees them tremble,
Fill futurity with wonder,
Strike even ſin itſelf with horror,
And ſhock hell even to the loweſt.

JORNADA III.

MONTE.

Sale GIL *con muchas Cruces, y una muy grande al pecho.*

Gil.

POR leña á eſte monte voy,
Que Menga me lo ha mandado,
Y para ir ſeguro, he hallado
Una brava invencion hoy.
De la Cruz, dicen, que es
Devoto Euſebio; y aſi
He ſalido armado aqui
De la cabeza á los pies.
Dicho y hecho; ¡ él es par diez!
No encuentro, lleno de miedo,
Donde eſtar ſeguro puedo;
Sin alma quedo. Eſta vez
No me ha viſto, yo quiſiera
Eſconderme hácia eſte lado,
Mientras paſa; yo he tomado
Por guarda una cambronera
Para eſconderme. ¡ No es nada!
Tanta pua es la mas chica:
¡ Pléguete Criſto! mas pica,
Que perder una trocada,
Mas que ſentir un deſprecio
De una dama Fierabras,

ACT III.

A WILD FOREST IN THE MOUNTAIN.

Enter GIL, *having his dreſs covered with numerous Croſſes, and with a large one on his breaſt.*

Gil.

THROUGH theſe wilds for wood I ſtray,
Driven abroad by Menga's dunning;
So, to go ſecure, a cunning
Stratagem I've plann'd to-day.
This Euſebio is, I hear,
Still to the Croſs devout, and ſo,
Thus all arm'd from top to toe,
Forth I venture without fear:—
Well and good. He's there, by Jove!
Looking glum and this way ſtriding,
And there's not a ſpot to hide in!
Oh! I cannot breathe or move!
But he ſees me not, this thickly
Twiſted thorn-buſh here may ſcreen me.
Oh! for ſomething ſoft between me
And theſe ſharp points bare and prickly!
Backwards, frontwards, under, over,
Where I ſtand the thorns are pricking,
Where I ſit the thorns are ſticking;
Ah! 'tis plain I'm not in clover,

Que á todos admite, y mas
Que tener zelos de un necio.

Though the graſs is thick about me.
Better bear with conſcience gnawing,
Better bear a fool's hee-hawing,
Or a ſcolding woman flout me.
[*Conceals himſelf.*

Sale Eusebio.

Euſebio.
No ſé adonde podré ir;
Larga vida un triſte tiene,
Que nunca la muerte viene
A quien le canſa el vivir.
Julia, yo me ví en tus brazos;
Cuando tan dichoſo era,
Que de tus brazos pudiera
Hacer amor nuevos lazos.
Sin gozar al fin dejé
La gloria que no tenia;
Mas no fue la cauſa mia,
Cauſa mas ſecreta fue;
Pues teniendo mi albedrío,
Superior efecto ha hecho,
Que yo reſpete en tu pecho
La Cruz que tengo en el mio.
Y pues con ella los dos,
¡Ay Julia! habemos nacido,
Secreto miſterio ha ſido,
Que lo entiende ſolo Dios.

Enter Eusebio.

Euſebio.
Still my days are dark and dreary,
Still along life's road I go,
Careleſs whither, death is ſlow
Only to the life-aweary.
Julia, O, my hoped-for wife!
When within thy arms I found me,
Then might love have twined around me
Garlands new to deck my life;
But the glory I repell'd,
Fled the untaſted joy I ſought,
Not through mine own ſtrength methought,
No, ſome ſecret force compell'd,
Since my will I could reſign
To that mightier power protecting,
On thy beauteous breaſt reſpecting
That ſame Croſs that's ſtamp'd on mine.
Then, ſince Heaven was pleaſed to ſend
Thee and me thus ſign'd to earth,
Some ſtrange myſtery marks our birth
God alone doth comprehend.

Gil (aparte).
Mucho pica, ya no puedo
Mas ſufrillo.
Euſebio.
Entre eſtos ramos
Hay gente. ¿Quién va?
Gil.
Aqui echamos
A perder todo el enredo.

Gil (aſide).
Ah! I'm prick'd in every joint;
More I can't endure!
Euſebio.
Quite near
Sounds a voice:—Who's there?
Gil.
I'm here,
Quite made up on every point.

Euſebio (*aparte*).
Un hombre á un árbol atado,
Y una Cruz al cuello tiene;
Cumplir mi voto conviene
En el ſuelo arrodillado.

Gil.
¿ A quién, Euſebio, enderezas
La oracion, ú de qué tratas ?
Si me adoras, ¿ qué me atas ?
Si me atas, ¿ qué me rezas ?

Euſebio.
¿ Quién es ?

Gil.
¿ A Gil no conoces ?
Deſde que con el recado
Aqui me dejaſte atado,
No han aprovechado voces
Para que alguien (¡ qué rigor !)
Me llegaſe á deſatar.

Euſebio.
Pues no es aqueſte el lugar
Donde te dejé.

Gil.
Señor,
Es verdad ; mas yo que ví
Que nadie llegaba, he andado,
De árbol en árbol atado,
Haſta haber llegado aqui.
Aqueſta la cauſa fue
De ſuceſo tan extraño.

Euſebio (*aparte*).
Eſte es ſimple, y de mi daño
Cualquier ſuceſo ſabré.—
Gil, yo te tengo aficion,
Deſde que otra vez hablamos,
Y aqui quiero que ſeamos
Amigos.

Euſebio (*aſide*).
Ah ! a man to a tree is bound,
On his breaſt's a Croſs, I now
Muſt fulfil my ſolemn vow,
Humbly kneeling on the ground.
[*Kneels.*

Gil.
Who, ſir, do you kneel before ?
Do you mean to deify me ?
If you adore me, why do you tie me ?
If you tie me, why adore ?

Euſebio.
Say, who *are* you ?

Gil.
Not know Gil ?
Since the time you left me tied here
With the meſſage, I have cried here
Without ſtint, out loud and ſhrill,
That ſome kind hand from this cord
Would releaſe me. (What a caſe !)

Euſebio.
But then this is not the place
That I left you in.

Gil.
My lord,
That is true ; but when 'twas clear
None would come, it ſeem'd to me
Beſt, thus tied, from tree to tree
On to glide, till I came here.
That's the ſimple explanation
Of ſo ſtrange a circumſtance.

Euſebio (*aſide*).
Through this ſimpleton perchance
I may get ſome information
Of my loſs.—Gil, I was quite
Taken with your worth when we
Laſt time met, ſo let us be
Friends henceforth.

Gil.

Tiene razon;
Y quiſiera, pues nos vemos
Tan amigos, no ir allá,
Sino andarme por acá,
Pues aqui todos ſeremos
Buñoleros, que diz que es
Holgada vida, y no andar
Todo el año á trabajar.

Euſebio.

Quédate conmigo pues.

Salen Ricardo *y Bandoleros, y traen á* Julia *veſtida de hombre y cubierto el roſtro.* [**Salen* Ricardo, *y* Julia, *de hombre; un* Pintor, *un* Poeta, *y un* Astrologo.†]

Ricardo.

En lo bajo del camino,
Que eſta montaña atravieſa,
Ahora hicimos una preſa,
Que ſegun es, imagino,
Que te dé guſto.

Euſebio.

Eſtá bien,
Luego della trataremos.

Gil.

You ſay quite right;—
And I'd wiſh, ſince friendſhip's tether
Binds us ſo, to go not near
My old cabin, but ſtay here
Bundoleering all together.
'Tis a pleaſant life, they ſay,
Not a ſtroke of work or bother
From one year's end to the other.

Euſebio.

Then with me you here may ſtay.

Enter Ricardo *and the other brigands, leading in* Julia, *dreſſed in man's clothes, and having her face covered.* [**Enter* Ricardo, *and* Julia *as a man; a* Poet, *a* Painter, *and an* Astrologer.†]

Ricardo.

On the road that 'neath heaven's cope
O'er this rugged mountain riſes,
We to-day have made ſome prizes
Of ſuch value that I hope
They may pleaſe you.

Euſebio.

Right, we'll ſee
Soon to that, but now behold

* Commencement of the ſcene in the edition of Hueſca.

† As mentioned in the introduction to this drama, *La Devocion de la Cruz* was firſt publiſhed in the *Parte Veinte y Ocho de Comedias de Varios Autores* (Hueſca 1634), under the title of *La Cruz en la Sepultura*, and as the work of Lope de Vega. Señor Hartzenbuſch mentions that this, the earlieſt impreſſion, exhibits many variations from the received text, which are of greater or leſſer importance. In this place an entirely new ſcene is introduced, which is not to be found in the edition of Vera Taſſis or in the later editions. This ſcene he prints in the notes to his Calderon. It was probably omitted from the acted play, as needleſſly breaking the continuity of the plot. Though ſlightly imperfect, it is ſufficiently curious to be preſerved, and I have therefore introduced it [between brackets] into the text both of the original and tranſlation. Señor Hartzenbuſch alſo prints the portion of this ſcene (in the edition of Hueſca), which is nearly the ſame as that in the later editions. A few of the verbal differences that exiſt between them, I have drawn attention to below.—See Hartzenbuſch's "Calderon," *Notas y Iluſtraciones*, t. iv. p. 701.

Sabe ahora, que tenemos
Un nuevo ſoldado.

Ricardo.

¿Quién?

Gil.

Gil; ¿no me ve?

Euſebio.

Eſte villano,
Aunque le veis inocente,
Conoce notablemente
Deſta tierra monte y llano,
Y en él ſerá nueſtra guia:
Fuera deſto, al campo irá
Del enemigo, y ſerá
En él mi perdida eſpía.
Arcabuz le podeis dar,
Y un veſtido.

*Celio.**

Ya eſtá aqui.

Gil.

Tengan láſtima de mí,
Que me quedo á embandolear.†

[*Euſebio.*

¿Quien eres tu?

Pintor.

Yo, ſeñor,
Soy de nacion jinoves;
A Florencia paſo, y es
Mi ejercicio el de pintor.
Llevo a Celio Batiſtela,
Un florentin poderoſo,
Aqueſte retrato hermoſo,
Que es de Madama Florela;
Que el me mandó que lo hicieſe.

Euſebio.

Mueſtra, a ver. ¡Hermoſa dama!
¿Como dice qui? *Madama*

A new comrade, juſt enroll'd
In our gallant troop.

Ricardo.

Who's he?

Gil.

Don't you ſee me? Gil.

Euſebio.

This ſwain,
Though ſo innocent appearing,
Knows each natural bound and mearing
Of this land here, hill and plain;
He will be our guide by-and-by
Through it, nay, he will repair
To the enemy's camp, and there
Act the deſperate part of ſpy.—
Give him then an arquebuſs,
And a ſoldier's dreſs.

*Celio.**

They're here.

Gil.

Woe the day that I appear
Robber-raw-recruited thus!

[*Euſebio.*

Who art thou?

Painter.

Sir, my confeſſion
I can make to you with eaſe:—
I'm by birth a Genoeſe,
And a painter by profeſſion.
I to Celio Batiſtela,
Of Florence, this fine picture bear
Of a lady young and fair,
Call'd Madama la Florela,
By him order'd, to him ſold.

Euſebio.

Let me ſee it. A fair dame
Truly! but why write her name

* "*Ricardo.*" Hueſca Edition.

† "*á bandolear.*" Hueſca Edition.

Florela.

Gil.

Oye: el cuento es efe
De un pintor que hizo un retrato
De un gato; y porque fupiefe
De quien era quien le viefe,
Pufo abajo: "Aquefte es gato."

Pintor.

No es defeto en la pintura
Traer efcrito fu nombre;
Que nadie habra a quien no afombre
Efta imitada figura.
Y yo foy el que pintar
Enfeño los naturales
Arboles y frutas, tales
Que fe pueden admirar
Los hombres; pues cuando imito
La variedad, y la veo
Queda fin hambre el defeo,
Sin defeo el apetito.

Eufebio.

Si en ti perfecion tan bella
Ha alcanzado la pintura,
Gran genero de locura
Es no aprovecharte della,
Atalde aqui; y fi mirare
La variedad de las flores,
Dadle paleta y colores;
Coma de lo que pintare.

Ricardo.

Vamos.

Gil.

Llevad de camino
Aquefta epigrama brava
Que * * * *
Hizo un ingenio divino,—
"Galanes, damas hermofas,
Baratas fueles vender,
Saliendo de tu poder

'Neath it?

Gil.

Lift! a tale doth run
Of a painter to whom fat
For her picture Pufs: below her,
So that every one might know her,
He infcribed, "This is a cat."

Painter.

No defect is't in a painting
That it fhould its own name bear;
Here's a figure, howfoe'er,
One can gaze at without fainting.
I am he who taught the art
Of depicting fruits and trees
After Nature: they fo pleafe
Thofe that fee them, that they ftart,
Wondering at them. My own fight,
Feeding on their fair variety,
Makes me furfeit to fatiety,
Takes the edge off appetite.

Eufebio.

If to fuch extreme perfection
Painting hath progreff'd with thee,
'Tis a great abfurdity
Not to ufe it for refection.
Tie him there: no fear he faints,
Flowers to him are like a falad;
Give him fome colours and a pallet,
Let him eat of what he paints.

Ricardo.

Let us go.

Gil.

And on the way,
Take with you this clever epigram,
Which * * * *
A great genius made one day:—
"Fabio, a many an hour,
To gallants and ladies fair,
Things you fell, nor rich nor rare

Eſtas y otras muchas coſas.
Fabio, con mano no eſcaſa
Pon tu mujer en la tienda,
Que aunque mil veces ſe venda
Siempre ſe te queda en caſa."

Euſebio.

Tu, ¿ quien eres ?

Aſtrologo.

Señor, ſoy
Aſtrologo.

Euſebio.

Buen oficio.

Aſtrologo.

Aunque ſe tiene por vicio ;
Pero ahora a Francia voy
A enſeñar aſtrologia.

Euſebio.

¿ Y tu la ſabes ?

Aſtrologo.

Yo he ſido
Quien los paſos ha medido
Al ſol que ilumina el dia.

Euſebio.

Si pudo tu ciencia ver
Tanto, ¿ por que no previno
Lo que en aqueſte camino
Te habia de ſuceder ?

Aſtrologo.

Ya tenia yo mirado
Que en el camino que ſigo
Habia de topar contigo.

Euſebio.

Pues dime que has alcanzado
De lo que he de hacer aqui.

Aſtrologo.

Ya he viſto en efetos llanos
Que he de morir a tus manos.

Euſebio.

Vete libre, porque aſi

Which muſt paſs from out your power.
Put into your ſhop your ſpouſe,—
Wondrous then will grow your pelf,
Since, though oft ſhe ſells herſelf,
Still ſhe never leaves your houſe.

Euſebio.

Thou, who art thou ?

Aſtrologer.

Sir, I am
An aſtrologer.

Euſebio.

A good employment.

Aſtrologer.

Yes, it's not without enjoyment:
I am going to France to cram
Pupils in the ſtarry art.

Euſebio.

And you know it ?

Aſtrologer.

I am one
Who hath track'd the path of the ſun
Through the heavens as on a chart.

Euſebio.

If your viſion is ſo clear,
Why did you foreſee not, ſay,
As you journey'd on your way,
What would happen to you here ?

Aſtrologer.

Nought of that, ſir, was conceal'd,
For I knew by deſtiny
I was doom'd to meet with thee.

Euſebio.

Tell me what has been reveal'd
Of thy fate here now with me.

Aſtrologer.

I have learn'd my fate commands
That I periſh by thy hands.

Euſebio.

Then, to prove fate wrong, go free.

Conozcas de tu ignorancia
El error, que deſde el ſuelo
No ſe ha de medir el cielo,
Que es infinita diſtancia.

Gil.

Eſcúcheme. A un licenciado
En eſtrellas, mató un dia
Una beſtia: aſi decia
Adonde eſtaba enterrado:
" Yace un aſtrólogo, cuya-
Ciencia a todos anunciaba
La ſuerte, y nunca acertaba
A pronoſticar la ſuya.
Un cadáver vió en cenizas
Su cadáver: que deſvelo
Tal entender pudo el cielo
Mas no a las caballerizas."

Euſebio.

¿Y tu?

Poeta.

Eſpanol; mi ejercicio
Hacer verſos: ſoy poeta
En efeto; que eſta ſeta
Algunos la han hecho oficio.

Euſebio.

Muchos he oido decir
Que ocupan aqueſa parte.

Gil.

Como ſe eſcriben ſin arte,
Son fáciles de eſcribir.

Poeta.

¿Que mas arte han de tener,
Señor, que haber de agradar
Entero á todo un lugar
Pues jueces vienen á ſer
El diſcreto, y ignorante,
Que juzgan ſin atencion
De mirar a cuyos ſon;
Pues quieren que un principiante

Thus thou'lt know thine auguries
Are but error's monſtrous birth,
Knowing little of the earth,
Knowing nothing of the ſkies.

Gil.

Hear me. A licentiate, read
In all ſtar-lore, by a horſe
Once was kill'd, and o'er the corſe
Where 'twas buried this was ſaid :—
" An aſtrologer, o'erthrown
By his ſteed, here lies: he told
Death-days round to young and old,
But could never tell his own.
The firſt corſe (ſo runs the fable)
That met *his* exclaim'd, 'My eyes!
You that underſtood the ſkies,
To know nothing of the ſtable!'"

Euſebio.

Thou art too . . . . ?

Poet.

A Spaniard: my
Buſineſs to write verſe; in fact
I'm a poet: few can act
Better in that way than I.

Euſebio.

There are many who, like you,
Try to play the poet's part.

Gil.

Thoſe who ſcribble without art
Find it eaſy work to do.

Poet.

Why, what greater art can be
Than to tickle a whole town,
Pleaſe the taſtes of clerk and clown,
Since your judges they muſt be—
Wiſe and fooliſh, ſaint and ſinner,
Paſſing ſentence like omniſcience,
Heedleſs of their own deficience;
Who require too a beginner

Tenga el miſmo eſtilo y ciencia
Que un anciano, ſin mirar
Que á eſo ſe han de aventajar
Ochenta años de experiencia?

Euſebio.

En tus razones ſe ve
Que ſiempre en voſotros lidia
Envidia y paſion.

Poeta.

Si envidia
Quien no tiene para qué
Dejen de envidiarme á mi.

Euſebio.

* * * *

Con irte vivo y dejarte.

Gil.

Copla hay tambien para ti.
De la comedia es dudoſo,
En fin: que indeterminado,
Lo que al ignorante agrado,
Canſa al fin al ingenioſo,
Buſca, Liſardo, otros modos,
Si fama quieres ganar;
Que es dificil de cortar
Veſtidos que venga á todos.]

Euſebio.

¿ Quién es† eſe gentil hombre,
Que el roſtro encubre?

Ricardo.

No ha ſido
Poſible, que haya querido
Decir la patria, ni el nombre;
Porque al Capitan no mas
Dice que lo ha de decir.

Should have the ſame ſkill and ſtyle
Of one older in ſuch matters,
Not reflecting on the latter's
Eighty years' uſe of the file?

Euſebio.

From your arguments 'tis ſeen
How for ever with you dwell
Spleen and envy.

Poet.

If to ſwell
'Gainſt injuſtice be call'd ſpleen,
I'm content it ſo ſhould be.

Euſebio.

* * * *

Go, I let thee live, be off!

Gil.

Take this rhyme along with thee:—
Since, howe'er the poet tries,
Doubtful is his drama's fate,
For what may the crowd elate,
The judicious may deſpiſe.
If you're ſeeking for fame's prizes,
Try ſome method leſs remote,
For 'tis hard to cut a coat
That will ſuit all ſorts of ſizes.*]

Euſebio.

Who's this gentleman, whoſe aim
Is to hide his face?

Ricardo.

In vain
Have we aſk'd him to explain
What's his country or his name;
To the captain of our band
Theſe he only will avow.

---

* "If this mutilated and erroneouſly attributed fragment," ſays Señor Hartzenbuſch, "is Calderon's, *The Devotion of the Croſs* muſt be one of his earlieſt dramas, written probably when he was a ſtudent at Salamanca, where he remained till his nineteenth year."

† "*y quien es el gentil hombre,*" &c. Hueſca Ed.

Eusebio.
Bien te puedes descubrir,
Pues ya en mi presencia estás.*

Julia.
¿Sois el Capitan?

Eusebio.
Sí.

Julia (aparte).
¡Ay Dios!

Eusebio.
Dime quien eres, y á qué
Víniste.

Julia.
Yo lo diré,
Estando solos los dos.

Eusebio.
Retiraos todos un poco.
[*Vanse, y quedan los dos solos.*
Ya estás á solas conmigo,
Solo árboles y flores
Pueden ser mudos testigos
De tus voces; quita el velo
Con que cubierto has traido
El rostro, y dime: ¿quién eres?
¿Dónde vas? ¿qué has pretendido?
Habla.

Julia.
Porque de una vez
[*Saca la espada.*
Sepas á lo que he venido,
Y quien soy, saca la espada;
Pues desta manera digo,
Que soy quien viene á matarte.

Eusebio.
Con la defensa resisto
Tu osadía y mi temor,
Porque mayor habia sido

* "*Con el capitan estas.*" Huesca Ed.

Eusebio.
Then you may declare them now,
Since before his face you stand.

Julia.
Are you the captain?

Eusebio.
True.

Julia (aside).
Too true!

Eusebio.
Tell me who you are, and why
You have come here.

Julia.
I'll reply
When we are alone, we two.

Eusebio.
All of you retire awhile.
[*Exeunt all but* Julia *and* Eusebio.
Now that thou'rt alone here with me,
Having only trees and flowers
Silently to look and listen
To thy words, remove the veil
With which cover'd thou hast hidden
Half thy face, and say who art thou,
Whither goest thou, here what brings
thee;—
Speak!

Julia.
That you may know at once
[*Draws her sword.*
What it is that brings me hither,
Who I am too, draw thy sword;
Since I mean to say in *this* way
That to kill thee I have come here.

Eusebio.
In defence I make resistance
To thy daring and my doubt,
Since it seems to me that bigger

De la accion, que de la voz.
Julia.
Riñe, cobarde, conmigo,
Y verás, que con tu muerte
Vida y confusion te quito.
Eusebio.
Yo por defenderme mas,
Que por ofenderte, riño;
Que ya tu vida me importa,
Pues si en este desafío
Te mato, no sé por qué,
Y si me matas, lo mismo.
Descúbrete ahora pues,
Si te agrada.
Julia.
Bien has dicho,
Porque en venganzas de honor,
Sino es que conste el castigo
Al que fué ofensor, no queda
Satisfecho el ofendido. [*Descúbrese.*
¿ Conócesme ? ¿ qué te espantas ?
¿ Qué me miras ?
Eusebio.
Que rendido
A la verdad y á la duda,
En confusos desvaríos,
Me espanto de lo que veo,
Me asombro de lo que miro.
Julia.
Ya me has visto.
Eusebio.
Sí, y de verte
Mi confusion ha crecido
Tanto, que si ántes de ahora
Alterados mis sentidos
Desearon verte, ya
Desengañados, lo mismo,
Que dieran antes por verte,

Is thine action, than thy voice.
Julia.
Fight then, coward, fight then with me,
And thou'lt see that with thy death
Life and doubt at once shall quit thee.
Eusebio.
I in my defence, much more
Than for thy least hurt, fight with thee,
Feeling even now an interest
In thy life; since if I kill thee
In this strife, I know not wherefore,
And 'tis so if me thou killest.
Then discover thyself now,
If it please thee.
Julia.
Thou speak'st wisely,
Since, when honour cries for vengeance,
If the hand of the chastiser
Is unknown unto the wronger,
Full revenge is not inflicted.
[*She discovers herself.*
Dost thou know me? Whence this terror?
Why thus gaze?
Eusebio.
Because bewilder'd,
Lost in mingled truth and doubt,
In confusions so conflicting,
I am shock'd at what I see,
I am scared at what I witness.
Julia.
Well, thou'st seen me.
Eusebio.
Yes, and seeing thee
So with new confusion fills me
That if but a moment hence
My disturb'd and doubting wishes
Long'd to see thee, even already
Disabused, they now would give here
The same price to see thee not,

Dieran por no haberte viſto.
¿ Tú, Julia, en aqeſte monte ?
¿ Tú con profano veſtido,
Dos veces violento en tí ?
¿ Cómo ſola aqui has venido ?
¿ Qué es eſto ?

Julia.

Deſprecios tuyos
Son, y deſengaños mios.
Y porque veas, que es flecha
Diſparada, ardiente tiro,
Veloz rayo, una muger,
Que corre tras ſu apetito,
No ſolo me han dado guſto
Los pecados cometidos
Haſta ahora, mas tambien
Me le dan, ſi los repito.
Salí del convento, fui
Al monte, y porque me dijo
Un paſtor, que mal guiada
Iba por aquel camino,
Neciamente temeroſa,
Por evitar mi peligro,
Le aſeguré, y le dí muerte,
Siendo inſtrumento un cuchillo,
Que él en ſu cinta traia.
Con eſte, que fue miniſtro
De la muerte, á un caminante,
Que corteſmente previno
En las ancas de un caballo,
A tanto canſancio alivio,
A la viſta de una aldea,
Porque entrar en ella quiſo,
Le pagué en un deſpoblado
Con la muerte el beneficio.
Tres dias fueron, y noches
Los que aquel deſierto me hizo
Meſa de ſilveſtres plantas,
Lecho de peñaſcos frios.

That to ſee thee they'd have given.
Thou here, Julia, in this mountain ?
Thou, profanely dreſſ'd, committeſt
Thus a two-fold ſacrilege
'Gainſt thyſelf: why haſt thou hither
Come alone ? What's this ?

Julia.

Thy ſcorn
And my diſilluſion is it:—
And to ſhow thee that an arrow
Shot in air, a burning miſſile,
A ſwift lightning-bolt's a woman
Who to paſſion doth ſubmit her,
Not alone do I feel pleaſure
In the ſins I have committed
Until now, but I do even
Feel it in their repetition.
I my convent left, and fled
To the mountain, where a ſimple
Shepherd having ſaid I was taking
The wrong pathway through the thicket,
Him, through fooliſh fearfulneſs,
And to ſilence thus a witneſs
Of my flight, I put to death,
A rude knife, which at his girdle
Hung ſuſpended, being the weapon.
With this weapon, the inflicter
Thus of death, a traveller,
Who had courteouſly provided,
On the haunches of his horſe,
Reſt for my long-travell'd tiredneſs,
When we came in ſight of a village,
Him, becauſe he wiſh'd to bide there,
In a lonely place I paid
Back with death for all his kindneſs.
Three long days and nights I ſpent
In that deſert, which provided
With its cold rocks for my bed,
For my ſcant food with its wild herbs.

Llegué á una pobre cabaña,
A cuyo techo pajizo
Juzgué pavellon dorado
En la paz de mis ſentidos.
Liberal huéſpeda fué
Una ſerrana conmigo,
Compitiendo en los deſeos
Con el paſtor ſu marido.
A la hambre y al canſancio
Dejé en ſu albergue rendidos
Con buena meſa, aunque pobre,
Manjar, aunque humilde, limpio.
Pero al deſpedirme dellos,
Habiendo antes prevenido,
Que al buſcarme no pudieſen
Decir: "noſotros la vimos;"
Al cortés paſtor, que al monte
Salió á enſeñarme el camino,
Maté, y entré donde luego
Hago en ſu muger lo miſmo.
Mas conſiderando entonces,
Que en el propio trage mio
Mi peſquiſidor llevaba,
Mudármele determino.
Al fin, pues, por varios caſos,
Con las armas y el veſtido
De un cazador, cuyo ſueño,
No imágen, traſunto vivo
Fué de la muerte, llegué
Aqui, venciendo peligros,
Deſpreciando inconvenientes,
Y atropellando deſignios.

Euſebio.

Con tanto aſombro te eſcucho,
Con tanto temor te miro,
Que eres al oido encanto,
Si á la viſta baſiliſco.
Julia, yo no te deſprecio,
Pero temo los peligros

I approach'd a lowly cabin,
Whoſe ſtraw roof appear'd to gliſten,
To my tired and languid ſpirits,
Lovelier than a gold pavilion.
There a ſhepherd's wife the part
Play'd of liberal hoſteſs with me,
Rivalling the ſwain, her huſband,
In all kindly acts and wiſhes.
Warineſs and hunger long
Could not in that lodging linger,
With its food though lowly, clean,
With its fare ſo good, though ſimple;
But at leaving I determined,
With a fatal fix'd previſion,
That to my purſuers never
Should they ſay, "Yes, here we hid her."
So I ſlew the courteous ſhepherd
Who had come ſome way to guide me
Through the mountain, and returning,
Did the ſame thing to his wife there.
But conſidering that I carried
A detector and a ſpier
In mine own dreſs, I determined
In another to diſguiſe me.
And at length, with various fortune,
In the arms and the equipment
Of a hunter, whoſe ſound ſlumber
No mere fancied type or image
Was of death, I here have wander'd,
Conquering every riſk and hindrance,
Every obſtacle deſpiſing,
Trampling all that would reſiſt me.

Euſebio.

With ſuch terror do I ſee thee,
With ſuch horror do I liſten,
To my ſight thou art a baſiliſk,
To my hearing thou'rt bewitchment;
I do not deſpiſe thee, Julia,
But I fear the ſure though hidden

Con que el cielo me amenaza,
Y por eſo me retiro.
Vuélvete tú á tu convento;
Que yo temeroſo vivo
De eſa Cruz tanto, que huyo
De tí.—¿ Mas qué es eſte ruido ?

Salen los Bandoleros.

Ricardo.

Preven, ſeñor, la defenſa;
Que apartados del camino,
Al monte Curcio y ſu gente
En buſca tuya han ſalido.
De todas eſas aldeas
Tanto el número ha crecido,
Que han venido contra tí
Viejos, mugeres y niños,
Diciendo, que ha de vengar
En tu ſangre la de un hijo
Muerto á tus manos, y jura
De llevarte por caſtigo,
O por venganza de tantos,
Preſo á Sena, muerto ó vivo.

Euſebio.

Julia, deſpues hablaremos.
Cubre el roſtro, y ven conmigo;
Que no es bien, que en poder quedes
De tu padre y mi enemigo.—
Soldados, eſte es el dia
De moſtrar aliento y brio.
Porque ninguno deſmaye,
Conſidere, que atrevidos
Vienen á darnos la muerte,
O prendernos, que es lo miſmo:
Y ſi no, en pública cárcel,
De deſdichas perſeguidos,
Y ſin honra nos veremos.

Dangers with which Heaven doth threat
me,
Therefore muſt I not ſtay with thee.
Thou return unto thy convent;
For ſuch holy awe doth give me
That ſtrange Croſs of thine, I fly
From thee.—But what noiſe comes
hither?

Enter Ricardo *and other bandits.*

Ricardo.

Sir, prepare for thy defence,—
For, departing from the highway,
Curcio and his people all
Up the mountain's ſides are climbing;
For from all theſe villages
Hath increaſed ſo his enliſtment,
That againſt thee now come on
Even the old men, women, children,
Saying that he comes for vengeance
In thy blood, for a ſon death-ſtricken
By thy hands, and he has vow'd
For thy chaſtiſement to bring thee,
Or for his revenge, in chains
To Siena, dead or living.

Euſebio.

Julia, more we'll ſpeak anon,
Veil thy face now and come with me,
Leſt thou fall into the hands
Of my enemy and thy ſire here.—
Soldiers, this is now the day
To diſplay your ſtrength and ſpirit!
That no craven heart be here,
Think that theſe expectant victors
Hither come to give us death,
Or, what's worſe, to make us priſoners;
If ſo in a public gaol,
By a thouſand ills afflicted,
Without honour we ſhall ſee us.

Pues ſi eſto hemos conocido,
¿ Por la vida, y por la honra,
Quién temió el mayor peligro ?
No pienſen que los tememos,
Salgamos á recibirlos ;
Que ſiempre eſtá la fortuna
De parte del atrevido.

Ricardo.

No hay que ſalir ; que ya llegan
A noſotros.

Euſebio.

Preveníos,
Y ninguno ſea cobarde ;
Que, vive el cielo ! ſi miro
Huir alguno ó retirarſe,
Que he de eſangrentar los filos
De aqueſte acero en ſu pecho
Primero que en mi enemigo.

Dentro Curcio.

Curcio.

En lo encubierto del monte
Al traidor Euſebio he viſto,
Y para inútil defenſa
Hace murallas ſus riſcos.

Voces (*dentro*).

Ya entre las eſpeſas ramas
Deſde aqui los deſcubrimos.

Julia.

¡ A ellos ! [*Vaſe.*

Euſebio.

Eſperad, villanos ;
Que ¡ vive Dios ! que teñidos
Con vueſtra ſangre los campos
Han de ſer undoſos rios.

Ricardo.

De los cobardes villanos
Es el número exceſivo.

If then this we have admitted,
Who is there for life, for honour,
That will fear the greater riſk here ?
Let them think not that we fear them ;
Let us forth and meet them firſt then,
Since is fortune on the ſide
Ever of the boldeſt ſpirits.

Ricardo.

There's no need to go, for they
Are already here.

Euſebio.

Be firm then,
And let no one play the coward ;
For, as Heaven lives ! if I witneſs
One of you or fly or falter,
I my ſword's edge ſhall encrimſon
In his heart's blood, rather than
In the enemy's that I fight with.

Curcio (*within*).

Curcio.

In the heart here of the mountain,
I have ſeen Euſebio hidden,
And the wretch, in vain defence,
Makes a rampart of theſe cliffs here.

Voices (*within*).

Through theſe thick o'erhanging boughs
We already can deſcry them.

Julia.

On them ! [*Exit.*

Euſebio.

Wait for us, baſe peaſants !
For, as God doth live ! beſprinkled
With your blood, the fields ſhall run
Rippling red like wavy rivers.

Ricardo.

Very numerous is the crowd
Of theſe craven herds and hinds here.

Curcio (*dentro*).
¿ Adónde, Eufebio, te efcondes ?

Eufebio.
No me efcondo, que ya te figo.
[*Vanfe todos, y difparan arcabuces dentro.*

Sale Julia.

Julia.
Del monte que yo he bufcado
Apenas las yerbas pifo,
Cuando horribles voces oigo,
Marciales campañas miro :
De la pólvora los ecos,
Y del acero los filos,
Unos ofenden la vifta,
Y otros turban el oido.
¿ Mas qué es aquello que veo ?
Desbaratado y vencido
Todo el efcuadron de Eufebio
Le deja ya al enemigo.
Quiero volver á juntaŕ
Toda la gente que ha habido
De Eufebio, y volver á darle
Favor ; que fi los animo,
Seré en fu defenfa afombro
Del mundo, feré cuchillo
De la Parca, eftrago fiero
De fus vidas, vengativo
Efpanto de los futuros,
Y admiracion deftos figlos. [*Vafe.*

Sale Gil *de bandolero.*

Gil.
Por eftar feguro, apenas
Fui bandolero novicio,
Cuando, por fer bandolero,
Me veo en tanto peligro.
Cuando yo era labrador,

Curcio (*within*).
Where, Eufebio, art thou hid ?

Eufebio.
Thee I feek, I am not hidden.
[*Exeunt all : fhots are heard within.*

Enter Julia.

Julia.
Scarcely have I trod the grafs
Of this mountain's fought-for ridges,
When I hear tumultuous cries,
When the ftrife of war I witnefs ;
By the echoes of the powder,
By the gleam of fwords that glitter,
Dazzled is the eye that fees them,
Deafen'd is the ear that liftens ;—
But, alas ! what's this I fee ?
Put to rout, and backward driven,
All the fquadron of Eufebio
Leave him to the enemy's will there.
I'll return and reunite
All the followers he had with him,
I'll return and give him aid ;—
For if them I thus infpirit,
I in his defence will be
The world's terror, the Fates' fwift fhears,
The fierce ruin of their lives,
To the future times the fymbol
Of revenge, and th' admiration
Of the ages that we live in. [*Exit.*

Enter Gil *dreffed as a bandit.*

Gil.
To preferve my fkin, I fcarcely
Have commenced my thieve's noviciate,
When the being a bandolero
Is, I fee, a dangerous bufinefs ;—
When I was a labourer,

Eran ellos los vencidos;
Y hoy, porque ſoy de la carda,
Va ſucediendo lo miſmo.
Sin ſer avariento traigo
La deſventura conmigo;
Pues tan deſgraciado ſoy,
Que mil veces imagino,
Que, á ſer yo Judío, fueran
Deſgraciados los Judíos.

My ſide was it that was lick'd then,
And to-day, for being a tramper,
With the ſame luck I'm afflicted!
Though no miſer, in my pocket
I misfortune carry with me;
Since ſo evil-ſtarr'd am I,
That it ſtrikes me many a minute,
That if ever I turn'd Jew,
Jews themſelves could be outwitted.

Salen Menga, Bras, Tirso *y otros villanos.*

Enter Menga, Bras, Tirso, *and other peaſants.*

Menga.
¡A ellos, que van huyendo!
Bras.
No ha de quedar uno vivo
Tan ſolamente.
Menga.
Hácia aqui
Uno dellos ſe ha eſcondido.
Bras.
Muera eſte ladron.
Gil.
Mirad,
Que yo ſoy.
Menga.
Ya nos ha dicho
El trage, que es bandolero.
Gil.
El trage les ha mentido,
Como muy grande bellaco.
Menga.
Dale tú.
Bras.
Pégale digo.
Gil.
Bien dado eſtoy y pegado:
Advertid . . .

Menga.
After them! for they are flying!
Bras.
On! no quarter muſt be given,—
Let not one ſurvive!
Menga.
See, here
One of them is ſlyly hidden!
Bras.
Kill the robber!
Gil.
Ah! now ſee
Who I am.
Menga.
That you're a brigand
Has your dreſs already told us.
Gil.
Then my dreſs lies like a villain
And a raſcal to have ſaid ſo.
Menga.
Give it to him!
Bras.
Pay him off quickly!
Gil.
I've been paid, and got it ſoundly,—
See, conſider! . . .

Tirſo.
No hay que advertirnos,
Bandolero ſois.
Gil.
Mirad
Que ſoy Gil, votado á Criſto!
Menga.
¿Pues no hablaras antes, Gil?
Tirſo.
Pues, Gil, ¿no lo hubieras dicho?
Gil.
¿Qué mas antes, ſi el yo ſoy
Os dije deſde el principio?
Menga.
¿Qué haces aqui?
Gil.
¿No lo veis?
Ofendo á Dios en el quinto,
Mato ſolo mas, que juntos
Un médico y un eſtío.
Menga.
¿Qué trage es eſte?
Gil.
Es el diablo.
Maté á uno, y ſu veſtido
Me puſe.
Menga.
¿Pues cómo, di,
No eſtá de ſangre teñido,
Si le mataſte?
Gil.
Eſo es fácil;
Murió de miedo, eſta ha ſido
La cauſa.
Menga.
Ven con noſotros,
Que victorioſos ſeguimos
Los bandoleros, que ahora

Tirſo.
We conſider
Only you're a thief.
Gil.
That *I* am
Gil, I call all Heaven to witneſs.
Menga.
Why not ſay ſo ſooner, Gil?
Tirſo.
Gil, why ſay not ſo at firſt, then?
Gil.
How, what ſooner, when I told you
From the firſt I was myſelf here?
Menga.
What are you doing?
Gil.
Don't you ſee?
I'm a-breaking juſt the fifth—tenth
Of the commandments, killing more
Than the ſummer and a phyſician.
Menga.
What's this dreſs?
Gil.
It is the devil,—
One of them I kill'd, and rigg'd me
In his dreſs then.
Menga.
But ſay, why
Is the dreſs not ſtain'd, if you kill'd
him,
With his blood?
Gil.
Oh! that is eaſy
To explain, the cauſe is ſimple,
'Twas of fear he died.
Menga.
Come with us,
For victorious the banditti
We purſue, for now the cowards

Cobardes nos han huido.

Gil.

No mas veſtido, aunque vaya
Titiritando de frio. [*Vanſe.*

Salen peleando Eusebio *y* Curcio.

Curcio.

Ya eſtamos ſolos los dos,
Gracias al cielo que quiſo
Dar la venganza á mi mano
Hoy, ſin haber remitido
A las agenas mi agravio,
Ni tu muerte á agenos filos.

Euſebio.

No ha ſido en eſta ocaſion
Airado el cielo conmigo,
Curcio, en haberte encontrado;
Porque ſi tu pecho vino
Ofendido, volverá
Caſtigado y ofendido.
Aunque no ſé qué reſpeto
Has pueſto en mí, que he temido
Mas tu enojo, que tu acero:
Y aunque pudieran tus brios
Darme temor, ſolo temo,
Cuando aqueſas canas miro,
Que me hacen cobarde.

Curcio.

Euſebio,
Yo confieſo, que has podido
Templar en mí de la ira,
Con que agraviado te miro,
Gran parte; pero no quiero,
Que pienſes inadvertido,
Que te dan temor mis canas,
Cuando puede el valor mio.
Vuelve á reñir; que una eſtrella,
O algun favorable ſigno

Fly before us panic-ſtricken.

Gil.

Catch me dreſs'd again, although
With the cold I ſhake and ſhiver!
[*Exeunt.*

Enter Eusebio *and* Curcio *fighting.*

Curcio.

Now we are alone, we two,
Thanks to favouring Heaven that giveth
Vengeance to my own right hand
On this day, without tranſmitting
To another's arm my wrong,
To another's ſword thy ſwift death.

Euſebio.

Curcio, on this occaſion
Heaven has not been angry with me,
In permitting me to meet thee;
Since if thou haſt carried hither
An indignant breaſt, thou'lt bear it
Back both puniſh'd and indignant.
Though I know not what reſpect
Thou haſt cauſed in me, that gives me
More fear for thy wrath than ſword:
And although thy ſtrength and ſpirit
Well might fright me, I but fear
When I ſee thoſe locks of ſilver,
Which a coward make me.

Curcio.

I
Own, Euſebio, thou art gifted
With ſome power, to appeaſe a part
Of the wrath with which, afflicted,
I behold thee; but I would not
Have thee careleſsly attribute
To theſe hoary hairs thy fear,
When my valour were ſufficient.
Come, renew the fight! one ſtar
Or one planet's favouring ſignal

No es baſtante á que yo pierda
La venganza que conſigo.
Vuelve á reñir.

Euſebio.

¿Yo temor?
Neciamente has preſumido,
Que es temor lo que es reſpeto;
Aunque, ſi verdad te digo,
La victoria que deſeo
Es, á tus plantas rendido,
Pedirte perdon; y á ellas
Pongo la eſpada, que ha ſido
Temor de tantos.

Curcio.

Euſebio,
No has de penſar, que me animo
A matarte con ventaja;
Eſta es mi eſpada. (Aſi quito [*Aparte.*
La ocaſion de darle muerte.)
Ven á los brazos conmigo.

[*Abrázanſe los dos, y luchan.*

Euſebio.

No ſé qué efecto has hecho
En mí, que el corazon dentro del pecho,
A peſar de venganzas y de enojos,
En lágrimas ſe aſoma por los ojos,
Y en confuſion tan fuerte,
Quiſiera, por vengarte, darme muerte.
Véngate en mí; rendida
A tus plantas, ſeñor, eſtá mi vida.

Curcio.

El acero de un noble, aunque ofendido,
No ſe mancha en la ſangre de un rendido;
Que quita grande parte de la gloria

Muſt not make me loſe the hope
Of the vengeance I ambition.
Fight anew, then!

Euſebio.

I to fear?
Oh! thou haſt preſumed too ſimply
Fear in that that was reſpect;
Though, if I the truth admitted,
The ſole victory I deſire
Is, thus kneeling, thy forgiveneſs
To implore; and at thy feet
To lay down this ſword, that has given
Fear to many a heart.

Curcio.

Euſebio,
Do not think that I could kill thee
At ſuch diſadvantage. Here
Alſo is my ſword; (I rid me [*Aſide.*
Of the means thus of his death.)—
Arm to arm then ſtruggle with me.

[*They cloſe, and ſtruggle together.*

Euſebio.

I know not by what charm poſſeſs'd,
Thus with thy heart againſt my breaſt,
My wrath expires, my vengeance dies,
In tender tears that guſh from out mine eyes.
So I implore thee, thus with trembling breath,
Confuſed, amazed, to give me inſtant death;
Take thy revenge, I terminate the ſtrife,
My lord, by laying at thy feet my life.

Curcio.

A brave man's ſword, how wrathful be his mood,
Is never ſtain'd in the defenceleſs blood

El que con ſangre borra la victoria.

Voces (dentro).

Hácia aqui eſtan.

Curcio.

Mi gente victorioſa
Viene á buſcarme, cuando temeroſa
La tuya vuelve huyendo.
Darte vida pretendo;
Eſcóndete; que en vano
Defenderé el enojo vengativo
De un eſcuadron villano,
Y ſolo tú, impoſible es quedar vivo.

Euſebio.

Yo, Curcio, nunca huyo
De otro poder, aunque he temido el tuyo;
Que ſi mi mano aqueſta eſpada cobra,
Verás, cuanto valor en tí me falta,
Que en tu gente me ſobra.

Salen Octavio *y todos los villanos.*

Octavio.

Deſde el mas hondo valle á la mas alta
Cumbre de aqueſte monte no ha quedado
Alguno vivo; ſolo ſe ha eſcapado
Euſebio, porque huyendo aqueſta tarde . .

Euſebio.

Mientes; que Euſebio nunca fue cobarde.

Todos.

¿Aqui eſtá Euſebio? ¡Muera!

Euſebio.

¡Llegad, villanos!

Of a fallen foe: for war's triumphant
ſtory, [half its glory.
If writ in needleſs blood, is ſhorn of

Voices (within).

Here, here they are.

Curcio.

My victor troop comes here
To ſeek me, while thy followers in fear
Fly from the unſucceſsful ſtrife.
I wiſh to ſave thy life;—
Conceal thyſelf, for I would vainly ſtrive
Thee to defend againſt a band
Of vengeful peaſants ſword in hand,
And thou againſt ſo many ſcarce couldſt
live.

Euſebio.

I, Curcio, never fly
From any power, though thine I've
fear'd to try;
But if my hand this ſword uplifts again,
Thou'lt ſee the valour that 'gainſt thee
proved weak
Can act its wonted part ſtill on thy men.

Enter Octavio *with a crowd of peaſants.*

Octavio.

From deepeſt valley to the higheſt peak
Of this vaſt mountain, not a ſoul our
wrath
Has left alive: Euſebio only hath
Eſcaped, for flying as the evening
lower'd . . . .

Euſebio.

Thou lieſt! Euſebio never was a coward.

All.

Euſebio here? The monſter let us ſlay!

Euſebio.

Villains, come on!

Curcio.

¡ Tente, Octavio, eſpera !

Octavio.

¿ Pues tú, ſeñor, que habias
De animarnos, ahora deſconfias ?

Bras.

¿ Un hombre amparas, que en tu ſangre y honra
Introdujo el acero y la deſhonra ?

Gil.

¿ A un hombre, que atrevido
Toda aqueſta montaña ha deſtruido ?
A quien en el aldea no ha dejado
Melon, doncella, que él no haya catado,
Y á quien tantos ha muerto,
¿ Cómo aſi le defiendes ?

Octavio.

¿ Qué es, ſeñor, lo que dices ? ¿ qué pretendes ?

Curcio.

Eſperad, eſcuchad, (¡ triſte ſuceſo !)
¿ Cuanto es mejor que á Sena vaya preſo ?
Date á priſion, Euſebio ; que prometo,
Y como noble juro, de ampararte,
Siendo abogado tuyo, aunque ſoy parte.

Euſebio.

Como á Curcio no mas, yo me rindiera,
Mas como á juez, no puedo ;
Porque aquel es reſpeto, y eſte es miedo.

Curcio.

Oh ! hold, Octavio, ſtay !

Octavio.

How, ſir, canſt thou, that ſhouldſt inſpirit us,
Now interpoſe and check our vengeance thus ?

Bras.

Canſt thou defend a man whoſe bloody aim
Thy name and blood has ſtain'd with blood and ſhame ?

Gil.

A man whoſe daring no reſtraint e'er bound,
Who ravaged all this mountain region round,
Who left no village in the wild unwaſted,
Nor melon's juice, nor maiden's lip untaſted ?
Is it for killing of ſo many people
Him thus you will defend ?

Octavio.

What is it, ſir, you ſay ? What thus intend ?

Curcio.

Oh ! liſten, ſtay ! (unhappy fate !) to me
Seems it far better in captivity
To lead him to Siena : yield, Euſebio, yield,
I give my knightly word to guard thy fate,
And though thy accuſer, be thy advocate.

Euſebio.

To thee, as Curcio, I perchance might yield me,
But to a judge I cannot ; ſince 'tis clear

Octavio.
¡ Muera Eusebio !

Curcio.
Advertid . . . .

Octavio.
Pues qué, ¿ tú quieres
Defenderle ? ¿ á la patria traidor eres ?

Curcio.
¿ Yo traidor ? Pues me agravian desta suerte,
Perdona, Eusebio, porque yo el primero
Tengo de ser en darte triste muerte.

Eusebio.
Quítate de delante,
Señor, porque tu vista no me espante ;
Que viéndote, no dudo,
Que te tenga tu gente por escudo.
[*Vanse todos peleando con él.*

Curcio.
Apretándole van. ¡ O quien pudiera
Darte ahora la vida,
Eusebio, aunque la suya misma diera !
En el monte se ha entrado,
Por mil partes herido,
Retirándose baja despeñado
Al valle. Voy volando,
Que aquella sangre fria,
Que con tímida voz me está llamando,
Algo tiene de mia ;
Que sangre, que no fuera
Propia, ni me llamara, ni la oyera.
[*Vase.*

The former were respect, the latter fear.

Octavio.
Eusebio, die !

Curcio.
Oh ! hear . . . .

Octavio.
What thus can move thee
Him to defend, and thus a traitor prove thee ?

Curcio.
A traitor I ?—since thus suspicion durst
Wrong me so much, Eusebio, forgive me,
That death's dark wound I'm doom'd to give thee first.

Eusebio.
Oh ! sir, stand not before me,
At sight of thee, it is not fear comes o'er me ;
No, but I do not doubt thy face will be
A shield betwixt thy followers and me.
[*Exit fighting with the peasants, who pursue.*

Curcio.
They press him hard. Oh ! who is there thy life,
Eusebio, now can save,
Though his for thine were offer'd in the strife ?
Through the mountain's rocky walls
Hath he enter'd wounded, bleeding
From a thousand wounds. He falls
Headlong to the vale ! I fly,
For that cold, cold blood outflown,
With its timid voice doth call me nigh,
As if it were a portion of mine own ;—
Were the blood not mine own, that voice so clear
Then had not power to call, nor I have power to hear. [*Exit.*

Baja deſpeñado Eusebio.

Euſebio.

Cuando, de la vida incierto,
Me deſpeña la mas alta
Cumbre, veo que me falta
Tierra donde caiga muerto:
Pero ſi mi culpa advierto,
Al alma reconocida,
No el ver la vida perdida
La atormenta, ſino el ver
Como ha de ſatisfacer
Tantas culpas una vida.
Ya me vuelve á perſeguir
Eſte eſcuadron vengativo;
Pues no puedo quedar vivo,
He de matar, ó morir:
Aunque mejor ſerá ir
Donde al cielo perdon pida;
Pero mis paſos impida
La Cruz, porque deſta ſuerte
Ellos me dén breve muerte,
Y ella me dé eterna vida.
Arbol, donde el cielo quiſo
Dar el fruto verdadero
Contra el bocado primero,
Flor del nuevo paraiſo,
Arco de luz, cuyo aviſo
En piélago mas profundo
La paz publicó del mundo,
Planta hermoſa, fértil vid,
Arpa del nuevo David,
Tabla del Moiſes ſegundo:
Pecador ſoy, tus favores
Pido por juſticia yo;
Pues Dios en tí, padeció
Solo por los pecadores.

[*The wildeſt part of the mountain.* Eusebio *is ſeen lying at the foot of a croſs.*]

Euſebio.

From this cliff ſo ſteep and tall
Falling headlong, almoſt dead,
Earth ſtill fails beneath my tread,
Where a living corſe I fall;
But when I my guilt recall,
Upward ſtill my ſpirit climbs,
Unregretting vaniſh'd times,
But with hope before I die,
Means to find to ſatisfy
With one life ſo many crimes.
Hither the revengeful foe
Comes my life's laſt drops to drain,—
Here the hope of life is vain,
I muſt give or meet the blow;
Though 'twere better far to go
Where for pardon I may pray;—
But this Croſs, athwart my way
Riſing up, in ſilence ſaith,—
They indeed can give you death,
I, the life that laſts alway.
Tree, whereon the pitying ſkies
Hang the true fruit love doth ſweeten,
Antidote of that firſt eaten,
Flower of man's new paradiſe,
Rainbow, that to tearful eyes
Sin's receding flood diſcloſes,—
Pledge that earth in peace repoſes,
Beauteous plant, all fruitful vine,
A newer David's harp divine,
Table of a ſecond Moſes;—
Sinner am I, therefore I
Claim thine aid as all mine own,
Since for ſinful man alone,
God came down on thee to die:

A mí me debes tus loores;
Que por mí ſolo muriera
Dios, ſi mas mundo no hubiera:
Luego eres tú, Cruz, por mí;
Que Dios no muriera en tí,
Si yo pecador no fuera.
Mi natural devocion
Siempre os pidió con fe tanta,
No permitiéſeis, Cruz ſanta,
Murieſe ſin confeſion.
No ſeré el primer ladron,
Que en vos ſe confieſe á Dios.
Y pues que ya ſomos dos,
Y yo no le he de negar,
Tampoco me ha de faltar
Redencion que ſe obró en vos.
Liſardo, cuando en mis brazos
Pude ofendido matarte,
Lugar dí de confeſarte,
Antes que en tan breves plazos
Se deſataſen los lazos
Mortales. Y ahora advierto
En aquel viejo, aunque muerto;
Piedad de los dos aguardo.
¡Mira que muero, Liſardo;
Mira que te llamo, Alberto!

Sale Curcio.

Curcio.
Hácia aqueſta parte eſtá.

Euſebio.
Si es que venis á matarme,
Muy poco hareis en quitarme
Vida, que no tengo ya.

Curcio.
¡Qué bronce no ablandará
Tanta ſangre derramada!
Euſebio, rinde la eſpada.

Praiſe through me thou haſt won thereby,
Since for me would God have died,
If the world held none beſide.
Then, O Croſs! thou'rt all for me,
Since God had not died on thee
If ſin's depths I had not tried.
Ever for thy interceſſion
Hath my faith implored, O Croſs!
That thou wouldſt not to my loſs
Let me die without confeſſion.
I, repenting my tranſgreſſion,
Will not the firſt robber be
Who on thee confeſſ'd to God;
Since we two the ſame path trod,
And repent, deny not me
The redemption wrought on thee.
Thou, Liſardo, though I could
Slay thee in my angry mood,
Still theſe arms were prompt to preſs thee,
Still could bear thee to confeſs thee,
Ere thy life flow'd out in blood.
And the reverend man, whom I
Now recall thus faint and weak:
Pity from ye two I ſeek,—
See, Liſardo, ſee, I die!
Hear, Alberto, hear my cry!

Enter Curcio.

Curcio.
Here he fell, adown this ſteep.

Euſebio.
If thou ſeek'ſt my life, 'twill be
Eaſy now to take from me
That which I no longer keep.

Curcio.
Oh! an eye of bronze would weep,
So much blood to ſee outpour'd!—
Yield, Euſebio, yield thy ſword.

Eusebio.
¿ A quién ?
Curcio.
A Curcio.
Eusebio.
Esta es. [*Dásela.*
Y yo tambien á tus pies
De aquella ofensa pasada
Te pido perdon. No puedo
Hablar mas ; porque una herida
Quita el aliento á la vida,
Cubriendo de horror y miedo
El alma.

Curcio.
Confuso quedo.
¿ Será en ella de provecho
Remedio humano ?
Eusebio.
Sospecho,
Que la mejor medicina
Para el alma es la divina.
Curcio.
¿ Dónde es la herida ?
Eusebio.
En el pecho.
Curcio.
Déjame poner en ella
La mano, á ver si resiste
El aliento. (¡ Ay de mí triste !)
[*Registra la herida, y ve la Cruz.*
¿ Qué señal divina y bella
Es esta, que al conocella,
Toda el alma se turbó ?

Eusebio.
Son las armas que me dió
Esta Cruz, á cuyo pie
Naci ; porque mas no sé

Eusebio.
Yield to whom ?
Curcio.
To Curcio.
Eusebio.
Yes ;
[*He gives his sword.*
And thy feet I likewise press
For that past offence, my lord,
Asking thy forgiveness. Here
Voice doth fail me, for a wound
Stops my breath, my sense hath swoon'd,
And a horror and a fear
Fill my soul.
Curcio.
Confused I hear ;—
Cannot human aid arrest
Thy swift-failing life ?
Eusebio.
The best
Cure for soul so sick as mine
Is, I feel it, the divine.
Curcio.
Where's thy wound ?
Eusebio.
'Tis in my breast.
Curcio.
Let me then my hand place there,
Thus to learn, (oh ! woe the day !)
What its troubled throb doth say ;—
[*He examines the wound, and sees the Cross.*
But what mark, divine and fair,
Is this sign my hand lays bare,
Which to see, my soul moves so ?
Eusebio.
'Tis my crest's emblazoned glow,
Given me by this Cross, whose base
Was my birth's mysterious place,

De mi nacimiento yo.
Mi padre, á quien no ſeñalo,
Aun la cuna me negó;
Que ſin duda imaginó,
Que habia de ſer tan malo.
Aqui nací.

Curcio.

Y aqui igualo
El dolor con el contento,
Con el guſto el ſentimiento,
Efectos de un hado impío
Y agradable. ¡Ay hijo mio!
Pena y gloria en verte ſiento.
Tú eres, Euſebio, mi hijo,
Si tantas ſeñas advierto,
Que para llorarte muerto
Ya juſtamente me aflijo.
De tus razones colijo
Lo que el alma adivinó.
Tu madre aqui te dejó
En el lugar que te he hallado;
Donde cometí el pecado,
El cielo me caſtigó.
Ya aqueſte lugar previene
Informacion de mi error;
¿Pero cual ſeña mayor,
Que aqueſta Cruz, que conviene
Con otra que Julia tiene?
Que no ſin miſterio el cielo
Os ſeñaló, porque al ſuelo
Fuérais prodigio los dos.

Euſebio.

No puedo hablar, padre, ¡á Dios!
Porque ya de un mortal velo
Se cubre el cuerpo, y la muerte
Niega, paſando veloz,
Para reſponderte voz,
Vida para conocerte,
Y alma para obedecerte.

For of *it* no more I know,
Since my father, of whom ne'er
I knew more, denied to me
Even a cradle: doubtleſs he
Then divined my dark career.
Here I firſt drew breath.

Curcio.

And here
Grief and joy contend in me,
Anguiſh and delight agree,
Sad and ſweet thoughts o'er me ſteal;—
O my long-loſt ſon! I feel
Pain and pride in ſeeing thee.
Thou, Euſebio, art my ſon,—
This a thouſand proofs have ſaid;
Ah! that I muſt mourn thee dead,
Ere thy life hath well begun.
What my ſoul by brooding on
Had divined, thy words make clear,
That thy mother left thee here,
In the place where I ſtand o'er thee;
Where I ſinn'd to her who bore thee,
Falls the wrath of Heaven ſevere.
Yes, deluſion diſappeareth,
All the more this place I ſee;
But what greater proof can be
Than that *thy* breaſt alſo beareth
The ſame Croſs that Julia weareth?
Not without ſome myſtery
Heaven has mark'd you out to be
The world's wonder thus, ye two.

Euſebio.

I can ſpeak no more, adieu,
Ah! my father, for on me
Falls the fatal veil, and death,
In its ſwift flight paſſing by me,
Life to know thee doth deny me,
Time to live thy ſway beneath,
And to anſwer thee even breath.

Ya llega el golpe mas fuerte,
Ya llega el trance mas cierto.
Alberto!

Curcio.

¡Que llore muerto
A quien aborrecí vivo!

Eusebio.

¡Ven, Alberto!

Curcio.

¡O trance esquivo!
¡Guerra injusta!

Eusebio.

¡Alberto! ¡Alberto!
[*Muere.*

Curcio.

Ya al golpe mas violento
Rindió el último aliento;
Paguen mis blancas canas
Tanto dolor.
[*Tirase de los cabellos.*

Sale Bras.

Bras.

Ya son tus quejas vanas;
¿Cuándo puso inconstante la fortuna
En tu valor extremos?

Curcio.

En ninguna
Llegó el rigor á tanto.
Abrasen mis enojos
Este monte con llanto,
Puesto que es fuego el llanto de mis ojos.
¡O triste estrella! ¡o rigurosa suerte!
¡O atrevido dolor!

Sale Octavio.

Octavio.

Hoy, Curcio, advierte

Now the final stroke draws nigh:—
O Alberto!

Curcio.

Strange that I
Mourn his death whose life I sought.

Eusebio.

Come, Alberto!

Curcio.

Fight hard fought!

Eusebio.

Haste, Alberto! haste, I die! [*Dies.*

Curcio.

In that last convulsive groan
Hath his troubled spirit flown.
Let these gray hairs for such pain
Pay now the price.
[*He pulls his hair distractedly.*

Enter Bras.

Bras.

Thy wailings all are vain:
Will fickle fate, relenting, ne'er give o'er
Trying thy courage thus?

Curcio.

I ne'er before
More keenly felt its ire;
The griefs I cannot drown
With scalding tears could burn this
mountain down,
For even the flood my tears let fall is fire.
O luckless star! O destiny of woe!
O bitter pang!

Enter Octavio.

Octavio.

To-day doth fortune show

La fortuna en los males de tu eſtado,
Cuantos puede ſufrir un deſdichado.
El cielo ſabe cuanto hablarte ſiento.

Curcio.

¿ Qué ha ſido ?

Octavio.

Julia falta del convento.

Curcio.

El miſmo penſamiento, di, ¿ pudiera
Con el diſcurſo hallar pena tan fiera ?
Que es mi deſdicha airada,
Sucedida aun mayor, que imaginada.
Eſte cadáver frio,
Eſte que ves, Octavio, es hijo mio.
Mira ſi baſta en confuſion tan fuerte
Cualquiera pena deſtas á una muerte.
Dadme paciencia, cielos,
O quitadme la vida,
Ahora perſeguida
De tormentos tan fieros.

Salen Gil, Tirso, *y villanos.*

Gil.

¡ Señor !

Curcio.

¿ Hay mas dolor ?

Gil.

Los bandoleros,
Que huyeron caſtigados,
En buſca tuya vuelven, animados
De un demonio de un hombre,
Que encubre de ellos miſmos roſtro y nombre.

In all thine ills, which vainly wait a cure,
How much one hapleſs mortal can endure :—
God knows I grieve to make the tidings known.

Curcio.

What are they ?

Octavio.

Julia from her cell hath flown.

Curcio.

Could wildeſt frenzy feign
A more o'erwhelming ſtroke or fiercer pain ?
Alas ! my hapleſs fate o'ercaſt
Makes each new ſorrow greater than the laſt.
This cold corſe here thou gazeſt on,
Octavio, is the body of my ſon ;
Think, 'mid the crowd of ill ſucceeding ill,
If one alone were not enough to kill.
Oh ! grant me patience, Heaven,
Or take this life away,
Afflicted day by day
With viſitations from thy ſcourging hand.

Enter Gil, Tirso, *and peaſants.*

Gil.

My lord !

Curcio.

Some newer grief?

Gil.

The robber band,
That but now chaſtiſed had fled,
Rallying, come to attack thee, led
By a man whom hell doth ſeem to inflame,
Who hideth even from them his face [and name.

Curcio.
Ahora que mis penas fuéron tales,
Que ſon liſonjas los mayores males.
El cuerpo ſe retire laſtimoſo
De Euſebio, en tanto que un ſepulcro honroſo
A ſus cenizas da mi deſventura.

Tirſo.
¿ Pues cómo pienſas darle ſepultura
Hoy en lugar ſagrado,
Cuando ſabes que ha muerto excomulgado ?

Bras.
Quien deſta ſuerte ha muerto,
Digno ſepulcro ſea eſte deſierto.

Curcio.
¡ O villana venganza !
¿ Tanto poder en tí la ofenſa alcanza,
Que paſas deſta ſuerte
Los últimos umbrales de la muerte ?
[*Vaſe llorando.*

Bras.
Sea en penas tan graves
Su ſepulcro las fieras y las aves.

Otro.
Del monte deſpeñado
Caiga, por mas rigor, deſpedazado.

Tirſo.
Mejor es darle ahora ſepultura
Entre de aqueſtos ramos la eſpeſura.*
[*Colocan entre las ramas el cuerpo de Euſebio.*

* "Mejor es darle agora
Rúſtica ſepultura entre eſtos ramos."
HARTZENBUSCH's *Ed.*

Curcio.
Such ſorrows rack my breaſt,
That now the greateſt ills appear a jeſt.
Take hence the body of Euſebio,
And place it where in time a tomb ſhall ſhow
How o'er his aſhes ſtill my tears endure.

Tirſo.
What! do you think of giving ſepulture,
In holy ground, unto a deſperate man,
Who died beneath the Church's heavieſt ban ?

Bras.
For one who died in ſuch a deſperate caſe,
The deſert ſeems a fitting burial-place.

Curcio.
O vengeance of a vulgar breaſt !
Has thy rude anger then no bounds, no reſt ?
Muſt thy coarſe appetite inſatiate crave
For food beyond the threſhold of the grave ? [*Exit weeping.*

Bras.
Wild beaſts and birds of prey ſhould limb from limb
Tear ſuch a wretch, and ſo thus bury him.

Another.
Let's throw his body o'er the rocks, that ſo
In fragments it may reach the ſands below.

Tirſo.
No, ſince the time no other mode allows,
Let's make his ruſtic grave beneath theſe boughs.
[*They place the body of* EUSEBIO *as deſcribed.*
Now ſince the night, wrapp'd in her mournful ſhroud,

Pues ya la noche baja,
Envuelta en eſa lóbrega mortaja :
Aqui en el monte, Gil, con él te queda;
Porque ſola tu voz aviſar pueda,
Si algunas gentes vienen
De las que huyeron. [*Vanſe.*

Gil.

¡ Linda flema tienen !
A Euſebio han enterrado
Alli, y á mí aqui ſolo me han dejado.
Señor Euſebio, acuérdeſe, le digo,
Que un tiempo fuí ſu amigo.
¿Mas qué es eſto? ó me engaña mi deſeo,
O mil perſonas á eſta parte veo.

Sale Alberto.

Alberto.

Viniendo ahora de Roma,
Con la muda ſuſpenſion
De la noche en eſte monte
Perdido otra vez eſtoy.
Aqueſta es la parte adonde
La vida Euſebio me dió,
Y de ſus ſoldados temo,
Que en grande peligro eſtoy.

Euſebio.

¡ Alberto !

Alberto.

¿ Qué aliento es eſte
De una temeroſa voz,
Que, repitiendo mi nombre,
En mis oidos ſonó ?

Finds too a grave in yonder murky cloud,
Let us away: thou on the mountain, Gil,
Hadſt beſt remain beſide the body ſtill;
Shouldſt thou ſee any of the troop that fled,
Call loud for aid, we'll hear. [*Exeunt.*

Gil.

That's eaſily ſaid :
Euſebio's corſe they bury out of ſight,
And leave but me to watch it through the night.
Señor Euſebio, recollect, I pray,
How you and I were friends the other day.
But what is this? Unleſs my eyes betray me,
At leaſt a thouſand perſons here waylay me.

Enter Alberto.

Alberto.

In the ſilent dark of night,
On my journey back from Rome,
I again have loſt my way
In this wild and mountain road :
'Tis the place that robber chieftain
Spared my life ſome time ago,
And new peril from his ſoldiers
Now again my fears forbode.

Euſebio.

Oh ! Alberto !

Alberto.

What faint breath
Of a trembling voice here blown
Falls upon my ear, my name
Sadly ſighing o'er and o'er ?

Euſebio.
¡ Alberto !
Alberto.
Otra vez pronuncia
Mi nombre, y me pareció
Que es á eſta parte ; yo quiero
Ir llegando.
Gil.
¡ Santo Dios !
Euſebio es, y ya es mi miedo
De los miedos el mayor.
Euſebio.
¡ Alberto !
Alberto.
Mas cerca ſuena.
¿ Voz, que diſcurres veloz
El viento, y mi nombre dices,
Quién eres ?
Euſebio.
Euſebio ſoy ;
Llega, Alberto, hácia eſta parte,
Adonde enterrado eſtoy ;
Llega, y levanta eſtos ramos ;
No temas.
Alberto.
No temo yo.
Gil.
Yo sí.
[ALBERTO *le deſcubre.*
Alberto.
Ya eſtás deſcubierto.
Dime de parte de Dios,
¿ Qué me quieres ?
Euſebio.
De ſu parte

Euſebio.
Oh ! Alberto !
Alberto.
Ah ! that voice
Syllables my name once more !
Here it ſeems to ſound from : nigher
Let me liſten.
Gil.
Holy God !
'Tis Euſebio ! fear like this
Have I never felt before.
Euſebio.
Oh ! Alberto !
Alberto.
Now 'tis nearer :
Voice that flieſt fleetly forth
On the wind, and call'ſt my name,
Say, who art thou ?
Euſebio.
I was known
As Euſebio : oh ! Alberto !
Hither come where I am thrown,
Take away theſe boughs that hide me ;*
Do not fear.
Alberto.
No fear I know.
Gil.
Not ſo *I*.
[ALBERTO *diſcovers him.*
Alberto.
Thou'rt now laid bare,—
Tell me, in the name of God,
What with me thou willeſt.
Euſebio.
I

* In Tirſo de Molina's *El Condenado por Deſconfiado*, the body of *Paulo* is alſo hidden under boughs, and laid bare in the ſame manner, with, however, a very different reſult.—See his *Comedias Ecogidas*. Madrid, 1850. p. 203. TR.

Mi fe, Alberto, te llamó,
Para que, antes de morir,
Me oyeſes de confeſion.
Rato ha que hubiera muerto,
Pero libre ſe quedó
Del eſpíritu el cadáver;
Que de la muerte el feroz
Golpe le privó de uſo,
Pero no le dividió. [*Levántaſe.*
Ven adonde mis pecados
Confieſe, Alberto, que ſon
Mas, que del mar las arenas,
Y los átomos del ſol.
¡Tanto con el cielo puede
De la Cruz la devocion!

Alberto.

Pues yo cuantas penitencias
Hice haſta ahora, te doy,
Para que en tu culpa ſirvan
De alguna ſatisfaccion.
[*Vanſe* EUSEBIO *y* ALBERTO.

Gil.

¡Por Dios, que va por ſu pie!
Y para verlo mejor,
El ſol deſcubre ſus rayos.
A decirlo á todos voy.

Salen por el otro lado JULIA *y algunos Bandoleros.*

Julia.

Ahora, que deſcuidados
La victoria los dejó
Entre los brazos del ſueño,
Nos dan baſtante ocaſion.

Uno.

Si has de ſalirlos al paſo,
Por eſta parte es mejor;
Que ellos vienen por aqui.

In his name, by faith made bold,
Call'd thee, ere my death, to hear
My confeſſion long untold.
I have been a brief while dead,
And my corſe without control
Of the ſpirit here has lain;
But although death's mighty ſtroke
Took its active uſe away,
Still unſever'd was the ſoul.
[*He ariſes.*
Come, Alberto, where my ſins
I to thee may tell, though more
Than the atoms of the ſun
Or the ſands upon the ſhore;—
All ſo powerful is with Heaven
The devotion of the Croſs.

Alberto.

Then on thee the various penance
Of my lifetime I beſtow,
That at leaſt to ſome extent
For thy ſins they may atone.
[*Exeunt* EUSEBIO *and* ALBERTO.

Gil.

There, by heavens! away he walks;
And to ſee him, I ſuppoſe,
See the ſun ſhines out on purpoſe.
Oh! I burſt to have it told!

Enter on the other ſide JULIA *and ſome bandits.*

Julia.

Now that in the careleſſneſs
Of ſucceſs they lie here prone,
Buried in the arms of ſleep,
Let us make the time our own.

A Bandit.

If thou wouldſt ſecure the paſs,
Better 'tis this way to go,
For in that way they advance.

Salen CURCIO *y villano.*

Curcio.

Sin duda que inmortal ſoy
En los males que me matan,
Pues no me mata el dolor.

Gil.

A todas partes hay gente;
Sepan todos de mi voz
El mas admirable caſo,
Que jamas el mundo vió.
De donde enterrado eſtaba
Euſebio, ſe levantó,
Llamando á un clérigo á voces.
¿ Mas para qué os cuento yo
Lo que todos podeis ver ?
Mirad con la devocion
Que eſtá pueſto de rodillas.

Curcio.

¡ Mi hijo es ! ¡ Divino Dios !
¿ Qué maravillas ſon eſtas ?

Julia.

¿ Quién vió prodigio mayor ?

Curcio.

Aſi como el ſanto anciano
Hizo de la abſolucion
La forma, ſegunda vez
Muerto á ſus plantas cayó.

Sale ALBERTO.

Alberto.

Entre ſus grandezas tantas,
Sepa el mundo la mayor
Maravilla de las ſuyas,
Porque la enſalce mi voz.
Deſpues de haber muerto Euſebio,
El cielo depoſitó
Su eſpíritu en ſu cadáver,
Haſta que ſe confeſó ;

Enter CURCIO *and his followers.*

Curcio.

Oh ! I ſurely muſt have grown
Deathleſs 'mid the deadlieſt ills,
Since I die not of my woe.

Gil.

Folks are round on every ſide,
Let my voice to all unfold
The moſt wonderful event
That the world has ever known :—
From the place that buried lay
Dead Euſebio, he aroſe,
Calling loudly on a prieſt !
But what need of words to ſhow
That which you yourſelves can ſee ?
Look there yonder, bending low,
See with what reſpect he kneels.

Curcio.

'Tis my ſon, divineſt God,
What a miracle is this !

Julia.

What a wonder here is ſhown !

Curcio.

And the ſaintly elder ſcarce
O'er his head doth make the form
Of abſolution, when he falls
At his feet a corſe once more

Enter ALBERTO.

Alberto.

'Mid its greateſt miracles
That the wondering world may know
Now the ſtrangeſt of them all,
Let my voice its praiſe extol.
After this Euſebio died,
Heaven was pleaſed to let his ſoul
Still within his body ſtay
Till he could confeſs the whole

Que tanto con Dios alcanza
De la Cruz la devocion.

Curcio.

¡ Ay hijo del alma mia!
No fue desdichado, no,
Quien en su trágica muerte
Tantas glorias mereció.
Asi Julia conociera
Sus culpas.

Julia.

¡ Válgame Dios!
¿ Qué es lo que estoy escuchando?
¿ Qué prodigio es este? ¿ Yo
Soy la que á Eusebio pretende,
Y hermana de Eusebio soy?
Pues sepa Curcio, mi padre,
Sepa el mundo y todos hoy
Mis graves culpas; yo misma,
Asombrada á tanto horror,
Daré voces: sepan todos
Cuantos hoy viven, que yo
Soy Julia, en número infame
De las malas la peor.
Mas ya que ha sido comun
Mi pecado, desde hoy
Lo será mi penitencia;
Pidiendo humilde perdon
Al mundo del mal ejemplo,
De la mala vida á Dios.

Curcio.

¡ O asombro de las maldades!
Con mis propias manos yo
Te mataré, porque sea
Tu vida y tu muerte atroz.

Julia.

Valedme vos, Cruz divina;
Que yo mi palabra os doy,
De hacer, volviendo al convento,
Penetencia de mi error.

Of his sins, such power with God
Hath devotion to the Cross.

Curcio.

Ah! my son, my much-loved son,
Thou wert not unlucky, no,
To obtain so much of glory
By the stroke that laid thee low;
Would that Julia now could know
Her transgressions!

Julia.

Help me! God!
What is this that now I hear?
What is this that shocks me so?
I Eusebio's sister? I
Am the same who sought his love!
Then let Curcio, let my father,
Let the world and all men know
My great guilt! I will myself,
Frighten'd by this horrid blow,
Publicly proclaim it:—Now
Let all living men be told
I am Julia, 'mid the crowd
Of all reprobates the worst;
But as my offence has been
Public, let my penance show
Publicly that I repent;
Humbly pardon I implore
From the world for bad example,
For an evil life from God.

Curcio.

Prodigy of wickedness,
By my own right hand alone
Shalt thou die: that life and death
Be with thee atrocious both.

Julia.

Aid me thou, O Cross divine!
And I plight to thee my word,
Back unto my cell returning,
For my error to atone.

[*Al querer herirla* CURCIO, *se abraza de la Cruz, que estaba en el sepulcro de* EUSEBIO, *y vuela.*

Alberto.

¡Gran milagro!

Curcio.

Y con el fin
De tan grande admiracion,
La Devocion de la Cruz
Felice acaba su autor.

[*As* CURCIO *is about striking her, she embraces the Cross that stands beside the grave of* EUSEBIO, *which rises into the air with her and disappears.*

Alberto.

What a miracle!

Curcio.

And thus,
With so wonderful a close,
Happily the author endeth
The Devotion of the Cross.

THE END.

CHISWICK PRESS:—PRINTED BY WHITTINGHAM AND WILKINS,
TOOKS COURT, CHANCERY LANE.

www.ingramcontent.com/pod-product-compliance
Lightning Source LLC
Chambersburg PA
CBHW021125270326
41929CB00009B/1056

* 9 7 8 3 7 4 4 6 9 5 7 0 1 *